S0-CAW-674

CONTEMPORARY AMERICAN
REFORM RESPONSA

OTHER BOOKS OF INTEREST TO THE READER

Walter Jacob AMERICAN REFORM RESPONSA, Central Conference of American Rabbis Press, (1983) 561 pp.

Elliot L. Stevens RABBINIC AUTHORITY, Central Conference of American Rabbis Press, (1982) 184 pp.

Simeon J. Maslin GATES OF MITZVAH, Central Conference of American Rabbis Press, (1979) 166 pp.

Peter S. Knobel GATES OF THE SEASONS, Central Conference of American Rabbis Press, (1983) 208 pp.

Solomon B. Freehof NEW REFORM RESPONSA, Hebrew Union College Press, (1981) 282 pp.

Solomon B. Freehof REFORM RESPONSA FOR OUR TIME, Hebrew Union College Press, (1977) 320 pp.

Walter Jacob THE PITTSBURGH PLATFORM IN RETROSPECT — With the Report of the Proceedings of 1885, Rodef Shalom Press, (1985) 123 pp.

Walter Jacob LIBERAL JUDAISM AND THE HALAKHAH. A Symposium, Rodef Shalom Press, (1988) 100 pp.

Available through the Central Conference of American Rabbis, 192 Lexington Avenue, New York, New York 10011

CONTEMPORARY AMERICAN REFORM RESPONSA

by Walter Jacob

Central Conference of American Rabbis
5747 New York 1987

Library of Congress Cataloging-in-Publication Data

Jacob, Walter, 1930—
    Contemporary American Reform responsa / by Walter Jacob. p. cm.
    Companion volume to: American Reform responsa. 1983.
    Includes index to both volumes.
    ISBN 0-88123-003-0 (pbk.):
    1. Reform Judaism—Customs and practices.
    2. Responsa—1800-
    3. Jewish law—Reform Judaism. I. Central Conference of American Rabbis. II. Central Conference of American Rabbis. American Reform responsa. III. Title.
BM197.J33 1987   87-21339
296.1'8—dc19   CIP

Copyright Central Conference
of American Rabbis 1987

Printed and Bound by Publishers Choice Book Mfg. Co.
Mars, Pennsylvania 16046

Dedicated to my brother
HERBERT JACOB
for warmth, scholarship, and good years shared together

Contents:

Orah Hayim

Preface

This volume, published by the Central Conference of American Rabbis, has benefited from a gift of the Rodef Shalom Congregation of Pittsburgh, Pennnsylvania. I am especially grateful to the Rodef Shalom Congregation for its generous support. I want to express thanks as well to Elliot Stevens for his advice. The typescript for this volume has been done with much devotion by Frances Stein, my thanks to her.

All of the responsa in this volume were written by the author, in contrast to the earlier volume, *American Reform Responsa* (1983), which I edited. That book presented 172 responsa of the Central Conference of American Rabbis; 57 of them represented my work; some of them were circulated to the committee. In this volume 30 responsa out of the total of 202 were presented to the Responsa Committee for their reaction and comments or discussed at meetings; they are marked with an *. Some of the comments by my colleagues have been incorporated in those responsa. The following individuals have been members of the Responsa Committee under my chairmanship at various times during the last twelve years: Robert Kirschner, Julius Kravetz, Leonard S. Kravitz, Yehiel Lander, Eugene Lipman, Eugene Mihaly, Isaac Neuman, Stephen M. Passamaneck, W. Gunther Plaut, Richard Rosenthal, Harry A. Roth, Herman Schaalman, Rav A. Soloff, Mark Washovsky, Sheldon Zimmerman, Bernard Zlotowitz.

Several of the Responsa printed in this volume have appeared previously in the *Yearbook of the Central Conference of American Rabbis* and in the *Journal of Reform Judaism*. They are now reprinted with the permission of the Central Conference.

December 1986
Kislev 5747

Introduction
Contemporary American Reform Responsa

The Reform Movement has been concerned with *halakhah* from its very beginning. The debates at the early European and American conferences inevitably dealt with *halakhic* issues. Yet the practical decisions and changes demanded by the times were usually made first and later discussions then justified them. This occurred with changes in liturgy, the introduction of the sermon and educational reforms (Jakob Petuchowski, *Prayerbook Reform in Europe*, pp. 84 ff; W. G. Plaut, *The Rise of Reform Judaism*; S. F. Temkin, *The New World of Reform*; W. Jacob, *The Changing World of Reform Judaism*). During the formative period of the Reform Movement, both in Europe and the United States, conferences and articles in learned and popular journals formed the context in which changes were adjusted or defended (Abraham Geiger, *Wissenschaftliche Zeitschrift für jüdische Theologie*; Samuel Holdheim, *Ueber die Autonomie der Rabbinen und das Princip der jüdischen Ehe*; Zacharias Frankel, *Monatsschrift für Geschichte und Wissenschaft des Judenthums*, Isaac Mayer Wise, *The American Israelite*, *Die Debora*, etc.) Some responsa were written early in the history of the movement, usually as answers to Orthodox critics (A. Guttman, *Struggle Over Reform in Rabbinic Literature*; Israel Bettan, "Early Reform in Contemporaneous Responsa," *Hebrew Union College Annual*, Jubilee Volume, 1925). This mode of argument was, however, not generally followed probably because liberal Judaism was struggling against Talmudic *pilpul* which had taken rabbinic studies far from the practical world and the average reader. Many nineteenth century traditional responsa followed this pattern which was very distant from the earlier more direct style. This then was hardly a medium for the intellectual debate which would provide an appropriate foundation for Reform Judaism. Furthermore, the early reformers were primarily interested in providing a historical view of the Jewish past. They sought to place the rabbinic literature into a framework, and so create a foundation for their reforms. Their detailed studies lent themselves far better to this purpose than responsa. The main works of many founders of the Reform Movement dealt with *halakhah* (Abraham Geiger, *Urschrift*; Zacharias Frankel, *Darkei Hamishnah*; L. Löw, *Die Reform des rabbinischen Ritus auf rabbinischem Standpunkt*," *Gesammelte Schriften*, [ed. Immanuel Löw]; *Ben Chanaja, Zeitschrift für jüdische*

Theologie etc.). Radical Reform often used as a whipping boy by enemies of the movement did not arise until the Frankfurt Conference of 1842. Then some individuals sought to eliminate the influence of the *halakhah* and rabbinic Judaism. Circumcision was debated, although no stand against circumcision was passed. This radical discussion gained few adherents, although antinomian views were aired. In America the Pittsburgh Platform leaned in the direction of rejecting aspects of "rabbinical laws" (IV, "Authentic Report of the Proceedings," in W. Jacob's *The Changing World of Reform Judaism*, p. 108). However, as I have shown, even the gathering in Pittsburgh of 1885 did not reject rabbinic Judaism; the deliberations and papers there (*Ibid.*, pp. 25 ff) and at every subsequent rabbinic conference (see *C.C.A.R. Yearbooks*) were concerned with the rabbinic development of the *halakhah*.

Although there have been voices in American Reform Jewish life which have rejected *halakhah*, that has not been the dominant trend. In the last decades precisely the opposite has been true with the renewed emphasis on Jewish practice and its *halakhic* background through S. B. Freehof's *Reform Jewish Practice and Its Rabbinic Background*, Vols. I and II (1944, 1963), D. Polish and I. Doppelt, *A Guide for Reform Jews* (1957), the *Shabbat Manual* (1972), as well as *Gates of Mitzvah* (1979) and *Gates of the Seasons* (1983), along with the much more traditional rubrics of *The Gates of Prayer* (1975). All of these books indicate a rabbinic and *halakhic* influence which may have been less apparent in the earlier age of rebellion.

We must also remember that the Reform Jewish revolution lasted almost a century in America; it began in the eighteen-forties and did not end till World War II. This contrasted vividly with the situation in Germany and the other lands of Central Europe in which two generations saw the movement firmly established with fixed approach and a well-defined relationship with the Orthodox minority. This occurred in Germany between the first Reform service of Israel Jacobson in Seesen (1808) and the last of the major German rabbinic conferences (Augsburg, 1868). The situation was similar in Austria and Hungary.

A modus vivendi was worked out quickly as the Jewish population in those lands was comparatively stable and as an official governmental relationship with the Jewish community existed. The newcomers to the German Jewish community, and there were tens of thousands from Eastern Europe, sought to combine modern culture with their Jewish heritage. They were amenable to minor religious innovations.

As the practical changes made by German, Austrian and Hungarian Reform were not radical, and as Hebrew remained the primary language of prayer, it was not difficult for Eastern European Jews to join the liberal congregations or the modern Orthodox congregations, which also modified their liturgy and other practices along the lines of Samson Raphael Hirsch's slogan, *"torah im derekh eretz"* (see Hirsch's *Horeb* and its major omissions of practice in fundamental areas as *nidah*, etc.).

In America matters were different as vast new groups reached these shores and the population multiplied geometrically. Many communities saw their numbers double each half decade as Jews fled from Tzarist persecution or the Balkan Lands. The immigrants themselves used traditional synagogues to help them adjust to the New World. The more radical American Reform was alien to them. As these immigrant groups Americanized and became acquainted with the modern world, they discovered Reform Judaism in succeeding waves over a period of a century. With each group of new congregants and enthusiastic rabbinic students the earlier debates were repeated and the underlying principles were discussed once more. The specific problems debated may have been different, but the basic approach to the rabbinic past had to be thrashed out again and again. Only following World War II after the last major wave of Jewish immigrants had Americanized did more settled conditions prevail.

Although each wave produced both conservative and radical views of changing Judaism the ultimate effect has been a renewed emphasis on *halakhah* and rabbinic Judaism. One may see this clearly by reviewing the responsa literature of the American Reform Movement. Although the Committee on Responsa was established by the Conference in 1906, very few questions seemed to have been directed to its chairman in the early years. It was the intent of the committee, as stated by Kaufmann Kohler, "to bring about some order within the Reform Jewish practices and to provide ready access for those who sought answers in rabbinic matters." There was relatively little interest by the Conference in the Responsa Committee nor did individual rabbis write their own responsa until the decade following World War II. In that period my predecessor, Solomon B. Freehof, found an increasing interest in answers based on the tradition. The seven volumes of responsa which he has written cover a period of twenty years and represent four hundred twenty-one responsa and inquiries. My own work as Chairman of the Responsa Committee covers eleven years with a total of three hundred responsa and an equal number of inquiries which have required no formal statements. The interest in rabbinic answers to questions has risen dramatically. This has been accompanied by a general concern with rabbinic literature. We should remember also that many questions nowadays are, of course, answered locally rather than by turning to the Responsa Committee.

As we look for the underlying philosophic approach of American Reform Judaism to *halakhah*, we must recall the statements of the rabbinic bodies from Pittsburgh to the Centenary Statement. Those gathered in Pittsburgh (1885) said:

"We recognize in the Mosaic legislation a system of training the Jewish people for its mission during its national life in Palestine, and to-day we accept as binding only its moral laws, and maintain only such ceremonies as elevate and sanctify our lives, but reject all such as are not adapted to the views and habits of modern civilization.

"We hold that all such Mosaic and rabbinical laws as regulate diet, priestly purity, and dress originated in ages and under the influence of ideas entirely foreign to our present mental and spiritual state. They fail to impress the modern Jew with a spirit of priestly holiness; their observance in our days is apt rather to obstruct than to further modern spiritual elevation."

At Columbus in 1935 we adopted a statement which read:

"Torah results from the relationship between God and the Jewish people. The records of our earliest confrontations are uniquely important to us. Lawgivers and prophets, historians and poets gave us a heritage whose study is a religious imperative and whose practice is our chief means to holiness. Rabbis and teachers, philosophers and mystics, gifted Jews in every age amplified the Torah tradition. For millennia, the creation of the Torah has not ceased and Jewish creativity in our time is adding to the chain of tradition.

"God reveals Himself not only in the majesty, beauty and orderliness of nature, but also in the vision and moral striving of the human spirit. Revelation is a continuous process, confined to no one group and to no one age. Yet, the people of Israel, through its prophets and sages, achieved unique insight in the realm of religious truth. The Torah, both written and oral, enshrines Israel's ever-growing consciousness of God and of the moral law. It preserves the historical precedents, sanctions and norms of Jewish life, and seeks to mold it in the patterns of goodness and of holiness. Being products of historical processes, certain of its laws have lost their binding force with the passing of the conditions that called them forth. But as a depository of permanent spiritual ideals, the Torah remains the dynamic source of life of Israel. Each age has the obligation to adapt the teachings of the Torah to its basic needs in consonance with the genius of Judaism.

"Judaism as a way of life requires in addition to its moral and spiritual demands, the preservation of the Sabbath, festivals and Holy Days, the retention and development of such customs, symbols and the ceremonies as possess inspirational value, the cultivation of distinctive forms of religious art and music and the use of Hebrew, together with the vernacular, in our worship and instruction."

The Centenary Statement adopted in 1976 stated:

"Judaism emphasizes action rather than creed as the primary expression of a religious life, the means by which we strive to achieve universal justice and peace. Reform Judaism shares this emphasis on duty and obligation. Our founders stressed that the Jew's ethical responsibilities, personal and social, are enjoined by God. The past century has taught us that the claims made upon us may begin with our ethical obligations but they extend to many others aspects of Jewish living, including: creating a Jewish home centered on family devotion; life-long study; private prayer and public worship; daily religious observance; keeping the Sabbath and the holy days; celebrating the major events of life; involvement with the synagogue and community; and other activities which promote the survival of the Jewish people and enhance its existence. Within each area of Jewish observance Reform Jews are called upon to confront the claims of Jewish tradition, however, differently perceived, and to exercise their individual autonomy, choosing and creating on the basis of commitment and knowledge."

Solomon B. Freehof, in the introduction to his various volumes of responsa, had indicated that he considers the responsa as "guidance not governance," (S. B. Freehof, *Reform Responsa*, 1960, p. 22). On the official level of the Conference there is still a good deal of hesitancy about rabbinic authority. Nevertheless, it has been possible to raise this issue and to publish a volume on this subject (E. Stevens, ed., *Rabbinic Authority*, 1982). The range of opinions is wide and there is reluctance to impose centralized control. Despite this, the authority of the rabbinic conference and of earlier rabbinic literature has been recognized by the vast majority of the members of the C.C.A.R. Autonomy and freedom have limits and there has been less concern about autonomy than with the danger of chaos. The books of guidance which the Central Conference has published indicate that mandates are very much desired by many in the American liberal community. The statements of *Gates of Mitzvah* and *Gates of the Seasons* are tentative with their wording, "It is a *mitzvah*," and skirt the issue of absolute obligation, but even in that form they reflect the stance of *halakhah* and commandments which would not have been acceptable to many American Reform Jews a few generations earlier. Yet, we must recall that the need for a guide had already been expressed by Kaufmann Kohler in 1907. Some movement in this direction existed from the beginning of the C.C.A.R. and earlier.

We must now turn to criteria of rabbinic authority. What do we consider acceptable and what do we reject? On what basis is this done? We view the rabbinic past as a historical development. The "Oral Law" is not seen as divinely given at Sinai, but rather as a reflection of our historic development and encounter with God in each succeeding generation. In this we follow Zunz, Geiger, Frankel, Graetz and others. We view God working through human agents. Each generation has produced capable and religiously inspired teachers. This, of course, means that we reject the often expressed traditional view which assigns greater holiness to those who lived in the past. Some individuals of our generation may equal or exceed those of the past. We have a healthy but not exaggerated respect for tradition or undue modesty about the best of our age. The reverse has led traditional Judaism to conservatism and great hesitation about change and innovations.

Historical and sociological studies of the rabbinic literature during the last two centuries have illuminated it. We view this vast literature as the product of human reaction to varying needs motivated by religious thought and the divine impulse. We feel no necessity to justify each segment of the literature in terms of every other portion as done through *hidushim* and *pilpul*. We see the differences among Talmudic and later authorities as reflections of particular points of view, different understandings of the divine mandate, as well as the needs of specific groups within their Jewish communities.

When we analyze each period of history we discover different strands in the *halakhah*. These appear both in the decisions and underlying philosophy. Tradition, of course, has chosen a single path and rejected the others, but we recall their existence and the fact that they were suggested and followed by loyal Jews in the past. Diversity has always been the hallmark of our literature and our people. When we find ourselves facing new situations in our age, we are justified in turning to the mainstream of rabbinic thought as well as its divergent paths for *halakhic* guidance. In our view, therefore, the *halakhah* is a vast repository whose old debates are often relevant to new situations.

Sometimes our solutions may parallel those of past generations. On other occasions we may diverge from them. Through this effort we seek solutions for a generation living in lands distant and distinct from those of the ancient Near East or medieval Europe.

Not every question can be resolved by reviewing the rabbinic literature and in some instances totally new legislation is appropriate. That may be buttressed by rabbinic precedent. We must with great care utilize the legislative process alongside responsa.

Our *halakhic* efforts intend to strengthen the role of Judaism in the lives of the million and a quarter American Reform Jews, the largest Jewish community in our land. Our forefathers in Europe and America sought to adapt Judaism to modern times. Their efforts have been justified by history as Judaism languished elsewhere. Our concern in the late twentieth century is less with adaptation and more with the strengthening of Jewish ties in a secular age. This has become especially important as secular Judaism in the form of Zionism has become less influential. Although the enthusiasm for Israel and the desire to help this young country continues, the idealism and fervor associated with early Zionism has disappeared. Modern Jewish philosophy must provide an intellectual basis for our Judaism. Modern *halakhah* and responsa must provide a practical expression for our daily Jewish existence. We are no longer satisfied with guidance but seek governance. It is the duty of liberal Jews to perform *mitzvot* on a regular basis as a part of their life.

As Reform Judaism has developed *halakhah*, the potential for conflict with traditional Judaism has increased. While our attitude toward *halakhah* was fluid and as long as some radicals rejected *halakhah* entirely, traditional Judaism could ignore us. They can not maintain this attitude in the face of our concern with *halakhah*. Therefore, the next decades will see considerable struggle here and in Israel. That should not trouble us. Our path in America is clear and our *halakhic* stance is akin to the pluralism of the past from the days of Hillel and Shammai in the first century through the entire rabbinic period to our own time. It is not our task as liberal Jews to complain about the Orthodox attitude or to be bullied by it, but rather to choose our legitimate path according to the inner logic and development of liberal Judaism.

Responsa are one way in which our rabbinic group the Central Conference of American Rabbis has set limits and defined its borders. Those limits may have seemed vague a century ago; as responsa have appeared over several generations, they have become clearer. It is the hope of this author that this volume of responsa will clarify the position of American Reform Judaism in the last decades of the twentieth century.

1. RABBINIC JURISDICTION**

QUESTION: A rabbi in a mid-western city in which there is a single Reform congregation wishes to know whether it is proper to exclude colleagues who may be willing to officiate at ceremonies which he is unwilling to conduct. This is not a question of establishing a new congregation but of seeking to bring someone to the community for a specific marriage or funeral against the wishes of the local rabbi. What are the prerogatives of the local rabbi according to tradition? Is he correct in his opposition?

ANSWER: The problem of rabbinic prerogatives within a community is an old one and has taken different forms in different ages. The *Talmud* dealt with it tangentially under the rabbinic rubric of *hasagat g'vul* which treated free enterprise and competition generally (*M. B.M. 4.12; 60a; B.B. 21b; Kid. 59a; San 81a* based on Deut. 19.14). Free enterprise without restrictions was generally favored, (B.B.21b). The medieval literature vastly amplified these discussions and applied them to the rabbinate. Rabenu Gershom, the eleventh century authority, discussed rabbis who were active communal leaders and judges but earned their livelihood through commerce; he decreed that no one in the community should interfere with their *ma-arufia*. As such a rabbis devoted time to communal purposes, they were to be spared commercial competition (S. B. Freehof, *A Treasury of Responsa*, p. 13). While there was agreement on this, there was a vigorous division of opinion on the question of the other prerogatives of the resident rabbi. What happened when an individual of greater stature arrived? May a visiting scholar deal with marriages, divorces, etc.? Some authorities like Isserlein and Weil permitted such competition and felt that it was good for the community (Weil, *Responsa* #151; Isserlein, *Terumat Hadeshen*, #128). In Weil's case neither of the two contesting rabbis had been officially selected by the community, so he felt that both had equal rights, although one had been in the community longer. Israel Isserlein made a similar decision to encourage the study of *Torah* (*Terumat Hadashen*). Some later authorities agreed with them. Many scholars felt that the appointed rabbi of the community had a right to protect his status both as a teacher and a judge; he could also protect the income from these and other sources (*Responsa Avnei Nezer*, Yoreh Deah 312.37; *Responsa Meshiv Davar*, I, 8 & 9; *Hatam Sofer*, Hoshen Mishpat #21; *Mayim Amuqim*, #70). The *Shulhan Arukh* and its com-

---

**The pronouns "he" and "she" have been used generically throughout this volume.

mentaries present both points of view (*Shulhan Arukh* Yoreh Deah 245.18 ff). This equivocation on the part of the medieval authorities was intended to encourage strong scholarly leadership.

Matters changed entirely when the modern rabbinate became a profession and the rabbis' livelihood depended upon services rendered to the congregation. Under these circumstances, it was forbidden to trespass on another rabbi's territory (Moses Sofer, *Hatam Sofer* Hoshen Mishpat #21; Yoreh Deah 32; *Meshiv Davar* #8). Some disagreement remained on the right of a newcomer to teach as this is a *mitzvah* and its fulfillment should not be denied to anyone (Elijah ben Hayim *Mayim Amuqim*, #70; Akiva Eger, *Responsa Tanina* #12; Abraham Mordecai Halevi, *Ginat V'radim* Yoreh Deah 3.7).

We in America are faced with a number of special problems as there is no chief rabbinate or any officially recognized jurisdiction for a rabbi either within the urban or rural setting as in so many European lands. The rabbi, therefore, has *de jure*, rights only, within the limited circle of his own congregation. They have elected him and through this agreed to his leadership. However, *de facto* the range of the congregational rabbi extends and is expected to extend considerably beyond his own congregation. He is constantly involved in communal activities and decisions. In addition, he is also expected to serve other members of the broader Jewish community who may not be affiliated with any congregation. We are in all of these instances not dealing with the income of the rabbi as that is assured through a salary which he receives from the congregation, but with the moral authority of the rabbi. That certainly should extend beyond the congregation especially in a smaller community in which he may be the only rabbi or the sole Reform rabbi.

The Code of Ethics of the Central Conference of American Rabbis (*Yearbook, C.C.A.R.*, 1976) indicates that the resident rabbi should be informed by the out-of-town visitor but need not have his consent. That is the official position of the Conference and governs our relationship with each other at the present time.

We would, therefore, conclude that the jurisdiction of the rabbi is clear among all those who are directly affiliated with the congregation (*de jure*) and those who are indirectly served by him (*de facto*). In the broader community the jurisdiction is somewhat less certain. A visiting colleague, of course, has the obligation to inform the local rabbi, but in accordance with our current policy, need not obtain his consent.

November 1986

2. THE DISABLED RABBI

QUESTION: May a rabbi who is temporarily disabled through a broken arm or leg continue to conduct services, preach, etc.?

ANSWER: We must differentiate between rabbinic functions in which the rabbi acts for a congregation as *sheliah tzibur* and teacher in contrast to his role as a judge. There are several kinds of situations in which he could not act as a judge because of the specific Biblical stipulations, at least according to the tradition. This would be true in capital cases in which, under some circumstances, the judge would be involved in the execution (Deut. 17.7; J. San. 8; 26b; Num. 5.11 ff; *Shulhan Arukh* Even Haezer 159.1; Hoshen Mishpat 7.2). As far as we are concerned, there is no likelihood of being involved in these kinds of cases, so there would be no problem with a physical disability and a rabbi's judicial function.

Much more important for us is the rabbi's function as a leader of the congregation and its religious services. The traditional statements connected with these duties are inevitably based upon those of the priests who officiated in the ancient temple. The main statement in Leviticus 21.19, which deals with *shever regel* or *shever yad*, is not as clear as it at first glance appears to be. It seems to exclude priests with a broken arm or leg from publicly officiating at the sanctuary, but this may very well have referred only to fractures which did not heal properly and, therefore, present a visible deformity to those watching the procedure (Bech. 45a). In any case, the lengthy *Talmud* discussions make it clear that a patient with a *mum* is only excluded from certain tasks at the sanctuary. Fractures of human limbs are rarely discussed in traditional literature.

The Biblical text and the various rabbinic sources state that those who limp or have a deformity of the leg are not fit to serve as priests (Lev. 21.18; *Sifra* Emor II, III, p. 95b; Bekh. 7.6; *Tosefta* Bekh 5.9; *Yad* Hil. Biyat Hamiqdash 8.13). Here we are dealing with defects of a permanent nature and visible to the worshipper.

These cautions have been carried into the synagogue, so a priest with a visible defect on his hands or feet may not recite the priestly blessing at a service as this may distract the people who may look at these disfigurements rather than think of the sacred words (M. Meg. 4.7; *Tosefta* Meg. 4.29; Meg. 24b). The regulations against defects extend to any deformities of the fingers (Yoma 2.1, 23a). An exception was made if everyone in the village is a dyer, and so all share the same visible defects; in that instance no one would notice (Meg. 24b; Mordecai; *Yam Shel Shelomo* Hul.; *Shulhan Arukh* Orah Hayim 53.8 with some disagreements). A visible deformity, such as discoloration of the face, etc., would disqualify a person from serving as *sheliah tzibur* (Ettlinger, *Binyan Zion* #5). These references also deal with permanent disabilities. If, however, such disabilities do not distract the congregation, then there is no obstacle to blessing the congregation or leading it in prayer (*Shulhan Arukh* Orah Hayim 128.30).

We might also note that tradition has no prohibition against the use of canes or crutches when they enable a person to walk to synagogue, even though they must be carried on *shabbat* (*Shulhan Arukh* Orah Hayim 301.17, 51, 346.13, 622.1).

If the defect is not visible, then there is no problem (*Yad* Hil. Tefilah 8.12). If the injury causes fainting or similar seizures and are frequent, then the individual should not lead the congregation in service; if infrequent, he remains capable of leading them in a service (Moses Sofer *Responsa* Yoreh Deah #7).

We can see from the sources that temporary disabilities do not disqualify as long as they do not distract the congregation. Certainly a congregation would soon become accustomed to a rabbi appearing in a sling, on crutches or with a cane, especially as it would only be for a short period of time. If this is not so, then someone should be designated to conduct services for the period of temporary disability and permit the congregation to worship undisturbed.

April 1983

3. PUNISHMENT OF MINORS

QUESTION: What is the status of the minor in Jewish law regarding punishment for serious offenses? (S. Levin, Pittsburgh, PA)

ANSWER: It is clear from a wide variety of statements that the father is completely responsible for the acts of his minor children. So, minors would not be punished no matter what their crime, but the father would face whatever monetary penalty is appropriate (M. K. 8.4; Yeb. 99b; Hag. 2b; Git. 23a; B. M. 10b; *Tur* and *Shulhan Arukh* Hoshen Mishpat 182.1, 348.81, 235.19).

In a similar vein, the father is compensated for any injury to his minor children, including the humiliation sustained by them (B. K. 86b). The value lost was figured as if they could still be sold into slavery, as was possible in an earlier period (B. K. 97b).

In the case of the seduction of minor females, the fine went to the father (Deut. 22.28). If the culprit married her, he paid no fine (Ex. 20.15). In case of rape, he had to pay a fine, marry her and could never divorce her (Deut. 22.28). The *Talmud* increased the fine and included psychological damage (Ket. 29a).

Individuals above the age of maturity (12 for girls and 13 for boys) are considered responsible and may be punished as adults, but no capital punishment is permitted until the age of twenty (*Yad* Hil. Genevah 1.10).

If damage to property occurs due to the action of a minor, liability is incurred only if proper precautions have been taken by the owner (B. K. 29a, 55b ff; *Tur* and *Shulhan Arukh* Hoshen Mishpat 421).

December 1981

4. PROFESSIONAL SECRECY AND AN ILLEGAL ACT

QUESTION: A lawyer has discovered that a fellow attorney is providing a client with advice which will lead to an illegal act and the possibility of considerable financial loss. The lawyer asking the question has gained this information in a confidential relationship. Should he break that confidence and inform the client in question?

ANSWER: It is clear that privacy and information gained as part of a professional relationship can generally not be divulged (Lev. 19.16; *Yad* Hil. Deot 7), yet this prohibition is not absolute. For example, if knowledge of certain medical information might change a marriage, such information should be presented (Israel Kagan, *Hofetz Hayim*, Hil. Rekhilut 9). The decision is based upon the principal of the "need to know." Such facts must not be given lightly or simply to complete existing information or for any personal gain.

If such information would lead to the protection of lives or prevent personal injury and financial loss, it must be divulged in accordance with the Biblical injunction of Leviticus, "You shall not stand idly by the blood of your neighbor" (Lev. 19.16). If an individual's life is endangered, immediate action to remove that danger must be undertaken. This was also the interpretation provided for our verse by tradition (San. 73b; *Yad* Hil. Rotzeah 1.13 f, 15; 4.16; Hil. San. 2.4, 5, 12; *Shulhan Arukh*, Hoshen Mishpat 425.10, 426.1). Maimonides considered it necessary to move in this direction in cases of idolatry (*Yad* Hil. A. Z. 5.4) and rape (*Yad* Hil. Naarah 3.1). This would apply, however, only if the client's life is endangered; that is not the case here.

Maimonides and some others go further through the exegesis of another verse from Leviticus (19.14), "Thou shalt not place a stumbling block before the blind." This would include reporting someone who provides incorrect advice which might lead to criminal acts or to a considerable financial loss (*Yad* Hil. Rotzeah 12.4; Jakob Breish, *Helkat Yaaqov* III 136; Elijah of Vilna, *Biur Hagra*, Yoreh Deah 295.2; Joshua Falk, *Peri Megadim*, Orah Hayim 443.5, 444.6).

We must also ask about the status of attorneys in Jewish law. Generally attorneys are not used in the traditional Jewish courts, although they have sometimes been appointed by the court (Ribash *Responsa* #235; Meir of Rothenburg *Responsa* #357). In other words, the litigants and the witnesses are present in person (*M.* Mak 1.9; *Yad* Hil. San. 21.8). Exceptions are only made when the individual involved is unavoidably absent or is too timid to defend himself (*Tos.* to Shev. 31a; *Tur* Hoshen Mishpat 123.16; also Bet Yosef).

When an attorney is appointed, the fiction is created that he acts entirely on his own behalf. He, therefore, has complete power of attorney for the defendant (B. K. 70a; *Yad* Hil. Sheluhin Veshutafin 3.7; *Shulhan Arukh* Hoshen Mishpat 122-123; *Arukh Hashulhan* Hoshen Mishpat 124).

There was, in other words, a reluctance to use attorneys, but by the late Middle Ages, they have been admitted to court, especially if the parties involved were present and their reaction could be watched. Such attorneys are paid by a fee for their services (Rif, *Responsa* #157; Rashba, *Responsa* II #393, III #141, V #287, etc.).

An attorney, therefore, acts as an agent and the laws of the agency apply to him. There is a legal presumption that an agent properly performs the duties assigned to him (Git. 64a); any agent is considered to have been appointed by a client to benefit and not to harm him (Kid. 42b). In this instance, the attorney might be considered akin to both an agent and an expert. Experts who are paid for their advice are liable if their opinion proves to be wrong (B. K. 99b ff; Simon ben Zemah of Duran, *Responsa* II, #174).

As the lawyer in question has not been ethical and has provided improper guidance to his client, it is the duty of the attorney to inform the Bar Association or other appropriate authorities of the misconduct which he suspects. This course of action should be followed in criminal and civil procedures.

December 1986

5. CONFIDENTIAL INFORMATION

QUESTION: A rabbi has been told by one of his congregants that she suffers from a rare disorder which may kill her prematurely. The congregant now intends to be married. The rabbi does not believe that the groom is aware of his wife's condition. Is it the rabbi's duty to inform the groom or should the information given in a confidential manner be kept secret by the rabbi? The woman in question has stated clearly that she will commit suicide if the information is divulged to her fiancé.

ANSWER: The Biblical prohibition against "being a tale bearer" is quite precise (Lev. 19.16) even when the information is true and accurate (*Yad* Hil. Deot. 7.2). However, in this case this Biblical citation is opposed by others in the same chapter of Leviticus, "You shall not place a stumbling block before the blind" (Lev. 19.14). In other words, one must prevent someone from committing a sin or placing themselves in a position of personal or financial loss (*Yad* Hil. Rotzeah 12.4, 1.13). Nor should "one stand idly by the blood of your neighbor" (Lev. 19.16). This has been interpreted to indicate that one should do everything possible to protect life and property from injury directly or indirectly, including providing information (*Yad* Hil. Rotzeah 1.13 *Shulhan Arukh* Hoshen Mishpat 426.1).

Hafetz Hayim (Israel Meir Kagan) argued vigorously for disclosure in a case specifically like this one especially as this may be a major factor in the perspective marriage and lack of such information may endanger the stability of the marriage in the future. Furthermore, in this instance, we are dealing with a life-threatening situation and not a vague problem which need not be revealed (*Sefer Hafetz Hayim* Hil. Rehilut #9).

In analogous situations involving physicians there is some difference of opinion whether he should volunteer or can be compelled to provide such information, but that is only because it may be contrary to the Hippocratic Oath. Most authorities feel that physicians may be forced to testify (Eliezer Waldenberg, *Tzitz Eliezer*, 13 #81; Jacob Breish, *Helkat Ya-akov* 3, #136). However, Barukh Rakover argues to the contrary and feels that a physician is bound by the oath (*Noam*, Vol. 2). A rabbi, however, would be duty-bound to divulge the information he possesses.

In this specific instance, the rabbi must weigh the danger of the woman commiting suicide against the problem of not providing adequate information to the fiancé. The quotation "do not stand idly by the blood of your neighbor" here weighs heavily on the side of the woman (Lev. 19.16). If the rabbi is convinced that her threat of suicide is real, he may *not* divulge the information.

November 1986

6. INFORMING ON OTHERS IN CRIMINAL ACTIVITIES

QUESTION: A prisoner has asked whether he is, according to Jewish law, duty-bound to inform on others in criminal matters with which he is charged. This will probably be part of "plea bargaining." What is his duty according to our tradition? (Rabbi W. J. Leffler, Lexington, KY)

ANSWER: Jewish tradition states that information which, if withheld, would harm individuals or the community, either through criminal activity or considerable financial loss, must be presented. This is based on a Biblical statement (Lev. 19.16) as well as later authorities (*Yad* Hil. Rotzeah 1.13; *Shulhan Arukh* Hoshen Mishpat 426.1; Elijah of Vilna *Biur Hagra*, Hoshen Mishpat 425.20; Isserles to *Shulhan Arukh* Hoshen Mishpat 388.11). Furthermore, in a criminal case every witness is obligated to testify if he possesses personal knowledge of the events (Lev. 5.1; B. K. 55b; Isserles to *Shulhan Arukh* Hoshen Mishpat 28.1).

It is also clear that a person is obligated to testify before a Jewish or non-Jewish court in order to save himself from threatened punishment. Under such circumstances, one is *moser beones* (*Tur* Hoshen Mishpat 388; *Shulhan Arukh* Hoshen Mishpat 388.8 ff; *Yad* Hil. Hovel 8.2). We should note that there is no problem of testifying before a non-Jewish court. We have records of a Jewish community handing a Jewish criminal who had injured a non-Jew to a Gentile court as early as the Gaonic Period (700 - 1000 C.E.; J. Mueller, *Mafteah*, p. 182).

It is quite clear, therefore, that Jewish law requires an individual to testify and that there is no reason to hesitate.

February 1983

7. INSANITY IN CRIMINAL CASES

QUESTION: Are there rabbinic opinions on insanity as a defense in a criminal trial? What is the status of the insane in criminal matters? (A. Adelstone, Flushing, NY)

ANSWER: When the *Mishnah* and the *Talmud* discussed individuals of limited ability, they frequently used the phrase, *heresh shoteh veqatan* - the deaf, the insane and the minor; insanity included any serious mental imbalance. No one in these categories may be punished for their offenses, and they are considered to have limited legal liability (*M.* Erub. 3.2; R. H. 3.8; Meg. 2.4; Hag. 1.1; Git. 2.5, 5.8; B. K. 4.4, 5.6, 6.4, 8.4, etc.) The later Jewish codes continue this classification. The insane are not considered responsible for injuries to others, though others who assault them are liable for the usual punishments (*M.* B. K. 8.4, 87a; *Yad* Hil. Hovel 24.20; *Shulhan Arukh* Hoshen Mishpat 424.8). However, if the individual has lucid moments, in other words, if insanity is temporary, then he is considered responsible (*Yad* Hil. Mekh. 29; *Shulhan Arukh* Hoshen Mishpat 235.23). If the rights or the estate of persons of unsound mind needed to be defended, then the court appoints an administrator (*epitropos*) who looks after their interests. They are not entitled to damages in cases of insult or defamation of character (B. K. 86b; *Yad* Hil. Hovel 3.4; *Shulhan Arukh* Hoshen Mishpat 300.27).

The status of the insane in rabbinic literature is, therefore, clear. The discussion in the later responsa deals almost exclusively with the problems of engagement, marriage, divorce or inheritance. Two problems remain for our discussion. How is insanity defined by rabbinic literature? What is temporary lucidity?

The *Talmud* attempted to define insanity as one "who wanders alone at night and spends the night in the cemetery and tears his garments" (Hag. 3b). This definition was immediately challenged by authorities on the same page, and no resolution was achieved. Others defined it to include individuals who were self-destructive or eccentric (Git. 78a; J. Ter. 40b). It was ultimately left to the judges to assess the situation and make a judgment according to the evidence in each case (*Yad* Hil. Edut. 9.9). In order to assure an appropriate decision, the judges were required to possess some knowledge of all the sciences including medicine (*Yad* Hil. San. 2.1).

Those temporarily insane are not considered liable for acts performed during periods of insanity. However, during times of lucidity, they are liable and could also act as witnesses (*Tos.* Ter. 1.3; J. Ter. 40b; B. B. 128a; *Yad* Hil. Mekh. 29; *Shulhan Arukh* Hoshen Mishpat 235.23). The court must decide whether an act has been committed in a period of insanity or lucidity. Furthermore, an individual so intoxicated as to be totally unaware of his actions is considered temporarily insane, and is treated accordingly by the court (Er. 75a; *Yad* Hil. Ishut 4.18). The cases cited in the responsa literature, however, deal with betrothal and marriage, not criminal acts.

Although some guidelines have been mentioned, they are vague and the decision of temporary insanity is left to the court. Individuals who are considered totally insane are not liable for any act which they may commit.

October 1982

8. DEBTS VERSUS A GIFT

QUESTION: A man's in-laws have sent him a catalogue from a prestigious department store and encouraged him to order one thousand dollars worth of clothing and merchandise as a *Hanukkah* present for himself, and to charge it to their account. The man is aware that the recent affluence of his in-laws enable them to offer such a gift. He also knows that they owe many times this amount to other family members who had made extensive loans during more difficult times. The man feels that these large debts should be repaid before he becomes the recipient of such largesse. For this reason, he wishes to refuse the gift. Should he accept the gift for the sake of *shalom bayit*, or should he refuse? (Rabbi R. A., Florida)

ANSWER: Let us begin this rather complex matter by looking at loans through the eyes of tradition. In the Talmudic period, there was some debate over whether the repayment of a loan is a *mitzvah* or a legal obligation. R. Papa felt it was a *mitzvah*, while R. Huna Ben Joshua considered it a legal obligation. Both lines of reasoning are continued in the later literature (B. B. 174a; Kid. 13b; Ket. 86a; *Semag* Aseh #93). In the final analysis, most scholars feel that there is a legal obligation, and that the concept of the repayment as a *mitzvah* refers to oral loans only (Rashban to B. B. 174a). Anyone who does not repay a loan is considered a wicked person (Ps. 37.21). Generally, when no period is specified in a loan, it is considered repayable after thirty days or less (*Yad* Hil. Malveh Veloveh 13.5; *Shulhan Arukh* Hoshen Mishpat 73.1).

Both lending money to the poor (Ex. 22.24; Shab. 63a; *Yad* Hil. Malveh Veloveh 1.1; *Shulhan Arukh* Hoshen Mishpat 97.1), and its repayment, are *mitzvot*. Everything possible has been done to encourage both of these *mitzvot*. Loans were stimulated through the institution of the *prosbul*, which protected lenders from the approaching sabbatical year which would normally have canceled the loan (Shev. 10.3; Git. 37a, 50a). It was specified that loans could be contracted before a court of three lay people, who were not experts in law (San. 3a), in order to further encourage them. Repayment has always been enforced by the courts. It is incumbent upon the member of the family to encourage repayment in keeping with the Biblical command not to "incur guilt" on account of a neighbor (Lev. 19.17).

The other issue which we must consider is the matter of honor due to in-laws. There are general statements of both *aggadic* and *halakhic* nature which deal with this subject. However, most of them refrain from specifics in this area full of potential conflict and misunderstanding. There are clear obligations to care for sick or indigent in-laws, as well as the obligation to show them proper respect and honor (*M.* Sotah 9:15; Ket. 61b; M. K. 20b; *Yalkut* to I Sam. 24:11; *Shulhan Arukh* Yoreh Deah 240:24; W. Jacob, *American Reform Responsa*, "Responsibility of Children to Their Parents," #53).

In the case which you have cited, it is the religious duty of the son-in-law to respectfully thank his in-laws for their demonstration of love, but he should remind them of their duty to repay their debts; this is both an obligation and a *mitzvah*. He should encourage them to perform that *mitzvah*.

November 1984

9. DEMANDS OF A WILL

QUESTION: What is the affect of a will which demands that a commitment to Judaism be made by the recipients and that they must promise to raise their children as Jews? (Rabbi P. Grumbacher, Wilmington, DE)

ANSWER: A properly executed will takes effect immediately upon an individual's death (B. B. 149a). Efforts were made to assure that the obvious wishes of the dying individual were followed, whether they were written or oral (B. B. 156b; Git. 15a; *Shulhan Arukh* Hoshen Mishpat 250.7). It could even lack the signature of proper witnesses (Git. 71a; *Yad* Hil. Nahalot 4.1). Naturally, nowadays, in all these matters we are guided primarily by the law of the land (*dina d'malkhuta dina*).

In our instance, we are dealing with a clear mandate of the deceased, and that wish should be conveyed to all of her heirs. Those who are already married, and are raising their children as Jews, present no problem. The others who have not yet reached the age of marriage must promise to do so in order to qualify for their part of the inheritance. This is all which can be required. We might add, however, that it remains a *mitzvah* to carry out the wishes of the deceased (Git. 14b; Ket. 70a). This would be true even if some aspects of the will are currently beyond the capacity of the beneficiary.

There is some debate among the authorities whether property is automatically transmitted upon a promise being made or whether actual action is necessary (Isserles to *Shulhan Arukh* Hoshen Mishpat 252.2; *Shulhan Arukh* Hoshen Mishpat 111.9, 257.6; *Responsa* Rosh 86.5; *Responsa* Ritba #54). Those instances, however, did not involve a potentially long waiting period, or one with as many complications as this woman's stipulation.

Here we are dealing with a situation that is akin to an ethical will through which an individual wishes to exert influence upon succeeding generations. The grandchildren should be made aware of the grandmother's wishes and have the moral obligation to execute them. There is nothing in Jewish law which would enable us to go further than this.

November 1984

10. SILENT PARTNERS IN A MEDICAL PRACTICE

QUESTION: What is the attitude of Jewish law to a partnership which provides the money for a medical practice? The individuals involved are not physicians, and therefore they would, on an indefinite basis, benefit from the income of that practice. Is it considered ethical to form a partnership in which the non-participating partners provide the funds for the medical practice which is carried out by a physician? May these individuals benefit from the healing which will occur through the medical practice? (Rabbi M. Staitman, Pittsburgh, PA)

ANSWER: Let us divide this question into two segments. The first will deal with partnerships and loans, and the second with medical ethics. It is clear that Biblical and Talmudic laws were opposed to interest bearing loans. This prohibition was absolute when Jews dealt with co-religionists within the community (Lev. 25.35 ff; Deut. 23.20 ff). The prohibition was amplified and expanded by the *Mishnah* and *Talmud* (*M. B. M.* 5.1, 60b ff, 75b; *Yad* Hil. Malveh 4.2 ff, 7.11, 10.1 ff; *Shulhan Arukh* Yoreh Deah 161.1 ff).

These restrictions, however, proved unrealistic in an economy which functioned on a monetary basis, and so a legal device known as *heter isqah* was invented and became common (*Pisqei Harosh* to B. M. 5.23; Mordekhai B. M. 3.19; *Nahalat Shivah* #40). In modern business transactions, the phrase *al pi heter isqah* remains sufficient, even if no formal document of this kind has been drawn up.

Interest from aliens or foreigners was permitted even in Biblical times (Lev. 25.35; *M. B. M.* 5.6, 70b f), but was frowned upon and discouraged in the Talmudic period (Mak. 24a). During the Middle Ages in Christian northern Europe, when money lending was among the few avenues of livelihood open to Jews, the taking of interest from non-Jews was defended because of the heavy financial burdens placed upon Jews by the non-Jewish authorities (*Tos.* to B. M. 70b; *Shulhan Arukh* Yoreh Deah 159.1). Furthermore, as the monetary economy developed, moral restrictions against lending to non-Jews were voided through reasoning similar to that described above with the *heter isqah*.

Some feel that loans to a teacher, physician or any other individual who helps the community should be considered in a highly positive manner. They are an investment which make it possible for him to continue in his profession, which he may otherwise abandon (Nathanson, *Hoel Umeshiv Mahadurah Kamma*, III, 160).

Other authorities limit loans to capital advanced for goods and not for services or the employment of an individual (*Imrei Yosher*, I, 108; Meir Arak; *Kitzur Shulhan Arukh* 66.10; *Shulhan Arukh Harav*, Hilkhot Ribit #42).

Let us now turn to the question of partnerships. Various forms of partnerships were reported in the *Mishnah* and *Talmud* (*M*. Ket. 10.4, etc.), and became widely accepted and used by the eleventh and twelfth century, particularly in Northern Europe (Mordekhai to B. K. 176; Rosh *Responsa* 89.13; Elon *Hamishpat Haivri* II, pp. 744 ff).

Frequently one partner furnished the capital and the other performed the work. In such instances, some difference in remuneration is stipulated by law, so that the working partner receives a greater benefit than the others (*M*. B. M. 5.4, 104 b; *Yad* Hil. Sheluhin 6.1 ff; *Tur* Yoreh Deah 177). Furthermore, the active working partner is protected, because he can withdraw more readily from the arrangement (*Tur* Hoshen Mishpat 176.28). It is clear from the above statements that silent partners are permitted, and funds earned in this fashion are perfectly acceptable under Jewish law. A variety of provisions have been made for such arrangements.

We must now ask whether there are any special restrictions on forming these kinds of arrangements for medical purposes. Fees were part of the acknowledged life of a physician, and the Biblical phrase, "cause him to be thoroughly healed," was interpreted by the *Targum* (Ex. 21.19) to indicate that a fee should be paid. It was considered normal and proper for services rendered. The service of those who took no fees was not considered to be worth much (B. K. 85a). Various arrangements were made for the payment of fees, sometimes in advance, and sometimes for a completed treatment, etc. (Ket. 52b, 105a). The skill and knowledge of a physician has been highly praised, and appropriate compensation is suggested (*Shulhan Arukh* Yoreh Deah 336.3). Although a physician may be motivated by humanitarian concerns, he should also receive a salary for his efforts. That portion of his life is governed by the same standards as any commercial venture.

A physician's business arrangements and fees are treated as any other business venture. There is some difference of opinion on the role of loans, as well as silent partners, in some types of commercial enterprise. This would hold true for our case as well, but it would generally be permitted. A permissive stance has made it possible for modern traditional Jews to participate in the stock market, various forms of partnerships and other enterprises previously not known by the traditional literature.

Jewish law does not distinguish between the employment of funds in a general partnership or a medical partnership. Nothing in Jewish law would prohibit silent partners in a medical practice.

June 1984

11. UNKNOWN DEFECT IN BUILDING MATERIAL

QUESTION: Our sanctuary and social hall contain asbestos tiles in their ceilings. The congregation is planning on removing them. At the last board meeting a directive was passed instructing our legal committee to file proceedings against an asbestos manufacturer. Is it moral to bring a liability suit against a manufacturer who was unaware of the potential health hazard of his product when it was installed? (Rabbi M. Levin, Kansas City, MO)

ANSWER: This entire matter is governed by a simple Biblical statement, "When you sell property to your neighbor, or buy anything from your neighbor, you shall not wrong one another" (Lev. 25:14). This law has been further developed in the *Talmud* and later codes. Maimonides made the seller responsible for disclosure of any defect to the buyer (Hul. 94a; *Yad* Hil. Mekhirah 18.1; *Tur Shulhan Arukh* Hoshen Mishpat 227; *Shulhan Arukh* Hoshen Mishpat 227.6; *Sefer Hamitzvot* Lo Ta-aseh #250). There is disagreement over the possibility of waiving such liability. Maimonides felt it could not be waived (*Yad* Hil. Mekhirah 15.6). Asher ben Yehiel disagreed (*Tur* Hoshen Mishpat 232.7); the discussion on waiver of responsibility was continued in the later responsa.

Traditional texts discuss specific items in which defects have been discovered. One of the primary grounds for recovering the purchase price involves an item which may have a dual use and the buyer finds it not suitable for his purpose. This would be true of eggs, which may be eaten or hatched, seed which may be consumed or planted, an ox which may be used for plowing or slaughtered for food, etc. If the buyer did not inform the seller of his intended use, then he has no recourse (B. B. 90a; *Yad* Hil. Mekhirah 16.2).

In these instances, and others like them, the seller had to provide a sum which made good on the defect, but the items purchased were not returned to him. However, if the defect was major and in a permanent item like a building, then the buyer generally had the right to return the building to the seller, though he might settle for payment of repair costs. For example, Asher ben Jehiel spoke of a building which had been severely damaged by vandals during the period of the sale. In that instance, the damage was repairable, and so the seller was responsible for payment of the repairs. However, if the damage had been more serious, and if the item could not have been restored to its original state, then the seller would have been forced to take it back (Asher b. Jehiel, *Responsa*, Section 96, #7; Joshua Falk to *Tur* Hoshen Mishpat 232.5; Joel Sirkes to *Tur* Hoshen Mishpat 232.4).

Each of these instances dealt with defects which were readily discernible and not latent as in the case of the asbestos. Furthermore, they dealt with defects which were discovered in a reasonable period of time, certainly before the item was heavily used. I have found no responsa which deal with a latent defect or cases in which damages and liability were claimed decades later.

The matter of damages is much more complex because it depends whether this situation is classified as *garmei* or *gerama*. *Garmei* implies liability and *gerama* does not. There is a considerable amount of discussion on these two terms without clear conclusions (B. K. 24b, 48b, 55b ff, 60a, 98b, 110a, 117b; B. B. 22b; *Tur* Hoshen Mishpat 232.21 and commentaries; *Shulhan Arukh* Hoshen Mishpat 232.20, 386.4 and commentaries). The general rule seems to be that the governing authorities impose damages when the public order makes it necessary or desirable. When the damages are indirect, can not be foreseen, and no public benefit is involved, then there is no liability (*Tur* Hoshen Mishpat 232.20; *Shulhan Arukh* Hoshen Mishpat 232.21). For a recent discussion of this, see Epstein, *Arukh Hashulhan* Hoshen Mishpat, Vol. 8, 386.1 ff; M. Elon, *Hamishpat Ha-ivri*, Vol. I, pp. 173 ff.

In each of the discussions cited above, the defect was found either immediately or after a reasonable length of time; it was apparent and not latent. That is not the case in the question which you have asked.

We must, therefore, conclude that traditional Jewish law would not hold the seller responsible for defects of damages after a long period of time has elapsed, especially as the defect was latent and unknown to both buyer and seller at the time of the transaction.

The entire matter may also be considered under the general classification *dina demalkhuta dina*, and as the courts of the United States have decided that the seller is responsible in this matter and that it is for the public good, it would be permissible for the congregation on those grounds alone to bring a liability suit.

April 1985

12. JUDAISM AND THE ENVIRONMENT

QUESTION: What is the attitude of Judaism toward environmental concerns expressed now by so many political groups? Is this an issue for Judaism? Or as we have been an urban people for such a long time, is this of relatively little concern to us? (F. P., Baltimore, MD)

ANSWER: As the amount of material on this question is immense, let me at the outset indicate that I will restrict myself to some *halakhic* sources and ignore entirely the vast *midrashic* literature, which is of a more homiletic character. It has, however, also played a major role in forming the Jewish attitude toward the environment. A good source for this material is Louis Ginzberg's *Legends of the Jews*, especially the volumes of notes.

Ancient Jewish sources were quite concerned with the destruction of man's natural environment and dealt with it from Biblical times onward. So, for example, the Biblical ordinance (Deut. 20.19, 20) against destroying fruit trees while besieging a city has been reinterpreted far more broadly to include any purposeless destruction during siege. This included the diversion of water from such trees as stated by Maimonides (*Yad* Hil. Malkhut. 6.8). Contrary citations from *Scripture* were interpreted as referring to very specific instances, but were not allowed to alter this basic attitude. Similarly, the land immediately outside a city was to remain clean and pure; it could not be sold, and its use could not be changed (Lev. 25.34; Num. 35; Ar. 33b).

There was specific concern about the environment of Jerusalem, especially as the problems of garbage, dung and remnants of sacrifices were considerable. No garbage or dung was permitted in the city

(B.K. 82b), and the ashes of the Temple sacrifices could not be scattered by the wind (*Yad* Hil. Tamid 2.15). Furthermore, no threshing was allowed within fifty cubits of Jerusalem, nor tanning within forty cubits or at an upwind location (B. B. 24b; B.K. 82b). Air pollution was of sufficient concern that altar fuel was limited to certain kinds of wood; other species which produced excessive smoke were prohibited (Tamid 29a, b).

The countryside further away from the city also needed to be watched; it should not be overgrazed, nor should goats or sheep be permitted in cultivated areas (B. K. 79b, 80a).

The mood expressed in these paragraphs, largely based on Talmudic sources, continued in the post-Talmudic rabbinic literature, and most of it can be summarized under the principle *bal tash-hit*, cause no wanton destruction. Naturally many exceptions were also cited in the literature. Trees could be destroyed to build the Temple, to cultivate a field, to remove an advantage from the enemy during a siege, and even to honor a ruler through some extravagant celebration. Yet the courts were permitted to intervene for the sake of ecology (*Shulkhan Arukh* Hoshen Mishpat 175.26). Special care for the environment had to be exercised in the land of Israel (Emden, *Sheelat Yabetz* #71).

A similar kind of feeling was expressed about animals through ordinances concerning hunting. Of course we Jews could not consume the meat of an animal taken during a hunt unless it had been ritually slaughtered. This was possible when the animal was trapped. Such hunting was permissible to provide food (*M.* Shab. 7.2), but it was considered wrong to hunt merely for sport. This was cruel to animals and was also considered wasteful (Maimonides, *Guide to the Perplexed*, Chap. 48; Meir of Rothenburg, *Responsa* #27). The same kind of attitude was expressed in more recent centuries by Ezekiel Landau, who felt that animals could be slain if they invaded a farm, were dangerous, or perhaps to obtain meat for someone else. Hunting for sport alone was considered wrong (*Noda Biyehuda* II, Yoreh Deah #10).

An appreciation for nature has been stressed by our liturgy; many benedictions regularly thank God for the wonders of nature. Some are conveniently listed in Hertz's *Daily Prayerbook*, pp. 584 ff. These include prayers of thanks for fruit, fragrant plants, spices, oil, the wonders of nature, lofty mountains, great deserts, lightning, beautiful trees, animals, a rainbow, upon seeing a tree in bloom, etc. Each of these prayers instills a feeling of reverence for the natural world and for its maintenance.

Judaism has emphasized an appreciation of the environment and nature since the Biblical period. These issues do not play a dominant role in Jewish life, but they remain important.

November 1984

13. A BAN ON SMOKING IN THE SYNAGOGUE

QUESTION: The congregation has recently constructed a new wing which includes multi-purpose rooms sometimes used as a small synagogue, as well as various assemblies and classrooms. We would like to ban smoking from the area sometimes used as a synagogue and would like to know whether it is appropriate to ban smoking entirely. (Rabbi J. Stein, Indianapolis, IN)

ANSWER: There has been some discussion of tobacco in the *halakhah* since the eighteenth century. It began with its use on festivals and fast-days (Mordecai Halevi, *Darkei Noam* #9). Other questions were discussed subsequently (Abraham Gumbiner *Magen Abraham* to *Shulhan Arukh* Orah Hayim 210 and 514; I. Z. Kahana, *Mehakrim Besafrut Hateshuvot*, pp. 317 ff). These early discussions of smoking dealt with this habit and the way in which it affected *shabbat*, holidays, studies and the decorum of the synagogue service. A few authorities even considered its use beneficial (Joshua Pollock; Jacob Emden in Kahanah, *op. cit.*, pp. 321, 323).

The question of tobacco in the synagogue was discussed, and it was generally prohibited (Moses Hagiz, *Leqah Hakemah* Hil Tisha B'Av; Isaac Lampronti, *Pahad Yitzhaq*; David Hoffmann, *Melamed Lehoil* Orah Hayim 15), but Hayim Palagi permitted it when there were no services (*Kaf Hahayim* 21.19). There was a division of opinion about its use while studying (Shimshon Hamburg, *Nezirat Shimshon* #92, Hayim Benjamin Puntrimoli, *Responsa*, Orah Hayim #103).

We, however, must view smoking differently as it is clear that smoking and any other use of tobacco are health hazards. Whatever lingering doubts existed earlier have been removed in the last decades by the Surgeon General's report of January, 1964. Therefore, we must treat this matter entirely on that basis.

It is incumbent upon every Jew to care for his health as well as the health of other human beings (Deut. 4.9, 15; 22.8), and no injurious product should be used. This applies as well to the health and well-being of one's neighbor (B. K. 91b; *Yad*. Hil. Rotzeah 11.4 ff; *Shulhan Arukh* Hoshen Mishpat 427; Yoreh Deah 116.5 and Isserles). These arguments have generally not been applied to smoking by Jewish authorities with the exception of Israel Meir-Hakohen Kagan, (*Kuntres Zekhor Miriam, Hofetz Hayim*) who dealt not only with the physical harm which cigarettes and cigars may bring but also with the neglect of study which the habit of smoking may cause.

Most modern Orthodox rabbis have been hesitant about prohibiting smoking as they felt that this was a popular habit difficult to change or that the danger to an individual was no greater than "crossing a street" (J. David Bleich, *Tradition*, Vol. 10, #3, Vol. 16, #4). After all, tradition has been opposed to prohibitions which will not be followed (B. K. 79b; Shab 148b; Moses Feinstein, *Igrot Mosheh*, Yoreh Deah II #49).

We, however, feel it is necessary to move beyond this cautious stance. When it is within our power to ban smoking, we should do so on the grounds of personal health as well as the health of our neighbors. It would, therefore, be appropriate for a synagogue to ban smoking entirely in its building or to restrict it to a few isolated areas.

December 1985

14. SUITABLE COSMETIC

QUESTION: A cosmetic manufacturer has begun to produce a new product which will use mink oil as its base. This product will emphasize "mink" to enhance the image of the product. Would there be any difficulty about Jews using this cosmetic product which would be produced as a facial cream lotion, etc., as the mink is not a kosher animal? (L. D., New York, NY)

ANSWER: Jewish tradition, beginning with the *Bible*, has spoken favorably of the use of cosmetics. Esther was anointed for "six months with oil of Myrrh, six months with sweet odors and with other ointments of this woman" (Esther 2.12). In addition, the Song of Songs also praised ointments. On the other hand, excessive use of cosmetics was attacked by the prophets (Jer. 4.30; Ez. 23.40). Later Jewish tradition in the *Talmud* continued to look favorably on the use of cosmetics by women as they might become unattractive if avoided

(J. Git. 50a). In addition, various Talmudic citations dealt with different kinds of facial creams or salves which enabled the face to look
fresh (Shab. 94b). The trade in cosmetics which seems to have been
quite extensive was also discussed. For example, there was concern
about the freedom of out-of-town peddlers, and they were guarded
against interference from local merchants (B. K. 82a). This may very
well have been done to maintain reasonable prices. The arrival of a
peddler led to some suspicion of the women who had been in contact
with him (Yeb 24b).

Another Talmudic tractate stated the husband should provide for
cosmetics in the dowry in accordance with local customs (Ket. 66b).
This custom was continued in Gaonic times (Lewin, *Otzar Hageonim*,
Vol. 8, pp. 199 ff). Elsewhere there was some concern about carrying a
vial of perfume around one's neck (akin to jewelry) on *shabbat*. This
was done to combat bad odors (Shab. 62a). A male student should not
use perfume (Ber. 43b). There are also various *Midrashim*, some not
too flattering toward women, which dealt with the use of perfumes.
One stated that men needed no perfume, in contrast to women as
men were created from earth which emits no bad odor, while women
were formed from the bone of Adam, and bones smell when left
standing for three days (*Midrash Rabbah* Gen. 17.8). This story may
also have sought to control the excessive use of perfumes by men. Of
course no kind of anointment was to be used during times of mourning (II Sam. 12.20; Dan. 10.3; Yoma 8.1) though they could be brought
into a house of mourning (M. K. 27a).

There was no Talmudic discussion about the contents of perfume.
The Biblical injunction against the use of anything akin to the incense
of the sanctuary remained (Ex. 30.33). One could object to the use of
mink oil only on the grounds that the mink is not a kosher animal.
This would not prevent the use of its fur, but matters might be
different with its oils as they could be absorbed through the skin or
swallowed in small amount accidentally. The psalmist seemed to
teach that anointing oil was absorbed by the user's body (Ps. 109.18),
but the *Talmud* specifically stated that this did not occur (Ber. 57b).
According to the Talmudic discussion that absorption was not a
consideration.

We must, therefore, consider the whole matter from the standpoint
of forbidden foods. Certain animals are prohibited, and everything
that comes from them in the way of food is included (Bek. 5b).
However, this principle only dealt with in items normally considered

as good, as for example, the milk of an unclean animal, the roe of an unclean fish, etc. This was taken by tradition also to cover the bone marrow used in gelatin; the Orthodox discussion about this question has dealt with its use in its natural or a chemically altered state. We might ask a similar question here, but it apparently will be used in its natural state.

We should note, however, that non-kosher food, when accidentally mixed with kosher food, would not cause the latter to be prohibited if the amount is smaller than one-sixtieth (*Shulhan Arukh* Yoreh Deah 94.4 ff). In this case the percentage of mink oil in the cosmetic is minute, probably less than one-sixtieth. So, if the oil were swallowed, or if it were accidentally mixed with kosher food through the handling of such food, the amount involved would be too small to present a question of *kashrut*. There could be no objection, therefore, for its use by Reform Jews or any Jews.

February 1979

15. INERT PIGMENT AS A PERMANENT COSMETIC

QUESTION: An eye surgeon has asked whether there would be anything in Jewish law against the procedure of inserting an inert pigment into the superficial dermis at the base of the eyelash. Its purpose is cosmetic in nature and has been requested by many individuals. Some have physical handicaps which make the application of normal cosmetics difficult or are allergic to a normal cosmetic. Others have requested it as a convenience.

The procedure has also been suggested to accompany a variety of surgical procedures used to correct defects or following serious accidents which lead to the loss of eye lashes. Appropriate tests to assure no allergic reaction will, of course, be made in each instance. As Judaism is opposed to tatooing, is it permissible to use this procedure on Jewish or non-Jewish patients? (Rabbi R. Agler, Boca Raton, FL)

ANSWER: The Biblical text of the Book of Leviticus (19.28) states, "you shall not make gashes in your flesh for the dead or incise any marks on yourself. I am the Lord." This passage has been interpreted by the *Talmud* to deal primarily with incisions made at a time of mourning for the dead (Mak. 20b). However, the next *Mishnah* prohibits any "incised imprint"; an offender was to be flogged. There was some discussion in the *Talmud* whether such an "imprint" refers only to incisions of the name of God or of idolatrous deities. One authority, Rabbi Malkiah, even prohibited the covering of a wound with burnt wooden ashes as it might appear like an "imprint" (Mak. 21a). This prohibition against tatooing included the permanent marking of slaves to avoid their flight (Git. 86a). Curiously, the writing of the Divine name on top of the skin, and covering it to avoid erasure during a bath, was permitted (Shab. 120b). In each of these instances in which tatooing is prohibited, it is done so on the basis of being an idolatrous practice or marring the human body.

Eye makeup and facial makeup is mentioned in the *Bible* (Jer. 4.30); it was a practice followed by women of doubtful morality, such as Jezebel (II Kings 9.30), and was condemned by the prophets (Ez. 23.40; Jer. 4.30). In the Mishnaic period, eye makeup was accepted although sometimes still frowned upon (*Tosefta* Sotah 3.3; Shab. 95a; M. B. K. 1.7; B. K. 117a; Ber. 18b, etc.) There was some discussion about which eye makeup might be provocative (Shab. 11b; 80a). Cosmetics are prohibited during the period of mourning (Ket. 4b).

These traditional sources make it clear that there would be nothing wrong with any temporary application of a cosmetic. They would prohibit its application in a permanent way as marring the human body.

When the procedure is used as a surgical procedure to restore the eye after an accident, or to correct some other deficiency, it is permissible as any other surgical procedure. It would also be appropriate for use with handicapped individuals. It would, however, violate the spirit of tradition to use this procedure in a broad, general manner.

January 1985

16. WHEN IS ABORTION PERMITTED?*

QUESTION: Assuming that abortion is *halakhically* permitted, is there a time span in which abortion may take place according to tradition? (Rabbi A. Klausner, Yonkers, NY)

ANSWER: Let us begin by looking at this assumption. There is currently considerable difference of opinion among Orthodox authorities about the permissibility of abortion as well as circumstances and time when it would be permitted. The laws have been analyzed by a growing number of scholars (V. Aptowitzer in the *Jewish Quarterly Review* [New Series], Vol. 15, pp. 83 ff; David M. Feldman, *Birth Control in Jewish Law*; Robert Kirschner, "The Halakhic Status of the Fetus with Respect to Abortion," *Conservative Judaism*, Vol. 34, No. 6, pp. 3 ff; Solomon B. Freehof, "Abortion" in W. Jacob *American Reform Responsa*, #171; *Noam*, Vols. 6 and 7, etc.). The fetus is not considered to be a person (*nefesh*) until it is born. Up to that time it is considered a part of the mother's body, although it does possess certain characteristics of a person and some status. During the first forty days after conception, it is considered "mere fluid" (Yeb. 69b; Nid. 3.7, 30b; M. Ker. 1.1).

The Jewish view of the nature of the fetus is based upon a statement in *Exodus* which dealt with a miscarriage caused by men fighting and pushing a pregnant woman. The individual responsible for the miscarriage was fined, but was not tried for murder (Ex. 21.22 f). We learn from the commentaries that payment was made for the loss of the fetus and for any injury done to the woman. Obviously no fatal injury occurred to her. This was the line of reasoning of the various codes (*Yad* Hil. Hovel Umazik 4.1; *Shulhan Arukh* Hoshen Mishpat 423.1; *Sefer Meirat Enayim* Hoshen Mishpat 425.8). If this case had been considered as murder, the Biblical and rabbinic penalties for murder would have been invoked.

The second source on the nature of the fetus is found in the *Mishnah*, which stated that it was permissible to kill a fetus if a woman's life is endangered by it during the process of giving birth. However, if a greater part of the fetus had emerged, or if the head had emerged, then the fetus possesses the status of a person and can not be dismembered, as one may not take one life in order to save another (*M. Ohalot* 7.6). This view considers the unemerged fetus entirely part of the woman's body; as any of her limbs could be amputated to save her life, so may the fetus be destroyed. The same point of view was taken in another section of the *Mishnah*, which discussed the execution of a pregnant woman for a crime. The authorities would not wait for her to give birth even if that process had already begun (Arackh. 7a). The statement from Ohalot is contradicted by San. 72b and led to controversy in recent centuries (Akiba Eger and *Tos.* to *M.* Ohalot 7.6; Epstein, *Aruk Hashulhan* 425.7, etc.)

A *tosefot* to another section simply stated that it was permissible to kill an unborn fetus; this passage, which stands in isolation, is taken seriously by some authorities, while others say that it represents an error (Nid. 44b) and is contradicted elsewhere (San. 59a; Hul. 33a).

The Mishnaic statement in Ohalot was based on two Biblical verses. In them the fetus was portrayed "in pursuit" (*rodef*) of the mother, and therefore, has endangered her life (Deut. 25.11 f; Lev. 19.16; *Yad Hil.* Rotzeah Ushemirat Hanefesh 1.9; *Shulhan Arukh* Hoshen Mishpat 425.2). Maimonides, who did recognize the fetus as possessing some status, and Caro were willing to use either drugs or surgery in order to save the life of the mother.

Modern rabbinic authorities have felt that the variety of attitudes toward the fetus and embryo in the *Talmud* also point to potential restrictions in the matter of abortion. When we review the discussion of fetus and embryo, as it arose in various situations, we see that it was not treated consistently. Different criteria were applied when dealing with slaves, the problems of animal sacrifice and issues of inheritance. No uniform definition from Talmudic sources can be achieved (see Robert Kirschner, *op. cit.* for a full discussion).

Some recent scholars have felt that only the argument of "pursuit" provides the proper basis for abortion when the mother's life is endangered. They reason that although the fetus is not a person (*nefesh*), it still possesses a special status, and therefore, should not be treated as nothing or destroyed for no good reason (Jacob Emden, *Responsa Sheelat Yavetz*, 1.43; Yair Bacharach, *Havat Yair*, #31; Eliezer Waldenberg, *Tzitz Eliezer*, Vol. #273, 9; *Noam* Vol. 6, pp. 1 ff). Others have felt a fetus may be aborted whenever there is any danger to a mother, as the status of a newborn child less than full term is in doubt until thirty days have elapsed, although it is, of course, considered a *nefesh* (Maharam Schick, *Responsa* Yoreh Deah #155; David Hoffmann, *Melamed Lehoil* Yoreh Deah #69).

On the other hand, a line of reasoning which dealt with the mother's psychological state has been based on Arakhin 7a; it would permit abortion for such reasons or for the anguish caused to the mother by a child's potential deformity or other problems. So, Ben Zion Uziel permits abortion when deafness is indicated in the fetus (*Mishpetei Uziel*, Hoshen Mishpat, #46). Uziel Weinberg permits it when rubella occurs in early pregnancy (*Seridei Esh* III, No. 727). Eliezer Waldenberg does so for Tay Sachs disease and other serious abnormalities (*Tzitz Eliezer*, Vol. 9, #236).

Other traditional rabbis have been very reluctant to permit abortion on the grounds that one is not permitted to inflict a wound on one's self (Joseph Trani, *Responsa Maharit* 1.99; Zweig, "Al Hapalah

Melahutit," *Noam*, Vol. 7, pp. 36 ff). Rabbi Unterman has argued against abortion as tradition permits the desecration of the *shabbat* in order to save an unborn fetus (Ramban to Nid. 44b); this would prove that the fetus possesses human status. An unborn child, although not yet a human being, is a potential human being, and abortion is "akin to murder"(I. Y. Unterman, "Be-inyan Piquah Nefesh Shel Ubar", *Noam*, Vol. 6, pp. 1 ff). Others have followed this line of reasoning. Unterman, however, also reluctantly permits abortion under some circumstances (*Ibid.* 52; *Shevet Miyehudah*, I, 29).

In summary, we see that there are some who agree with Rabbi Unterman and reluctantly permit abortion to save the mother's life. Others permit abortion when the mother faces a wider array of life-threatening situations, such as potential suicides, insanity, etc. Both of these groups would permit abortion only for serious life-threatening dangers.

Those authorities who do not consider abortion "akin to murder" are more lenient, but would not permit an abortion lightly either (Solomon Skola, *Bet Shelomo*, Hoshen Mishpat 132). They would permit it for rape (Yehuda Perlman, *Responsa Or Gadol*, #31) or to avoid undue pain (Jacob Emden, *Sheelat Yavetz*, #43), but not in the case of a woman who seeks an abortion after adultery (Yair Hayim Bachrach, *Havot Yair*, #31). This group also permits abortion when there is serious danger to the mother's mental health (Mordechai Winkler, *Levushei Mordekhai*, Hoshen Mishpat #39), or when serious fetal impairment has been discovered in the first three months (Eliezer Waldenberg, *Tzitz Eliezer*, Vol. 9, #327).

We can see from the recent discussion that there is some hesitancy to permit abortion. A number of authorities readily permit it if the mother's life has been endangered, or if there is potentially serious illness, either physical or psychological. Others are permissive in cases of incest or rape. A lesser number permit it when a seriously impaired fetus is known to exist - not for the sake of the fetus, but due to the anguish felt by the mother.

The Reform Movement has had a long history of liberalism on many social and family matters. We feel that the pattern of tradition, until the most recent generation, has demonstrated a liberal approach to abortion and has definitely permitted it in case of any danger to the life of the mother. That danger may be physical or psychological. When this occurs at any time during the pregnancy, we would not hesitate to permit an abortion. This would also include cases of incest and rape if the mother wishes to have an abortion.

Twentieth century medicine has brought a greater understanding of the fetus, and it is now possible to discover major problems in the fetus quite early in the pregnancy. Some genetic defects can be discovered shortly after conception and more research will make such techniques widely available. It is, of course, equally true that modern medicine has presented ways of keeping babies with very serious problems alive, frequently in a vegetative state, which brings great misery to the family involved. Such problems, as those caused by Tay Sachs and other degenerative or permanent conditions which seriously endanger the life of the child and potentially the mental health of the mother, are indications for permitting an abortion.

We agree with the traditional authorities that abortions should be approached cautiously throughout the life of the fetus. Most authorities would be least hesitant during the first forty days of the fetus' life (Yeb. 69b; Nid. 30b; M. Ker. 1.1; Shulhan Arukh Hoshen Mishpat, 210.2; Solomon Skola, Bet Shelomo, Hoshen Mishpat 132; Joseph Trani, Responsa Maharit, 1.99; Weinberg, Noam, 9, pp. 213 ff, etc.) Even the strict Unterman permits non-Jews to perform abortions within the forty day periods (Unterman, op. cit., pp. 8 ff).

From forty days until twenty-seven weeks, the fetus possesses some status, but its future remains doubtful (goses biydei adam; San. 78a; Nid. 44b and commentaries) as we are not sure of its viability. We must, therefore, be more certain of our grounds for abortion, but would still permit it.

It is clear from all of this that traditional authorities would be most lenient with abortions within the first forty days. After that time, there is a difference of opinion. Those who are within the broadest range of permissibility permit abortion at any time before birth, if there is a serious danger to the health of the mother or the child. We would be in agreement with that liberal stance. We do not encourage abortion, nor favor it for trivial reasons, or sanction it "on demand."

January 1985

17. A DANGEROUS MEDICAL EXPERIMENT

QUESTION: A man with a severe heart disease and no more than six months to live wants to know whether he may participate in a controlled experiment with a new drug; he is anxious to do so. Since the purpose of the experiment is to save lives in the future, may he participate even though there is some danger of shortening his life-span? His own chance for a cure at this late stage of the disease is slight. (H. T., Los Angeles, CA)

ANSWER: It is a general rule that every person should avoid danger to life. So, the *Talmud* (Ber. 3a; Shab. 32a) said that a person should not walk among ruined buildings because of the danger that a shaky wall may collapse. The *Talmud* (Hul. 10a) stated that danger to life and health was of greater concern than religious prohibitions (*sakanta tamira meissura*). In other words, one must exercise greater care to avoid danger than a religious prohibition.

The general rule of guarding against danger is, however, confronted by the duty of rescuing a fellow human from danger. This has been discussed from early times by our tradition (Lev. 19.16; San. 73a; *Shulhan Arukh* Hoshen Mishpat 426). The question then is whether we may endanger ourselves in order to help others. There is no doubt that we must assist our fellowman through our means or influence, but are we permitted or required to go further? This question has been discussed in a rather picturesque way by David Ibn Zimri of Egypt (16th century). In his responsa (Vol. III, #627), the following incident was cited: The Pasha told a certain Jew to allow his leg to be amputated or else he (the Pasha) would kill another Jew. May this man endanger his life (since the amputation was dangerous) in order to save the life of a fellow Jew? David Ibn Zimmi considered this beyond the call of duty.

The medieval *Sefer Hassidim* (#467, ed., Margolis) described a medicine which cured or killed the patient in nine days. The book prohibited the drug on the basis that it might kill the patient before his time (*qodem simno*). A number of later authorities have agreed with this assessment (*Shevut Yaaqov*, Vol. I, #13, Vol. 3, #75; *Binyan Zion*, #111, *Hatam Sofer* Yoreh Deah #76).

The general principles governing our question are fully discussed by the modern Israeli authority, A. Abraham (*Lev Avraham*, Vol. II, pp. 75-76). He states that no doctor has the right to subject another person to a medical experiment even though such an experiment may eventually help others. The doctor may expose himself to danger (*sofeq sakana*) when he attends an infectious patient, as that is his duty as a physician, but he cannot ask a patient to submit to a dangerous experiment. The author adds that if the experiment is *not* dangerous, then the patient may participate in it and that would be reckoned as a *mitzvah*. Eliezer Waldenberg (*Tzitz Eliezer*, Vol. XIII, #103) disagrees with this view of safe experiments and denies any religious obligation even when there is no danger. At the most, one may permit such participation, but it is in no sense a religious duty (*mitzvah*).

We would generally agree with the tradition and the decision reached by Dr. Abraham, yet our patient's desire to participate must also be considered. The need and *mitzvah* to help others through his part in such experiments is important. Tradition would reject any participation, but we may argue that as we have benefited from medical progress, we must help to continue it.

We must ask many questions before we reach a decision. Is the patient fully informed? Does he have the capacity to understand the implications of his choice? Has this been discussed by him with his family? What actually is the risk/benefit ratio?

We would permit participation in an experiment of limited risk and doubtful benefit by this patient if these questions have been answered and if he is certain that this would give meaning and purpose to the last phase of his life. Many individuals search for some useful act during this period, and the experiment may provide it for this individual and his family. If successful, it may, of course, also prolong his life somewhat.

August 1985

18. TEST TUBE BABY

QUESTION: Recently an embryo was successfully formed from an egg fertilized by her husband's sperm. It was then implanted in the wife's womb and developed into a full-term baby. Is this form of insemination permissible for Jewish parents who otherwise could not have children? Is it permissible to fertilize several such eggs, store the embryos and implant them in others? (S. M. L., Pittsburgh, PA)

ANSWER: It is clear that these techniques are now available. Although some refinements still need to be made before they can be widely practiced, it is possible to fertilize an egg under laboratory conditions and implant it in the mother's womb. It is also possible to freeze the embryos of livestock and keep them over long periods of time. On subsequent implantation, they develop into full-fledged, normal animals. This has been done regularly with livestock and could, presumably, be done with human beings. Various aspects of these questions will be discussed separately.

Jewish authorities have favored the principle that every individual at least reproduce himself, and so a couple should have a minimum of two children (Yeb. 62b; *Yad* Hil. Ishut 15.16; *Shulhan Arukh* Even Haezer 1.8). This was Hillel's interpretation of *peru urvu*. Parents have been encouraged to have at least two children. This remains high on the Jewish agenda despite the general mood of birth control, as we remain a very small endangered minority.

In keeping with this principle, it has always been considered a sin to emit sperm for an act other than procreation (San. 108b; Nidah 13a; R. H. 12a; *Yad* Hil. Issurei Biah 21). This has led Orthodox authorities to prohibit various methods of birth control. Here, however, we are not dealing with the misuse of the sperm, but simply the fertilization outside of the normal channels. This matter has been discussed and approved by Mosheh Feinstein (*Igrot Mosheh* Even Haezer #10) if the sperm utilized was that of the husband, while he and most others would prohibit using the sperm of a donor. Solomon B. Freehof would permit it in either case, while Alexander Guttmann would exercise great caution with donor sperm (W. Jacob, *American Reform Responsa*, #157, 158) As we are dealing with the husband's sperm, all the cautions cited are irrelevant. There would be nothing which would prohibit the actual fertilization of the egg taking place in a test tube and its implantation in the wife's womb. It would enable some childless Jewish couples to have children and should be encouraged when available.

The second part of the question deals with the freezing of embryos (fertilized eggs) and keeping them indefinitely. This, of course, raises an entirely different set of problems. If it is the intent to preserve the embryos for this couple only, and insert them into the wife at a later time, perhaps if the first pregnancy fails or to create subsequent children, no objection could be raised. However, adequate safeguards must be assured with, perhaps, a time limit for the preservation. Such frozen embryos should not be used for genetic experimentation or engineering. Both of these areas need much careful further study.

August 1978

19. *IN VITRO* FERTILIZATION WITH COUSIN'S *OVA* *

QUESTION: A couple is unable to have children. The wife's first cousin had agreed to donate *ova* for *in vitro* fertilization with the husband's sperm. It will be subsequently implanted into the wife's womb. Is there a question of incest? (Rabbi H. Silver, West Hartford, CN)

ANSWER: The question of artificial insemination has been dealt with in two responsa by Solomon B. Freehof and Alexander Guttman in 1952 (W. Jacob, *American Reform Responsa*, #157, 158). There are, however, two substantial differences between the question raised here and these responsa. In that instance the sperm of a stranger was used to fertilize the *ova* of the wife; the situation here is reversed as the husband's sperm will be used and the *ova* will be that of another person. Secondly, in the previous responsa the donor was not known while here the *ova* of the cousin will be used. As the source of the *ova* is known, one of the traditional objections to artificial insemination is removed. Orthodox authorities fear that the youngster produced by such insemination might inadvertently marry incestuously. In this case, as he would know his ancestry, that could not occur.

Now we must ask whether it is possible to use the *ova* of the wife's first cousin. It is clear that in the days of bigamy or other forms of multiple marriage like concubinage, it was possible for a first cousin to marry the same husband. The details of concubinage are discussed in a separate responsum (W. Jacob, *American Reform Responsa*, # 133). Polygamy has, of course, been prohibited for Ashkenazic Jews since the decree of Rabenu Gershom in the eleventh century. If it were still permitted offsprings of such a marriage would be considered *kasher*. In this instance no marriage will take place; the *ovum* will be fertilized *in vitro* and then placed in the womb of the wife.

We must carefully consider some other potential problems, however. As the source of the *ovum* will be known to both the parents and possibly the child, this may cause psychological difficulties. In case of normal family strife, will this situation aggravate matters? Are any pressures for donation being applied to the cousin? These and other issues must be carefully discussed with competent experts and a good deal of counselling must occur with the couple and also with the prospective donor. As the current divorce rate is high it would be wise to discuss this possibility and its ramifications also, painful though it may be. The possibility of a defective child should also be discussed.

Peru ur'vu is of course a major *mitzvah* and children are mentioned as an essential element of marriage many times by the traditional sources (M. Ye. 6.6; Nidda 13b; Ket. 8a; Yeb 61b; *Yad* Hil. Ishut 15.6; *Tur* and *Shulhan Arukh* Even Haezer 1.5) and lack of children was considered grounds for divorce (*Shulhan Arukh* Even Haezer 1.3 f, 154.10) although others disagreed. The *mitzvah* may, of course, be fulfilled through adoption ("Adoption and Adopted Children," W. Jacob, *American Reform Responsa,* # 63); this couple has chosen a different route. We would give reluctant permission to use *in vitro* fertilization in the manner you have described. The potential problems are numerous and should lead to great caution.

November 1986

20. GENETIC ENGINEERING

QUESTION: Would a person produced through genetic engineering rather than natural reproduction possess a soul? Does a clone have a soul? (Z. Shtohryn, St. Joseph, MO)

ANSWER: We should divide this question into two segments. First we must deal with the question of when a soul enters the human body. There are a number of *midrashic* and *halakhic* responses to this, but the practical *halakhic* implication is that a baby becomes a person only at the moment of birth. Therefore, if a woman in labor can not give birth, and her life is endangered, it is permissible to destroy the child as long as its head has not come out of the womb. Until that time it is considered an integral part of the woman, and so may be treated like any other limb of the body rather than a separate human being (M. Ohalot 7.6, *Shulhan Arukh* Hoshen Mishpat 425.2). Many safeguards have been built around this statement by the rabbinic tradition to assure that it would not be misused for broad scale abortions. This practical decision developed independently from the Talmudic conceptions of the soul.

The rabbis of the *Talmud* developed several doctrines of the soul, but they have not been systemized. A prayer from this period taken into the liturgy expresses a leading motif. It states: "My God, the soul which You have given me came pure from You," (Shab. 152b). A dualism between body and soul was assumed by many scholars of that period (Ber. 10a; Shab. 113b; Yoma 30b; etc.). There is considerable discussion among the rabbis about the moment at which the soul enters the body. Is it at the instant of conception, of embryonic formation, or of birth (San. 91b; *Gen. Rabbah* 34.10)? All three were possible for those rabbis who followed the Neo-Platonic three-fold division of the soul. An additional element of the soul would then have been added at each of the above mentioned stages.

In the Middle Ages, when Jewish philosophy was influenced by Greek thought transmitted by Arab scholars, other ideas of the soul developed and many thinkers divided the soul into three forms in accordance with Islamic Neo-Platonists. The first was equated with man's active intellect, while the other two were connected with lower forms of life (Saadiah, Bakhya Ibn Paquda, Ibn Gabirol and Maimonides). Maimonides and some others considered the three forms of the soul to be animal, vegetative and human, and so felt that the lower forms of life also contained souls.

The *Zohar*, the leading mystical work of medieval Judaism, also divided the soul into three elements. The first was rational, the second moral and the third vital. All three were then connected to the *Sefirot*, which link God and man. There is a considerable amount of speculative literature about the nature of the soul, and many different philosophical patterns have appeared in Jewish thought. Anything produced asexually like a clone would be akin to a plant, would also be considered to have at least a lower form of the soul. The soul in its human form, according to the *halakhic* tradition, however, enters a *body* only at the time of birth as the references above have indicated.

The only references in traditional literature to man-made creatures are the legends of the *Golem*. These stories arose in the Middle Ages and are akin to those found in other folk mythologies. The *Golem* was thought to be a clay or wooden figure brought to life by its master through the insertion of the divine name in its mouth, or the placement of the name on its forehead. *Golems* were sometimes considered dangerous and had to be restrained through removal of one of the letters of God's name, otherwise they could become destructive (Gershom Scholem, *The Kabbala and Its Symbolism*, 1965, pp. 185-204; A. D. Eisentein, "Golem," *The Jewish Encyclopedia*, Vol. 6, p. 36 f). The *Golems* which appear in various legends were completely controlled by their master or maker. They, therefore, were akin to modern robots which can perform tasks upon command, but are controlled by a human master. No one would consider a computer to possess a soul. When Zvi Ashkenazi and Jacob Emden were asked whether a *Golem* could be counted as part of a *minyan* they responded that it could not (*Hakham Zevi* #93).

We are, however, concerned with an entirely new being which might conceivably begin its life in a test tube from a fertilized *ovum* or a variety of genetic material and would be capable of sexual reproduction itself. We shall not discuss the desirability of such an undertaking, but at some time in the future it will, undoubtedly, occur with or without approval. We could well consider such a being to have a soul. It will have been formed from human material despite all genetic alterations. Its development will have taken place in an artificial environment rather than the womb, but at some point it will emerge as a human being. Hopefully, it will then not be enslaved to its maker or master, but will develop independently as other human beings. Unless such possibilities of independent intellectual and moral development are genetically removed, this would be a human being.

We must add that these conclusions remain speculative as knowledge in this field remains limited. The parameters and possible consequences of genetic engineering remain to be explored; until this has been done, only preliminary guidance can be provided.

February 1978

21. FETUS USED FOR EXPERIMENTATION

QUESTION: Under what circumstances, if any, would it be permissible to conduct medical research involving an aborted fetus? A member of a congregation is doing research in Alzheimer's Disease which requires live brain tissue otherwise unavailable. (Rabbi H. Jaffe, Minneapolis, MN)

ANSWER: Jewish tradition looks upon the fetus in a manner similar to that of a severed limb. In other words, it has some special status and is considered part of a human being, but it does not possess a soul of its own and is not considered a separate human being in its own right until it has reached a certain age. Even then there is some disagreement. A fetus, therefore, needs to be treated with reverence, but not in the same manner as a deceased person.

A fetus which is less than forty days old does not possess human status (Shab. 135b; Solomon Skola, *Bet Shelomo* Hoshen Mishpat #139). Even when the fetus is older than forty days, it is not considered as a living soul by most traditional authorities (San. 72b; Rashi to San. 72b; Joshua Falk, *Meirat Enayim* to *Shulhan Arukh* Hoshen Mishpat 425; Ben Zion Uziel, *Mishpetei Uziel*, III, #46, 47). There is, therefore, no formal obligation to bury the fetus. It is treated as a severed limb. In Talmudic times, limbs and organs severed from the human body, and fetuses, were disposed of informally and needed no formal burial (Ket. 20b; *Tur* Yoreh Deah 266; *Shulhan Arukh* Yoreh Deah 266). A few recent authorities disagree and feel that a fetus must be buried (David Cohn, *Kol Torah* Adar, Sivan, 5730). Moses Feinstein (*Igrot Mosheh* Yoreh Deah I #231) also stipulates that all segments of the body must be buried as a matter of law.

Severed limbs and fetuses are generally buried for two reasons; first in order to assure their dignified disposal as a part of a human body, and second, in order to prevent the ritual uncleanliness of priests who might come in contact with them (*Yad* Hil. Tumat Okhlin 16.8; *Shevut Yaaqov*, II, #10; Ket. 20b).

As there is no mandate to bury a fetus, and as it has not been viewed as a human being with its own soul, there is no objection to its use for medical experimentation. This has been the general view expressed by some traditional authorities (*Noda Biyehudah* II Yoreh Deah #209; Eliezer Waldenberg, *Tzitz Eliezer*, X, #25, Chapt. 8).

We should mention one additional negative argument which might be raised, i.e., not benefiting from the dead (*asur behana-ah*). This, however, is not involved in our case, as this referred only to a deceased "person," a status which the fetus has not attained (*Shulhan Arukh* Yoreh Deah 364.1). The experimentation, which this scientist intends to conduct is, therefore, in keeping with Jewish tradition as well as with our interpretation of it.

November 1984

22. NAZIRITE VOW

QUESTION: Occasionally inmates in various prisons have decided to take the "Vow of Nazirite." Their refusal to cut their hair brings them into conflict with prison officials, and leads to punishment for insubordination. What is the position of Reform Judaism on the "Nazirite Vow?" (Rabbi L. Sussman, Middletown, OH)

ANSWER: Let us begin by looking at the historic background of the "Nazirite Vow" (Nu. 6). Restrictions are placed upon a Nazirite: He may not be in contact with any dead, including his father and mother. He may not cut the hair of his head. He may not drink wine or utilize any product of the grape and possibly all alcohol, [*shekhor*], (Nazir 4a, etc.). In this state he is considered "holy to God" (Nu. 6.8). And if for some reason he becomes unclean during this period, he must bring a sacrifice. Upon the completion of his vow, he also brought a sacrifice.

We actually hear very little about Nazirites in the *Bible*. The only well-known examples are those of Samson (Ju. 13.5) and possibly Samuel (I Sam. 1.11 ff). There are also references to Nazirites in a few other isolated passages such as Jeremiah 7.29 and 35.

The *Mishnah* developed the laws of the Nazirite as this state of semi-asceticism had become popular; it was open to any Jew, but not to Gentiles or slaves (Nazir 61a). An entire tractate was devoted to the details of the vow, the offerings which were to be brought, the status of the Nazirite within and outside the land of Israel, the rights of women and slaves to take this vow, the questions of grape leaves and other prohibitions (34b). The later Talmudic tractate further developed and discussed the laws of the Nazirite. The laws set the duration of the vow from a few hours to a lifetime, although the actual minimum was thirty days (*M. Nazir* 1.3). It also provided for various categories of Nazirites with different rules for each. For example, a Nazirite who had made the vow for life was permitted to cut his hair once a year (*M. Nazir* 1.4). He was permitted to clean and arrange his hair as long as no comb touched it (Nazir 42a). He might also trim it in certain other ways (Nazir 39b ff). Despite all the details, we have no clear picture of the heightened spiritual state which may have been sought or attained through these vows.

We should note that there was opposition to the Nazirite in Talmudic times, and some authorities considered asceticism as sinful even if the vows were completely fulfilled (Nazir 4a; Taanit 11a; Ned. 9a ff, 20a, 77b, etc.) It is clear, nevertheless, that this state of asceticism remained popular for a number of centuries. Much was made of the fact that the Maccabean Queen, Adiabne, was a Nazirite, and rabbinic tradition included the Biblical figure of Absolom in this circle due to his long hair.

Modern scholars have speculated that it was the rabbinic opposition to asceticism which led to the abandonment of this vow. Others felt that it ceased because of the destruction of the Temple and the end of the sacrificial cult. Neither answer is satisfying and both raise many additional problems.

The medieval literature virtually ignores the Nazirite, and we find a thorough discussion only in Maimonides' Code (*Yad* Hil. Nazirut). To the best of my knowledge, there are no responsa on this matter. In other words, it is a custom which died long ago.

As Reform Jews, we must ask ourselves whether there is any good reason to re-institute this custom. Certainly the sacrifices once connected with it lost their meaning with the destruction of the Temple, nor does the issue of defilement of the dead play a role in our lives. This leaves abstinence from wine and the grape, along with the refusal to cut one's hair, and whatever undefined heightened spiritual commitment might accompany this status. As this rite is not practiced by the Reform Jewish community, nor has it become an accepted custom within any segment of the Jewish community, it would be inappropriate for an occasional prisoner to adopt this ancient rite merely to trouble his jailers. There are no grounds for a Reform Jew to claim a special status because of the Vow of the Nazirite.

June 1985

23. HISTORICAL BASIS FOR JEWISH SOCIAL SERVICES

QUESTION: What is the historical basis for social services as we now know them? (Dr. S. Busis, Pittsburgh, PA)

ANSWER: If we turn to the Biblical period, we find most emphasis placed upon alleviation of poverty either through outright charity (Deut. 15.10 ff, etc.), tithing for the benefit of the poor (Deut. 14.28 f), participating in the harvest and the produce of the sabbatical year (Lev. 19.9 f, 23.22, etc.). In addition to this, there was an attempt to bring about economic equality every fifty years through the Jubilee Year when all Hebrew slaves were set free and all land was returned to its original owner (Lev. 25.8 ff). Those legislative statements of the *Torah* were constantly reenforced by the message of the prophets. A similar emphasis on charitable acts was continued in the *Mishnah* and *Talmud* reflecting the period of the second Temple and the Babylonian exile. Perhaps the grandest statement about charitable acts is to be found in Maimonides' *Yad Hazaqah*, which listed eight degrees of philanthropy with emphasis upon helping the poor toward independence (*Yad.* Hil. Matnat Aniyim 10.7 ff). "The highest degree is attained by those who give him a gift or a loan, or go into partnership with him, or find work for him to strengthen his hands so that he need no longer appeal for help." A discussion of some other aspects of charity and charitable gifts will be found in the responsa "Priorities for an Adoption Agency" and "Priorities in Charitable Distribution."

All such charitable directives were addressed to the individual and were more concerned with the physical needs of the poor than with their psychic and emotional needs. As the former matters are now part of the services of the secular government, the emphasis of Jewish social services is on the latter. This, too, has a long tradition in our history.

Sick-care societies on a communal basis did not appear until the Spanish-Jewish period. They may have begun as early as the thirteenth century in Spain (A. A. Neuman, *Jews in Spain*, II, 161 ff). Such societies were responsible for the physical and spiritual welfare of all who were ill, burial of the dead, and counseling of the bereaved.

Similar societies were founded in Germany in the seventeenth century, probably under the influence of Spanish-Jewish immigrants (J. R. Marcus, *Communal Sick-Care*, p. 64). At the same time, we find such societies beginning in Italy. Throughout Central Europe they patterned themselves somewhat after Christian groups which also cared for the sick, but two major differences continued to exist between the Jewish organizations and their Christian counterpart. The Christian organizations were also social clubs and tended to look only after their own sick members. The Jewish Brotherhood had few social overtones and worked for the benefit of the entire community. These societies, often called "Holy Brotherhood" or "Brotherhood of Loving-kindness," were motivated by strong religious forces. Their constitutions often quote Psalm 41 or the *Ethics of the Fathers* — "by three things is the world upheld, by *Torah*, service, and by deeds of loving-kindness," or "you shall love your neighbor as yourself" (Lev. 19.18).

The Brotherhoods were tightly organized and funded through the community. All the members of the Brotherhood were duty-bound to serve in whatever capacity they could. There were rigid schedules of visiting the sick and caring for the bereaved. As much attention was given to the religious and emotional needs as to the physical needs of the sick. The basic feeling of these groups has been best stated by Dr. Abraham Wallich, a seventeenth century university trained physician, who in his *Sefer Dimyan Harefuot* felt that the sickness must be cured not only by physical but also by spiritual means. Manuals were written for the guidance of those who counseled the sick and the bereaved. Many of them, like *Sefer Hahayim* or *Maaneh Lashon*, were very popular and went through many editions.

We also find Jewish hospitals as specific Jewish institutions beginning in Germany in the thirteenth century. Through communal pressure, they became modernized in the eighteenth century. Often they were guided by a Brotherhood as well as the general community. It was felt necessary to have Jewish hospitals as their counterparts were specifically Christian rather than secular. Both the Brotherhoods and the Jewish hospitals could also be found in the Eastern European Jewish communities. Brotherhoods were present in communities both large and small in the last two centuries, while hospitals existed only in the large Jewish centers.

We may then see that there is a long history of continuous Jewish social service through well organized groups which looked after the physical, spiritual and emotional needs of the members of the community during times of personal stress and crisis.

March 1974

24. PRIORITIES IN CHARITABLE DISTRIBUTION

Question: Does tradition set priorities in the distribution of charitable funds which have been collected? In this community there are day schools, afternoon schools, Jewish community center programs, senior adult housing, nursing homes and many other groups which claim priority from the charitable funds. What kind of priorities does the *halakhah* set? (Rabbi B. Greenspan, Pembroke Pines, FL)

Answer: Charity has been emphasized in Judaism since Biblical times. The *Torah* suggested that one tenth be collected for the poor, and that corners of the field and the gleanings of the harvest be left for them so that they could participate in the harvest. This was a way of providing for individuals who needed food and basic sustenance (Lev. 19, 27.30 ff; Nu. 18.26; Deut. 12.17; II Ch. 31.5 f; Neh. 13.12).

Many Biblical books continue this emphasis and frequently chastise those who neglect the poor while amassing fortunes themselves (Deut. 15.7 f; Amos 2.6 ff; Isaiah 1.17; Jeremiah 7.6; Mal. 3.5; Prov.

31.10; Job 29.16; etc.). Categories of poor, such as widows, orphans and the sick were mentioned, but no priorities were established.

These thoughts were reinterpreted by the later Mishnaic and Talmudic literature. By that time, portions of the Jewish population lived in urban settings, so the earlier manner of distribution through gleanings and abandoned corners of the field were no longer appropriate. The *Mishnah* provided for the poor through the continuation of the tithe as well the placement of gifts in a special area of the Temple from which individuals could help themselves according to their need without shame.

There are a variety of rules in the *Talmud* which deal with the poor and define those eligible for gifts. So, for example, those who still have enough provisions for two meals may participate in public food distribution in a soup kitchen, while those who still possess enough for twenty-four meals may not participate in distributions from a charitable box. Furthermore, those whose possessions consist of two *zuzim* could not glean in the fields (*M.* Peah 8.7, 8; *J.* Peah 29b). There were, of course, other rules, too, about the sale of possessions and family responsibility for those relatives who were poor (Ket. 68a; *Shulhan Arukh* Yoreh Deah 253.1; 257.8).

Local poor individuals were always given priority over those at a distance, and members of the family over outsiders (B. M. 71a; *M.* B. K. 11.9; *Shulhan Arukh* Yoreh Deah 251.3).

The Jewish community took care of its own poor and except under special circumstances charity from non-Jews was not accepted. On the other hand, non-Jews could be beneficiaries of Jewish charity (*M.* Git. 5.8; 61a f; *Shulhan Arukh* Yoreh Deah 254.2).

Charity in the form of food or clothing was arranged by loans to the poor (Yeb. 62b f); items were sold below cost when the prices had risen excessively (*Sefer Hassidim* #1049).

Every effort was made to adopt orphans (San. 19b; Ket. 50a) or to arrange for orphanages although the latter is a development of modern times. The first Jewish orphanage was opened in London in 1831.

Different forms of giving were listed but unsystematically and few priorities on distribution were provided; among the noblest was the anonymous gift through which the recipient and the donor were unknown to each other. A large number of sayings which encourage charity are scattered through the *Talmud* and the *Midrashic* literature (*M.* Avot 1.2; B. B. 9a, b, 109b; Ber. 55a; Ket. 67b; Shab. 156b; Taan 20b, etc.). Even the poor are to be charitable (Git. 7b).

A system for the collection of charitable funds was established in every community and one or two treasurers took care of this task. In fact, no community was to be without such individuals who looked after the poor (*Yad* Hil. Matnat Aniyim, 9.1-3). Efforts to organize patterns for the distribution of charity were undertaken by the twelfth century *Sefer Hassidim*, and Maimonides (1135-1204) in his *Yad* (Hil. Matnat Aniyim), as well as Caro (*Shulhan Arukh* Yoreh Deah 250 f) and subsequently by Elijah ben Avraham of Smyrna (*Meil Tzedaqah*). Each of these works listed various gradations of giving and distribution independently without much reference to any earlier effort. The loftiest goal was the procurement of employment for the poor or the provision of a dowry for an orphaned girl; both would remove the recipients from the rolls of the poor and would eliminate a drain on the community (Shab. 63a.; Mak. 24a; *Yad* Hil. Matnat Aniyim 10.7 f). No distinction was made between Jew and non-Jew (Git. 61a) nor of rank within the Jewish community (Ket. 6, 7a: *Yad* Hil. Matnat Aniyim 8; *Shulhan Arukh* Yoreh Deah 251).

Much effort was expanded on ransom for captives, or if that was not possible, at least proper provisioning for those who were held captive (Rieger, *Geschichte der Juden in Rom*, II, p. 316; *Shulhan Arukh* Yoreh Deah 252.1). This could extend to selling items from the synagogue in order to help captives (Israel Abraham, *Jewish Life in the Middle Ages*, pp. 337 ff). Funds were made available for Israel and they were collected by *Sheluhim* who regularly visited communities (Abraham Yaari, *Shiluheh Eretz Yisrael*).

In the medieval period, vigorous charitable organizations looked after the feeding, housing, educational and dowry needs of the poor (M. Güdemann, *Geschichte des Erziehungswesens und Kultur*, I, 50 ff; A. Cronbach, "Me'il Tzedakah," *Hebrew Union College Annual*, Vols. 9-14). This was necessary as poverty was endemic in a sizable portion of the Jewish community during many centuries.

Hospitals are mentioned early in the literature, however, they were actually hostels for traders and poor travelers. The first reference to such a Jewish "hospital" is in 1210. A leper hospital existed in Heidelberg, in 1349, but this seems to have been an exception (Abraham Cronbach, *Religion and Its Social Setting*, p. 131). Few financial provisions were made for sick care, unless the sick were indigent. Every effort was made to assure that they were regularly visited (*Or Zarua* 2.51). In some cases, individuals unwilling to make such visits were fined (Abraham Cronbach, *op. cit.* p. 137).

Educational institutions were not recipients of charity, although wealthy individuals endowed them. In the Talmudic and later Medieval periods, it was the duty of each community to establish and support such institutions. Elementary schools were always provided for in conjunction with synagogues; parents of the children paid tuition according to their ability, while poor students were fed and housed by the community (Cronbach, *op. cit.*, p. 128). Considerable sums were expanded on direct support for educational institutions but this was not considered charity. It was an obligation supported by taxes and tuition. Scholarships for poor students were provided in the form of food, lodging or books as a charitable contribution (Turei Zahav to *Shulhan Arukh* Yoreh Deah 249.2; S. Dubnow, *Pinqas Hamedinah*, #528 and #588). Institutions of higher learning were established and supported by patrons. Their future depended on this help, and when the economic conditions changed, they closed or moved to a new location.

None of these sources dealt with institutions which are now the major recipients of charitable funds such as vocational institutions, special education units, social service agencies, hospitals, etc. In other words, the earlier Jewish communities faced so many basic needs that other matters could not be considered.

We may conclude from this that tradition provides little guidance for our age, especially as we have been fortunate enough to overcome the basic problems of previous ages. All sources agree that communities need primary education, sick care, and centers of higher learning. They do not deal with their funding in detail.

July 1986

25. GIFTS TO ORGANIZATIONS INIMICAL TO REFORM JUDAISM*

QUESTION: Should Reform Jews contribute to organizations which advocate changes in the Law of Return in Israel? (Rabbi D. Taylor, Highland Park, IL)

ANSWER: If we begin by asking the broader question, "Who has the right to expect some help from us or any other fellow Jew," we must turn to the Biblical demands which deal with the maintenance of the sanctuary as well as charity toward the poor. The temple in Jerusalem, and the earlier Tent of Meeting, were maintained through a gift of the half-*sheqel* by every adult male. In addition a tithe, as well as portions of all the sacrifices, were provided for the priests and the Levites. The other gifts mandated by the *Bible*, and later literature are intended to deal with the poor, the widow, the orphan, etc. (Lev. 19, 27.30 ff; Nu. 18.26; Deut. 12.17; II Ch. 31.5 f; Neh. 13.12; see "Priorities in Charitable Distribution").

As Judaism developed, numerous institutions became part of each Jewish community. These included a system of schools, both for the education of the young and advanced scholars, hospitals, as well homes for the aged and destitute (J. Marcus, *Communal Sick-Care in Medieval Germany*; M. Güdemann *Geschichte des Erzieungswesens*; L. Löw, *Die Lebensalter*; Israel Abrahams, *Jewish Life in the Middle Ages*). These institutions served the entire Jewish community despite differences of opinion about interpretations of Jewish law.

When major disagreements appeared on the Jewish communal scene in various periods of Jewish history, such common ventures ceased. We can see this clearly in the century long bitter struggle between Hassidim and Mitnagdim. They not only refused to support each other's institutions, but fought with every weapon at their command including the intervention of the hostile Czarist government (S. Dubnow, *Geschichte des Chassidismus*, Vol. 2, p. 149 ff). We find a similar situation when we look at the vigorous rising Reform Movement in Germany and Hungary during the last century. In Germany, for example, the Orthodox community fought hard to withhold financial support and to keep the liberal community from obtaining government funds to which all religious communities were entitled. These struggles also led to the secular courts in encounters like the Geiger-Tiktin Affair in which a segment of the community sought to keep the great liberal Jewish scholar, Ludwig Geiger, from the position of rabbi in Breslau (D. Philipson, *The Reform Movement in Judaism*, pp. 51 ff). When the battle was lost by the Orthodox, they successfully sought legislation in Prussia which would permit a segment of the community to withdraw from the general community and still receive government support. This effort was led by Samson Raphael Hirsch (Ismar Ellbogen, *A Century of Jewish Life*, p. 99 ff; W. G. Plaut, *The Rise of Reform Judaism*, Vol. 1, pp. 63ff; N. H. Rosenbloom, *Tradition in an Age of Reform*).

We see similar hostility when we review the history of the Zionist Movement in Europe and America. Certainly anti-Zionists strongly opposed all financial support for Zionism. The ultra-Orthodox *neturei karta*, as well as various Hassidic anti-Zionist groups, still deny support and do their best to lobby against it both within the Jewish community and with the United States Congress.

We as Reform Jews should *not* contribute to organizations which advocate a change in the "Law of Return" and should do everything within our power to see to it that others do not contribute to them either. This not only represents enlightened self-interest, but also will help maintain some semblance of unity within the broader Jewish community. We must remember that it is militant Orthodoxy which threatens to divide, and thereby, weaken the modern Jewish community. This threat should not be taken lightly, but must be fought with all the vigor and power at our command.

May 1986

26. CHILDREN'S SUPPORT OF PARENTS

QUESTION: Can the community force children to support their parents? Can the community refuse to support them on the basis of the children's obligation? (Rabbi R. Kahn, Houston, TX)

ANSWER: The basis for the support of parents by their children is the fifth commandment: "Honor your father and your mother..." (Ex. 20, 12). This has been taken as one of the main sources for most aspects of the child-parent relationship. The question of financial support of parents by their children led to a division of opinion between the scholars of Babylonian and Palestinian *Talmud*. The authorities of the Palestinian *Talmud* felt that children had to support their parents, and of course, were also obligated to honor them through their personal service and devotion. This could be compelled by the community (J. Kid. 71b). The Babylonian authorities, in one long discussion, felt that although honor and devotion was due to the parents from their children; financial support was debatable. Arguments were presented on both sides, but ultimately the decision freed a son from any obligation to support his parents (Kid. 30a). Emphasis was placed upon personal service rather than on financial obligation. That service was to be rendered by a son, even if it led to a considerable financial loss. Such service could be forced by the community. Other discussions indicate that sons were forced to support their parents financially (Hul. 110b; Ket. 49b, 50a). There are also numerous stories in the *Midrash* which emphasize this. This was the position ultimately taken by tradition.

The debate among the later authorities does not deal with the need to support parents, which is taken for granted, but whether this could be compelled. The answer in most instances turned out to be positive, as this is a charitable duty and the community may compel charitable contributions. On the other hand, scholars felt uneasy about compelling devotion and respect.

Rabbi Meir of Rothenburg indicated that charity must begin with close relatives; parents are first, then brothers and sisters; other relatives follow, and the total stranger comes last (*Responsa*, Vol. II, p. 118 f; *Seder Elijahu*, Chap. 27, p. 135). It was normal in medieval Europe to support family members from the tithe allocated to the poor (Meir of Rothenburg, *Responsa* #75, p. 10b, ed. Bloch; Isaac of Vienna, *Or Zarua*, Tzedaqa, Sec. 26). The community could go to considerable length to force a son in this direction. Solomon ben Aderet, for example, suggested that the synagogue be closed to a son and he be publicly shamed until he supported his father, yet he should not be placed under a ban (*Responsa*, Vol. 4, #56). In this case there was some doubt about the economic deprivation of the father. Somewhat similarly, David ben Zimiri felt that children could be compelled to support their parents in a manner appropriate to the financial status of the children (*Responsa*, Vol. 2, p. 664). A decision akin to this was rendered much later by Moses Sofer (*Hatam Sofer*, Yoreh Deah 229). It further indicated that anything which the son possessed must be placed at the disposal of the parents.

There are, of course, many other responsa which deal with specialized problems in which there is controversy between parents and children over other matters which cloud the nature of these obligations. We may, therefore, conclude that the community may go to considerable length to force children to support their parents. The traditional authorities, naturally, mentioned only the responsibility of sons; we would broaden that to include all children. If the community does not succeed in obtaining such support as the enforcing powers of the modern community are limited, then the community itself is obligated to support the parents.

June 1982

46

27. DRESS CODE FOR RELIGIOUS SCHOOL

QUESTION: Our religious school has insisted on a dress code for young people both in school and especially for the attendance at synagogue services. Is there anything in Jewish tradition that points to "proper attire" for attendance at synagogue services? (Kenneth G. Jacob, Pittsburgh, PA)

ANSWER: This question leads us to look at the sumptuary legislation in the past. The question may be restated as follows: Does the Jewish tradition give the synagogue community or the rabbinate the right to legislate on the question of dress? We will find that such legislation began in Mishnaic times (*M*. Sotah 9.14) when the rabbis prohibited the use of "crowns of the bridegroom" during the war of Vespasian and "diadems of the bride" during the war of Titus.

Restrictions applicable to synagogue services became frequent in the Middle Ages. Many decrees may be found beginning with the early fifteenth century. These represented reactions to the danger of envy by Gentiles. The decrees passed at Forli, Italy, in 1416, dealt with extravagant dress worn in public. Some idea of the detailed nature of such sumptuary legislation may be given through a short quotation from acts passed in Metz in 1690: "On Saturdays and festive occasions women are allowed to wear only ordinary veils. God-mothers are allowed to wear others only on the evening before circumcision or the Saturday following the birth of a boy. Veils of gold or silver are expressly forbidden, except on the Saturday preceding a wedding, to the mother of the bride, her mother-in-law, sisters-in-law, sisters, grandmothers and aunts. This privilege lasts for the two days before the wedding and extends to women who conduct the bride to the synagogue on the morning of the wedding and those who accompany her under the *hupah*" (Alfred Rubens, *A History of Jewish Costume*, p. 196). Similar details curbing extravagant clothing of men may be found in a wide variety of medieval sources (Louis Finkelstein, *Jewish Self-Government in the Middles Ages* and Cecil Roth, *Gleanings*).

A discussion of special garments to be worn on the Sabbath appeared in the *Talmud* (Shab. 113a), and declared that those who possessed a change of clothing should wear the new clothing on the Sabbath, and those who do not simply should make the old clothing look a little better in order to honor the Sabbath. The passage sought to assure that the Sabbath was distinguished from other days in every possible way, "dress, speech, manner of walking, etc." Even here one rabbi opposed this on the grounds of ostentation, but that opinion was rejected. David ibn Zimri (16th century) mentioned special clothing worn by men and women on the Sabbath; in Egypt these were white (*Responsa* II, 693; IV, 62), while Lampronti cited a number of sources which indicated that a woman's special Sabbath garb might only be sold if one needed money for sustenance (*Pahad Yitzhaq*). None of this, however, was concerned specifically with dress in the synagogue.

There were also strong prohibitions against wearing clothing akin to the costume of non-Jews. A *taqanah* was mentioned by Güdemann against wearing clothing of monks and nuns in the synagogue (*Geschichte*, Vol. I, pp. 260 ff; Meir of Rothenburg, *Responsa* #18). We know from other sources that medieval Jewish travelers often found safety in dressing themselves like monks and nuns (*Sefer Hassidim*, ed. Margolis, #702). This prohibition was codified by Maimonides (*Yad* Hil. Avodah Kokhavim 11.1) and in the *Shulhan Arukh* (Yoreh Deah 1.78). Isserles, however, stated that the prohibition applied only to religious vestments used in actual services, not to clothing which happens to be similar to that of Gentiles. Both Caro and Isserles agreed that such garments may be worn if required for attendance at court or government functions (for a recent brief discussion of this, see Moseson, "Hukat Akum," *Hadarom*, #40, pp. 47 f).

Another medieval *taqanah* dealt with the problem of dirt caused by wooden shoes worn in the synagogue and prohibited them inside the building (Güdemann, *Geschichte*, Vol. III, pp. 267 ff, quoting Moses Cohen, *Book of the Pious*). This regulation was akin to contemporary church rules which were concerned with the ostentation of wearing such shoes as well as the noise caused by them; it forbade the worshipper to bring a second clean pair for wear in the church.

We can see from this and other sources which might be cited that rabbinic authorities had the authority to regulate dress within and outside the synagogue. Certainly, this would have been used to assure the proper attire had such legislation been necessary. A modern rabbi must also insist that dress in the synagogue be appropriate, but not ostentatious.

March 1976

28. BERIT MILAH

QUESTION: Is it Reform practice to observe the *berit milah* on the eighth day, or can it be done at the convenience of the parents by a Jewish or Gentile physician? In addition, should the comparable naming ceremony for girls also be observed on the eighth day? (Rabbi E. Sapinsley, Bluefield, WV)

ANSWER: The Biblical statement about circumcising a male on the eighth day is very clear and is provided in Genesis 17.11 (*Shulhan Arukh* Yoreh Deah 261 ff; *Yad* Hil. Milah). Reform Jews observe this practice on the day stipulated. Of course if a medical reason makes the circumcision dangerous, it may be postponed virtually indefinitely until the child can be circumcised safely. All traditional authorities agree completely on this. If the parents do not arrange for a boy's circumcision as a child, it becomes his responsibility as an adult.

It is clear as well (A. Z. 26a) that a Jew must perform the actual operation of circumcision. In the Reform tradition, if no Jewish doctor is available, then a non-Jew may perform the operation while the rabbi or father recites the appropriate prayers. In fact, someone totally removed from Judaism [a pagan] would be preferable to an individual close to Judaism [like a Samaritan] who is a sectarian, according to Rabbi Meir (A. Z. 26b). In his notes to the *Shulhan Arukh*, Moses Isserles indicated that a non-Jew might also perform the operation during a period of duress or danger (*Shulhan Arukh* Yoreh Deah 264.1).

The treatment of girls, as far as the "convenant" is concerned, varies (S. J. Maslin, *Gates of Mitzvah*, p. 15). Many congregations name girls in the synagogue at a Sabbath close to birth when both parents can attend and participate in the service. This makes the event a happy congregational celebration. The recently introduced ceremony of "convenant of life" should probably also occur on the eighth day if we wish to indicate complete equality for girls. As no medical impediments can arise, and as there is no need to return to a hospital, it is possible to conduct this ceremony on the eighth day, but postponement for the sake of family convenience is equally acceptable.

January 1978

29. NAMING AN UNCIRCUMCISED CHILD

QUESTION: May we name an uncircumcised male child in the synagogue? In this case the child was not circumcised as the mother has been influenced by current medical fashion which indicates that circumcision may not be necessary for health reasons. She fears that circumcision may actually harm the child. (Rabbi R. Raab, Wantagh, NY)

ANSWER: Let me refer you to a rather recent responsum, "The Circumcision of Infants," 1982, (*American Reform Responsa*) which indicates that we consider the circumcision of male infants an essential and fundamental commandment. Of course those who are not circumcised would still be considered Jews (San. 44a; David Hoffmann, *Melamed Lehoil* Yoreh Deah #79; *C.C.A.R. Yearbook*, 1890, pp. 118 ff; S. B. Freehof, *Reform Jewish Practice*, Vol. I, p. 113; S. J. Maslin, *Gates of Mitzvah*, pp. 118 ff). Current medical fashions are irrelevant for us as we consider circumcision to be a religious rite, not a health matter. Unless there is a serious medical problem, all male children should be circumcised on the eighth day. Circumcision remains for us as the sign of the covenant followed by Judaism since the days of Abraham, our Father.

As this boy will be raised as a Jew, the lack of circumcision will embarrass him throughout life. Furthermore, if the operation is postponed, it will only become more difficult and painful.

We urge that every effort be made to convince the parents that the boy should be circumcised. Such a youngster should *not* be named at a synagogue service and everything should be done to assure his circumcision.

August 1986

30. ROLE OF A GODFATHER IN THE CIRCUMCISION CEREMONY

QUESTION: What is the role of the godfather in the circumcision ceremony? Is it possible for a godfather to withdraw his consent for this act some years later? (Rabbi J. Folkman, Columbus, OH)

ANSWER: The primary role of godfather is that of helping at the time of the circumcision. Among oriental Jews where a table was not used for the circumcision, someone specially designated simply held the child upon his knees. The *Midrash* (to Ps. 36.10) stated that each portion of the body was designated for a *mitzvah*, and the knees were for holding a child during circumcision (*Roqeah* 108). This was the practice during the many centuries when the circumcision was held at home and also subsequently when the ceremony was moved to the synagogue, which seems not to have occurred before the ninth century in Persia, and probably reflected an imitation of the Muslim custom to circumcise in the mosque. This custom was then followed by both rabbinic and Karaite Jews (L. Löw, *Die Lebensalter in der Jüdischen Literatur*). From there the custom was introduced to Europe and is mentioned in northern France in the eleventh century and in Germany in the thirteenth.

The Hebrew term used for godfather, *sandeq*, is from the Greek and later Latin *syndicus*. (French, *comprere*, German or Yiddish, *gevatter*, Spanish, *padrino*, Hungarian, *koma*, Hebrew, *baal berit*). Various *midrashim* refer to the *sandeq*, as did *Or Zaruah* Hil. Milah in the thirteenth century (for example, *Midrash* to Gen. 18.1; Ps. 35.10; Neh. 9.8). The office was discussed by Isserles at length in a note (*Shulhan Arukh* Orah Hayim 65.11).

As the office is considered an honor, the individual fulfilling it has to be of good character and pious. He, in turn, possesses certain rights, as that of being called to the *Torah* on the day of the circumcision if it fell on the day when the *Torah* is read (*Maharil* 84a). He, of course, sits in the special chair provided in many synagogues if the circumcision is customarily held there.

It seems that the *sandeq* was also responsible for certain financial contributions to the festivities of the circumcision. Usually the meal connected with it was prepared at his expense. In order to prevent this from becoming an unusual burden, the Tosafists, Peretz De Corbeil and Judah, the Pious, stated that an individual was only permitted to serve in this capacity once (*Maharil* Hil. Milah). Ezekiel Landau (1713-1793) disagreed with this and stated that the same individual could be asked a number of times. He also reported that in Poland in his time the rabbi was often appointed as the permanent *sandeq* and participated in this fashion in each *berit* (*Nodah Biy'hudah*, Vol. I #86). Moses Sofer rejected Landau's interpretation and cited astrological reasons for having a *sandeq* officiate only once in this role

(*Hatam Sofer*, Orah Hayim #158, 159.) Various opinions were cited by Elijah Gaon (*Beer Hagrah* to Yoreh Deah 265).

It is possible for women to participate in this role, although Isserles suggested that this not be done (*Shulhan Arukh* Yoreh Deah 265.11). Women participated among German Jews, while other Jewish communities discouraged it. Christians also have assisted in this fashion, as for example, in 1484 in Castrogiovanni, Sicily (L. Zunz, *Zur Geschichte und Literatur*, p. 499). Several medieval councils tried to prohibit such Christian participation (Council of Terracinana in 1330). Similar prohibitive statements are found in Protestant ordinances.

In modern times, the role of *sandeq* and godfather has sometimes been separated, but there is no basis for this in the earlier tradition. In all the traditional material there is no discussion whatsoever of any additional responsibility on the part of the *sandeq* beyond the circumcision. In other words, his privileges and his responsibilities end with the ceremony. Therefore, it would not be possible for the individual to withdraw his participation at a later time.

July 1978

31. RABBI OR *MOHEL* AT A MOSLEM CIRCUMCISION

QUESTION: May a rabbi or *mohel* participate in the circumcision of a Moslem boy? (Rabbi E. Sapinsley, Bluefield, WV)

ANSWER: This question involves a number of different matters which should be discussed separately. We must ask about the status of Islam in Jewish eyes, the responsibility of Jews toward non-Jews, and the extent to which a Jew may become involved in conducting ceremonials or rituals for another religious group under extraordinary conditions.

The ancient statements dealing with idolaters do not apply to followers of Islam. Their status is clearly that of *ger toshav*, one who has rejected the worship of idols (A. Z. 64b; Isserles to *Shulhan Arukh* Yoreh Deah 146.5; D. Hoffmann *Shulhan Arukh*, pp. 20 ff; J. Lauterbach, "The Attitude of the Jew Towards A Non-Jew," *C.C.A.R. Yearbook*, Vol. 31, 1921, pp. 200 ff). As Islam is strictly monotheistic and has no doctrine akin to trinitarian Christianity, it is even closer to Judaism than the latter, though Christianity has also been considered as non-idolatrous monotheistic religion (Rabenu Tam in the *Tosefot* to San. 63 f; Bekh. 2b; *Shulhan Arukh* Orah Hayim 156, etc.) We would, therefore, treat all followers of Islam as monotheist or as *gerei toshav*.

There is, of course, no problem with a Jewish doctor treating non-Jewish patients and we have examples of such medical practices from early times. A Jew named Theudas was a famous physician in Alexandria (J. Betzah I, 60). The emperor, Antonius Pius (96-161), asked Judah Hanasi to send him a physician for his slaves from among his own students. The great scholar Samuel, who died about 254 C.E., was an outstanding doctor who served the general community. This tradition continued and perhaps reached its climax with Moses Maimonides who was the physician at the court in Cairo. Any Jewish encyclopedia will provide a long list of physicians past and present, many of whom attended non-Jews as well as Jews. In this instance, however, we are not dealing with general medical practice, but specifically with circumcision. This rite has always been of unusual significance for us as Jews, so it is treated differently than other medical procedures. The *Shulhan Arukh* presents contradicting opinions about a Jew circumcising non-Jews. Joseph Caro prohibited such a circumcision (*Shulhan Arukh* Yoreh Deah 268.9) as did Moses Isserles (*Shulhan Arukh* Yoreh Deah 263.5.) However, Isserles' later notation (*Shulhan Arukh* Yoreh Deah 268.9) concluded, "in those lands where it is permitted to heal Gentiles, it would be permitted to perform a medical circumcision for them," (also *Yad* Hil. Milah 317 and *Shakh.* to Yoreh Deah 268.9). It is clear, therefore, that this medical procedure can be performed by a Jewish physician or *mohel* upon non-Jews.

In our case, however, the procedure is not purely medical, but is intended as the circumcision required by Islam, called *khitaan*. Although there are several different sets of rules for Islamic circumcision, it is clear that circumcision is obligatory. Although it is not prominently treated in books of Islamic law, it is of great importance to the followers of Islam. The operation is performed at varying ages from seven days to thirteen years depending on the specific sectarian and national tradition. When the ceremony takes place at a mosque in the presence of an Ima'm, it is accompanied by prayers for the preservation of the child (H.A.R. Gibbe and J.H. Kramers, *Shorter Encyclopedia of Islam*, pp. 254 f). The ritual has religious significance with folklore overtones. Is it appropriate for a Jew to involve himself in this?

We might make a number of distinctions here from a practical point

of view. It would be fully permissible for a Jewish physician to participate and let a Moslem recite the appropriate prayers. He would
clearly be there only in his medical capacity. This, of course, would
also be true for a *mohel*, although his presence might raise some
confusion in the community, as a *mohel* specializes in circumcising
Jewish youngsters. It would be permitted *mipnei darkhei shalom* - "for
the sake of peace." We must remember that this statement refers to
positive deeds done for our fellowmen (Git. 59b) and not merely
avoiding ill-will. That thought is expressed through the phrase *mishum
evah* (A. Z. 26a).

It would not be proper for a Jew to recite the prayers normally said
at the Islamic circumcision for a number of reasons. As the Islamic
circumcision may be conducted during such a long span of time, it
can be arranged when an *Ima'm* or other appropriate Islamic religious
leader is present. In addition, it does not seem to be a rite which is
absolutely essential, so it is not akin to baptism, which must be given
to a dying new-born Catholic infant or final rites which must be given
to a dying Catholic adult. In both those cases under special emergency circumstances, such as wartime, a Jew could be the agent for
the Catholic Church — at least from a Jewish point of view (S. B.
Freehof, *Recent Reform Responsa*, 1963, pp. 67 ff). He would not consider himself as a "agent for sin" (Kid. 42b) as Catholicism is a
monotheistic religion. In this instance we are, however, not dealing
with an emergency.

We would, therefore, conclude that nothing would restrain a Jewish physician from participating in an Islamic circumcision. It would,
however, not be appropriate for a Jew to say the words of prayer
which generally accompany this rite.

February 1978

32. THE CHANGING OF A JEWISH NAME

QUESTION: A woman with two children has been divorced. She
has now married another man. Her first husband takes no interest
in her children, nor does he support them. The second husband has
already formally adopted the children. Their last name has been
changed to the new family name. Can the Jewish name also be
changed to reflect the role of their new adoptive father? (Rabbi J.
Salkin, Doylestown, PA)

ANSWER: This kind of a question arose frequently in the past when orphaned children were raised in a new household. They were considered legally part of the household (Isserles to *Shulhan Arukh* Hoshen Mishpat 42.15). Appropriate changes in legal documents, of course, had to be made in order for them to inherit from their new household. They had the right to say *qaddish* for their adoptive parents as well as their natural parents. The name of their adoptive father could be used in all documents (Isserles to *Shulhan Arukh* Even Haezer 129), although it is equally appropriate to use the name of the natural father. Occasionally a question has been raised about using the name of the adoptive father in a *get*; *bediavad* this was always accepted (*Teshuvat Yehuda*; *Shulhan Arukh* Even Haezer 129.9). Even the strictest authority simply added the word *"hamgadlo"* to the adoptive father's name whenever an occasion demanded its use (*Nahalat Shiva* 12.15). It is, therefore, clear that nothing would stand in the way of changing the name of the children to that of the adoptive father.

April 1984

33. CHANGING HEBREW NAME

QUESTION: Does anything need to be done in order to change a Hebrew name from the name given at birth, but now only vaguely remembered and never used, to a totally different name in memory of a deceased ancestor?

ANSWER: There are, of course, Biblical sources which indicate a change of name. God did so with Abraham and Sarah; in another story an angel blessed Jacob through changing his name (Gen. 17.5, 32.29, 35.10). On other occasions such changes were made by human beings, so Jacob changed Benjamin's name (Gen. 35.16) and Moses altered Joshua's name (Num. 13.16), among others. Since Talmudic times, Hebrew names have usually been given to boys at the time of circumcision. Girls are named when their father is called to the *Torah* on the *shabbat* following the child's birth. Nowadays we may also use the home ceremony of *berit hayim* for the naming of girls (*Gates of the House*, p. 114; S. Maslin, *Gates of Mitzvah*, p. 13 ff).

A good deal has been written on the choice of names. Among Ashkenazim, it is the general practice to name children after a deceased ancestor, while among the Sephardim both deceased and living forebearers' names are used. The history of the development of naming in Jewish tradition is long and complex (Jacob Z. Lauterbach, *C.C.A.R. Annual*, 1932, Vol. 42, pp. 316 ff).

The primary occasion which led to formal name changes in the past was critical illness. This was done to confuse the angel of death (Bet Yosef to *Tur* Orah Hayim 129; *Toldot Adam Vehavah* I, 28). Similar fear of the angel of death led individuals in the Middle Ages to avoid the name of someone who had died a violent death or at a young age. If they, nevertheless, wished to preserve the name of that individual, this was accomplished through a double name which used the dangerous name in a changed context and so neutralized the danger (*Sefer Hassidim* #363 f; Isaac Shmelkes *Bet Yitzhaq* to Yoreh Deah, Part II, #163). The practice of changing a name in order to confuse the angel of death was already mentioned in the *Talmud*. The ritual for that purpose was established by the Gaonim (*Sefer Toldot Adam Vehavah*, I, #28; Baer, *Liqutei Tzvi*, p. 46).

A name was chosen in a number of different ways, either at random or through opening a *Torah* scroll and utilizing the name of the first Biblical figure which appeared, excluding names prior to Abraham (Joseph Trani, *Responsa* I, #189). Sometimes names like Hayim, Rafael or Azariel, with positive overtones, were used. The medieval *Sefer Hassidim* also mentioned a different method of foiling the angel of death; it suggested that we do not change the individuals name, but that of his parents, so that the child was transferred to another set of parents (*Sefer Hassidim* #635).

In each of these instances, the changing of the name was a formal ceremony and was done with a *minyan* present. One person held a *Torah*, and the appropriate words were recited. A simpler ceremony with a brief prayer may be found in *Hamanhig* (pp. 103 ff), or Isaac Baer's *Totzaot Hayim* (pp. 45 ff). We must remember that such procedures were followed in an emergency. For that reason the occasion was made as formal and as impressive as possible.

Although names were readily changed in order to escape the angel of death, there were legal problems involved in the changing of a name, especially if the original name had been used in a *ketubah* or a *get*. In both of these documents the name must be precisely and accurately given (*Shulhan Arukh* Even Haezer 129).

Some caution should be used in changing a name. In this instance, we would advise the individual not to change his name entirely, but to simply add the name of the deceased relative whom he wishes to honor to the name originally given. That would serve the additional purpose of honoring the individual after whom he was originally named and not obliterate that name.

Through utilizing both names, the one originally given and that now desired, the honor due to both deceased individuals would be provided.

November 1984

34. HEBREW NAME FOR CHILD WITH ONE JEWISH PARENT*

QUESTION: What parental names should be used at the *berit*, naming or later Jewish life-cycle events for an individual who has one Jewish parent and one non-Jewish parent and is to be raised as a Jew? (Rabbi C. Abramson, Memphis, TN)

ANSWER: On initial reflection we might turn for guidance to the analogy of the *asufi* and *shetuki* - foundlings whose parents are unknown or whose father is unknown. A child would use only his/her own name, and no name of a father would be used in any document which he/she might be called upon to issue (*Shulhan Arukh* Even Haezer 129.9; Solomon ben Aderet, *Responsa*). This has been generally followed, but it would also be appropriate procedure to use the name of the maternal grandfather (Isserles to *Shulhan Arukh* Orah Hayim 139.3). If the name of that grandfather is not known, then the individual could simply be called *ben Avraham* - as we are all children of Abraham (Isserles to *Shulhan Arukh* Orah Hayim 139.3). *Peri Megadim* asserted that we are careful to call such a boy the son of Abraham, our father, but not the son of Abraham the proselyte.

These citations are, however, not helpful as they take it for granted that the father is missing or unknown, and that he is presumed to be Jewish. In our instance, it is clear that the father or mother is non-Jewish.

Let us look at the possibility of using only the Jewish mother's name. This practice is sometimes followed in the *mi sheberakh* of the *Torah* service recited for someone who is sick. This was based by the *Zohar* on Psalms 86.16, and on the notion that God would have mercy (*rahamim*) upon a child because he/she had come from the mother's womb (*rehem*) (*Otzar Dinim Uminhagim "Mi Sheberakh"*). I am indebted to my colleague, Louis A. Rieser, for this reference.

This presents a precedent for using a Jewish mother's name alone, although it comes from a crisis situation rather than the normal course of events.

We, therefore, need to augment this solution. The most appropriate path would be to utilize only the name of the Jewish parent. It would be wrong to assign a Hebrew name to the non-Jewish parent; that would further blur the lines of identity. If, of course, the non-Jewish partner converts, then a Hebrew name can be inserted into any existing document.

It would, therefore, be appropriate that the name of the Jewish partner be used, and that name alone.

December 1984

35. ADOPTED CHILDREN AND THEIR BIOLOGICAL PARENTS*

QUESTION: A number of adopted children have requested that they automatically be told the names of their natural parents. They are prompted to do so for a variety of Jewish reasons. If the natural parents are Jewish, they wish to recite *qaddish*; in the various life cycle ceremonies they want to use the name of their biological parents. Furthermore, they want to be sure of not accidentally marrying a relative who is forbidden to them. What is the relationship of adopted children to their biological parents according to Jewish tradition? (Rabbi D. Gluckman, Olympia Fields, IL)

ANSWER: The entire question of legal adoption by parents who are unable to have children for a variety of reasons is a modern matter. Formal adoption in the modern sense was known to the ancient Romans and others, but not to the ancient Jewish community. Jewish law, however, contains a great deal of discussion about children raised by those not their parents. In virtually all instances, these children were orphans brought into the home to be raised by relatives or friends. There is discussion about their status, names to be used, rights of such children, etc. Some of these matters have been discussed in an earlier responsum entitled "Adoption and Adopted Children" (W. Jacob, *American Reform Responsa*, #63).

When tradition deals with rearing orphaned children, the question of parental names and inheritance and matters of concern. These adopted orphans also continue to have different rights within their new home which are distinct from those of any natural children who were in the household. In matters of inheritance it is clear that the orphaned child is entitled to anything left by the biological parents. On the other hand, unless special provisions are made in a will, the "adopted" children (in this case, orphans), do not possess the automatic right of inheritance of the biological children, yet provision can be made for them as a person may dispose of his estate as he wishes (B.B. 134a, 127b; Kid. 78b; *Tur* Hoshen Mishpat 279.1; *Moreh Nivukhim* 3.41; *Yad* Hil. Nahalot 6.1).

In the matter of *qaddish*, one view has stated that it is the duty of the natural children to say *qaddish* for their biological parents. This commandment is incumbent upon them, while for adopted children the obligation is assumed. It is prompted by love and conscience, but it is not their duty (Jacob Colon, *Responsa*; Hatam Sofer, *Responsa* Orah Hayim #164). On the other hand, the earlier Isserles disagreed and stated that children have the same rights in this matter as biological children (Isserles to *Shulhan Arukh* Orah Hayim 118), as for example, in leading congregational services at the time of *yahrzeit*, etc.

If we turn to marriage and the fear of marrying a relative, we must view this discussion in the perspective of earlier times; we were principally dealing with orphans who were sometimes scattered to various households due to poverty or accident. The likelihood of marriage to a forbidden relative, even under those circumstances, was considered too small to be considered a danger (*Shulhan Arukh* Even Haezer 4.26).

In a marriage of adopted children the *ketuvah* usually gives the name of the adoptive parents and *b'diavad* was valid in a *get* (*Shulhan Arukh* Even Haezer 129.10). Those who were strict used *hamgadlo* with the name in the documents and possibly also on other occasions (*Shemot Rabbah*, 46 end; Isserles to *Shulhan Arukh* Even Haezer 129.10; Steinberg, *Responsa on Adoption*, p. 20). If the adoptive parents wish to preserve the family name of an orphan's biological parents (if known), then these names may be used. In our times the names of these parents are known only to the court and the biological parents wish their name to be forgotten.

In all these matters ancient Jewish law and customs, and modern American or Israeli law, are primarily concerned with the welfare of the child. Most decisions were made according to this principle

(Aderet, *Responsa* #28; Radbaz, *Responsa* I, #123; *Shulhan Arukh* Even Haezer 82 and *Pit-hei Teshuvah*; *The Law of Adoption*, Israel, 1957).

Of course the majority of modern adoptions deal with children who are not born of Jewish parents. Therefore, the various considerations raised by the questioner will not arise. When such a child is brought into a Jewish home, that child should be converted to Judaism and introduced to Judaism in the same way as any other young convert (W. Jacob, *American Reform Responsa*, # 63). Although a convert may recite *qaddish* for non-Jewish parents, this is not obligatory (S. B. Freehof, *Recent Reform Responsa*, p. 137), nor obviously is there any obligation or desire to continue the former family name, so this question does not arise; this is also true as Jewish law considers a convert a new person without relatives (Yeb. 22a). The issue of marriage to a prohibited relative, therefore, is mute.

We must also concern ourselves with the right to privacy of the biological parents. In most instances, social or family problems have led the biological mother (and sometimes the father) to release the child for adoption. The laws of most states protect the privacy of the natural parent/parents. The information possessed by the court is confidential and must not be released (based on Lev. 19.16; *Yad* Hil. Deot. 7.2). Such confidential information may only be divulged to save lives or to protect against serious injury and financial loss (*Yad* Hil. Rotzeah 1.13; *Shulhan Arukh* Hoshen Mishpat 426.1; Jacob Breish, *Helkat Yaakov*, III, #136.) We would, therefore, respect the privacy of the biological mother and father.

In conclusion, we would urge the adopted children to view their adoptive parents as their natural parents and treat them in precisely the same way as biological children treat their parents. This course should be followed in every instance including the recitation of *qaddish*.

April 1983

36. PRIORITIES FOR AN ADOPTION AGENCY

QUESTION: The Jewish Family Service of this city has given first priority to families in which both parents are Jewish. Now a family in which the mother is Jewish and the father is Christian has approached the agency as they wish to adopt a child. They have a Jewish home and are committed to raising the child as a Jew. According to tradition, as well as the feelings of Reform Judaism, should the policy of the agency remain as it is or be changed to accommodate such families? (A. Marks, Dallas, TX)

ANSWER: There is, of course, nothing that deals specifically with this kind of situation in the traditions of the past. For that matter, the entire matter of adoption is rarely discussed in the traditional *halakhic* literature (W. Jacob, *American Reform Responsa*, #63). However, we may draw some conclusions from the system of priority worked out for the recipients of charitable donations.

In this instance, as with charitable gifts, the need has always been greater than the supply and so a procedure had to be established. Charity begins at home and, therefore, members of one's own family had an initial claim on any funds available (*Sefer Hassidim*, #895, 918, 1039, 1049, etc.) They were followed by individuals in one's own city and one's own country, and only then were funds provided for the poor elsewhere (*Sefer Hassidim* #869; *Shulhan Arukh* Yoreh Deah 251.3). Earlier, the same section explained that a woman is provided with food before a man and then in the sequence of priest, *kohen*, Levite, and Israelite. An exception is made for an Israelite scholar or even a *mamzer* who is a scholar; these take precedence over a *kohen* (Ket. 67a; *Yad* Hil. Matnat Aniyim 8.15, 10.18; *Shulhan Arukh* Yoreh Deah 251.8).

The twelfth century *Sefer Hassidim* also preferred scholars and students who were poor (#860, 862, 902 ff) as well as the pious over those who were less pious (#1029).

The great work on charity, *Meil Tzedaqah*, by Elijah Hakohen ben Solomon (18th century), provided a similar sequence of distribution along with specific reasons (#92 f, 1435 f, 1500, 1433 f). It also indicated that we act on behalf of Jews first and Gentiles subsequently (#1434 f). Non-Jewish poor also had a claim on charity (Git. 61a) and are supported whenever possible. Jews who were open and willful transgressors were to be refused support from all sources (*Shulhan Arukh* Yoreh Deah 251).

When we look at the other rather substantial sections of the traditional literature which deal with precedence in the distribution of charity to the poor, we see that they are primarily concerned with obtaining proper gifts from the rich and only secondarily with a system of distribution. However, the above mentioned sources are in general agreement on preferences.

We may conclude by analogy that it is proper to establish a similar system of priority in the matter of adoption. As Reform Jews we would agree with the traditional priorities. In other words, the priority which your agency has set is appropriate. Families in which both parents are Jewish (by birth or conversion) should be given preference. Within that category priority should be given to families with a real commitment to Judaism, whether Reform, Conservative or Orthodox. Families in which only one party is Jewish, and who intend to raise their children as Jews, should be placed in a second category and be given children when the first category has been exhausted. Since the passage of the Resolution on Patrilineal Descent in March of 1983 (W. Jacob, *American Reform Responsa*, Appendix), we make no distinction between families in which the mother is Christian and the father Jewish, or vice versa.

May 1984

37. ADOPTION AND MIXED MARRIAGE

QUESTION: What is the status of a child whose natural parents are both Gentiles, who is adopted by a couple where one partner (in this case the husband) is Jewish and the other is not? (Rabbi R. Block, Riverside, CT)

ANSWER: This child should be treated as any other adopted child, in other words named in the synagogue, with a *berit* for a male, and if the family desires, *tevilah*. All this should be done in accordance with the responsum, "Adoption and Adopted Children," (W. Jacob, *American Reform Responsa*, #63). As this child has been brought into a mixed marriage, we should be especially careful about her education.

The ritual acts at the beginning of life (*berit*, *tevilah*, naming) are a prelude to the education of the youngster. In other words, the conversion conducted at the time of infancy would designate this youngster as Jewish and her future education would confirm that Jewishness.

April 1984

38. PATRILINEAL AND MATRILINEAL DESCENT

QUESTION: What are the origins of matrilineal descent in the Jewish tradition; what *halakhic* justification is there for the recent Central

Conference of American Rabbi's resolution on matrilineal and patrilineal descent which also adds various requirements for the establishment of Jewish status?

ANSWER: We shall deal first with the question of matrilineal and patrilineal descent. Subsequently we shall turn to the required positive "acts of identification."

It is clear that for the last two thousands years the Jewish identity of a child has been determined by matrilineal descent. In other words, the child of a Jewish mother was Jewish irrespective of the father (Deut. 7.3, 4; M. Kid. 3.12; Kid. 70a, 75b; Yeb. 16b, 23a, 44a, 45b; A. Z. 59a; J. Yeb. 5.15 (6c), 7.5 (8b); J. Kid. 3.12 (64d); *Yad* Issurei Biah 15.3 f; etc.). The Talmudic discussion and that of the later codes indicate the reasoning behind this rule.

The rabbinic decision that the child follow the religion of the mother solves the problem for offspring from illicit intercourse of unions which are not recognized, or in which paternity could not be established, or in which the father disappeared. This practice may have originated in the period of Ezra (Ezra 10 3; Neh. 13.23 ff) and may parallel that of Pericles of Athens who sought to limit citizenship to descendants of Athenian mothers (G. F. Moore, *Judaism*, Vol. 1, p. 20). It may also have represented temporary, emergency legislation of that period. We hear nothing about such a permanent change till early rabbinic times, then the union between a Jew and a non-Jew was considered to have no legal status (*lo tafsei qiddushin*). At one stage in the Talmudic discussions, an authority, Jacob of Kefar Neburya, considered a child of such a union Jewish, but subsequently retracted his opinion when faced with a verse from Ezra quoted by R. Haggai (J. Kid. 64d; J. Yeb. 4a; see Shaye J. D. Cohen, "The Origin of the Matrilineal Principle in Rabbinic Law," *Judaism*, Winter, 1984, note 54). R. Judah in the name of R. Assi considered a union between a Jew and non-Jew valid in "his time" as the non-Jew might be a descendent of the lost ten tribes (Yeb. 16b). Many authorities considered children of all such unions as *mamzerim*. They felt that the danger lay with non-Jewish women who could not be trusted to establish the Jewish paternity of their child, though that was contested by others.

The statement which grants the status of the mother to the child saves that child from the status of *mamzerut* or other similar disabling category. There was considerable disagreement before the decision later universally accepted was reached (Kid. 66b ff; *Shulhan Arukh*

Even Haezer 4.19 and commentaries). The discussions demonstrate that this decision represented rabbinic reaction to specific problems.

We should contrast the rabbinic position to the view of the earlier Biblical and post-Biblical period. Patrilineal descent was the primary way of determining the status of children in this period. The Biblical traditions and their early rabbinic commentaries take it for granted that the paternal line was decisive in the tracing of descent, tribal identity, or priestly status. A glance at the Biblical genealogies makes this clear. In inter-tribal marriage paternal descent was likewise decisive (Nu. 1.2, *l'mishpehotam l'veit avotam*); the line of the father was recognized while the line of the mother was not (*mishpahat av keruyah mishpahah, mishpahat em enah keruyah mishpahah*, B. B. 109b; Yeb. 54b; *Yad* Hil. Nahalot 1.6, etc.).

We should also recognize that later rabbinic tradition did not shift to the matrilineal line when conditions did not demand it. Therefore, the rabbinic tradition remained patrilineal in the descent of the priesthood; it was and remains the male *kohen* who determines the status of his children. The child is a *kohen* even if the father married a Levite or an Israelite. Thus lineage was and continues to be determined by the male alone whenever the marriage is otherwise proper (*M.* Kid. 3.12; Kid. 29a; *Shulhan Arukh* Yoreh Deah 245.1).

If a marriage is valid but originally forbidden, (marriage with someone improperly divorced, etc.), then the tainted parent, whether mother or father, determines lineage (Kid. 66b; *Shulhan Arukh* Even Haezer 4.18). The same rule applies to children born out of wedlock if both parents are known.

Matrilineal descent, although generally accepted for the union of a Jew and a non-Jew, has rested on an uncertain basis. Some have deduced it from Deuteronomy 7.4, others from Ezra 9 and 10. Still others feel that the dominant influence of the mother during the formative years accounted for this principle. A few modern scholars felt that the rabbinic statement followed the Roman Paulus (*Digest* 2.4 f), who stated that the maternity was always known while paternity was doubtful; this, however, could be extended to the offspring of any parents. Shaye Cohen has also suggested that the rabbis may have abhorred this type of mixture of people as they felt negatively toward mixtures of animals and materials. A full discussion of this and other material may be found in Aptowtizer's "Spuren des Matriarchats im jüdischen Schrifttum," *Hebrew Union College Annual,* Vols. 4 and 5 and Shaye J. D. Cohen's "The Origin of the Matrilineal Principle in

Rabbinic Law," *Judaism*, Winter, 1984.

We should note that the Karaites considered the offspring of a Jewish father and a Gentile mother to be a Jew. It is, however, not clear from the sources available to me whether the conversion of the mother to Judaism may not have been implied (B. Revel, "The Karaite Halakha," *Jewish Quarterly Review* III, pp. 375 f.) The matter continues to be debated.

These discussions show us that our tradition responded to particular needs. It changed the laws of descent to meet the problems of a specific age and if those problems persisted, then the changes remained in effect.

The previous cited material has dealt with situations entirely different from those which have arisen in the last century and a half. Unions between Jews and non-Jews during earlier times remained rare. Furthermore, the cultural and sociological relationship with the people among whom we lived did not approach the freedom and equality which most Jews in the Western World now enjoy.

We in the twentieth century have been faced with an increasing number of mixed marriages, with changes in the structure of the family, and with the development of a new relationship between men and women. This has been reflected in the carefully worded statement by the Committee on Patrilineal Descent (W. Jacob, *American Reform Responsa*, Appendix).

We may elaborate further with the following statements which reflect the previously cited historical background, the introduction to the resolution as well as other concerns. We shall turn first to the question of descent and then to the required "acts of identification."

1. In the Biblical period, till the time of Ezra or beyond, patrilineal descent determined the status of a child, so the children of the kings of Israel married to non-Jewish wives were unquestionably Jewish. This was equally true of other figures. Furthermore, our tradition has generally determined lineage (*yihus*) through the father, i.e., in all valid but originally forbidden marriages. This was also true for priestly, Levitical and Israelite lineage which was and continues to be traced through the paternal line (Nu. 1.2, 18; *Yad* Hil. Issurei Biah 19.15; *Shulhan Arukh* Even Haezer 8.1). If a marriage was valid, but originally forbidden, then the tainted parent (mother or father) determines status (Kid. 66b; *Shulhan Arukh* Even Haezer 4.18). The same rule applies to children born out of wedlock if both parents are known.

Yihus was considered significant, especially in the Biblical period, and long genealogical lines were recorded; an effort was made in the time of Ezra and, subsequently, to guarantee pure lines of descent and precise records were maintained (Ezra 2:59 ff; genealogies of I, II Chronicles). An echo of that practice of recording genealogies remained in the *Mishnah* and *Talmud* despite the difficulties caused by the wars of the first and second century which led to the destruction of many records (*M.* Kid. 4.1; Kid. 28a, 70a ff). In the Biblical period and in specific later instances, lineage was determined by the father.

2. Mishnaic and Talmudic authorities changed the Biblical laws of descent, as shown earlier in this responsum, as well as many others when social or religious conditions warranted it. Family law was changed in many other ways as demonstrated by the laws of marriage. For example, the Talmudic authorities validated the marriage of Boaz to Ruth, the Moabitess, despite the strict ruling against such marriages (Deut. 23.4); they indicated that the Biblical rule applied only to males, not to females (Yeb. 76b ff). Earlier the *Mishnah* (Yad. 4.4) claimed that the various ethnic groups had been so intermingled by the invasion of Sennacherib that none of the prohibitions against marriage with neighboring people remained valid. In this instance and others similar to them, we are dealing with clear Biblical injunctions which have been revised by the rabbinic tradition. We have followed these examples in our own twentieth century revision.

3. The Reform movement has espoused the equality of men and women, virtually since its inception (J. R. Marcus, *Israel Jacobson*, p. 146; W. G. Plaut, *The Rise of Reform Judaism*, pp. 252 ff). As equality has been applied to every facet of Reform Jewish life, it should be applied in this instance.

4. We, and virtually all Jews, recognize a civil marriage between a Jew and a Gentile as a marriage although not *qiddushin*, and have done so since the French Sanhedrin of 1807 (Tama, *Transactions of the Parisian Sanhedrin* - Tr. F. Kerwan, p. 155 f; Plaut, *op. cit.*, p. 219). We are morally obliged to make provisions for the offsprings of such a union when either the father or mother seek to have their children recognized and educated as a Jew.

5. We agree with the Israeli courts and their decisions on the matter of status for purposes of *leam*, the registration of the nationality of immigrants and the right to immigrate under the Law of Return. Such rulings are secular in nature and do not bind the Israeli rabbinic courts or us, yet they have far reaching implications for all Jews. In the Brother Daniel case of 1962, this apostate was not judged to be Jewish

although he had a Jewish mother (1962 - 16 - P.D. 2428). The court decided that a Jew who practiced another religion would not be considered Jewish despite his descent from a Jewish mother. "Acts of religious identification" were determinative for secular purposes of the State of Israel. The court recognized that this had no effect on the rabbinic courts; nonetheless, it marked a radical change which deals with new conditions.

Earlier in March, 1958, the Minister of Interior, Israel Bar-Yehuda, issued a directive which stated that "any person declaring in good faith that he is a Jew, shall be registered as a Jew." No inquiry about parents was authorized. In the case of children, "if both parents declare that the child is Jewish, the declaration shall be regarded as though it were legal declaration of the child itself" (S. Z. Abramov, *Perpetual Dilemma*, p. 290; *Schlesinger v. Minister of Interior* 1963 - I - 17 P.D. 225; *Shalit v. Minister of Interior* 1968 - II - 23 P.D. 477-608). This was for the purposes of immigration and Israeli registration. It represented the farthest stance away from *halakhah* which any official body in the State of Israel has taken in this matter. It remained law until challenged and later legislation replaced it. There have been a number of other decisions which have dealt with this matter.

The current law, passed in 1970 after a government crisis over the question of "Who is a Jew," reads, "for the purpose of this law, Jew means a person born to a Jewish mother, or who has become converted to Judaism, and who is not a member of another religion" ("Law of Return -Amendment, March, 1970, #4b; M. D. Goldman, *Israel Nationality Law*, p. 142; *Israel Law Journal*, Vol. 5, #2, p. 264). Orthodox efforts to change this to read "converted according to *halakhah*" have been defeated on various occasions. We should note that although the definition of a Jew was narrowed, another section of the law broadened the effect of the Law of Return and included "the child and grandchild of a Jew, the spouse of a Jew and the spouse of the child and grandchild of a Jew - with the exception of a person who was a Jew and willingly changed his religion" (*Law of Return Amendment* #2, #4a, March, 1970). This meant that a dual definition (descendants from Jewish mothers or fathers) has remained operative for immigration into the State of Israel.

The decision of an Israeli Court is a secular decision. It is, of course, not determinative for us as American Reform Jews, but we should note that their line of reasoning is somewhat similar to ours. We also see flexibility to meet new problems expressed in these decisions.

For the reasons cited in the introduction to the Resolution, those stated above and others, we have equated matrilineal and patrilineal descent in the determination of Jewish identity of a child of a mixed marriage.

Now let us turn to the section of the resolution which deals with "positive acts of identification." There are both traditional and modern considerations for requiring such acts and not relying on birth alone.

The clause which deals with the "appropriate and timely acts of identification with the Jewish faith and people ..." has gone beyond the traditional requirements for consideration as a Jew. Here we have become stricter than traditional Judaism. We have done so as the normal life of Jews has changed during the last two centuries.

In earlier periods of our history, individuals whose status was doubtful were limited in number. The question became significant only during the period of the Marranos. When such individuals identified themselves and lived as part of the Jewish community, they joined a semi-autonomous corporate community largely cut off from the surrounding world. Its entire way of life was Jewish. Emancipation changed this condition. It is difficult for those of doubtful status to integrate in an effortless way as was possible in earlier periods of our history. They and virtually all Jews live in two worlds.

We are dealing with a large number of individuals in our open American society as well as in all western lands. The Jewish status of a potentially large number of immigrants from the Soviet Union is also doubtful.

In order to overcome these problems as well as others, we now require "appropriate and timely public and formal acts...." The requirement has been worded to permit some flexibility for individual circumstances. With time and experience, custom will designate certain acts as appropriate and others not. It would be wrong, however, to set limits now at the beginning of the process.

We are aware that we have made more stringent requirements than our tradition. We believe that this will lead to a firmer commmitment to Judaism on the part of these individuals and that it will enable them to become fully integrated into the Jewish community.

We have taken this step for the following additional reasons:

1. We do not view birth as a determining factor in the religious identification of children of a mixed marriage.

2. We distinguish between descent and identification.

3. The mobility of American Jews has diminished the influence of the extended family upon such a child. This means that a significant informal bond with Judaism which played a role in the past does not exist for our generation.

4. Education has always been a strong factor in Jewish identity. In the recent past we could assume a minimal Jewish education for most children. In our time almost half the American Jewish community remains unaffiliated, and their children receive no Jewish education.

For those reasons the Central Conference of American Rabbis has declared:

"The Central Conference of American Rabbis declares that the child of one Jewish parent is under the presumption of Jewish descent. This presumption of the Jewish status of the offspring of any mixed marriage is to be established through appropriate and timely public and formal acts of identification with the Jewish faith and people. The performance of these *mitzvot* serves to commit those who participate in them, both parents and child, to Jewish life.

"Depending on circumstances, *mitzvot* leading toward a positive and exclusive Jewish identity will include entry into the covenant, acquisition of a Hebrew name, *Torah* study, *Bar/Bat Mitzvah*, and *Kabbalat Torah* (Confirmation). For those beyond childhood claiming Jewish identity, other public acts or declarations may be added or substituted after consultation with their rabbi."

October 1983

39. PATRILINEAL DESCENT AND A QUESTIONABLE BACKGROUND*

QUESTION: A young man who grew up in England was a child of a mixed marriage and now wishes to marry an American Jewish girl. His father was Jewish and his mother was Anglican; both are deceased. The father was affiliated with the United Synagogue and the youngster believes he was ritually circumcised (*berit milah*) and named in the synagogue, although no formal record of this exists. He has had virtually no Jewish education. What is his status as far as we are concerned? We should note that the couple intends to settle in England. (A. D., New York, NY)

ANSWER: We base our decision on the resolution of the Central Conference of American Rabbis, March, 1983, and the responsum "Patrilineal and Matrilineal Descent." The Resolution reads:

"The Central Conference of American Rabbis declares that the child of one Jewish parent is under the presumption of Jewish descent. This presumption of the Jewish status of the offspring of any mixed marriage is to be established through appropriate and timely public and formal acts of identification with the Jewish faith and people. The performance of these *mitzvot* serves to commit those who participate in them, both parents and child, to Jewish life.

"Depending on circumstances, *mitzvot* leading toward a positive and exclusive Jewish identity will include entry into the covenant, acquisition of a Hebrew name, *Torah* study, *Bar/Bat Mitzvah*, and *Kabbalat Torah* (Confirmation). For those beyond childhood claiming Jewish identity, other public acts or declarations may be added or substituted after consultation with their rabbi."

As this young man can produce no evidence that he was ritually circumcised and named in the synagogue, and as he has had no Jewish education nor been involved in any subsequent acts which would affirm his Jewish identity, we would require conversion on the part of this young man as the affirmative way of establishing his Jewish identity.

October 1983

40. A NON-JEW RAISING JEWISH CHILDREN*

QUESTION: A non-Jewish spouse has lost her Jewish husband. Prior to their marriage the couple promised to raise their children as Jews; the children, ages eight and ten, have received some Jewish education. The widow, however, does not wish to continue that Jewish education. She lives in a small town and has little contact with her Jewish in-laws. Can anything be done to assure a Jewish education for these children? Furthermore, let me also ask about a similar situation in which there has been a divorce. In this instance, the husband is Jewish and the wife is not Jewish. The children are approximately the same age. The wife has custody of the children who see their father only during vacations. (D. F., New York, NY)

ANSWER: Although tradition would classify these children of non-Jewish mothers to be non-Jews, unless they had been formally converted, we presume them to be Jewish if they act on that presumption and receive a Jewish education (Resolution Central Conference of American Rabbis, March, 1983). We would insist that the parents affirm that presumption through a Jewish education and other acts of identification.

It will be very difficult to do anything aside from moral persuasion with the young widow. Undoubtedly this has been attempted. As you indicate, the relationship with her former in-laws is poor and the children will rarely see their Jewish grandparents, so it is doubtful whether anything can be done. A promise made at the time of marriage, even if written into the original marriage contract, would not be enforceable in most North American jurisdictions. Furthermore, even if the courts would rule positively in this matter, it would be self-defeating to force an unwilling widow to provide a Jewish education. So much of the education depends upon the home, which in this instance would have a negative rather than a positive effect.

In the case of a divorce, it would be possible in the divorce proceedings to stipulate that the children continue their Jewish religious education and to make the father financially responsible for it. This has frequently succeeded. If, however, the mother lives in a small town without a Jewish community, as you indicate, then the father must do whatever can be done during the long summer vacation and at holiday time.

It is quite clear that these children are presumed to be Jewish by us, and fortunately, they have at least begun the process of Jewish education. Hopefully, as they grow older they will continue along this path of their own volition.

June 1983

41. STATUS OF A CHILD GENETICALLY NOT JEWISH

ANSWER: A Jewish woman is married to a Gentile. She is unable to conceive. However, doctors are planning to fertilize an egg from another woman, *in vitro*, with the husband's sperm, and then implant the fertilized *ovum* in the wife. Since genetically neither the father nor the *ovum* donor is Jewish, although gestation will take place within the womb of a Jewish woman, would the child require conversion? (Rabbi B. Lefkowitz, Taunton, MA)

ANSWER: The issues raised by this question are not akin to anything else which has been discussed in Jewish literature. The traditional material which has some bearing on the subject has been cited in an earlier responsum on surrogate mothers (W. Jacob, *American Reform Responsa*, #159). Somewhat akin to the question is the situation of adoption in which the child has been born to Gentile parents, or a child whose origins are not clearly known, and raised by a Jew from early infancy. In that case, we have decided that the child should be treated as any other Jewish infant with an option of *tevilah* (W. Jacob, *An American Reform Responsa*, "Adoption and Adopted Children," #63).

Our questions differ from adoption as the child has been part of the mother throughout the period of gestation. The intent of this procedure is to provide the parents with a child which is as much theirs as possible. It, therefore, goes one step further than adoption and means that the child should never feel the anxieties of an adopted child. As the Jewish community has always placed a strong emphasis upon family and upon children as an essential part of the family, this technique, which raises other questions also, will enable a large number of families to have children and will certainly be utilized.

As this child has been part of the mother throughout the period of gestation, we should consider this child born of a Jewish mother as potentially Jewish without any formal act of conversion. The child, of course, will need to participate in "positive acts of identification," and just as in the case of any other child of mixed marriage, this would be in keeping with the resolution of the Central Conference of American Rabbis of March, 1983 (W. Jacob, *American Reform Responsa*, Appendix). This child is, therefore, considered as potentially Jewish and no act of conversion is necessary.

February 1984

42. JEWISH STATUS AND MISTAKEN IDENTITY

QUESTION: A young woman has been raised to consider herself as Jewish. Her mother assured her that her "real" father was Jewish and that she herself had some Jewish lineage in her genealogy. She did not receive any kind of Jewish education, but had Jewish friends and occasionally attended some Jewish ceremonies at home and in the synagogue. Upon reaching maturity she discovered that there was, in fact, no Jewish ancestry at all. What is her status? (Rabbi E. H. Hoffman, Brookline, MA)

ANSWER: This young woman will undoubtedly need some counseling in regard to her Jewish identity and probably also in connection with her family life. After all, she grew up thinking that someone who was actually her father was not her father. We should be sympathetic to her and guide her in every way possible so that she may overcome whatever difficulties are present.

As far as her Jewish identity is concerned, we would follow the ruling of the Central Conference of American Rabbis:

"The Central Conference of American Rabbis declares that the child of one Jewish parent is under the presumption of Jewish descent. This presumption of the Jewish status of the offspring of any mixed marriage is to be established through appropriate and timely public and formal acts of identification with the Jewish faith and people. The performance of these *mitzvot* serves to commit those who participate in them, both parents and child, to Jewish life.

"Depending on circumstances, *mitzvot* leading toward a positive and exclusive Jewish identity will include entry into the covenant, acquisition of a Hebrew name, *Torah* study, *Bar/Bat Mitzvah*, and *Kabbalat Torah* (Confirmation). For those beyond childhood claiming Jewish identity, other public acts or declarations may be added or substituted after consultation with their rabbi."

This statement indicates that identity is conferred through lineage and acts of identification. In this instance the young woman in question has not fulfilled either one of these requirements, so we would encourage her to become Jewish through conversion. It might make her feel better to realize that even if there had been one Jewish parent and she lacked a formal Jewish education, the requirements would have been the same.

A young woman like this will need some special attention above and beyond what we normally provide for those who join us, and that should certainly be given.

July 1985

43. ORIGIN OF THE MIQVEH FOR CONVERSION

QUESTION: What is the origin of the *miqveh* for the purpose of conversion? When was this practice instituted? (Rabbi C. Levy, Pittburgh, PA)

ANSWER: It is clear that there was no Biblical requirement of immersion in any body of water for the purpose of conversion. Males who wished to join the community needed to be circumcised (Gen. 17.11,12, 34.14; Ex. 4.25), while females who wished to join us did so simply through marriage to a Jew. As far as we know nothing was required, for example, of Ruth, who married Boaz and earlier had married one of Naomi's sons (Ruth 1.4, 4.13), Jezebel who married Ahab (IK 16.31) or Moses who married Zippora, a Midianite (Ex. 2.21). Conversion is presumed by later authorities, though none may have taken place.

In Mishnaic times the well known tale of the pagan who wished to learn about Judaism while standing on one foot may indicate that no ritual was required (Solomon Zeitlin, "Proselytes and Proselytism"); other scholars feel that we can not argue from silence in this matter; the ritual requirements were simply not mentioned there. Subsequent discussions of rites to be followed by converts were conducted between the followers of Hillel and those of Shamai. They argued whether there was a need for both immersion and circumcision for males as a conversion rite. They agreed that the convert had to bring a sacrifice to the Temple. Immersion in a *miqveh* was obviously not yet an established custom although it existed (Ker 9a; Yeb. 46b ff; *Tosefta* Shab. 31a, 135a). Solomon Zeitlin, on the other hand, felt that the ritual was not intended as an introduction to Judaism, but dealt with ritual uncleanliness which was extended to pagans in the first century (Solomon Zeitlin, "Proselytes and Proselytism"; Harry Wolfson, *Jubilee Volumes*, Vol. 2, pp. 587 ff). We can see from the *New Testament's* John the Baptist (Matthew 3.7) and from the rites of the Essenes (Josephus, *Wars*, 2.129 ff, 148), as well as the Qumram community (*Manual of Discipline*), that immersion of a special nature was mandatory to join these pietistic groups. That would place the ritual in the first century before our era. As there is no discussion of this practice as something new or unusual, it probably antedated this period. There is, however, nothing in the older literature to indicate the beginning of the custom. We can safely say that it has been conducted as a Jewish rite for the admission of proselytes since the first century of our era.

June 1983

44. THE *MIQVEH* AND REFORM CONVERTS

QUESTION: Has liberal Judaism taken a position of the use of a *miqveh* as part of the conversion ceremony to Judaism? Should this ancient custom be reintroduced? (Simon Levy, Harrow-on-the Hill, England)

ANSWER: The traditional requirements for conversion are clear (Yeb. 46, 47; *Shulhan Arukh* Yoreh Deah 268; *Yad* Hil. Issurei Biah 15); a court of three is necessary. Prospective converts must be warned that they are joining a persecuted community and that many new obligations will be placed upon them. They were then to bring a sacrifice in the days when the Temple stood, take a ritual bath, and in the case of males, be circumcised. To this day the requirements of a *bet din*, *tevilah* and *berit* remain for traditional Jews. The sources are clear on the requirements, but considerable discussion about them exists in the *Talmud*. For example, R. Eliezer stated that if a prospective male convert was circumcised or took a ritual bath, he was considered a proselyte. R. Joshua insisted on both and his point of view was adopted (Yeb. 46b); Hillel and Shammai disagreed about a prospective male convert who was already circumcised; *Bet Shammai* insisted that blood must be drawn for him, while *Bet Hillel* stated that one may simply accept that circumcision without drawing blood (Shab. 135a). The rabbinic authorities decided in favor of *Bet Shammai* (*Shulhan Arukh* Yoreh Deah 268.1; *Yad* Hil. Issurei Biah 14.5). Clearly there were differences of opinion about steps necessary for the ritual of conversion in ancient times. These may reflect historic competition with Christianity, persecution, etc., in the early centuries of our era.

The Talmudic discussions insist that the convert must join Judaism without any ulterior motives, and if such are present, the conversion is void (Yeb. 24b). Of course this opinion applies only prospectively, not retrospectively and *bediavad* they were accepted. Some authorities were more lenient in regard to ulterior motives, so Hillel (Shab. 31a) readily accepted a convert who stated that he wished eventually to become a high priest. R. Hiya accepted a woman who wanted to marry one of his students (Men. 44a). In modern times, although most Orthodox authorities would reject converts who seek to join us for the sake of marriage, some would accept them in order to avoid the conversion by Reform rabbis (Mendel Kirshbaum, *Menahem Meshiv* #9), because civil marriage has preceded or because the couple is living together (Yoreh Deah 85). Similar arguments have been advanced by Meshullam Kutner in *Uketorah Yaasu*, Mosheh Feinstein (*Igrot Mosheh*, Even Haezer Vol. 1, #27). However, the greatest number of Orthodox authorities have rejected these arguments (Joseph Saul Nathenson, Jacob Ettlinger, Yehiel Weinberg). Their rejection was based upon ulterior motivation and the likelihood that they would not accept all the commandments especially as they are not generally observed in the modern Jewish community and probably not kept by the Jewish partner (Isaac Herzog, *Hekhal Yizhoq*, Even Haezer Vol. 1, #20; Meir Arak, *Imrei Yosher*, Vol. 1, #176; Abraham Kook, *Da'at Kohen*, #154; Mosheh Feinstein, *Igrot Mosheh* Yoreh Deah, Vol. 1, #157, 160; Even Haezer III, #4).

I have quoted all of these modern Orthodox authorities to show that our future path in this matter should not be based on the false assumption of bringing greater unity to the Jewish community. The Orthodox would, in any case, not accept a liberal conversion; they would consider our *bet din* invalid and would certainly feel that our converts have not accepted the yoke of the commandments.

As we view the rite of conversion from a Reform point of view, we should note that the Reform movement has stressed careful instruction with more attention to intellectual rather than ritual requirements. The Central Conference of American Rabbis, in 1892, abolished the requirement of any ritual including circumcision. Most liberal rabbis, however, require circumcision or accept the existing circumcision in accordance with the opinion of Hillel (Shab. 135b). Converts were to be accepted after due instruction before "any officiating rabbi assisted by no less than two associates."

Except in a cursory way, no discussion of *tevilah* has been undertaken by liberal Jewish authorities. The custom has fallen into disuse, but was never actually rejected by liberal Judaism. Ritual immersion has completely ceased to be practiced for *nidah* and is followed only by a small percentage within the Orthodox community. The practice has further been hindered by endless Orthodox debates about the technical requirements of the *miqveh*. A ritual immersion has, therefore, not been considered necessary for conversion among most Reform Jewish communities. There are, however, a number of cities in the United States and Canada in which *tevilah* has been encouraged or required for Reform conversions.

We might conclude that if the custom possesses meaning for the community and for the prospective convert, it should be encouraged. This would make it more difficult for traditionalists to challenge liberal conversions, although Orthodox authorities will never willingly accept anything we do as our basic premises differ sharply.

December 1977

45. A SWIMMING POOL AS A *MIQVEH**

QUESTION: May a swimming pool be used as a *miqveh*? What are the requirements for immersion which we would follow with converts in those communities in which ritual immersion is indicated or where the rabbi feels strongly about the inclusion of this ritual? (Rabbi D. Shapiro, White Plains, NY)

ANSWER: We will deal briefly with the question of the use of the *miqveh* for conversion in Reform *gerut* as that has been dealt with in earlier responsa ("Origin of the *Miqveh* for Conversion" and "The *Miqveh* and the Reform Convert"). The question of rituals which should be used to accept converts was debated in Germany in the eighteen-forties. This centered mainly around the requirement of circumcision (*milah*). Samuel Holdheim and the Reform Society were opposed to circumcision. Abraham Geiger and the vast majority emphasized it as a necessary rite. The issue was raised in America at the Philadelphia Conference of 1869 and again at the Pittsburgh meeting in 1885; between these conferences various Reform rabbis had written pamphlets and articles on the question. *Tevilah* was not debated and only generally included in these discussions. This was equally true in 1893 when considerable time was spent on debating "Initiatory Rites of Proselytes." The resolution which was passed called for acceptance of proselytes "without any initiatory rite" (*C.C.A.R. Yearbook*, Vol. III, p. 36). Those rabbis who recorded the reason for their opposition to the resolution dealt only with *milah*, not *tevilah*.

The ritual of *tevilah*, therefore, quietly vanished without debate; it has similarly reappeared on the scene as a larger number of American

Reform rabbis have made *tevilah* optional or mandatory for *gerut*. In many instances the traditional *miqveh* has been used. When none was available, immersion has taken place elsewhere. Let us turn to the requirements for a *miqveh*.

We should begin with the regulations connected with a traditional *miqveh* which are clear. It should be at least three cubits long, a cubit wide and a cubit deep and contain forty seahs of water (Er. 4b; Yoma 31a; *Shulhan Arukh* Yoreh Deah 201.1). In other words, a space which contains between 171 and 191 gallons of water would be sufficient.

The water must be from a natural source. It may be from a spring, a lake or a river which has been fed by a natural spring in accordance with a statement in Leviticus (11.36): "Nevertheless a fountain or a cistern wherein is a gathering of water shall be clean." The opening word of that statement has been interpreted to be restrictive (*akh*) according to tradition (Hul 84a; *Sifra* to Lev. 11.36). Rain water is also appropriate as is water melted from ice or snow (M. Miq. 7.1; *Yad* Hil. Miqvaot 3.1 ff; *Shulhan Arukh* Yoreh Deah 201.2; 201.30).

It is clear from the rabbinic sources that the only usable liquid is water (*Shulhan Arukh* Yoreh Deah 201.23) and that it must be still water (*Sifra* to Lev. 11.36; Rashi to Shab. 65b, to Nid. 67a; Tos. to Hag. 11a; *Yad* Hil. Miqvaot 10.16; *Shulhan Arukh* Yoreh Deah 201.2). The water which enters the *miqveh* may not be drawn or poured into it (*Smag* Positive Commandment #248; Tos. to B. B. 66b, to Pes. 17b; *Shulhan Arukh* Yoreh Deah 201.3). It must enter through a system of pipes not subject to uncleanliness; this excludes pipes of metal, wood or clay unless specifically treated to turn them into "vessels" (*Rosh* Miq. 5.12; *Yad* Hil. Miq. 5.5; *Shulhan Arukh* Yoreh Deah 201.34; Hatam Sofer *Responsa* Yoreh Deah 199). The *miqveh* itself must be constructed in the ground or be located in a building which is built into the ground. The *miqveh* may not consist of a tub (B. B. 66b; Tos. to Pes. 17b; *Shulhan Arukh* Yoreh Deah 201.6).

We should also note that if a pool has attained the status of a *miqveh*, then one may add any amount of water, such as tap water, by other means and the *miqveh* does not lose its status. Furthermore, the original *miqveh* may be connected with another through a pipe. If this is done and it flows into the neighboring pool it is considered an appropriate *miqveh* (Rashi to Yeb. 47b).

The main problem in building a *miqveh* are the rules connected with the piping, and the vessels through which the water must pass. The vessels can not be of such a size that objects can be placed into them;

the pipe itself is not considered a vessel (*M.* Miq. 4.1; *Yad* Hil. Mikvaot 6.1). The problem of using a modern water system are the reservoirs, holding tanks, and filters, through which spring or river water flows before reaching the user. Most *miqvaot* in modern cities, therefore, use rain or melted snow water as the basic supply to which other water is added as needed (*Shulhan Arukh* Yoreh Deah 201.36; Ezekiel Landau, *Noda Biyehuda* Yoreh Deah 136, 137; Hatam Sofer *Responsa* #198, #199, #203ff; Rosh *Responsa* #30, #31).

Now let us turn to the matter of a swimming pool seen in a traditional setting. It is clear from the outset that in many ways a swimming pool satisfies the provisions of a *miqveh*. Most pools are built into the ground or into buildings which are in the ground. There would be no difficulty of properly guiding two hundred gallons of rain water or melted snow into the pool at the outset and then adding other water. Similarly a small neighboring splash pool could be properly prepared and connected. The problem of recirculated water which causes a flow and drainage holes in the bottom of the pool are among the chief obstacles for traditional Jews in using a swimming pool as a *miqveh*. This is true even though the flow of water is entirely internal as the pumps pass water through the filters and return it to the pool. For a complete discussion of these problems see Benjamin Kreitman, "May a Swimming Pool Serve as a Kosher *Miqveh*," (*Proceedings of the Rabbinical Assembly*, Vol. 33, 1969 pp. 219 ff). The nineteenth and twentieth century traditional authorities have turned more and more to technical discussions about the *miqveh* and even questioned the appropriateness of *miqvaot* in long use. For our purposes these details upon details are irrelevant.

We must ask about the purpose of this ritual. If we return to the Biblical and early rabbinic statements connected with purification for *gerut* or other purposes, we can see that the authorities sought a ritual which used pure water in an appropriate setting. This symbolic purification changed the status of the individual involved (*Yad* Hil. Miqvaot 4.1, 11.12). This symbolism is meaningful to many modern converts as it helps them to make the transition to Judaism.

Symbolic purification for *gerut* can be properly provided by a natural body of water, a *miqveh* or a swimming pool. If a pool is used, the ritual should take place only when no other use is made of it. The ceremony should be conducted in an appropriately dignified manner.

We should remember that our use of *tevilah* for *gerut* has gradually developed among us as we have changed since 1893. No rituals have been mandated by the Central Conference of American Rabbis which stipulated that acceptance of Judaism occur before a rabbi and two associates for *gerut*; however both *milah* and *tevilah* have been widely used.

November 1986

46. PRIVACY OF A CONVERT

QUESTION: The congregation keeps a public register in its library of all the life cycle events such as birth, *Bar/Bat Mitzvah*, confirmations, marriages, and deaths. All conversions are also included. Does such a public register of conversions invade the privacy of the convert? Is it appropriate to maintain it in the congregational library? (Rabbi J. Edelstein, Monroeville, PA)

ANSWER: Conversion in Judaism is a public rite conducted before a court of three (Yeb. 47b; *Yad* Hil. Issurei Biah 13.14, *Shulhan Arukh* Yoreh Deah 268, 269). Such requirements obviously makes it initially a public act and assures proper status in the community for the convert. We, however, are concerned with the sensitivity of converts at a later time. Two discussions provide some insight into this question. All converts receive a Hebrew name. Although nothing is said about this in the major codes, it has become a general custom. New male converts are generally named "the son of Abraham"; Abraham is considered the father of all proselytes (*Tanhuma* Lekh Lekha 32, ed. Buber). Although this custom is frequently followed (*Shulhan Arukh* Even Haezer 129.20; Felder, *Nahalat Tzevi* 1.31, 124), it is not mandatory, nor is anything said about naming female proselytes, although we often name them "the daughter of Ruth," the most famous Biblical female proselyte. As such names are publicly used particularly in the *Torah* service, they are a public reminder of conversion.

We should also remember that individuals who are converted as infants may be given the opportunity to determine their own religious status at the age of maturity (*Bar Mitzvah* for boys and slightly earlier for girls). They may reject Judaism without prejudice, if they wish (*Shulhan Arukh* Yoreh Deah 268.7). This has made it necessary for the status of young convert to be remembered. Traditionally, there have also been some matters of marriage law which specifically involve converts. They have been given broader latitude about whom they may marry, and this includes individuals of doubtful descent (Kid. 72b; *Shulhan Arukh* Even Haezer 4.22). In this discussion, tradition has stated that this special status would continue until the tenth generation, or until the fact that "the family stemmed from a proselyte had been forgotten." A number of famous individuals have been specifically recalled as proselytes (Adiabne and Antipater in Josephus *Antiquities* XX 2; Onkelos in Meg. 3a; etc.)

Conversion to Judaism remains public knowledge. However, there is no intent to embarrass the convert. It would, therefore, be proper to have a public register of all life cycle events and conversions in the congregational library, yet it should be placed in such a way that it will not be used simply to satisfy idle curiosity.

February 1984

47. INFANT CONVERSION

QUESTION: A young couple is in the process of converting. In this instance, the conversion, or the study toward conversion, has been spread out over a period of two years due to desire for a thorough study, as well as business problems. The couple is committed to Judaism and the conversion should be finished in January. The couple expects a child, most likely a male, in September. The local *mohel* refuses to do a *berit milah*, even *leshem gerut*, as neither parent is Jewish. What can be done in this instance to start this young lad in life as a Jew? (Rabbi J. Adland, Indianapolis, IN).

ANSWER: Tradition makes clear provisions for the conversion of Gentile infants to Judaism. The conversion was undertaken by a *bet din* who stand in place of the father (Ket. 11a; *Yad* Hil. Isurei Biah 13.7; *Tur, Shulhan Arukh* Yoreh Deah 268.7). This procedure was followed when a father and mother do not convert to Judaism but wish their son or daughter to be Jewish (Rashi, Ritba to, Ket. 11b). There was some discussion as to whether a formal *bet din* was necessary for such conversion. In the case of the boy there was also controversy as to whether the circumcision must be done at the request of the *bet din* or independently (Smak in the name of Aderet; also Ritba and Meiri to Ket. 11b).

Although there is a fair amount of discussion on the details of the conversion and whether, in the case of a boy the *berit milah* precedes or follows the immersion in a *miqveh*, there is no debate on *whether conversion under these circumstances is possible*. It is clearly possible and obviously occurred regularly in the past.

An infant convert always has the right, whether conversion is done at the request of his father or at the request of a *bet din*, to renounce his conversion on reaching maturity. If such renunciation takes place, it is not held against the individual in any way (Ket. 11a; Rashi to Ket. 11a; see also Ritba, Aderet, Meiri; *Tur, Shulhan Arukh* Yoreh Deah 268.7). This question is raised upon reaching maturity, i.e., the age of thirteen for boys, or twelve for girls.

It would, therefore, be perfectly possible for you to convert this youngster at the time of his *berit*, or if it is a girl, shortly after her birth. This may be done with or without *miqveh* according to local custom. This would be completely in keeping with tradition, as well as Reform Jewish practice. If the local *mohel*, because of some individual idiosyncrasy, refuses to do so, then the *berit* may be conducted with equal validity by a Jewish physician. The rabbi would recite the appropriate prayers for *gerut* and *berit milah*.

August 1984

48. CONVERSION OF A YOUNG CHILD OF A FIRST MARRIAGE

QUESTION: How shall we deal with the children of a non-Jewish divorced parent, now converted to Judaism, who has married a Jew in her second marriage and wishes her children to be Jewish? (Rabbi J. Folkman, Columbus, OH)

ANSWER: Such a family situation, of course, demands care and sensitivity about the concerns of all parties. The children currently find themselves in a family with Jewish parents, while they remain Christian, but we should not take their conversion or education as Jews for granted. In most, though not all instances, this would require the consent of the natural father. He should also be consulted and in some way he must be included in the ceremonial occasions in the lives of his children.

If there is agreement on these matters, then we should proceed with these children as with any other children who seek to become Jewish. In the previous generation, the religious education of such children and their *Bar/Bat Mitzvah* and Confirmation were considered by the Central Conference of American Rabbis as equivalent to their conversion ("Report on Mixed Marriage and Intermarriage," *C.C.A.R. Annual*, pp. 158 ff). Today it would be preferable to proceed somewhat differently. Young children in the religious school should not be left uncertain about their Jewish status. Therefore, we should provide an understanding of Judaism at the level appropriate for the child and convert them fully while still young (Ket. 11a).

In the case of boys who are not circumcised, circumcision should occur if at all possible. If a child was already circumcised, some parents may want to undertake *tipat dam*, but that remains optional. Girls should be entered into the *berit* with a special ceremony (See S. J. Maslin, *Gates of Mitzvah*, p. 15).

More traditional parents may also want to have the child undergo *tevilah* (Yeb. 46a ff; *Yad* Hil. Issurei Biah 14; *Shulhan Arukh* Yoreh Deah 268). It is quite clear from tradition that if such a child at any later time undergoes *tevilah*, even though not specifically for the purpose of conversion, it would be considered the same as if he had undergone it for this purpose (*Shulhan Arukh* Yoreh Deah 268.3). The *Talmud* debated the need for both circumcision and ritual bath. R. Eliezer (*Talmud* Yeb. 46a) indicated that a proselyte who was circumcised, and did not take the ritual bath, was considered fully Jewish. The decision went against him. Orthodox and Conservative rabbis in our day require it, but we as a movement do not, though in certain areas this has become standard practice as well. *Tevilah* should, therefore, be considered as optional, as it is with adult converts. The children should be given a Hebrew name, and a certificate of conversion would then be presented to them and their families.

This procedure, as outlined, has the advantage of making the children completely Jewish. They would possess that status throughout their religious education. No question about their status would rise during these years and their education would follow the same pattern as that of every other Jewish child. It should be pointed out that such conversion, while full and complete ritually and legally, obligates the parents to provide a Jewish education, *Bar/Bat Mitzvah* and Confirmation for these children. Only through years devoted to learning will Judaism become meaningful to the children.

According to tradition, of course, such children have the right to challenge their conversion upon reaching majority. When such children reach the age of thirteen for boys and twelve and a half for girls, there is a traditional mechanism by which converted children may reject Judaism without prejudice (*Shulhan Arukh* Yoreh Deah 468.7). In earlier days, a formal process of rejection was required because of the rigidity of the Jewish-Gentile relationship. Nowadays, no such rejection mechanism is necessary, because belonging to the Jewish people and faith is essentially voluntary. This is, therefore, not necessary for us, and *Bar/Bat Mitzvah* and Confirmation would be an equivalent to a young adult's reaffirmation of Judaism.

In summary, we urge that a complete conversion take place for the young individual if it is agreeable to both parents, and then insist that the youngster be provided with a Jewish education.

April 1981

49. CONVERSION OF A YOUNG CHILD

QUESTION: What should be done for a four year old who was baptized as a Catholic and born to a Roman Catholic mother? The mother has now married a Jew who has legally adopted her son. Both have agreed that the child should be converted to Judaism and raised as a Jew. He is surgically circumcised. What procedure should this conversion follow? (O. R., Pittsburgh, PA)

ANSWER: We should begin by reviewing the traditional requirements for conversion. They are clear (Yeb. 46, 47; *Shulhan Arukh* Yoreh Deah 268; *Yad* Issurei Biah 15); a court of three is necessary. Prospective converts must be warned that they are joining a persecuted community and that many new obligations will be incumbent upon them. They were then to bring a sacrifice (in the days when the Temple stood), take a ritual bath, and in the case of males, be circumcised. To this day the requirements of a *bet din*, *tevilah* and the *berit* remain for traditional Jews. The sources are clear on the requirements, but considerable discussion about them exists in the *Talmud*. For example, R. Eliezer stated that if a prospective male convert was circumcised, or took a ritual bath, he was considered a proselyte. R. Joshua insisted on both, and his point of view was adopted (Yeb. 46b). Hillel and Shammai disagreed about a prospective male convert who was already circumcised. *Bet Shammai* insisted that blood must be drawn from him, while *Bet Hillel* stated that one simply accept that circumcision without drawing blood (Shab. 135a).

The rabbinic authorities decided in favor of Bet Shammai (*Shulhan Arukh* Yoreh Deah 268.1; *Yad* Issurei Biah 14.5). Clearly, there were differences of opinion about steps necessary for the ritual of conversion in ancient times. The *Talmud* also contains a variety of opinions about the desirability of accepting converts. These reflect historic competition with Christianity, persecution, etc. in the early centuries of our era.

The Talmudic discussions insist that the convert must join Judaism without any ulterior motives, and if such are present, the conversion is void (Yeb. 24b). Of course this opinion applies only prospectively, not retrospective, and *bediavad*, they were accepted. This is hardly at issue here, but let us understand this line of reasoning as well. Some authorities were more lenient in regard to ulterior motives, so Hillel (Shab. 31a) readily accepted a convert who stated that he wished eventually to become a high priest. R. Hiya accepted a woman who wanted to marry one of his students (Men. 44a). In modern times, although most Orthodox authorities would reject converts who seek to join us for the sake of marriage, some would accept them in order to avoid conversion by Reform rabbis (Mendel Kirshbaum, *Menahem Meshiv*, #9), because civil marriage has preceded, or because the couple is living together (David Hoffmann, *Melamed Lehoil*, Even Haezer 8, 10; Yoreh Deah 85). Similar arguments have been advanced by Meshullam Kutner in *Uketorah Yaasu* and Moses Feinstein in *Igrot Mosheh* (Even Haezer I, 27). However, the greatest number of Orthodox authorities have rejected these arguments (Joseph Saul Nathenson, Jacob Ettlinger, Yehiel Weinberg). Their rejection even for consideration as converts is based upon ulterior motivation and the likelihood that they would not accept all the *mitzvot* as they are generally not observed in the Jewish community today, and probably not kept by the Jewish partner (Isaac Herzog, *Hekhal Yizhoq*, Even Haezer I, #20; Moses Feinstein, *Igrot Mosheh* Yoreh Deah, I, #157, 160; Even Haezer III, #4). I have quoted all of these modern Orthodox authorities to show that our *gerut* may not be accepted by traditional authorities. The Orthodox would, in any case, not accept a liberal conversion. They would consider our *bet din* invalid and would certainly feel that our converts would not have accepted the yoke of the commandments, the entire system of *mitzvot*.

As we view the rite of conversion from a Reform point of view, we should note that the Reform movement has placed its stress on careful instruction with more attention on intellectual rather than ritual requirements. The Central Conference of American Rabbis, in 1892, abolished the requirement of any ritual including circumcision. Most liberal rabbis, however, require circumcision in accordance with the opinion of Hillel (Shab. 135b). Converts are to be accepted after due instruction before "any officiating rabbi assisted by no less than two associates." There are, of course, definite limits to instruction in this instance, but some initial education can be undertaken.

Except in a cursory way, no discussion of *tevilah* has been undertaken by liberal Jewish authorities. The custom has fallen into disuse, but was never actually rejected. It is followed for *niddah* by only a small percentage even within the Orthodox community. The practice has been further hindered by endless Orthodox debates about the technical requirements of *miqveh*. A ritual immersion has, therefore, not been considered necessary for conversion in many Reform Jewish communities. There are, however, a number of cities in the United States and Canada in which *tevilah* has been encouraged or required for Reform conversion. In others it is optional.

We might conclude that if the custom possesses meaning for the communities and for the prospective convert, it should be encouraged. This would make it more difficult for traditionalists to challenge liberal conversions, although Orthodox authorities will never willingly accept anything we do as our basic premises differ sharply.

When infants who are adopted become Jewish, it may also be done through the naming ceremony conducted either at home or in the synagogue. In many Reform congregations, this would be considered sufficient ritual conversion for girls and also for a large number of boys. This act, along with Jewish education, would bring the child into the covenant of Judaism in the same manner as a child born Jewish.

We have several possibilities which might be followed in the conversion of this young boy about whom you ask. He should certainly begin to receive some Jewish education. As he is already circumcised, his parents might want to undertake *tipat dam*. Although tradition would encourage this, we would not suggest it for a child four years old. It would certainly provide a negative initial experience with Judaism. However, *tevilah*, with an appropriate ceremony, or a Hebrew name bestowed either in the synagogue or at home, would provide a proper initiation into Judaism through something meaningful and understandable to the young boy and his parents.

October 1980

50. TEENAGERS AND *GERUT*

QUESTION: A number of teenagers have indicated a serious interest in Judaism. The first is a girl whose divorced mother married a Jew. The youngster was raised as a Presbyterian until age eight with no subsequent religious training. She would like to formally convert and participate in Confirmation at the age of sixteen. The mother has not converted, and the stepfather, although affiliated with the congregation, is not active in it.

The second individual is a boy whose mother moved to Israel when he was two and lived there for ten years as part of the Beta Yisrael Movement of Black Americans in Dimona. The boy speaks fluent Hebrew and has a fairly well developed Jewish education. The mother never converted, nor did any member of the family. The young man has disavowed any Christian attitudes or theologies which were originally part of the group when he moved to Israel.

The third is a young girl from a non-Jewish home in which neither parents practice Christianity, but certainly are not interested in Judaism; she has attended religious school with a friend and requested permission to come regularly. She has also indicated the desire to participate in Confirmation with or without conversion. (Rabbi J. Stein, Indianapolis, IN)

ANSWER: Traditionally a sixteen-year-old individual was considered an adult and could, therefore, make his own choice as far as *gerut* (conversion) was concerned. Such an individual would be accepted like any other convert and simply join the Jewish people (W. Jacob, *American Reform Responsa*, #65). However, in our age sixteen is still part of childhood, and such an individual is not an adult in any legal or formal sense. Therefore, we should treat such an individual as a minor.

We must acknowledge that these three youngsters come from very different backgrounds and with different motivations; we must begin by asking some fundamental questions. To what extent is their interest in Judaism part of a teenage rebellion? Are family or psychological problems present? What is the attitude of the parents toward the wish of their child to become Jewish? Is a friendship with a Jewish child the primary motivating factor? These and other similar questions must be properly answered before any further steps are taken.

In addition we should clearly indicate to each youngster that although it is possible theoretically for us to accept teenagers as converts, we would as a matter of principle not do so. A teenager is a minor for us in twentieth century America. We also recall that we have frequently suffered from efforts to convert children and teenagers to Christianity in the past, and fully understand the potential problems involved. We, therefore, suggest that these youngsters participate in all informal programs of the congregation, but in no formal instruction. If their interest is serious, and endures, then they may follow the path of *gerut* when they are adults.

In summary, we would strongly discourage conversion at age sixteen, nor should the ceremony of conversion and confirmation be combined.

June 1984

51. JAPANESE JEWISH CHILD

QUESTION: A young couple consisting of a Jewish father and a Japanese mother have raised their child in the synagogue, and at the same time made every effort to imbue him with some knowledge of his Japanese heritage in a series of classes held each week. This includes the Japanese language and customs, as well as a knowledge of the Shinto religion. Is this a conflict with the young man's Jewish identity? (O. T., Pittsburgh, PA)

ANSWER: It is clear that this individual has been introduced to Judaism from his earliest age onward. There was a *berit milah*, and Jewish customs are observed in the home. The family attends synagogue with some regularity, and so although there has been no conversion on the part of the child's mother, it is clearly the intent of these parents to raise their child as a Jew. He is currently enrolled in *Bar Mitzvah* classes and has a considerable knowledge of Hebrew, as well as Jewish history and customs.

The effort to also provide a Japanese cultural background should not stand in the way of his Jewishness. The introduction to the Shinto religion may very well have religious overtones for several of the other children in the group, as they are neither Jewish nor Christian. They are seeking an identity in the Shinto/Buddhist religious life of Japan. However, for this young man, who is a committed Jew, such instruction will be similar to hearing about Catholicism or Episcopalianism in a parochial school. As long as the instructors realize that this young man is Jewish and do not try to infringe upon his Jewish identity, there is no harm in learning about the Shinto religion and the part in which it has played, and continues to play, in Japan. We should consider this young man as fully Jewish through his identification with the Jewish community.

October 1983

52. HOMOSEXUAL CONVERT*

QUESTION: "In our community there is a small group of 'gay' Jews who have gathered together to form a *havurah*. (Some of them are members of my congregation). The *havurah* meets on a regular basis and holds a monthly *shabbat* service. Occasionally members of the *havurah* attend regular services at the Temple or join us for special programs. We have attempted to be as open to them as possible. Recently a few non-Jews have been attracted to the *havurah*. Several of them have indicated an interest in Jewish life, and one individual in particular has approached me in regards to the possibility of studying in order to convert to Judaism." In light of the strong antipathy of Judaism to homosexuality, should we accept a known and active homosexual who desires to convert to Judaism? (Rabbi R. Safran, Ft. Wayne, IN)

ANSWER: The attitude of traditional Judaism to homosexuality is clear. The Biblical prohibition against homosexuality is absolute as seen in the verses — "Do not lie with a male as one lies with a woman; it is an abhorrence" (Lev. 18.22); "if a man lies with a male as one lies with a woman, the two of them have done an abhorrent thing; they shall be put to death - their blood-guilt is upon them" (Lev. 20.13). Other statements are equally clear. The Talmudic discussion of the matter makes no substantive changes and continues the prohibition. It deals with the question of minors, duress and various forms of the homosexual act (San. 53a ff; Yeb. 83b; Ker. 2a ff; Ned. 51a, etc.). In the subsequent codes, the matter is briefly mentioned with the same conclusions (*Yad* Hil. Issurei Biah 1.5, 22.2; *Tur* and *Shulhan Arukh* Even Haezer 24). There is very little material in the responsa literature which deals with homosexuality, as it does not seem to have been a major problem. The commentators to the above mentioned section of the *Shulhan Arukh* felt that suspicion of homosexuality could not arise in their day, and so various preventive restrictions were superfluous. For example, Moses Rifkes (seventeenth century Poland) stated that this sin did not exist in his time (*Be'er Hagolah*). Until the most recent modern period, there has been no further discussion of this matter.

The Central Conference of American Rabbis has dealt with the issue of homosexuality over a number of years. In 1977, the following resolution was adopted:

Whereas, the Central Conference of American Rabbis consistently supported civil rights and civil liberties for all people, especially for those whom these rights and liberties have been withheld, and

Whereas, homosexuals have been in our society long endured discrimination,

Be it therefore resolved, that we encourage legislation which decriminalizes homosexual acts between consenting adults, and prohibits discrimination against them as persons, and

Be it further resolved, that our Reform Jewish religious organizations undertake programs in cooperation with the total Jewish community to implement the above stand.

We will not discuss the modern Jewish attitude toward homosexuals which has been shaped by two factors: (a) the attitude of tradition towards homosexuality, (b) our contemporary understanding of homosexuality, which sees homosexuality as an illness, a genetically-based disfunction or a sexual preference and life style. There is disagreement whether homosexuality represents a willful act or a response to which the individual is driven.

If a homosexual comes to us and seeks conversion, we should explain the attitude of traditional Judaism and that of our Reform Movement to him quite clearly. After that, if he continues to show an interest in Judaism and wishes to convert, then we may accept him as any other convert.

The entire matter is somewhat complicated by the fact that this group of homosexuals has organized itself into a *havurah*. We must ask ourselves whether it is simply for the purpose of companionship, or if this is a group who will seek to attract others to a homosexual lifestyle. In the case of the latter, we could certainly not accept a convert who intends to influence others in that direction. Otherwise, a homosexual who wishes to convert to Judaism should be accepted as any other convert.

June 1982

53. CONVERT WITH A JEWISH FATHER

QUESTION: A young woman whose father is Jewish and mother Christian was raised as a Christian. Now as an adult she is in the process of converting to Judaism and has gone through the formal conversion requirements. In choosing a Hebrew name she would like to include the name of her father. Although he did not transmit Judaism to her, she wishes to retain this family tie through her name. (Rabbi N. Cohen, St. Louis Park, MN)

ANSWER: It has long been customary to designate proselytes as *ben Avraham* or *bat Rut* (*Shulhan Arukh* Even Hazer 129.20; I. Felder, *Nahalat Tzevi* I, 31, 124 ff). This identifies the individual as a convert and provides a Jewish lineage for someone who obviously does not possess it and proudly links her with Abraham, who, according to the *agadah*, was responsible for the first proselytes to Judaism or with Ruth, an ancestor of David and so also a link to the Messianic Age.

In this instance, matters are a little different as the young lady does have a Jewish father, although he did nothing to encourage her Judaism. It would be appropriate, therefore, to use his name in keeping with the general emphasis within Judaism on family ties even when the bond is remote. For example, in the case of an *asufi* or *sh'tuki* - foundlings whose parents were unknown or whose father was unknown, one of the procedures suggested was the use of the name of the maternal grandfather (Isserles to *Shulhan Arukh* Orah Hayim 139.3).

We have continued this emphasis on family ties and should encourage the young woman in this direction, especially as there is nothing in tradition which demands the use of *ben Avraham*, the proselyte or *bat Rut*.

June 1985

54. CONVERT WITH CHRISTIAN FAMILY*

QUESTION: A young man wishes to convert to Judaism. His wife and very young children do not share that interest, and the husband and wife have agreed that their children should be raised as Christians despite the young man's interest in Judaism. She is active in her church, and it is doubtful whether she will convert at any time in the future. Should we accept this young man as a serious candidate for conversion? (M. K., Baltimore, MD)

ANSWER: Both traditional Judaism and Reform Judaism suggest a period of study and inner reflection before the step of conversion to Judaism is seriously contemplated (Yeb. 46, 47; *Shulhan Arukh* Yoreh Deah 268; *Yad* Hil. Isurei Biah 15; W. Jacob, *American Reform Responsa*, #65). Furthermore, the difficulties which an individual might face upon joining us as a Jew are to be clearly explained. All this indicates that the step is to be taken with greatest care. We should certainly exercise such care in this case.

The motivation of the individual involved should be thoroughly examined. The individual should then be instructed that although the current mood of America leaves religion very much in the private realm, and sees it primarily as an individual decision of conscience, this is not the view of Judaism. We see Judaism as part of a pattern of family life and the life of an entire people. As this man's family life will not be Jewish, it will be extremely difficult for him to live in accordance with Jewish ideals and daily practices. As he views the *mitzvot*, he is bound to meet frustration again and again when he realizes that there are many which are beyond his ability to execute because of his Christian family.

Such obstacles and frustrations may eventually lead to the destruction of his family life. We do not wish to encourage such a weakening of the family; it is the object of Judaism to strengthen the family unit.

In this instance, we recommend that the individual be strongly discouraged from converting to Judaism. We would encourage him to remain a "righteous Gentile," close to Judaism and friendly to its causes. We would invite him to participate in all of the activities of the synagogue and the Jewish community. In this way, he may feel close to Jews and Judaism and yet not bring unusual problems to his family life.

December 1984

55. CONVERSION WITH RESERVATIONS

QUESTION: Several Christians who seek to become Jews have indicated that they are convinced of their ability to become Jews but can not absolutely abandon the divinity of Jesus. May such individuals be accepted as converts? (Rabbi H. L. Poller, Larchmont, NY)

ANSWER: The traditional requirements for conversion are clear (Yeb. 46, 47; *Shulhan Arukh* Yoreh Deah 268; *Yad* Hil. Isurei Biah 15) — a court of three is necessary. Prospective converts must be warned that they are joining a persecuted community and that many new obligations will be incumbent upon them. They were to bring a sacrifice in the days when the Temple stood, and males had to be circumcised and take a ritual bath. The *Bet Din* has asked the prospective convert a number of questions which deal with his education and commitment to Judaism. One of the questions which has traditionally been asked is whether the convert receives upon herself the entire *Torah* without exception (Bekh. 30b; *Yad* Hil. Issurei Biah 14.8; *Tur* and *Shulhan Arukh* Yoreh Deah 268.2 ff). Traditional Judaism would interpret this as an obligation to observe all of the commandments. We state that the convert has an obligation to practice Judaism according to our Reform tradition. Both would, however, agree that this indicates a clear willingness to abandon all other former beliefs. This would definitely include belief in the divinity of Jesus.

Individuals who believe in the divinity or a special status of Jesus may, of course, study Judaism. It will help them understand Judaism better, but we can not accept them as converts until they are willing to give up their belief in Jesus without any mental reservations.

February 1984

56. TWO SOVIET JEWS OF DOUBTFUL DESCENT

QUESTION: A young Soviet Jewish man has met a young Soviet Jewish woman. Both have come to the United States recently from the Soviet Union. Their parents are deceased and neither one is absolutely certain whether their mothers were Jewish. While living in the Soviet Union, they suffered the disabilities of all Jews. Since their arrival in the United States, they have participated in programs at the Jewish Community Center and a number of synagogues in various cities in which they have lived. Shall we consider them Jews and marry them, or shall we demand certain prerequisites before marriage? (A. M. - L. Z., Pittsburgh, PA)

ANSWER: Let us begin by inquiring about the identity of these two young people while they lived in the Soviet Union and now that they have settled in the United States. As they suffered the disabilities of Soviet Jews certainly the Soviet government considered them to be Jews, and they were accepted as Jews by their co-religionists in the Soviet Union. To the best of their knowledge no one has ever questioned their Jewish identity. Although the Russian Jewish community possesses very little Jewish knowledge the tradition of matrilineal descent remains widely known among them. We may, therefore, presume that the mother was Jewish in both instances and that the parents wished to have their children recognized as Jews. During their stay in the Soviet Union they suffered because of their Jewish identity and emigrated. It is, therefore, likely that the mothers of both young people were Jewish if we follow the initial assumption, and so we may marry them as any other Jewish young people in accordance with tradition. Furthermore, we may do so in keeping with our recent Reform resolution on patrilineal descent as these individuals have identified themselves with the Jewish community and participated in Jewish life to the best of their ability.

March 1984

57. RUSSIAN IMMIGRANT COUPLE WITH MIXED BACKGROUND

QUESTION: A Jewish man from the Soviet Union married a non-Jewish woman simply for the purpose of enabling her to emigrate from the Soviet Union. They also brought a teen-aged child along, who is really not their child but needed to leave the Soviet Union. During the period that this family has lived in the United States, they have identified with the Jewish community, although neither wife nor daughter are Jewish. The young lady has fallen in love with a Jewish man and wishes to marry him. What is her status?

ANSWER: It is not our concern that her entrance to this country may have occurred under somewhat cloudy circumstances. She has maintained herself within this country, has been of no trouble to the

94

authorities or the community. And as the general status of immigrants in this country is currently under debate, that matter need not be discussed.

It is clear that this young woman should be considered as a non-Jew who wishes to join us. Although her adoptive parents are reluctant to say much about her background or her parents in the Soviet Union for fear of the authorities, their influence on this young woman, and the fact that they have led a Jewish life for several years during the period of transition in their lives, has brought her to Judaism in an informal manner. It would be appropriate now to formalize this through converting the young woman as we would convert anyone else.

Many of us have experiences with individuals who have been attracted to Judaism through Jewish friends, customs, practices and ideas. Some of them have moved in Jewish circles for a long time, yet we would not consider them Jewish without some more formal instruction and an official acceptance into the Jewish community. The same path should be followed by this young woman. This would resolve all questions about her identity on her part or that of her family.

September 1983

58. INTERMARRIED RUSSIAN JEWISH FAMILY

QUESTION: A Russian Jewish man has been married twice. His first wife was not Jewish and a daughter resulted from that union. The second wife is also not Jewish. They have a son and a daughter. All five have immigrated to the United States. The oldest daughter is twelve; the second is six and the third child is three years old. The husband has joined a synagogue and has now inquired about the status of his children.

ANSWER: We would answer this inquiry in keeping with the Resolution of the Central Conference of American Rabbis of March 1983:

"The Central Conference of American Rabbis declares that the child of one Jewish parent is under the presumption of Jewish descent. This presumption of the Jewish status of the offspring of any mixed marriage is to be established through appropriate and timely public and formal acts of identification with the Jewish faith and people. The performance of these *mitzvot* serves to commit those who participate in them, both parent and child, to Jewish life.

"Depending on circumstances, *mitzvot* leading toward a positive and exclusive Jewish identity will include entry into the covenant, acquisition of a Hebrew name, *Torah* study, *Bar/Bat Mitzvah*, and *Kabbalat Torah* (Confirmation). For those beyond childhood claiming Jewish identity, other public acts or declarations may be added or substituted after consultation with their rabbi."

These children would need to perform acts of Jewish identification to be considered as Jews. In this instance, it would mean their enrollment in religious school and subsequent *Bar/Bat Mitzvah*, as well as Confirmation. As the twelve-year-old girl can not fulfill the normal requirements for *Bat Mitzvah* before her thirteenth birthday, we would suggest that she undertake an intensive program, or better yet, delay her *Bat Mitzvah* until such a time as she has fulfilled those requirements.

If these children are raised as Jews and receive a Jewish education, we will consider them as Jews.

March 1984

59. THREE GENERATIONS OF MIXED MARRIAGE

QUESTION: A young man who grew up in the South is the product of three generations of mixed marriage. His great grandfather was Jewish and his great grandmother was Christian. His grandmother was raised as a Christian, but married a Jew. Both of his parents come from mixed marriages, and have provided him with no formal religious education. He would now like to claim his Jewish heritage and feels that the recent decision of the Central Conference of American Rabbis would make this easier for him. (H. S., Washington, DC)

ANSWER: The resolution of the Central American Rabbis, passed in 1983, has stated:

"The Central Conference of American Rabbis declares that the child of one Jewish parent is under the presumption of Jewish descent. This presumption of the Jewish status of the offspring of any mixed marriage is to be established through appropriate and timely public and formal acts of identification with the Jewish faith and people. The performance of these *mitzvot* serves to commit those who participate in them, both parents and child, to Jewish life.

"Depending on circumstances, *mitzvot* leading toward a positive and exclusive Jewish identity will include entry into the covenant, acquisition of a Hebrew name, *Torah* study, *Bar/Bat Mitzvah*, and *Kabbalat Torah* (Confirmation). For those beyond childhood claiming Jewish identity, other public acts or declarations may be added or substituted after consultation with their rabbi."

This resolution deals with the current generation and cannot be applied retroactively. In any case, there was no Jewish education or commitment in the previous generations. This young man has been raised in a secular fashion which has been colored by Christian traditions. Although there was very little formal Jewish education for three generations, some Jewish heritage survived. Otherwise, the young man in question, who now lives in a slightly larger town, would not be interested in reclaiming his Jewish identity. From a traditional Jewish point of view, he would not be considered Jewish as the link was broken in the second generation in which the father was Jewish and the mother non-Jewish. Had this not been the case, traditional Judaism might consider him as a Jew in accordance with the view of Solomon ben Simon of Duran (Rashbash, *Responsa* #89). He was concerned with the offsprings of Marranos and considered them Jewish indefinitely if the female Jewish lineage remained unbroken. Most authorities would insist on some form of *haverut* to mark a formal re-entry into the Jewish community (*Shulhan Arukh* Yoreh Deah 268.10 f; Ezekiel Landau, *Noda Biyehudah*, #150, etc.)

We, however, feel that there must be a strong educational component which will create a positive identity, and so would demand more regardless of matrilineal or patrilineal descent.

As this young man and his forefathers had no Jewish education or contact, we should treat him as a convert to Judaism and welcome him to Judaism. In the process of conversion and the final ceremony, we should stress his links to a Jewish past which he now wishes to establish firmly for himself and for future generations.

September 1983

60. PROBLEMS IN A FAMILY TREE

QUESTION: A young man who intends to make *aliyah* has raised a question about his family tree. He, his parents and grandparents have been active in the Jewish community. The young man in question has received an excellent Jewish education, both at the high school and university level. Recently, while looking into his family tree, he has discovered that one great grandmother may not have been Jewish. The matter is somewhat doubtful, but he suspects that it is so. Should he undergo formal conversion to Judaism in order to correct this "blemish"? (D. P., NY)

ANSWER: Let us look at this question first from a traditional point of view and then from our own Reform view. Tradition looks for matrilineal descent and asks about the Jewishness of the mother. Generally this is done in that generation, and only rarely are inquiries made about grandmothers. The presumption of tradition always favors "no blemish" and inquiries are only made reluctantly.

In the period of the Marranos, individuals who claimed Jewish identity appeared in Europe or North Africa generations after the expulsion of Jews from Spain. They were almost always accepted without detailed questions about their background (H. J. Zimmels, *Die Marranen in der rabbinischen Literatur*). It is, therefore, very doubtful whether even a strict traditional authority would engage in this kind of inquiry. Furthermore, we must note that it is not absolutely certain whether the great grandmother in question was a Christian. No accusation of that kind has ever been raised against the family. It has been sufficiently prominent within the community for comments to have been made. Tradition would, therefore, generally ignore the possible "blemish."

Let us now review this matter from our Reform perspective and through the statement of the Central Conference of American Rabbis, made in March, 1983:

"The Central Conference of American Rabbis declares that the child of one Jewish parent is under the presumption of Jewish descent. This presumption of the Jewish status of the offspring of any mixed marriage is to be established through appropriate and timely public and formal acts of identification with the Jewish faith and people. The performance of these *mitzvot* serves to commit those who participate in them, both parents and child, to Jewish life.

"Depending on circumstances, *mitzvot* leading toward a positive and exclusive Jewish identity will include entry into the covenant, acquisition of a Hebrew name, *Torah* study, *Bar/Bat Mitzvah*, and *Kabbalat Torah* (Confirmation). For those beyond childhood claiming Jewish identity, other public acts or declarations may be added or substituted after consultation with their rabbi."

This statement makes it quite clear that acts of identification are necessary along with descent. The family in question has been clearly identified with the Jewish community. The young man in question has demonstrated his loyalty and interest in Judaism. The consideration of *aliyah* demonstrates this further. There would, therefore, be no question in our mind that the young man is to be considered as Jewish.

March 1984

61. A CHILD RAISED IN TWO RELIGIOUS TRADITIONS

QUESTION: A couple in which the wife is Jewish and the husband is Christian were married by a priest and a rabbi. Their child has been baptized and circumcised. During the early years of the boy's life, he went to religious school sporatically, but now the parents wish to enroll him in Hebrew classes as well as regular religious school class in preparation for *Bar Mitzvah*. Further probing shows that they also intend to have him prepared for First Communion. What is the status of this child? Should he be enrolled in the *Bar Mitzvah* program? Would the answer to the question be different if the mother were Christian and the father Jewish? (M. K., St. Louis, MO).

ANSWER: The status of a Jewish child, according to tradition, is determined by the Jewishness of the mother. We, as Reform Jews, changed this through a resolution passed by the Central Conference of American Rabbis, in 1983, which stated:

"The Central Conference of American Rabbis declares that the child of one Jewish parent is under the presumption of Jewish descent. This presumption of the Jewish status of the offspring of any mixed marriage is to be established through appropriate and timely public and formal acts of identification with the Jewish faith and people. The performance of these *mitzvot* serves to commit those who participate in them, both parents and child, to Jewish life.

"Depending on circumstances, *mitzvot* leading toward a positive and exclusive Jewish identity will include entry into the covenant, acquisition of a Hebrew name, *Torah* study, *Bar/Bat Mitzvah*, and *Kabbalat Torah* (Confirmation). For those beyond childhood claiming Jewish identity, other public acts or declarations may be added or substituted after consultation with their rabbi."

This means that the child of a Jewish mother or a Jewish father is potentially Jewish if the parents act to assure the Jewish identity of the child through education, appropriate ceremonies, etc. Here, of course, the parents have done that, but have also, and at the same time, provided the youngster with a Christian identity. Furthermore, we are faced with two religious traditions which place exclusive claims upon a child. Traditional Judaism would insist that this child, by virtue of its Jewish mother, remains Jewish regardless of any actions which may be taken on its behalf or which the child may take. He would be considered an apostate because he is affiliated with Christianity, but he would always be welcome to return to Judaism with a minimum of ceremony. On the other hand, Catholicism places a similarly exclusive claim on the child by virtue of his baptism, although this need not concern us.

We would say to the parents that although their family life thus far has followed a dual path, they have now come to a juncture at which a decision must be made. It would have been much simpler if such a decision had been made at the time of their marriage, then some of these problems would not have arisen. Now, however, the child must follow one religious tradition or another. We can not in good conscience prepare a child for *Bar Mitzvah* with the knowledge that at the same time he is being prepared for First Communion. Furthermore, the child will not be helped by this equivocal stand of the parents, for he will merely be confused, both now and in the future when his status will remain a puzzle to him. This matter must be settled at this moment, and we must insist on a decision for this child. The rabbi and the congregation should be absolutely certain that the path upon which the parents agree will be followed and should ask for such an agreement in writing.

September 1983

62. RETURN TO JUDAISM OF A BAPTIZED JEWISH GIRL

QUESTION: A student in this year's Confirmation Class has a brother who is a "Jew for Jesus." Her mother, although born Jewish, practices Christianity. The girl was privately baptized when she was five. The father is a committed Jew and wants his daughter confirmed. Under what conditions can we confirm this girl? (Rabbi M. Feinstein, San Antonio, TX)

ANSWER: It is clear that we have a confused religious situation in this family, as every member seems to be going in a different direction. It is, therefore, necessary to ascertain whether this young girl and her father are sincere in their motivations, or whether her interest in a confirmation at the synagogue represents part of a family quarrel. If these problems have been resolved, then we should approach the young woman as an adult, and ask for an affirmation of her Judaism, a declaration of *haverut*, as for any repentant apostate.

Most of the traditional material which discussed apostates is only peripherally relevant, as it deals with those who converted under duress. Here the conversion of the mother and the baptism of the child were voluntary acts. Those converted under duress should be permitted to return to Judaism in as simple a manner as possible.

In cases of duress such individuals were readmitted to the Jewish community (and we must remember that this was a corporate community, not merely a congregation) without any action on their part except their desire to rejoin the Jewish community. No ritual bath or anything else is necessary. This is the law as finally stated in the *Shulhan Arukh* (Moses Isserles to *Shulhan Arukh* Yoreh Deah 268.12; Abraham Gombiner, Magen Avraham, to *Shulhan Arukh* Orah Hayim 326), based upon a verse in Jeremiah (3.22), "Return you recalcitrant children." This Biblical statement, as well as similar Talmudic statements, is cited by Elijah Gaon of Vilna in his discussion of the above mentioned passages of the *Shulhan Arukh*.

It has been generally felt that one should not embarrass such unfortunate individuals and make it easy for them to return to the Jewish community. So Rabenu Gershom, who lived in the Rhineland in the eleventh century, felt that one should simply admit such individuals and not in any way remind them of their previous apostasy (*Mahzor* Vitry, pp. 96 ff). Solomon ben Simon Duran (*Responsa* #89) also felt that no ritual bath or any other act was required. These thoughts were incorporated by Joseph Caro in his *Bet Josef* (to *Tur* Yoreh Deah 268).

However, in instances where the apostasy was not under duress, and where the apostate may have caused considerable trouble to the community, then a process akin to conversion was demanded (Hai Gaon in Aderet, *Responsa*, Vol. 4, #292; Rashi to Kid. 68b and Lev. 24.10). At the very least, a ritual immersion in the *miqveh* was demanded (Moses Isserles to *Shulhan Arukh* Yoreh Deah 268.12) as well as a promise to become an observant Jew before three witnesses

(Joseph Ibn Habib to *Alfasi* Yeb. Chap. 4). Examples of this more demanding point of view may be found in Zimmel's *Die Marranen in der rabbinischen Literatur*.

The young lady involved in this instance does not quite fall into either historic category. She was not converted under duress. On the other hand, she is also not an apostate who left us and caused us any problems. We, therefore, recommend a middle road. We would admit her with a simple ceremony which will impress the seriousness of her decision on her and formally make her part of the Jewish community. Whether immersion in a *miqveh* is required will depend on the traditions of the community.

January 1984

63. CONCEALING JEWISH IDENTITY*

QUESTION: Is it permissible to deny our identity as Jews if we find ourselves in a life threatening situation caused by terrorists? This question has been prompted by the events surrounding the highjacking of the *Achille Lauro* by terrorists. What should we do if we find ourselves in such a situation? Should we instruct our children to conceal their Jewish identity under such circumstances? (Rabbi S. Priesand, Tinton Falls, NJ)

ANSWER: It is a clear statement of Jewish tradition that one must give up one's life rather than violate three prohibitions. They are idolatry, incest and killing another person (San. 60b ff; A. Z. 43b, 54a; Ket. 33b; Shab. 149a; *Sefer Hazmitvot* Lo Ta-aseh #2 ff, 10 and 14; *Shulhan Arukh* Yoreh Deah 157.1). Unfortunately, this question has arisen many times, and there is considerable literature on the subject. Frequently in the Middle Ages Jews were threatened with death unless they accepted Christianity or Islam. (A good summary of the literature is provided by H. J. Zimmel's *Die Marranen in der Rabbinischen Literatur*). Many from the time of the Crusaders onward became martyrs under those circumstances. Others simulated an acceptance of Christianity or Islam while they privately remained Jews and escaped when that possibility arose (W. Jacob, "Status of Children," *American Reform Responsa*, #145). Such individuals who publicly proclaimed another religion, but privately remained Jews, were to be considered Jews in most ways even though *lehat-hilah*, another course of action was mandated (*Shulhan Arukh* Yoreh Deah 119.12; Orah Hayim 128.37; Even Haezer 42.5). These were the decisions of the *Shulhan Arukh*. Earlier opinions varied according to: (a) the danger presented by such apostasy to the Jewish community; (b) the conditions under which they returned to Judaism, as I have discussed in the responsum cited above.

Maimonides prohibited a feigned acceptance of another religion in accordance with the *Talmud*; no Jew was to abandon his religion for another religion (*Sefer Hamitzvot*, Ta-aseh 9), as did Caro (*Shulhan Arukh* Yoreh Deah 157.1). The *Shulhan Arukh* had also stipulated very clearly that even at the risk of death, one can not declare, "I am not a Jew" (Yoreh Deah 157.2). The question of permitting apostasy was faced by Ephraim Oshry (*Responsa Mema-amakim* 13) and others during the Holocaust. And he answered it negatively, and stated that a Jew may not save himself through the purchase of a forged baptismal certificate, and thereby, try to join the partisans in the forest. However, there is also another line of thought which states that if the Jew is able to provide an ambiguous answer, which does not require an outright declaration that he is a Christian, such a declaration is considered acceptable (Isserles to *Shulhan Arukh* Yoreh Deah 157.2, in accord with *Nimukei Yosef*).

There were also instances, particularly in the medieval period, in which Jews wore Christian garb to save themselves. The surrounding world considered them to be Christians, and asked no questions. This, too, won the approval of the *Shulhan Arukh* (Yoreh Deah 157.2), although Maimonides disagreed (*Sefer Mitzvot* - Lo Ta-aseh #30).

For Oshry during the Holocaust there was a difference between following a path which had the appearance of permanently abandoning Judaism, like using a baptismal certificate which he prohibited, and on the other hand using a forged Christian passport, a temporary measure, which he permitted. Similarly, he allowed an individual with a non-Jewish name to enter the letters R. K. into a passport, which stood for Roman Catholic in German, to the Nazis, but could be interpreted differently by the Jewish bearer. A parallel decision was given by Hayim Shor (*Torat Hayim* #17) and Samuel Ungar (*Mekadshei Hashem*, p. 214; R. Kirschner, *Anthology of Holocaust Responsa*, pp. 97 ff). It is clear from these statements that these rabbis took a hard line with a baptismal certificate which seemed like an outright denial of Judaism, but were willing to go along with anything less.

Other authorities during the Holocaust, however, decided differently even on the matter of baptismal certificates. They realized that (a) the Nazis were not interested in converting anyone to Christianity; (b) they made such conversions punishable by death; (c) they severely punished any Christian clergy involved in such an act of mercy. For these reasons the number of *Batei Din* in Poland, Czechoslovakia and Hungary, as well as Lithuania, permitted such baptismal certificates to be held by Jews, and treated these Jews as any other member of the Jewish community despite protests within the community. Any other action seemed to play directly in the hands of the Nazis, and the rabbis certainly did not wish to do that (H. J. Zimmels, *The Echo of the Nazi Holocaust in Rabbinic Literature*, pp. 77 ff). Similarly, it was permitted for individuals to declare themselves Karaites as they were not considered Jews under various Nazi rulings (Ibid. 81 ff).

The main line of thought among both Medieval and modern commentators prohibits an outright denial of Judaism, but permits an ambiguous statement which can be interpreted as a denial by the persecutor. It also permits a disguise which would not cause any questions to be asked.

The Medieval authorities also distinguished types of persecution. If the persecutor wished to force Jews to accept another religion, then it was the duty of the Jew to resist even if it meant death. If, however, it was the intent of the persecutor merely to persecute the Jew and threaten him with death without any interest in turning him into an idol worshipper, then he could simulate idol worship in order to save his life (*Azei Levonah* Yoreh Deah 179; *Turei Zahav* Yoreh Deah 179; *Shulhan Arukh* Yoreh Deah 157.1).

In the period of the Holocaust and the Expulsion from Spain, the identification of Jews and their persecution was a matter of government policy. In 1492, the authorities demanded conversion to Christianity. During the Holocaust everyone of Jewish descent, even Christians, were to be slain. Those conditions were very different from a temporary act of terrorism.

Terrorists usually do not hold their hostages beyond a brief specified period. Furthermore, such terrorists are not interested in bringing about a change in religion, but want to use Jewish hostages for whatever leverage can be exercised through them upon Israel. It is the duty of the remainder of the Jewish community to obtain the freedom of captives whenever this does not endanger the community itself (B.

B. 8b; *Yad* Hil. Matnat Aniyim 8.10; *Shulhan Arukh* Yoreh Deah 252). One great medieval hostage, Meir of Rothenburg, forbade payment of any ransom after he had been taken captive as he felt that this would hurt the community and set a bad precedent (Graetz, *Geschichte der Juden* Vol. VII, pp. 173 f; 423 f). In the case of modern hijacking by terrorists potential hostages can help Israel to avoid blackmail and guard themselves from additional danger by hiding their Jewish identity.

It would, therefore, be appropriate for children and adults, if taken hostage by terrorists, to conceal their Jewish identity first through passive acts and then through any other way which is possible.

November 1985

64. RETURN TO JUDAISM OF AN APOSTATE

QUESTION: An elderly man, both of whose parents were Jewish and who had no Jewish education, married a non-Jew early in life and was baptized. Later in his life he became a member of the Congregational Church, and eventually he was even ordained as a minister of the United Church of Christ. He served in several pulpits. Eventually he became disillusioned with Christianity and dropped his ministerial status. He is now actively studying Judaism. Is anything required aside from *haverut* for readmission to Judaism? What ceremony and what words should actually be used? (Rabbi N. Hirsch, Seattle, WA).

ANSWER: The question of someone returning to Judaism after leaving it goes back to Talmudic times where there is a discussion of this matter (Bekh. 31a; A. Z. 7a). The entire matter, however, became crucial in the Middle Ages. There we deal with two kinds of apostates who have returned to Judaism. The first are those who are forced to convert individually or as a community. This occurred from time to time in virtually all the countries of Europe, especially in Spain which led to the problems of the Marranos. The second instance included those who converted under little duress or who remained Marranos for a longer period of time when it was quite possible to escape that status.

In the first instance, it is clear that such individuals were readmitted to the Jewish community (and we must remember that this was a corporate community not merely a congregation) without any action on their part except their desire to become formally part of the Jewish community once more. No ritual bath or anything else was considered necessary. This was the law as finally stated in the *Shulhan Arukh* (Moses Isserles to *Shulhan Arukh* Yoreh Deah 268.12; Abraham Gombiner, *Magen Avraham* to *Shulhan Arukh* Orah Hayim 326), based upon a verse in Jeremiah (3.22) - "Return you recalcitrant children." This Biblical statement, as well as various Talmudic statements similar to it, were cited by Elijah Gaon of Vilna in his discussion of the above mentioned passages of the *Shulhan Arukh*.

There was a general feeling that one should embarrass such people as little as possible and make it easy for them to return to the Jewish community. So Rabenu Gershom, who lived in the Rhineland in the eleventh century, felt that one should simply admit such individuals and not in any way remind them of their previous apostasy (*Mahzor Vitry*, pp. 96 ff). Solomon ben Simon Duran (*Responsa #89*) also felt that no ritual bath or any other act was required. These thoughts have also been followed by Joseph Caro in his *Bet Josef* (to *Tur* Yoreh Deah 268).

However, in instances where the apostasy was not under duress, and where the apostate may have caused considerable trouble to the community, then it was considered advisory to demand a ritual bath (Moses Isserles to *Shulhan Arukh* Yoreh Deah 268.12). This entire ceremony, as well as a promise to become an observant Jew, had to be made before three witnesses (Joseph Ibn Habib to *Alfasi* Yeb., Chap. 4). Examples of this more demanding point of view may be found in Zimmel's *Die Marranen in der rabbinischen Literatur*.

In this instance we are dealing with an individual who has been a leader in another religious group and, therefore, may be looked upon by some in the community in a different fashion than an ordinary apostate. We should require more of him. Certainly a rather specifically worded statement of *haverut* made before three witnesses would be in order. The statement should be worded in a manner appropriate for this individual.

March 1983

65. DRIFTING APOSTATE

QUESTION: A young woman has moved through Christianity to Bahai and then to Judaism. After what appeared to be a sincere conversion, along with active synagogue participation, she and her twelve-year-old daughter suddenly disappeared upon reconciliation with an ex-husband. She subsequently moved into "neo-paganism" and Unitarianism. Now she has returned and once more seeks membership in the congregation. The time elapsed since her disappearance from the community is approximately nine months. The woman appears to be a spiritual "drifter." Should she be accepted as an active *haverut*? How should the child be treated? (Rabbi D. Zucker, Springfield, MO)

ANSWER: It is quite clear that a proselyte who has become an apostate remains, nevertheless, a Jew. In modern times we can not deny the right of an individual to join another religion, but for our purposes, that individual, nevertheless, remains a part of the Jewish people (see "An Apostate Proselyte," W. Jacob, *American Reform Responsa*, #71). Now we must ask what should be done to readmit this individual as we are unsure of her stability.

Most of the traditional material which deals with apostates is irrelevant for this situation as it treats apostasy under duress. Here the act was entirely voluntary and may reflect the instability of the young mother. When apostates under duress reappeared in a Jewish community (principally Marranos), they were generally welcomed and made part of the community with as little fuss as possible.

It has been felt that one should not embarrass such unfortunate individuals and make it easy for them to return to the Jewish community. So Rabenu Gershom, who lived in the Rhineland in the eleventh century, felt that one should simply admit such individuals and not in any way remind them of their previous apostasy (*Mahzor Vitry*, pp. 96 ff). Solomon ben Simon Duran (*Responsa* #89) also felt that no ritual bath or any other act was required. These thoughts were incorporated by Joseph Caro in his *Bet Josef* (to *Tur Yoreh Deah* 268).

However, in instances where the apostasy was not under duress, and where the apostate may have caused considerable trouble to the community, then a process akin to conversion was demanded (Hai Gaon in Aderet, *Responsa*, Vol. 4, #292; Rashi to Kid. 68b and Lev. 24.10). At the very least, a ritual immersion in the *miqveh* was demanded (Moses Isserles to *Shulhan Arukh* Yoreh Deah 268.12) as well as a promise to become an observant Jew before three witnesses (Joseph Ibn Habib to *Alfasi* Yeb. Chap. 4). Examples of this more demanding point of view may be found in Zimmel's *Die Marranen in der rabbinischen Literatur*.

In this instance, as the woman seems unstable, it should be impressed upon her that conversion to Judaism is serious and that a return from the status of apostasy is not easy, so a declaration along with perhaps immersion in a *miqveh* are in order. As presumably the daughter followed her mother into neo-paganism and Unitarianism, the same requirements should be applied to her.

July 1986

66. CHILDREN OF "MESSIANIC JEWS"

QUESTION: A couple previously affiliated with a "Messianic Jewish" congregation has returned and affiliated with my Congregation and became quite active. The children are enrolled in religious school and are doing well in school. Recently, I found out that the couple had not actually abandoned their "Messianic Jewish" conviction. They hope, in fact, that the rabbi and the remainder of the congregation would eventually adopt their philosophy. May this couple be permitted to continue as members of my congregation? How should we treat their children who are currently enrolled in religious school and seem to be normative Jews? (Rabbi N. Cohen, St. Louis Park, MN)

ANSWER: The Responsa Committee has dealt with the question, "Status of a Completed Jew in the Jewish Community." It indicates that such individuals should be treated as apostates. They have become apostates willingly without the duress frequently felt in the medieval period; we should, therefore, take the strictest position of our tradition toward them (see also "Apostate Proselyte," W. Jacob, *American Reform Responsa*, # 71). We should follow the suggestions of the previously cited responsum.

"We can not, and should not, exclude such individuals from attendance at services, classes or any other activity of the community, for we always hold the hope that they will return to Judaism and disassociate themselves from Christianity, but they should be seen as outsiders who have placed themselves outside the Jewish community. This should be made very clear to them and to the Jewish and general community, especially as many such individuals are active proselytizers.

Such individuals should not be accorded membership in the congregation or treated in any way which makes them appear as if they were affiliated with the Jewish community, for that poses a clear danger to the Jewish community and its relationships with the general community. We certainly do not want these individuals to speak for Judaism in any public forum.

In conclusion, we should make the distinction between ourselves and these individuals very clear to them, to the Jewish community and the general community around us."

In the question you have asked, the matter is somewhat complicated by the children who are enrolled in the religious school, and appear to be normative Jews. We should continue to permit the enrollment in religious school and do our best to raise them as Jews. It may be necessary to arrange a school membership, or other category with equivalent dues, but without the parents being considered members of the congregation. Similar situations have arisen in the case of a Christian widow of an intermarriage who wishes to continue to raise her children as Jews. There the congregation arranged for a special category for this individual and her children.

In other words, we should not deprive the children of a Jewish education. On the other hand, we should not permit the parents to proselytize, openly or quietly, within the congregation, or to be considered as normative Jews, either within or outside the Jewish community.

July 1984

67. BURIAL OF "MESSIANIC JEWS"

QUESTION: An active member of the group called "Messianic Jews" recently died. His family, which is also active in this movement, has requested that he be buried in a Jewish cemetery. Should that request be granted? (Rabbi S. Prystowsky, Laffayete Hill, PA)

ANSWER: "Messianic Jews" claim that they are Jews, but we must asked ourselves whether we identify them as Jews. We can not do so as they consider Jesus of Nazareth as the Messiah who has fulfilled the Messianic promises. In this way, they have clearly placed themselves within Christianity. They may be somewhat different from other Christians as they follow various Jewish rites and ceremonials, but that does not make them Jews. After all, Seventh Day Adventists celebrate Saturday as their day of rest, and various Black Christian churches continue to celebrate a number of Jewish festivals throughout the year. The theology and underlying beliefs of "Messianic Jews" remove them from Judaism and make them Christians.

The early *Evel Rabbati* (*Semahot* II) listed apostates among those whom the community has no obligation to bury. Although the later codes agreed, they were lenient under special circumstances and the law developed along those lines, mandating burial even for apostates. The division of opinion centers around the question of what is done for the "honor of the dead" and what for the "honor of the living." The latter are more readily performed; this means burial in a Jewish cemetery, but without eulogy or *takhrikhim*, nor a period of mourning, as these are "for the honor of the dead" (Moses Sofer, *Responsa* Yoreh Deah #341; *Tur*, Yoreh Deah 344, 345 and commentaries). Of course, if the death of the apostate was sudden, then it is assumed that he has repented (Isserles to *Shulhan Arukh* Yoreh Deah 340.5; Hoshen Mishpat 266.2). In our case, the family of the deceased also consider themselves "Messianic Jews," so there is no question of doing anything for "the honor for the living."

We should also note that when special conditions endangered the community, burial could be, and was, refused (Nahmanides, *Responsa* #224; Jacob Levi, *Responsa* #49). "Messianic Jews" present such a danger as its members masquerade as Jews and mislead Jews, while they are actually Christians. We should refuse to bury this "Messianic Jew," despite his self identification he was a Christian.

November 1985

68. STATUS OF A "COMPLETED JEW" IN THE JEWISH COMMUNITY*

QUESTION: There are a number of individuals in the community who consider themselves as "completed Jews" or "Messianic Jews"; they accept Jesus as their savior, but, nevertheless, still feel Jewish "in their hearts." How should the congregation view such individuals? (Rabbi A. S. Task, Greensboro, NC)

ANSWER: Individuals who feel a vague attachment to one or another religion pose no problem for those religious groups which leave identification solely in the hands of the individual. Judaism, however, does not do so. It is not the individual who defines whether she is Jewish but the group. For us in the Jewish community anyone who claims that Jesus is their savior is no longer a Jew and is an apostate. Through that belief she has placed herself outside the Jewish community. Whether she cares to define herself as a Christian or as a "fulfilled Jew," "Messianic Jew," or any other designation is irrelevant; to us she is clearly a Christian. It is true that this individual may be somewhat different from other Christians as she continues to follow certain Jewish practices and folkways, but we should remember that various Christian sects do likewise. For example, the Seventh Day Adventists observe *shabbat* as their day of rest. There are some Black Christian groups who also follow specifically Jewish observances, and there have been other groups like this in the past centuries.

We should, therefore, consider a "completed Jew" as an apostate. What would her status be for us? Judaism has always considered those who left us as sinners, but still remaining as Jews. They could always return to Judaism through *teshuvah*, and the exact response of Judaism depended very much on the conditions of the time. Hai Gaon (as quoted by Aderet *Responsa*, VII #292) felt that an apostate could not be considered as a Jew. Centuries later the rabbis of the Mediterranean Basin had to face the problems of the Marranos (*anussim*). Their attitude differed greatly and may be summarized under five headings:

(1) Apostates were Jews who had sinned but, nevertheless, remained Jewish (Isaac ber Sheshet; Simon ben Zemah of Duran, but on some occasions he did not grant this status; Solomon ben Solomon; Zemah ben Solomon).

(2) Those who considered the apostate as Jewish only in matters of matrimony (and so their offsprings were Jewish), but not in any other area (Samuel de Medina).

(3) Marranos (*anussim*) were non-Jews in every respect including matters of marriage; their children were not considered to be Jews (Judah Berab, Jacob Berab, Moses ben Elias Kapsali, etc.).

(4) An apostate was worse than a Gentile (ben Veniste, Mercado ben Abraham).

(5) Descendants of the Marranos who have been baptized were like Jewish children who have been taken captive by non-Jews, and their children are Jewish (Samuel ben Abraham Aboa). A full discussion of

the problem may be found in H. J. Zimmel's *Die Marranen in der Rabbinischen Literatur*, pp. 21 ff. One extreme position was held by Solomon ben Simon Duran (Rashbash *Responsa* #89) who felt that not only the apostate but also the children would continue to be considered Jewish forever into the future as long as the maternal line was Jewish. He also felt that nothing needed to be done by any generation of such apostates when they returned to Judaism. No ritual bath or any other act was considered necessary or desirable. In fact, he emphasized that no attention be given to their previous state, for that might discourage their return. Rabbenu Gershom similarly urged the quiet acceptance of all who returned to Judaism (*Mahzor Vitry*, pp. 96, 97).

The other extreme has been presented by Hai Gaon as cited in a slightly different fashion by Rashi (in his commentary to Kid. 68b and Lev. 24.10). He felt that any returning apostate, or the children of a Jewish mother who had apostasized, were potentially Jewish but must undergo a process akin to conversion if they wished to become part of the Jewish community. That point of view was rejected by most later scholars, as for example, Nahmanides (in his commentary to Leviticus 24.10; *Shulhan Arukh* Yoreh Deah 268.10 f; Ezekiel Laudau, *Noda Biyehudah* #150, etc.). We, therefore, have two opposing positions in rabbinic literature; both, of course, represented reaction to particular historic conditions. Solomon ben Simon of Duran wished to make it easy for a large number of Marranos to return to Judaism; unfortunately this did not occur. Even when it was possible for Jews to leave Spain, the majority chose to remain. Rashi's harsh attitude probably reflected the small number of apostates who were a thorn in the side of the French community. The later tradition chose a middle path and encouraged the apostate's return along with some studies, but without a formal conversion process. Even if an apostate indicated no desire to return to Judaism, he would, nevertheless, be considered as part of the Jewish people (San 44a).

A summary of special laws which were applied to apostates would include a number of matters mainly connected with family law. The marriage of an apostate who left Judaism under duress, if performed according to Jewish law, was valid (Yeb 30b; *Shulhan Arukh* Even Haezer 44.9). The rules of divorce when apostates were involved were modified; such individuals were not considered to be reliable witnesses except in the case of an *agunah*. Penalties could be imposed on their inheritance (Kid. 18a) although they did possess the right of inheritance (B. B. 108a, 11a). Normal mourning rites should not be observed for such persons (*M.* San. 6.6; *Shulhan Arukh* Yoreh Deah 345.5). Clearly apostates stood outside the community in all but relatively few matters until their repentance.

Each of these cases cited above, of course, dealt with apostasy under greater or lesser duress. Outside pressures played a major role in the lives of the individuals involved. This is not the case with the "Completed Jew." We would, therefore, be stricter with her than with individuals who were forced into a position of becoming Christian. For us such modern willing apostate is a non-Jew. In this matter we would disagree with the *Talmud* and later tradition (Bech. 30b; see "An Apostate Proselyte," *American Reform Responsa,* #71 for further references).

We can not, and should not, exclude such individuals from attendance at services, classes or any other activity of the community, for we always hold the hope that they will return to Judaism and disassociate themselves from Christianity. But they should be seen as outsiders who have placed themselves outside the Jewish community. This should be made very clear to them and to the Jewish and general community, especially as many such individuals are active proselytizers.

Such individuals should not be accorded membership in the congregation or treated in any way which makes them appear as if they were affiliated with the Jewish community, for that poses a clear danger to the Jewish community and also to its relationships with the general community. We certainly do not want these individuals to speak for Judaism in any public forum.

In conclusion, we should make the distinction between ourselves and these individuals very clear to them, to the Jewish community and to the general community around us.

September 1983

69. A PRINTED *SEFER TORAH*

QUESTION: A new Jewish community in Soviet Russia wishes to know whether a photocopy of a *Sefer Torah* may be used at regular services. The congregation does not possess a *Torah* Scroll now; it may be possible for one to be brought to them by visitors from the United States, however, the risk of confiscation is very great. While it would be relatively easy to replace a photocopied *Torah*, it would be difficult and expensive to replace a *Torah* Scroll. May a photocopied scroll be used during this time of emergency and persecution? (Rabbi M. Staitman, Pittsburgh, PA)

ANSWER: We should, of course, do everything possible to help our fellow Jews in the Soviet Union physically and spiritually. The *Torah* Scroll possesses great symbolic value for all Jews alongside its practical use in the synagogue service. As the Soviet Jews can not meet in a regular synagogue, but conduct services in apartments or other temporary sites which are constantly changed, the normal furnishings and appertinences of the synagogue are difficult to arrange. Everything connected with the service must be readily movable. A *Torah* Scroll, therefore, becomes even more important to such a congregation.

The actual problem revolves around the nature of the text and permission to recite the traditional blessings which should not be recited in vain (*levatalah*), and the "honor of the congregation."

The question of a photocopied *Torah* takes us to a Talmudic statement which deals with engraving (*haqiqah*) and inquires whether this may be considered the equivalent of writing (*ketivah* Git. 20a). The question asks whether the letters are sunken into the text or raised from it. The ancient discussion gained new prominence and the debate was renewed with the invention of printing, as the early printer's type created a depression in the paper and that was akin to engraving, which was not considered akin to "writing."

Despite questions about printed texts they have been shown reverence; even though they do not possess the sanctity of the *Torah*, they are to be buried just as worn out *Torah* Scrolls (Ezekiel Katzenellenbogen, *Keneset Yehezqel* #37, etc.). The problem of depressed letters does not exist with modern printing or photography. We could, therefore, say that a photographed *Torah* which precisely reproduces spaces, lines and the letters, possesses a high level of sanctity on these grounds, although not on the same level as a *Sefer Torah* itself.

However, questions concerning the sanctity of photography versus printing have been raised on other grounds. Photography is clearly more automatic and less manual than printing; printing is, of course, less manual than writing by hand as performed by a scribe. If personal, manual involvement determines sanctity, then the photographed item would be less holy. Though some feel that a photographed text possesses less sanctity, this line of reasoning has not been followed further. Books produced by this method (and almost all modern books are so produced) are considered sacred and must be buried when worn out if they contain the divine name. (Benjamin Weiss, *Even Yeqarah Tinyana* #39; Shalom Mordechai Shwadron, Responsa, *Maharsham*, 3.357; Wolf Leiter, *Bet David* #8).

We may, therefore, follow Solomon ben Aderet who permitted the reading from a *humash* in place of a *Torah*. In his time the *humash* in question was in the form of a scroll (but was not written precisely as a *Torah*). He allowed this while prohibiting the use of a *humash* in book form (*Responsa*, Vol. I, #805). Earlier, Maimonides had also stated that the most important matter connected with the *Torah* reading was the reading itself rather than the nature of the scroll from which the reading might be made. Therefore, if only an imperfect *Torah* were available, it could be used (Maimonides, *Responsa*, #42). We should add, however, that later in his *Mishneh Torah*, Maimonides stated that only those scrolls which fulfilled all the technical requirements were appropriate for use in a regular service (*Yad* Hil. Sefer Torah, 10.1). This was the path followed by the *Shulhan Arukh* as well (Orah Hayim 143.1 ff; *Bet Yosef* to *Tur*, 143). Isserles, on the other hand, was willing to be more lenient and permitted the use of an imperfect *Sefer Torah* when none other was available (Comments to Orah Hayim, 143.5). We should note that a rabbi of Marrakeesh was asked whether Jews who traveled across the Sahara by caravan could use a *humash* for *Torah* reading (Joseph Mesas *Mayim Hayim*, #79). He concluded that if their journey lasted only a few weeks, they should not read the *Torah* during those Sabbaths, but if their journey lasted for many weeks, it was preferable to read from a *humash* but not to pronounce the traditional blessings.

The second issue discussed by tradition deals with the honor of the congregation (*kavod hatzibur*). It was considered inappropriate for a congregation to read from a *humash* or an imperfect *Torah* scroll (Git. 60a) for this reason, yet is also clear that a congregation has the right to forego its honor (Solomon ben Aderet, *Responsa*, Vol. 1, #805; Isserles to *Shulhan Arukh* Orah Hayim 143.5).

The major codes of Maimonides and Caro do not permit a *Torah* reading at a public service except from a perfect handwritten *Torah*. They, of course, deal with a normative congregation in normal times. On the other hand, Maimonides in his responsum, Aderet and Isserles permitted such a *Torah* reading.

The problem of reading from a photographed text finally involves not the reading itself but the issue of reciting a blessing in vain (*levatalah*). We must weight that consideration against the importance of reading the *Torah* as well as the symbolism connected with the *Torah*, even a photocopied *Torah*. Clearly, in the prolonged emergency which affects Soviet Jews, we would agree with Maimonides' responsum that the *mitzvah* of reading a *Torah* far outweighs the nature of the scroll. The burden of a *berakhah levatalah* is rather minimal when compared with that of the lack of public *Torah* reading and symbolic union with the remainder of the Jewish people on each occasion when the *Torah* is read. We would, therefore, agree to the use of a photographed *Sefer Torah* under these emergency conditions in the Soviet Union.

August 1986

70. MARKING A *TORAH**

QUESTION: A number of *Torah* Scrolls have been stolen from synagogues in various cities across the country. Is it possible to mark a *Torah* in order to indicate ownership? What can be done in the framework of tradition? (V. Kavaler, Pittsburgh, PA)

ANSWER: We should remember that tradition from early times has been quite specific about the manner of writing a *Torah* (Shab. 108a; Meg. 19a; Shab. 79b; *M.* Sofer 2.9; Men. 30a, etc.). These laws have later been restated by the codes (*Yad* Hil. Sefer Torah; *Shulhan Arukh* Yoreh Deah 270 ff). These statements deal with the nature of the parchment, the type of writing permitted, the composition of the ink, the form of writing, divisions into paragraphs, etc. In addition, there is a long list of matters which cause a *Torah* to be unfit (*pasul*). In theory, every adult male Jew must write a *Torah* during his lifetime. In case he is unable to fulfill this *mitzvah*, he may designate someone else to write it, while he merely completes the last letters. These regulations clearly state that nothing additional can be written on the Scroll itself, or even on the sheet at the beginning or at the end, which is partially blank. Nothing may be written on the back. A palimset, i.e., a parchment which has been once used, may not be used for the purpose of writing a *Torah*. The restrictions on marking the *Torah* are absolute.

It would be possible, however, to mark the wooden staves at both ends of the Scroll. They have frequently contained the names of donors as well as the city and congregation to which the *Torah* has belonged. This would be an easy way to identify a particular *Torah*.

This course of action would not solve the problem of theft, for it would be a simple matter to remove the staves or the writing on the staves and then dispose of the *Torah*.

It has been suggested that a Scroll be marked in some way that is not obvious, either ink visible only through infrared light or through attaching some agents to the current ink formula which would make it readable through infrared, ultraviolet or other technical means. If such methods change the basic formula of the ink, or write upon the Scroll itself (although in an invisible fashion), they would make it *pasul*. If, however, certain portions of the ink with which a *Torah* is normally written can be given trace-elements or some others means of identification, such a sophisticated method of identification would be acceptable.

The problem with these methods is that they can be incorporated into a new *Torah*, but not into an an already existing *Torah*, unless this is done during repair work. Furthermore, devices needed to read them are not readily accessible. It would be simpler to make exact photographs of sections of the *Torah*, as every scribal version is slightly different; even small differences will show, especially in a major enlargement. This would provide accurate tracing devices and identify a *Torah*. It would, however, not make it possible for a potential purchaser to see whether a *Torah* has been stolen.

The maintenance of a central registry of *Torahs* which have been stolen from our synagogues is desirable, but that is cumbersome and unlikely to be useful in the near future.

It would be easiest and most appropriate that any synagogue which is offered a *Torah* from a questionable source make a thorough inquiry about its origin. Every attempt should be made to identify such a *Torah*.

If danger of theft is acute, then we would suggest that the *Torah* be visibly marked with the name of the congregation on the first and last sections. This would restrain the thief and, on the other hand, would enable the congregation to replace those segments when the danger had passed.

It is unlikely that a potential thief would follow the same procedure, as that would clearly indicate that the *Torah* had been obtained illegally.

Few other devices are available to us except to take the obvious precautions of locking the Ark and the synagogue so that theft becomes more difficult.

January 1981

71. CASING OF A MEZUZAH

QUESTION: A member of the Adath Israel Youth Group has collected some seashells. After cleaning the shells, they will mount them on a piece of walnut and insert a kosher scroll to form a *mezuzah*. Would it be improper or violate Jewish law to use seashells as the casing of a *mezuzah*? This is a fund raising effort of the Youth Group (Rabbi John Adland, Lexington, KY)

ANSWER: The commandment of the *mezuzah* is found in Deuteronomy (6.4 ff; 11.13 ff). The text deals with affixing a *mezuzah* on the doorpost. Later discussions turn to three questions, the nature of the text, the way in which the text is written, the places which do or do not require a *mezuzah*.

The text itself has always included the appropriate paragraphs from the *shema* (Deut. 6.4-9; 11.13-21), which was inscribed on a piece of parchment rolled up in such a way that the text was on the inside, while the empty portion of the parchment faced outward (*M.* Mezuzah, 2.10; *Sof.* Mezuzah 1.1; Shab. 108a; *Yad* Hil. Tefillin Umezuzah V'sefer Torah; *Shulhan Arukh* Yoreh Deah 271). The laws, at least in the *Talmud*, were a little more lax about writing a *mezuzah* than writing a *Torah*. It need not be copied but could be done from memory (Men. 32b), however, it had to be completely accurate and no letter could be missing.

The text itself must always be handwritten, be free of errors and be inscribed on parchment (*M.* Men. 3.7). Originally it could be written in any form as long as it did not imitate the decorative practices of pagans (Franz Landsberger, "The Origin of the Decorative Mezuzah," *Hebrew Union College Annual*, Vol. 31, pp. 157 f). The pattern for a *mezuzah* called for a twenty-two line document with the material on each line specified, so the first line began with the word *shema*, the second with *adonai* and the third with *had'varim*, etc. Although if written differently, it would be (*bedivad*) acceptable as long if the text was accurate (*Shulhan Arukh* Yoreh Deah 285).

In the early Middle Ages additional material was often included on the back of the *mezuzah* as there was no prohibition against that. The name of God, *Shadai*, was inscribed there and that became common practice (*Kol Bo* 90, *Yad* Hil. Telifin, Umezuzah Vesefer Torah 5.4). It is interesting to note that Maimonides did not disapprove of this practice which has remained current to this day. On some *mezuzot* we find longer names of God added (J. Trachtenberg, *Jewish Magic and Superstition*, p. 148).

From Gaonic Times until the late Middle Ages, the names of angels were sometimes added to the text side especially by Ashkenazic Jews. This practice is first mentioned by Judah Hadassi. It was considered normal by the *Mahzor Vitry* and the *Sefer Hapardes* (V. Aptowitzer, "Les Noms de Dieu et des Anges dans la Mezouza," *Revue des Etudes Juives*, Vol. 60, p. 38 ff). Maimonides and others vigorously fought against this practice and by 1300 it had disappeared. The works of Aptowitzer and Landsberger provide examples of specific angels as well as the placement of their names in the text.

The use of angels enhanced the feeling that a *mezuzah* possessed special power to ward off evil spirits. A hint of this was already found in the *Talmud* (A. Z. 11a; Men. 32b f; *Gen. Rabba* 35.3). Various medieval figures felt that the *mezuzah* possessed protective powers. Among them were Rashi, Meir of Rothenburg, Solomon Luria, Isaiah Horowitz, etc. (Rashi to Men. 33b; Meir of Rothenburg, *Responsa*, #108; *Shelah*, Vol. I, 187a).

The use of the name of angels represented a difference of custom between Askenazim and Sephardim. The Northern Europeans favored the practice while Maimonides and those of the Mediterranean Basin opposed it vigorously (*Yad* Hil. Tefillin Umezuzah Vesefer Torah; 5.4). The custom eventually disappeared.

There was a problem about exposing the name of God, *Shadai*, if the room was occupied by children, was a bedroom, etc. Moses of Coucy, therefore, covered the word, *Shadai*, with a bit of wax (*Sefer Mitzvot Hagadol* Aseh #23), while the *Shulhan Arukh* and its commentaries suggest that under those circumstances it might be wise to cover the entire *mezuzah* (*Shulhan Arukh* Yoreh Deah 286.5). This led to *mezuzah* cases which had hinged openings over the word *Shadai*).

There are lengthy discussions of the place which required a *mezuzah* as well as how it is to be affixed to the door (*Sof.* Mezuzah 114 ff). Maimonides lists ten places which require or should not have a *mezuzah* (*Yad* Hil. Tefillin Umezuzah Vesefer Torah). The *Shulhan Arukh* follows a similar pattern. In the discussion of how the *mezuzah* should be affixed, some mandated a vertical position while other commentaries prefer a horizontal position. Isserles suggested the slanted position now customary as a compromise between these two points of view. It is placed on the right hand door as one enters the house slanting inward with the upper portion pointing outward.

Relatively little is said in the traditional literature about the casing of the *mezuzah*. Landsberger suggests that the original way of affixing a *mezuzah* to the door was by inserting it into a hole which had been drilled in the doorpost (*Sof.* Mezuzah 1.10; *M.* Mez. 2.10; *Yad* Hil. Tef. 5.6; see also F. Landsberger, *op. cit.*, p. 152 f). In addition, it was suggested that the *mezuzah* be placed in a reed or similar protective covering of wood or metal (*Sof.* Mezuzah 1.10). Only slowly did the *mezuzah* container become decorative and Landsberger feels there were virtually no decorated *mezuzot* until the seventeenth or eighteenth century (Landsberger, *op. cit.*, p. 162 f). In the last few centuries, a wide variety of decorated *mezuzot* have evolved with abstract decorations, floral designs, animals as lions, griffins, as well as Hebrew inscriptions of various kinds (Wolpert and others).

The traditional literature, as well as artistic practice during the last century, indicate that there are no restrictions on the decoration of the casing of the *mezuzah*. It would be permissible to use an animal shell as any other form of decoration. The young people should be encouraged in this project which shows imagination and should add beauty to the *mezuzah*.

August 1986

72. MEDICAL USE OF PSYCHEDELIC DRUGS

QUESTION: What is the Jewish attitude toward using addictive psychedelic (mind altering) drugs as part of the healing process? Such drugs would be used under the direction of a physician to deal with severe psychological disturbance. (M. S., Cleveland, OH)

ANSWER: A wide variety of drugs have been described by the *Talmud*, although none of them seem to have been mind altering (Julius Preuss, *Biblical and Talmudic Medicine*, translated by Fred Rosner, pp. 433 ff). Various medieval physicians have given us the name of the drugs which they used. The most extensive list is that of Maimonides which contains more than two thousands items. We recognize that the medicinal use of drugs has expanded vastly in the last century and has become a regular part of medical treatment. This form of treatment, as well as all others, should be used under the general permission provided by the statements, "And he shall surely be healed," and "You shall live by them" (Ex. 21.19). When there is danger to life, the physician is encouraged to utilize all means at his disposal (*Shulhan Arukh* Yoreh Deah 116). The use of drugs in order to aid healing under the prescription of a physician is, therefore, permitted. It makes no difference whether the drugs are mind altering or not, as long as they have been prescribed to heal those who are ill.

May 1985

73. MIND ALTERING DRUGS FOR PLEASURE

QUESTION: What is the Jewish attitude toward using addictive psychedelic (mind altering) drugs for pleasure in a manner akin to the use of alcohol, tobacco, coffee or tea? (M. D., Miami, FL)

ANSWER: There is very little discussion in the traditional *halakhic* literature about the use of drugs. The codes, as well as earlier sources, and the responsa occasionally refer to *samim* (drugs) and their use; this category includes all drugs. Furthermore, the paucity of references indicate that this was not a serious problem until the latter part of the twentieth century. Even when Jews lived in societies which utilized addictive drugs widely among certain classes, we seem to have escaped that phenomenon.

The *Talmud* quotes Rav Hiyah who was cautioned by his father, Rab, "not to get into the habit of taking drugs" (Pes. 113a), but we do not know their nature. This work also recognized that some individuals react distinctively to drugs and that they affect various parts of the body differently (Eruv 54a; Nid. 30b). It warned against use of eye paint which had been mixed with drugs, as the vapors might be injurious when inhaled (Nid. 55b). Interestingly enough, when Rashbam commented on Pes. 113a, he mentions that this was a caution against drugs which may become habit forming, and, therefore, expensive. Then he concluded by stating that drugs should never be used if some other form of medicine was available. From his perspective there was no danger of drug abuse among the Jewish population.

Alcohol was the substance most likely to be abused; tradition was well acquainted with this problem, and it dealt with it in a straightforward fashion.

In the Biblical period, abstinence was admired and was one qualification for becoming a Nazirite (Nu. 6.8). This state entered by a vow seems to have been of limited duration. For most people the maximum period was six years (*M.* Nazir 1.4; Ber. 73a; Ned. 3b). Some people in Talmudic times abstained without taking the vow of a Nazirite (Shab. 139a; B. B. 60b).

Alcohol was rendered partially harmless through its continual ritual use in the *qiddush*, which is part of virtually every Jewish holiday and all joyful life cycle events. The limit of consumption was defined as a *reviit*. Beyond that there are two states of inebriation: *shetui* and *shikur*. *Shetui* refers to a person who may be shaky but can speak coherently in the presence of a king; a *shikur* is one who can not do so (Eruv 64a). Such an individual may also be called "drunk as Lot" and is likely to be totally incoherent similar to a *shoteh* (*Shulhan Arukh* Orah Hayim 99.1; Yoreh Deah 244.13). If an individual in this state orders a divorce, the scribe may not write it (*Yad* Hil. Gerushin 2.14). Such an individual is not criminally responsible for his actions even if he causes an injury (Joel Sirkes, *Responsa* #62). However, when he becomes sober he must pay for the damages done.

An individual who is to act as a judge may not take the slightest drink (Joel Sirkes, *Responsa* #41), although if this individual sleeps or walks a certain distance after drinking a small amount, and so counters the effect of the alcohol, he may act as judge (*Ibid.* #140). There is some discussion about the weaker nature of modern wines in contrast to wines of former times, but the conclusion remains that those who drink can not render judgment (Bet Yosef to *Tur*; *Shulhan Arukh* Hoshen Mishpat 7.4)

There is even some discussion in the traditional literature about the statement which exempts a groom from various *mitzvot*, such as the recitation of the *shema*. Some authorities felt that this was because the groom should devote himself to conjugal *mitzvot* (Tosafot; Rosh) while others, like Isserlein, felt that he was not obligated as he might be under the influence of alcohol (*Terumat Hadeshen*, Vol. I #42; *Havot Yair*, #66).

The *Midrashic* literature contains numerous citations which deal with the positive effect of wine as well as its negative influence. Moderation is encouraged while over-indulgence should be avoided (Ps. 104.15; Jud. 9.13; Prov. 31.6, 21.17, 9.1-6; Ez. 44.21; Is. 1.13; Ned. 20b; San. 70b; Eruv 65a; Ket. 8b; Meg 7b; *Gen. Rabbah* 36.7, etc.). For example, Ilai indicated that an individual was judged in three ways, by his drinking, his spending and his temperament (Eruv 65b). Drunkenness, in both men and women, was recognized as an evil which could only lead to wickedness (Ket. 65a; *Lev. Rabba* 12.4). There was some discussion by Rambam and others about those who occasionally imbibed too much and those who have become alcoholics (Maimonides, *Responsa* #16 and 17. Such an individual is disqualified as cantor (Isaac Spector, *Ein Yitzhak*, Vol. 1, #1).

Tradition has been much slower in dealing with the other habit forming items such as tobacco, coffee or tea. These can all be considered hazardous to health to a greater or lesser degree. Jewish tradition has prohibited individuals from wounding themselves. In fact, a person should remove all possible dangers to life (Deut. 4.9, 4.15, Ber. 32b; B. K. 91.b; *Yad* Hil. Rotzeah Ushemirah Hanefesh 11.4; Hil. Shevuot 5.57; Hil. Hovel Umaziq 5.1). Smoking has only recently been condemned through a number of strongly worded responsa and articles (M. Aberbach, Smoking and the *Halakhah, Tradition*, Vol. 10, pp. 49 ff; F. Rosner, *Modern Medicine and Jewish Law*, pp. 25 ff; M. Feinstein *Noam*, Vol. 24; "Ban on Smoking in the Synagogue" in this volume). Moses Feinstein has followed the classical pattern in this matter by stating that as a great many individuals are involved, it is better to leave them ignorant of the prohibition so that they "sin unwittingly rather than knowingly" (*Igrot Mosheh*, Yoreh Deah, Vol. 2, #49). As a large number of scholars and pious individuals, including Baal Shem Tov, smoked, it was difficult for traditional authorities to move in this direction. The real danger of tobacco did not become known until the middle of the twentieth century.

Although coffee and tea contain drugs which may be dangerous, it is not currently felt that this is a major health hazard comparable to psychedelic drugs, alcohol or tobacco.

The traditional attitude toward alcohol and tobacco, which are habit-forming, has been to encourage moderation. Psychedelic drugs are far more dangerous to health and are used without the social controls provided by Judaism for the ritual use of alcohol. We would, therefore, conclude that the use of psychedelic drugs for pleasure is forbidden by Judaism. We should also note that they are also prohibited under the well-known principle of *dina d'malakhuta dina* (the law of the land is the law). As the law of the United States makes the use of these drugs illegal, we must abide by that law.

May 1985

74. DRUGS AND MYSTICAL EXPERIENCE

QUESTION: Is it possible to use mind altering drugs in order to attain a mystical experience? (K. V., Los Angeles, CA)

ANSWER: The Jewish attitude toward mystical experience is shaped by *halakhic* and *kabalistic* views. Normative Judaism has been anti-mystical, or at least suspicious of mysticism. The *Talmud* cautioned that such literature not be studied until the student is mature (M. Hag. 2.1; 13b). Sometimes this struggle between the two forms of Judaism may be found in a single individual, such as Joseph Caro, author of both the *Shulhan Arukh* and the mystical *Magid Mishnah* (R. J. Z. Werblowsky, *Joseph Karo, Lawyer and Mystic*).

The various Jewish philosophical and mystical works, which deal with heightened states of awareness of whatever form, demand that they be attained through study, introspection, the observance of the *mitzvot*, and a life of piety. External stimulants are, to the best of my knowledge, not mentioned by authorities in this field, like Gershom Scholem.

As psychedelic drugs promote no assurance that a "heightened state of awareness" will be attained, we would, therefore, have to classify such a use of these drugs as seeking pleasure. This is prohibited by Judaism; that question has been treated in another responsum.

Mind altering drugs, therefore, may not be used by Jews to induce a "heightened sense of religious awareness" or to seek a mystical experience.

May 1985

75. DAMAGES FOR A PHYSICIAN'S ERROR

QUESTION: An elderly woman suffering from a variety of ailments was mistakenly given an excessive dosage of a drug. This led to her serious rapid deterioration and hastened her death. The physician in question immediately admitted his error and did everything possible to rectify it. Is the family entitled to damages on moral and ethical grounds? Should this course be pursued to make the doctor more careful in the future? (M. M., Pittsburgh, PA)

ANSWER: The *Talmud* dealt with the general problem of a physician's liability while healing the sick. The *Talmud* considered the task of healing a *mitzvah* and not interference with God's intentions [as He may have sent the disease] (B. K. 85a; *Bet Yosef* to *Tur* Yoreh Deah 336). It was a person's duty to seek the best physician in case of illness (Shab. 32a). Furthermore, it was permitted to violate all *shabbat* and ritual laws to save a human life (Yoma 85b; *Shulhan Arukh* Orah Hayim 329.3). If the physician failed and the patient died, he is free from liability as long as the remedies were tried in good faith (*Tosefta* Git. 4.6). This *Tosefta* discussed other situations of inadvertent injury incurred while performing a *mitzvah*. As long as the injury is inadvertent, no liability is incurred. The traditional statements are very specific about the physician's responsibility and free him from general liability for unintentional harm. Without such assurance it would be impossible for a physician to practice (David Pardo in J. Preuss, *Biblical and Talmudic Medicine*, p. 28). It is, of course, assumed that the physician has been trained and properly licensed (Nachmanides; *Torat Ha-adam* 12b; Simon ben Zemah of Duran, *Responsa*, Vol. 3; *Tur* Yoreh Deah 336; *Shulhan Arukh* Yoreh Deah 336; Eliezer Waldenberg, *Tzitz Eliezer*, Vol. 5, #23).

When, however, the physician has clearly made a mistake, then he is liable for the same damages as anyone engaged in other professional or commercial transactions (*Tosefta* B. K. 9.11). The general laws of liability apply here. The surviving family is entitled to damages on moral and ethical grounds and should pursue this course of action. The physician may well be willing to assume this obligation in keeping with tradition.

November 1986

76. PIERCED EARS

QUESTION: The custom of piercing the earlobe in order to insert an ear ring has again become widespread. What does Jewish tradition have to say about this? Is it permissible according to tradition? (V. Kavaler, Pittsburgh, PA)

ANSWER: The piercing of the earlobe is one of the few surgical procedures mentioned in the *Bible*, however, in a totally different connection. If a Hebrew slave, who was to serve for six years and be freed in the seventh year, declared that he loved his master, and his wife and children did not wish to be freed, then "he shall be brought to the door or the doorpost and his master shall pierce his ear with an awl; and he shall then remain his slave for life," (Ex. 21.6; *Tosefta* B. K. 7.5). Pierced ears in Biblical times, therefore, clearly indicated lifelong slavery and were a permanent form of branding the individual. It was considered appropriate to pierce the cartilage so that the wound site would never close again, although there was some controversy about this (Bekh. 37a; Kid. 21b).

In our instance, however, we are not dealing with permanent marks on the ear, but rather with a way of holding decorative items of female ornamentation. Piercing for this purpose was known in Talmudic times (*M. Shab. 6.6*). For that matter, not only were ornaments worn in the ear during the Talmudic period, but also as signs of various trades and professions. So, a writer would carry a quill, a carpenter a little piece of wood, and a money changer, a coin, while other professions carried other items (*Tos. Shab. 1.8; Shab. 11b; J. Shab. 3b*). It is clear, therefore, that such a surgical procedure was permitted in Talmudic times, nor was it prohibited later, although during frequent periods it was not fashionable.

Generally this matter is related to the Talmudic willingness to encourage women to beautify themselves. For example, spices are frequently mentioned, and a dealer in spices could visit women in the women's quarter, although such visits were prohibited to anyone else (B. K. 82a; B. B. 22a). Furthermore, women could continue to beautify themselves even during the semi-holiday period (*Shulhan Arukh* Orah Hayim 346.5) and a husband had to provide the means for such beautification (Ket. 64b). Many other references along these lines could also be provided.

We may, therefore, conclude that piercing one's ears for the sake of beautification would be permissible to Jewish women according to tradition.

September 1983

77. DANGERS OF SURGERY CORRECTING CONGENITAL CRANIOFACIAL MALFORMATIONS

QUESTION: A twenty-six-year-old man was born with Apert's syndrome, a disorder which is known as craniofacial dysostosis. This illness is found in a severe form in my patient, Albert. His strange appearance frightens children. He can not chew food properly. His nasal airway is small, so he can not breathe through his nose. He is disturbed and he suffers from many colds, etc. due to poor breathing. Surgery would correct some of these problems and improve his appearance. A social service agency favors surgery and would pay for it.

It is not entirely clear whether this individual wishes to have the surgery. His intelligence is limited as he is educably retarded. His mother is very much dependent on him for companionship and transportation, and has cared for him all his life. The risks of the operation are formidable and might lead to blindness, meningitis, seizure disorder and coma, or even death. The issues in this situation are the following: Albert, due to his limited intellect and his long standing physical deformity, may experience little impact from this extensive surgery and its attendant risks. In addition, the potential sacrifice and suffering the mother will experience are also disquieting. Finally, the expenses to achieve this result will be tens of thousands of dollars, and perhaps more if there are complications. Is it appropriate to proceed? (Dr. L. Hurwitz, Pittsburgh, PA)

ANSWER: A number of different questions have been raised by this case. The first is the extent to which one should risk someone's life for an operation whose results, because they are principally psychological, will not be known in advance. The social agency, which will pay for the extensive surgical procedure, feels that it will be beneficial. However, the patient and his mother have their doubts, each for different reasons.

Jewish tradition indicates that one should not wound one's self or endanger one's life. In fact, it stipulates that an individual should remove all possible dangers from himself (Deut. 4.9; 4.15; Ber. 32b; B. K. 91b; *Yad* Hil. Rotzeah Ushemirat Hanefesh 11.4; Hil. Shevuot 5.57; Hil. Hovel Umaziq 5.1). However, later responsa agree that even if there is considerable risk in the surgical procedure, it may be taken if there is a small chance that a cure will be effected (Jacob Reisher,

Shevut Yaakoq, III, 75; Hayim Grodzinski *Ahiezer*, Yoreh Deah 16). The recent Chief Rabbi of Israel, Untermann, sanctioned such an operations solely on the grounds that the chance of success was greater than possible failure (Address to the Congress of Oral Law, Jerusalem, August, 1968; several articles in *Noam* have also discussed this matter (Vol. 12, 13, etc.).

The patient may, therefore, undergo the operation even if the risk involved is considerable as long as some medical benefit is likely.

The second question deals with of the relationship of mother and child. What role should this play in our decision? We shall view this first from the point of view of the child's continued responsibilities to her parent. There is considerable discussion in the traditional literature of this matter. It deals with two aspects of a child's responsibility towards parents. One is the fiscal responsibility. This rests upon children generally, but of course, not in this case. The other aspect deals with the emotional dependence of the parents upon the child. Conflict in this area often became acute when an adult child moved away from his parents for marriage or another reason. Our tradition stressed the child's independence through comments on Biblical tales which dealt with this theme, as for example Genesis 2.24, "Therefore shall a man leave his father and his mother...," and on God's command to Abraham, "Get yourself out of your country and from your family and from your father's house....." (Gen. 12.1). The rabbinic interpretation of these citations provided for independence of the child from his parents, although the rabbis felt the need to defend Abraham (*M. Ber.*, 6.4; *Genesis Rabbah*, II, p. 369). The medieval *Sefer Hassidim* stated that any son who had made financial provisions for his parents was free to move (#564, p. 371). When dealing with a sick parent, or one who was mentally incapacitated, there was a difference of opinion between Maimonides and Rabad. Both agreed that the son may need to leave the parents, but Rabad felt that the obligation of emotional support remained with the son (*Derishah* to *Tur* Yoreh Deah 240). The *Shulhan Arukh* followed Maimonides in this matter (Yoreh Deah 240.10). Clearly the son remains responsible for the physical and mental welfare of his parents unless an extraordinary difficult situation makes this impossible.

The normal situation of a child leaving a home in order to marry presents potential problems. It is a *mitzvah* for a father to assure the marriage his children (Kid. 29a ff; Ket. 52b; San. 93a). We will not consider the matter of choice of mate, which has been discussed at great length in the literature. Marriage, with the normal move from the original home, is considered a *mitzvah* (Kid. 29a), and the traditional literature insists that a father is obliged to guide the child toward independence. In our case, the mother is similarly dutybound to assure her son's independence, or at least to take him as far as possible. He, in turn, must continue to support his mother emotionally and help her according to his ability. The mother's fear of the child's independence should not be a factor in any decision about this operation.

The third issue concerns the resources to be expended upon this individual. The social agency obviously feels that the money spent in this fashion will enable him to be less of a public charge both now and later in life. Jewish tradition lauds expenditures for this purpose. When Maimonides listed degrees of charity, the highest prepared the individual to be independent (*Yad* Hil. Matnat Aniyim, 10.7 ff).

Some doubts have been expressed whether the individual involved would actually be able to benefit from the operation and make the psychological adjustment to his new, improved status. That clearly is a matter of judgment which only a physician with considerable experience can decide. However, the surgeon should see himself primarily as the agent who sets the stage for possible future improvement. Unless this has been done, no improvement is possible. This willingness to take a chance and to risk failure is a basis of many aspects of life and religious life. For example, the entire notion of atonement connected with the *yamim naraim*, and especially *Yom Kippur*, suggests that we may be forgiven for past errors and begin anew; yet, there is no guarantee of such improvement. True repentance is sought, but the goal remains allusive (Yom. 86b; *Yad* Hil. Teshuvah 1.1 ff).

Tradition would have us note the problems connected with this operation. However, if the surgeon feels that it will be successful, and beneficial to the patient then the risk should be taken.

February 1984

78. BANKS FOR HUMAN ORGANS

QUESTION: Is there any objection to the establishment of repositories for organs like kidneys, heart, liver, cornea, and segments of skin, so that they can be used to help victims at the proper time? It is now only possible to store organs for a short period. Would

Reform Judaism object to long term storage as it becomes feasible in order to save lives? Skin banks now help burn victims survive. (Rabbi M. Beifield, Jr., Raleigh, NC)

ANSWER: Tradition has demanded the quickest possible burial of the dead and considers it shameful to leave a body unburied overnight unless the delay is for the honor of the dead (Deut. 21.23; San. 46b; M. K. 22a; *Shulhan Arukh* Yoreh Deah 357.1). Burial according to the Talmudic discussion in *Sanhedrin* is an act of atonement and also prevents any dishonor to the corpse. The thought of atonement through burial is based on the Biblical verse, "And he makes atonement for the land of his people." In other words, burial in the earth will make atonement for the individual (Deut. 32.43). In addition it prevents the ritual impurity of the priests (*kohanim*) who are to have no contact with the dead (Lev. 21.2 ff; *Shulhan Arukh* Yoreh Deah 373.7 f; Greenwald, *Kol Bo Al Avelut*, pp. 249 ff).

Burial of limbs is carried out by extension and was known by Talmudic sources (Ket. 20b). However, almost all authorities who discuss burial of limbs indicate that it is done only to prevent ritual impurity of the *kohanim* (M. Eduyot 63), and that the other two motivations for general burial, i.e., atonement and the honor of the dead, are not applicable (Jacob Reisher, *Shevut Yaaqov*, Vol. II, #101; Ezekiel Landau, *Noda Biyehudah*, Vol. II, Yoreh Deah #209). Maimonides limited the possibility of ritual impurity to a limb which had been completely preserved with skin, sinew, etc. and felt that other sections of the human body like liver, stomach, or kidneys, did not transmit ritual uncleanliness (*Yad* Hil. Tumat Hamet 2.3).

It is clear from this discussion as well as recent responsa that there is no obligation to bury the vital internal organs as they do not transmit ritual uncleanliness. That is true for traditional Jews, and of course, for us as Reform Jews. As the *kohanim* have no special status among us, the precautions connected with them have no significance for us.

There are no problems about the removal of the organs, however we must now attempt to define the turning point when "independent life" has ceased and can best do so by looking carefully at the traditional Jewish and modern medical criteria of death. The traditional criteria was based on a lack of respiratory activity and heart beat (M. Yoma 8.5; *Yad* Hil. Shab. 2.19; *Shulhan Arukh* Orah Hayim 329.4). Lack of respiration alone was considered conclusive if the individual lay as quietly as a stone (*Hatam Sofer* Yoreh Deah #38). All of this was discussed at some length in connection with the provision by the *Shulhan Arukh*, that an attempt might be made to save the child of a woman dying in childbirth even on *shabbat*; a knife might be brought to make an incision in the uterus in order to remove the fetus (*Shulhan Arukh* Yoreh Deah 339.1). If one waited until death was absolutely certain, then the fetus would also be dead.

Absolute certainty of death, according to the *halakhic* authorities of the last century, had occurred when there had been no movement for at least fifteen minutes (*Gesher Hayim* I, 3, p. 48) or an hour (*Yismah Lev* Yoreh Deah #9) after the halt of respiration and heart beat. On the other hand, a recent Israeli physician, Jacob Levy, has stated that modern medical methods permit other criteria, and the lack of blood pressure, as well as respiratory activity, should suffice (*Hamayan*, Tamuz 57.31).

This discussion was important in connection with the preparation for burial, as well as other matters. When death was certain, then the preparation for burial must begin immediately (*Hatam Sofer* Yoreh Deah 338; Y. Z. Azulai, *Responsa* Hayim Shaul II, #25). In ancient times, it was considered necessary to examine the grave after a cave burial to be certain that the individual interred had actually died. This was recommended for a period of three days (*M. Semahot* 8.1). This procedure was not followed after Mishnaic times.

In the last years, it has been suggested that Jews accept the criteria of death set by the ad hoc committee of the Harvard Medical School which examined the definition of brain death in 1978 (*Journal of American Medical Association*, Vol. 205, pp. 337 ff). They recommend three criteria: (1) lack of response to external stimuli or to internal need, (2) absence of movement and breathing as observed by physicians over a period of at least one hour, (3) absence of elicitable reflexes, and a fourth criteria to confirm the other three, a flat or isoelectric electroencephalogram. They also suggested that this examination be repeated after an interval of twenty-four hours. Several Orthodox authorities have accepted these criteria while others have rejected them. Mosheh Feinstein felt that they could be accepted along with turning off the respirator briefly in order to see whether independent breathing was continuing (*Igrot Mosheh* Yoreh Deah II, #174). Moses Tendler has gone somewhat further and has accepted the Harvard criteria (*Journal of American Medical Association*, Vol. 328, #15, pp. 165.1 ff). Although David Bleich (*Hapardes*, Tevet 57.37; Jacob

Levy, *Hadarom*, Nisan 57.31, Tishri 57.30; *Noam* 5.30) vigorously rejected these criteria, we can see that though the question has not
been resolved by our Orthodox colleagues, some of them have certainly accepted the recommendations of the Harvard Medical School
committee. We are satisfied that these criteria include those of the
older tradition and comply with our concern that life has ended.
Therefore, when circulation and respiration only continue through
mechanical means as established by the above mentioned tests, then
the suffering of the patient and his family may be permitted to cease,
as no "natural independent life" functions have been sustained.

In addition to this, we may be well guided by the statements on
medical ethics made by the Committee of the Federation of Jewish
Philanthropies of New York. They have suggested that the following
criteria be used:

"1. Acceptance of total cessation of brain-stem function as a crite-
rion of death is in keeping with *halakhic* standards for determining
death, provided the Harvard Criteria are met.

"2. The Committee expressed confidence in the medical profession's
ability to provide needed safeguards and to set proper standards.

"3. Our support of this new legislation is necessary to correct the
lack of uniformity presently found among hospitals and staff in
determining the fact or moment of death. This legislation is, therefore,
viewed as a 'tightening up' of standards.

"4. The neurological definition of death serves an important function in view of the widespread introduction of respiratory-assist
technology in hospitals.

"5. Radiological methods for determining cessation of blood flow to
the brain's respiratory centers are considered a particularly valid test
for neurological (i.e., brain-stem) death," (M. D. Tendler, ed., *Medical
Ethics*, 5th ed., 1975, with addendum 1981).

Hanaah, the problem of "benefiting from the dead," has been
discussed by Solomon B. Freehof (W. Jacob, *American Reform Responsa*,
#86). A transplant lies outside the scope of what tradition has normal-
ly understood as *hanaah*; this potential objection does not exist.

As we view the traditional reluctance in this matter, we feel that the
desire to help a fellow human being, especially in these dire circumstances of *piquah nefesh*, is of primary significance. From our liberal
understanding of the *halakhah*, this is the decisive factor. The act of
donating organs does honor to the deceased; many of those about to
die would gladly forgo any other honor and donate organs for this

purpose (Kid. 32; *Shulhan Arukh* Yoreh Deah 364.1, 368.1; Isserles *Responsa* #327). As the donation of an organ will help to save the life of another human being, storage until the time of proper use presents no problem. Progress in the future may raise new issues of use and lead us to reexamine this matter. At the present time we should insist that storage and handling be done with appropriate respect and that the disposal organs which are not used be done with reverence.

March 1986

79. SELLING A HUMAN KIDNEY FOR TRANSPLANT*

QUESTION: The sale of kidneys and other bodily organs is illegal within the United States. Can a doctor who suspects that a donor who claims to be a close relative and states that he is donating his organ but who is is actually selling it, perform a transplant operation in good conscience? Can he perform such an operation upon citizens of the United States in a country in which the sale of bodily organs is permitted? (Rabbi M. Staitman, Pittsburgh, PA)

ANSWER: We must first concern ourselves with the general question of transplants and the dangers which lie in the operation. There is a clear line of reasoning in the Jewish tradition which demands that a person remove all possible danger to himself (Deut. 4.9, 4.15; Ber. 32b; B. K. 91b; *Yad* Hil. Rotzeah Ushemirat Hanefesh 11.4; Hil. Shevuot 5.57; Hil. Hovel Umaziq 5.1). This has led modern traditional authorities to limit operations to those matters in which there was a high likelihood of success ("Dangers of Surgery").

In the case of a kidney, we face danger to both the donor and the recipient. The donor possesses two kidneys, and the loss of one may at a later stage in life cause health problems. The recipient of a kidney transplant undergoes an operation which, while not routine and often successful, is dangerous. The recipient benefits greatly from the new kidney which restores that person to a normal life in place of regular dialysis. The general question of such transplants has been discussed from a Reform point of view (S. B. Freehof, *New Reform Responsa*, pp. 62 ff; *Current Reform Responsa*, pp. 118 ff) and from a traditional point of view by many authorities (Mosheh Feinstein, *Igrot Mosheh* Yoreh Deah 229 and 230; Eliezer Waldenberg, *Tzitz Eliezer* IX, 45, X, 25; Obadiah Yoseph *Dinei Yisrael*, Vol. 7). There is a consensus that although it is permissible to give a kidney to a close relative, no one should urge such a donation because of the potential danger involved.

In our instance we are going a step further as we are discussing the sale of such a kidney from a living person. The sale of all organs is illegal in the United States. We, in this case however, are discussing the morality of transplanting a kidney which may have been sold elsewhere and whether Judaism permits the transplant when a sale is suspected.

Individuals in the third world have been particularly tempted to sell organs because of dire poverty. It is reprehensible to solicit organs in such lands. The practice has been defended by those engaged in it as an act of *gemilat hasadim*; despite the commercial transaction the "donor" is saving the recipient's life which is currently in danger, so the donor, whether he makes a gift or a sale, is saving a fellow human being. We recognize this line of reasoning, but are not convinced by it. There is a somewhat parallel case reported by David Ibn Zimri of Egypt (16th century). In his responsa (Vol. III, #627) the following was cited: The Pasha told a certain Jew to allow his leg to be amputated or else he would kill another Jew. May this man endanger his life (since the amputation was dangerous) in order to save the life of a fellow Jew? David Ibn Zimri considered this beyond the call of duty.

As people often search desperately for a donor, such sales are bound to continue despite our disapproval and their illegality. We must help to assure alternative sources for transplant organs; we urge that the public be educated to donate their organs. The 40,000 annual fatal automobile accidents alone are sufficient to supply most needs. If foreign sources are closed by the refusal of surgeons to use organs when a sale is suspected, then we may become serious about a national donor program.

The surgeon in this case should not perform the operation on moral grounds.

March 1986

80. SELLING HUMAN BLOOD FOR MEDICAL PURPOSES

QUESTION: May a donor sell blood for medical purposes, i.e., plasma, transfusion or medication? (Rabbi M. Staitman, Pittsburgh, PA)

134

ANSWER: There is a clear line of reasoning in the Jewish tradition which demands that a person remove all possible danger to himself (Deut. 4.9; 4.15; Ber. 32b; B. K. 91b; *Yad* Hil. Rotzeah Ushemirat Hanefesh 11.4; Hil. Shevuot 5.57; Hil. Hovel Umaziq 5.1). This has led modern rabbinic tradition to limit operations to those matters in which there is a high likelihood of success (see "Dangers of Surgery" in this volume). In the matter of blood donation there is virtually no danger to the donor, although there may be some danger to the recipient, as he may unwittingly receive a disease.

We must, therefore, ask whether the ownership of one's body is such that we can dispose of it as we wish. The traditional view holds that no harm can be permitted to the human body (Shneir Zalman of Ladi, *Shulhan Arukh*, Shemirat Haguf #14; Eliezer Waldenberg, *Tzitz Eliezer*, Vol. X, #7). Waldenberg goes further and claims that man is only the temporary possessor of his body. It is provided by God on loan, and so, must be carefully guarded.

In the case of blood donations, however, no real change in the body's material occurs, as the blood will be replaced fairly quickly. Nothing irreplaceable has been removed.

We must, therefore, turn from the questions of physical harm and ownership to the commercial aspect of the transaction. Clearly there would be no problem with simply donating blood. We might go even a step further and state that it is our duty to help a fellow human being through donating blood. This should be encouraged. Tradition has stated that we should not stand idly by while our neighbor is harmed (Lev. 19.16; San. 73a; *Shulhan Arukh* Hoshen Mishpat 426). Helping a person is, therefore, a duty whether it involves physical effort or a gift. In the later rabbinic discussion of this *mitzvah*, the only question raised is that of *pikuah nefesh*, in other words, how far should an individual endanger his own life in such an effort. As we have pointed out, there is little danger to the donor.

The nearest similarity to the sale of blood is the sale of milk by a wet nurse. There a nursing mother is willing to sell some of the fluid produced by her body, in this case milk during her period of lactation. Her milk will save the life of a child and nourish it. The use of wet nurses has continued throughout the ages from Biblical times onward (Gen. 35.8). Sometimes this was done as an act of friendship, but frequently such an individual was hired for this specific task. Such wet nurses were often engaged for a period of two or three years (Ket. 60b; 65b). There is some discussion about the acceptability of a non-Jewish wet nurse; the *Tosefta* permitted this practice. The only stipulation added was that she should live in the household of the baby (*Tosefta* Nidah 2.5; A. Z. 26a). A woman might even milk her body's milk into a bowl and feed a baby in this fashion, though this was frowned upon (*Tosefta* Sab. 9.22). Clearly, the rabbinic tradition had no hesitation about such a transfer of life giving fluid from one person to another as a commercial transaction.

We have no hesitation about the commercial sale of blood at plasma centers on these grounds. We have concerns on other grounds, however. The individual involved in these transactions are generally the poor and homeless who have absolutely no other resources except their blood. Their plight should move us to help them rather than encourage commerce in blood.

There is a constant medical need for human blood. Its donation will help to save lives. We encourage and urge individuals to participate in this effort and are willing to accept the sale of blood as it, too, saves lives.

November 1985

81. HUNTINGTON'S DISEASE AND SUICIDE*

QUESTION: I am writing about a young woman who has been definitely diagnosed as having Huntington's Disease (sometimes called Huntington's Chorea). It is a genetic disease which is incurable and results in inevitable, severe neurological deterioration causing loss of mental and physical facilities. She has told me that she is contemplating taking her own life when she feels that the disease will rob her of control over her own life and before she deteriorates completely. She asks what would be the Jewish response to her decision? (Rabbi J. Miller, Rochester, NY)

ANSWER: All of the material relevant to this question has been presented in previous responsa directed toward slightly different questions; the answers were provided by Israel Bettan, Solomon B. Freehof, and Walter Jacob (*American Reform Responsa*, #76 ff). In each instance, the writer of the responsum felt that despite the severe problems involved, euthenasia could not be encouraged. This would be equally true of suicide here.

The path of this disease is clearly known and the degenerative affects are terrible, both for the individual involved and those dear to her. Although we can empathize with her wish to commit suicide, it would be difficult for us to approve of this act as Judaism has and continues to object strongly to suicide. The problems which arise under slightly different conditions with other diseases or other circumstances do not make it possible for us to assent to her wish, but we understand it.

June 1983

82. JEWISH REACTION TO EPIDEMICS (AIDS)*

QUESTION: The current AIDS epidemic has led to much fear in various communities. Individuals afflicted with this disease have been removed from positions, ostracized socially, and their children excluded or segregated in schools. What has been the traditional approach of Judaism to such epidemics for which there is no known cure? (Rabbi G. Stern, New York, NY)

ANSWER: We must be concerned with the victims of AIDS as the disease is fatal; they need our compassion. We will not deal with the problems of sexual morality raised by AIDS in this responsum, but only with fear of the potential epidemic. The fear of the general population is understandable as little is known about the disease, its incubation period, or potential cure. Concern for both the individual and the community when a member is afflicted with a dangerous disease has been shown since Biblical times. The book of Leviticus contains detailed instructions of how a skin disease (*metzora*) is to be diagnosed and handled (Lev. 13). During the period of his illness the afflicted person was isolated. The priest who made the diagnosis examined that person after seven days, as well as subsequently. When the disease had come to an end, a complex ritual of purification was provided (Lev. 14 ff). The precautions extended from the individual to the house in which he lived and it, too, was examined, and if necessary scraped and replastered and a ritual of purification was mandated.

Although we do not know the nature of the disease called *metzora* by the *Bible*, it was clearly contagious and led to vigorous efforts to isolate the individuals involved. These procedures were developed further by the *Mishnah* and *Talmud*. There are fourteen chapters in the

Mishnah Negaim which deal with the subject in considerable detail.

Metzora was treated only from a ritual point of view by some authorities, so they did not apply the rules of non-Jews (*M.* Neg. 3.1). All contact with Jews who were afflicted was to be avoided. This included the sick person, his room, any food near him and even the air near the sick room (San. 76b; *Lev. Rabba* 17.3). Insects and flies which had contact with the diseased person were to be avoided (Ket. 77b). For example, when the diseased person came to the *bet hamidrash* in order to study, he was separated from the other students by a wall which was to be "ten handbreadths high and four wide." It was also mandated that he enter the building first and leave it last (*M.* Neg. 13.12). These individuals were excluded from the community and usually lived outside of the cities (II Kings 7.3). If a man was afflicted by this illness his wife had a right to divorce and vice versa (*M.* Ket. 7.9) Those who suffered from such diseases were to avoid sexual intercourse (Ket. 77b).

In the Talmudic period, individuals so afflicted were considered akin to the dead (Ned. 64b). In the *New Testament* some such diseased individuals called to Jesus from a distance as they were obviously prohibited from approaching anyone in the community (Luke 17.12).

Discussions in the *Talmud* and the later responsa literature which dealt with other epidemic diseases usually were less drastic; they suggested that a fast be decreed as the pestilence was thought to be the result of community sins (*M.* Avot 5.12; Ta-anit 3.4, 19b). Jews in the Middle Ages like the rest of the population often fled whenever a plague or epidemic threatened. An epidemic existed if a smaller city suffered three deaths from a known disease on three consecutive days, or nine deaths in three days in a larger city [one which could provide 1500 young men as soldiers] (Ta-anit 21b).

The Jewish medical works of the seventeenth century contain regulations which govern epidemic diseases. As the garments of the sick were considered to provide a source of contagion, they were to be avoided until thoroughly aired. All drinking water was to be purified as a preventive against the epidemic (Tobiah Hakohen *Ma-aseh Tuvyah*, Frankfurt, A. M., 1707, in Max Grunwald's *Die Hygiene der Juden*, p. 262). Dr. Leon Elias Hirschel suggested a number of ways of fighting smallpox; they included quarantine and washing with vinegar by those who came in contact with the ill ("Abhandlung von den Vorbauungs - und Vorbereitungsmitteln bei den Pocken," Berlin, 1770, *Ibid.* p. 265). Israel Salanter took a humane and courageous approach to a cholera epidemic in Vilna during his lifetime as he urged the community to assist the victims (D. Katz *Tenu-ot Hamusar*, Vol. I, pp. 156 ff).

It is clear from all this that our forefathers sought to protect themselves through whatever ways were available from epidemics. The avenues of quarantine and flight were used.

In the current situation as we deal with AIDS, we should begin by following the advice of the medical community. The current medical opinion suggests that the disease is spread through sexual contact (homosexual or heterosexual), intimate contact and blood transfusions. Little is yet known, however, and there is no cure or preventive vaccine for AIDS, nor is anything known about its incubation period.

The fear and anxiety of employers, parents and others, therefore, can be understood. It is our duty to calm that fear and counteract the pressure of the media. In some instances quarantine or other measures may be appropriate, but they should not be undertaken lightly.

We should do whatever we can to minimize the suffering of the victims of this disease and help them and their families adjust to its tragic consequences. We should follow the advice of public health authorities in our attitude to employees and school-aged children.

November 1985

83. QUALITY OF LIFE AND EUTHANASIA*

QUESTION: Does Jewish tradition recognize the "quality of life" as a factor in determining medical and general care to preserve and prolong life? I have four specific cases in mind. In the first the patient is in a coma, resides in a nursing home and has not recognized anyone for several years. In the second, the patient is in a nursing home, completely paralyzed and can not speak or make his wishes known in any way. The third is a victim of a stroke, sees no hope for recovery or even major improvement, wishes to die and expresses this wish constantly to anyone who visits. The fourth is slowly dying of cancer, is in great pain and wants a prescription which will relieve her of pain but will probably also slightly hasten death. All of these patients are in their early eighties; none is receiving any unusual medical attention. Should we hope for a new medical discovery which will help them? (Rabbi R. H. Lehman, New York, NY)

ANSWER: The considerations which govern euthanasia have been discussed by the Committee in a recent responsa (W. Jacob, *American Reform Responsa*, #79, 1980). The conclusion of that responsum stated:
"We would not endorse any positive steps leading toward death. We would recommend pain-killing drugs which would ease the remaining days of a patient's life.

"We would reject any general endorsement of euthanasia, but where all 'independent life' has ceased and where the above-mentioned criteria of death have been met, further medical support systems need not be continued."
The question here goes somewhat further as we are not dealing with life threatening situations, but with the general question of prolonging life when its quality may be questionable. In none of these situations has any current extraordinary medical attention been provided. In two of the cases the cognitive and/or communicative ability seems to have ended. In the third there is a strong wish for death. In the fourth, the primary concern is relief from pain. Let us look at each of these cases individually.

For the patient in a coma and the one completely paralyzed and unable to communicate, a segment of the brain which provides intelligence seems to be damaged beyond repair. Judaism does not define human life only in terms of mental activity. Every person has been created in the image of God (Gen. 1.26), and so even those individuals who may be defective, i.e. the retarded, the blind, the deaf, the mute, etc., have always been considered as equally created in the image of God; their life is as precious as any other. It is necessary to guard their life and protect it just as any other human life. This is also true of an elderly individual who has now lost some of her mental ability or power of communication. In fact, we owe a special duty toward these individuals who are weak and more likely to be neglected by society just as to the orphan, the widow and the poor (Deut. 14.29, 27.13, Jer. 7.6; Is. 1.17; Shab. 133b; Meg. 31a; San 74a; Yoma 82b).

Let us turn to the individual who seeks death and constantly reiterates his wish to die. Although some rabbinic authorities feel that neither an individual nor his family may pray for his death (Haim Palagi *Hiskei Lev*, Vol. I, Yoreh Deah #50), most of our tradition would agree that a person may ask God to be relieved of suffering. The decision, of course, lies with God. A servant of Judah Hanasi prayed for his release (Ket. 104a). Other ancient authorities pointed to similar examples (Ned 40a and Commentaries). We would, however, discourage the individual from such prayer and rather seek to encourage a different attitude toward life. The growing field of psychology for the aged has succeeded in developing a variety of techniques for dealing with such long term depression. We would encourage the family and the patient to utilize these methods or any other form of counseling and therapy available.

The individual who seeks relief from her pain should receive drugs which may help, even though they may slightly hasten death. As this is a very long term process, the drug can not be seen as actually causing her death. Suffering itself has never been seen as an independent good by Judaism. Even criminals destined for execution were drugged to alleviate their suffering (San. 43a). Similarly the executioner of the martyr Hanina ben Teradyon was permitted by him to increase the temperature and remove wool sponges from his heart in order to make death a little easier, though Hanina was unwilling to pray for his own death as his disciples suggested (A. Z. 18a). We would, therefore, see no objection to relieving the suffering of the woman who is dying from cancer and for whom the drugs are not life threatening.

It is clear that in each of these cases, and in others like them, we should do our best to enhance the quality of life and to use whatever means modern science has placed at our disposal for this purpose. We need not invoke "heroic" measures to prolong life, nor should we hesitate to alleviate pain, but we can also not utilize a "low quality" of life as an excuse for hastening death.

We can not generalize about the "quality of life" but must treat each case which we face individually. All life is wonderful and mysterious. The human situation, the family setting and other factors must be carefully analyzed before a sympathetic decision can be reached.

December 1985

84. AUTOPSY FOR FUTURE KNOWLEDGE

QUESTION: Can autopsy be performed for the sake of future medical knowledge? A man who is terminally ill with Alzheimer's Disease wishes to have an autopsy performed and would like a portion of his brain to be used for medical research. (Rabbi H. Waintrup, Abington, PA)

ANSWER: There are three different issues involved in the matter of autopsy. We must ask whether an autopsy is objectionable to Judaism. Is it permissible to disfigure the dead? Finally, is it necessary to bury portions removed from a corpse? We will assume that the individual has given his consent for an autopsy and wishes his brain tissues to be used for research.

The entire matter of autopsy was discussed in detail in a lengthy responsum by Jacob Lauterbach decades ago. He came to the conclusion that neither the *Talmud* nor the later rabbinic literature including the eighteenth century Ezekiel Landau or the nineteenth century Moses Sofer prohibited autopsy. The latter felt that it is permissible if it benefits an ill person in the same place. The classical literature explicitly and implicity permitted autopsy as demonstrated by Jewish physicians from *Talmudic* times onward who possessed considerable anatomical knowledge (W. Jacob, *American Reform Responsa*, #82).

In the last century and in modern Israel objections to autopsy have arisen on the grounds of disfiguring the dead which is considered dishonorable; it may not be permitted even for the benefit of the living (Jacob Ettlinger, *Binyan Tzion*, #170, 171). This authority, however, also agreed that it is permissible if the individual consented to an autopsy as a person may reject any honor due to him. On the other hand other authorities felt that an individual had no right to consent, as the human body belongs to God and is only lent to the individual for safekeeping (Moses Sofer, *Hatam Sofer* Yoreh Deah #336; *Maharam Schick*, Yoreh Deah #347). Contemporary Orthodoxy follows this stricter line of reasoning. We, however, do not and feel that the individual may permit an autopsy if he wishes.

There is a general stipulation that all portions of a body be buried, yet this is *minhag* rather than law (Ezekiel Landau, *Noda Biyehudah*, II Yoreh Deah #209). Mosheh Feinstein disagreed and felt that every portion of a body must be buried (*Igrot Mosheh*, Yoreh Deah I, #231), while still others like Eliezer Waldenberg felt that burial was mandated only to prevent the possible defilement of a *kohen* (*Tzitz Eliezer*, #25, Chap. 8). We accept the more lenient view and feel no necessity to bury the organs which have been removed for study.

In our age of rapid medical progress and worldwide communication, an autopsy anywhere may help someone else. We would also encourage the use of a portion of the body, in this case the brain, for the purpose of long range research which may help many others in a few years. Such a use would be as helpful as alleviating the immediate suffering of another person in a nearby community.

November 1986

85. SURGERY AT NINETY-SIX*

QUESTION: A ninety-six-year-old woman who lives in a nursing home has recently been informed that severe hardening of the arteries necessitates the amputation of her foot. As a result of the shock of hearing this news, she has become severely disoriented. Her family was subsequently advised of her situation and several alternatives were presented. She may submit to amputation with a chance that her condition will be permanently corrected. However, there is no assurance that she may not die during surgery or soon thereafter. Furthermore, her other foot may be similarly affected, or her rehabilitation may not be successful. The alternative is a slow and painful death which can be partially relieved by sedation. The family wants the mother to make the decision. She refuses to sign the release for surgery. But as her lucid moments are brief, it is not clear whether that is what she actually wishes. Should there be surgery or should matters simply be allowed to take their course? (Rabbi, Illinois)

ANSWER: We shall look at both the traditional and modern components of this question. Rabbinic tradition from Talmudic times onward has encouraged the utilization of all possible medical procedures for life threatening situations. Sanhedrin (23a) advocates this direction on the basis of "you shall not stand idly by the blood of your fellow" (Lev. 19.16). Baba Kama (85a) bases itself on "he shall cause him to be thoroughly healed" (Ex. 21.20). There are other parallel passages in which the citations are a little less clear. Nahmanides, (13th century) in his commentary on Leviticus 25.36 ("and your brother shall live with you"), followed this path, earlier proposed by Hai Gaon (10th century). Yehuda Lev Zirelson (20th century) applied this line of reasoning to less dangerous, non-life threatening situations (*Teshuvat Atzei Levanon* #61). The general principle that medical intervention is to be widely used has thus been established.

We must ask three further questions. Is this appropriate when the procedure is dangerous? Is there an age limit beyond which tradition would not advocate rigorous medical intervention? Shall this ninety-six-year-old woman face the trauma of an amputation?

The fact that considerable risk may be undertaken to save or restore life is based on a Talmudic discussion (A. Z. 27b), which interprets a story from II Kings (7.3 f). In this tale a group of lepers about to starve in the siege of Samaria decided to risk the mercy of the Syrian army rather than face certain death in the city. The *Talmud* used this discussion to show that in life threatening situations one might place oneself even into the hands of idolaters. In modern times this passage has been cited in order to permit the use of drugs whose side effects may be hazardous (J. Reischer, *Shevut Yaakov* III, #85; Posner, *Bet Meir* Yoreh Deah 339.1). There are further discussions about use of hazardous drugs when the chance of survival is low. Eliezer Waldenberg (*Tzitz Eliezer* 10, #25, Chap. 5, Sec. 5) felt that a 50% survival rate was necessary to recommend usage. Others like Mosheh Feinstein (*Igrot Mosheh*, Yoreh Deah 2, #59) felt that hazardous procedures and drugs may be used even when there is only a remote chance of survival. This path was also followed by I. Y. Unterman (*Noam* 12, p. 5). There is considerable debate on this matter. It is quite clear, however, that the use of medical procedures with a high risk have been encouraged by traditional Judaism whenever there is an opportunity to save a life.

In the literature cited, and in other instances, there has been no discussion of an age limit beyond which such procedures should not be utilized. If an individual is close to death, she should be permitted to die peacefully, and it is not necessary to subject them to needless pain through therapy which can not succeed (*Sefer Hassidim* #723; W. Jacob, *American Reform Responsa*, # 79). However, if there is a chance for success, it should be undertaken.

Although the life span throughout the rabbinic and Biblical period was low, the Psalmist's ideal of three score years and ten, or by reason of strength four score years (Ps. 90) and Moses' life of one hundred and twenty with his "eyes undimmed and his vigor unabated" (Deut. 34.7), as well as the ages of patriarchs and others, pointed to the ideal of an advanced age. As medical practice has advanced and made a longer life possible, we, too, should encourage medical procedures on individuals who have reached an advanced age.

However, we must also take into consideration the psychological factors which our forefathers only partially considered. In this instance even the news of a possible amputation was devastating, and the woman was not able to overcome it. This indicates a doubtful prognosis for her future. Here the psychological disadvantages

144

may outweigh the medical advantages. We must remember that the efforts of tradition was solely concerned with saving life and not with its quality.

The medical prognosis is doubtful in our case and the psychological prognosis negative. Under these circumstances we would be reluctant to encourage an operation and inclined to let the woman live out her remaining days with the help of drug therapy to provide all possible comfort.

September 1984

86. ALZHEIMER'S DISEASE

QUESTION: A sixty-three-year-old man has been diagnosed as suffering from Alzheimer's Disease. In nine months he has deteriorated drastically and now needs constant skilled nursing care. His wife, a school teacher, has discovered that her insurance does not cover such expenses which are more than $2,000.00 a month. The couple's savings will be entirely exhausted in a few years. Medicaid will not help until nothing except the house in which they live remains. The wife's lawyer has counseled her to seek a legal divorce, which will shield her resources so that she may have some income when she reaches retirement in a few years. Without such a step she will become dependent upon the charity of her children and the general community. If she takes this step she will, of course, feel that she has abandoned her husband. His condition has degenerated to such an extent that he is unaware of his surroundings and does not fulfill his marital responsibilities. (Rabbi D. D. Weber, Elyria, OH)

ANSWER: These circumstances which you have described are tragic. Unfortunately, as modern medicine progresses an ever increasing group within our population reaches an advanced age, and frequently one member is afflicted with an incurable debilitating disease which slowly destroys that life and drastically affects the life of the healthy spouse.

Let us see whether a marriage may be dissolved under these circumstances. Marriage, as the Hebrew designation *qiddushin* implies, is a sacred act which brings special sanctity to the relationship established between husband and wife. The blessings recited (*sheva berakhot*) indicate the sanctity of the status into which the couple entered.

Marriage and all aspects of family life have been discussed at great length in Jewish literature since the Mishnaic period. Provisions have, of course, also been made for divorce (Deut. 24.1 ff) and the Talmudic Tractate *Gitin*, as well as discussions elsewhere, deal with causes and the subsequent implementation of divorce.

Among the reasons for divorce is the affliction of either party with an incurable disease which makes intercourse impossible or dangerous (*Shulhan Arukh* Even Haezer, 117.1 ff, 154.1 ff). A wife may also seek a divorce if the husband is squandering the family assets so that she feels that her maintenance is endangered (*Ibid.* 154.3). Although no age restrictions are mentioned in these discussions, marriages of the young or middle-aged are implied. In other words, these reasons were not intended to deal specifically with the problems of old age which may, naturally, lead to illness, impotence and unusual expenses.

We may approach the entire question from another point of view as noted by Professor Mark Washofsky, to whom I am indebted, and turn to the duty of one spouse to pay the other's medical obligations. *Shulhan Arukh* Even Haezer (69, 79) obliges the husband as part of the *ketubah* to provide medical care for his wife. In our Reform context we would, of course, extend this obligation to the wife. Paragraph one states that this obligation holds whether the illness is of a temporary or a chronic nature. Paragraph three deals directly with our problem. It provides an escape in the event of a long-term and expensive illness (*Yad* Hil. Ishut 14.17); the husband may set a limit for her medical bills; should she refuse this offer, the husband divorces her and she receives the *ketubah*. *Rambam* and Caro argue against this arrangement on ethical grounds (see also *Magid Mishneh*), but neither denies that the husband possesses this right. On the other hand, some authorities do deny this right; the Rabad limits the husband's power of divorce to a case where the wife is not terminally ill (Ran to Alfasi, Ket. 19a); Solomon Luria argues that in our day, when the *taqanah* of R. Gershom forbids divorce without the wife's consent, the husband can not compel her to choose between these alternatives (Joel Sirkes to *Tur* Even Hazer 79). At any rate, whether a spouse possesses this right or not, it is definitely not in keeping with the spirit of marriage and its sanctity.

Just as the wife has the obligation to provide medical care for the husband, the husband is also obligated to provide economic sustenance to his wife. This is a *tenai bet din* (*Yad* Hil. Ishut 12.2 ff). The wife has the right to renounce this support; if she does, her husband no longer has any claim to her income. The wife in this instance could be encouraged to establish herself in a state of financial independence; under Jewish law she need not be divorced in order to gain control of her own finances (Ketubot 58b; *Yad* Hil. Ishut 12.4). In addition, the *bet din* is empowered to seize the husband's property in the event of his mental incapacity in order to fulfill her requirement of *mezonot* (*Ibid.*, 12.17). In this case, the husband's "property" would include the *ketubah* or its equivalent; under Jewish law the husband's estate is mortgaged in order to provide the required support for the wife. This also means that his children as his heirs are obligated to support his wife; this is not charity, but a debt which is owed her. These thoughts help us within the framework of *halakhah*, but not with the current requirement of American law.

We must balance these statements with our general view of *qiddushim* and see it in the light of this particular couple. There is nothing in the question which indicates that they have become estranged from each other. Only this debilitating illness has led to thoughts of divorce. They surely entered into marriage with the understanding that they would help each other irrespective of what the future might bring.

Although there might be some technical justification for a divorce from a *halakhic* point of view, it would be morally wrong to follow that route in order to preserve the estate. A divorce may affect the husband despite his current condition and would certainly affect the wife and children.

We should seek an alternative way to help her both now and in the future, especially as these questions arise frequently and the social security administration is generally responsive to such efforts. Furthermore, *halakhah* also encourages such practical solutions which will continue the marriage bond and avoid poverty.

The wife is dutybound to care for her husband even though there is no hope of recovery and although it may destroy her resources. We should seek alternative ways to help her both now and in the future. The lawyer in question should be encouraged to look for other ways to protect the resources of this client.

March 1986

87. A LONG DELAYED FUNERAL

QUESTION: The mother of a member of my Temple died in New York.

A daughter is traveling with her husband in Australia and New Zealand and will return within a month. The Funeral Director indicated that it would be possible to hold the body for a month. However, the rest of the family felt that the funeral should be held immediately as it was. Would it have been possible, according to Jewish Law, to delay the funeral until the daughter's return? (Rabbi A. Task, Greensboro, NC).

ANSWER: The *Talmud* and the later Codes insisted that burial take place immediately. Therefore, traditional Jews do their best to bury on the same day. This ruling is based on a specific Biblical injunction which deals with an individual who has been executed for a crime. Tradition has generalized from this single instance for all burials (Deut. 21.23; San. 46b; *Shulhan Arukh* Yoreh Deah 357.1). It has, however, also been traditional to delay burial overnight and possibly longer for the sake of the honor of the dead (*Shulhan Arukh* Yoreh Deah 357.2 ff). Such a delay permitted the acquisition of proper shrouds or a coffin, as well as close relatives to journey to the funeral (M. K. 22a). Most funerals in our time are delayed as families are widely scattered and need a day or two in order to arrive in the city of the deceased.

It would, however, be wrong to delay the funeral for as much as several weeks or a month in order to accommodate the travel schedule of a child. Such a delay would dishonor the deceased. If for some reason it is impossible for that child to return before such a long period has elapsed, it would be appropriate to conduct a memorial service at the time of the *sheloshim*, thirty days after the death. This is customary in many communities in any case.

August 1985

88. WIDOWER'S RIGHTS

QUESTION: A young woman has died and been buried. Now her parents wish to move her grave to another location. The widower, who was left with young children and is now remarried, has objected to this request and denied it. According to Jewish law, who has the ultimate authority and obligation in connection with the deceased wife? (Rabbi M. Staitman, Pittsburgh, PA)

148

ANSWER: The *ketubah* stipulates that the husband must support his wife in every way. This includes normal obligations of food, shelter and clothing (Ket. 47b; 65a ff; Yeb. 66a). Furthermore, if his standard of living rises, he is obligated to provide for his wife an increased level. If it diminishes, he can not, however, decrease her maintenance (Ket. 48a, 61a). He is obligated to take care of her medical expenses (Ket. 51a ff; *Yad* Hil. Ishut 14.17; *Shulhan Arukh* Even Haezer 79), to ransom her (Ket. 52a ff) and to bury her (Gen. 23.19, 48.7, 49.31; Ket. 46b ff; *Yad* Hil. Ishut 12.2; *Shulhan Arukh* Even Haezer 111). If he is poor, he must provide a decent funeral (Ket. 46b), and otherwise make provisions in accordance with local custom (Ket. 28a).

These obligations grant him complete authority to make final determination in each of these matters. The remarriage of the widower has no bearing on this. Such remarriage is encouraged as soon as an adequate mourning period has passed. That is normally considered to be the passage of three pilgrimage festivals, but if there are young children, remarriage may take place sooner (*Shulhan Arukh* Yoreh Deah 392.2).

According to rabbinic tradition, and according to the practice of Reform Judaism, the widower has absolute and complete rights in this matter.

January 1985

89. EXTENDING THE PRIVILEGE OF BURIAL FROM THE SYNAGOGUE

QUESTION: The congregation, which has already permitted funerals of members and their children to use the synagogue, wishes to discuss an extension of that permission to parents and other close relatives of members. Is this in keeping with Jewish tradition? What is the underlying principle through which the *Talmud* distinguishes between "public and private funerals?" What is the basic objection to any funeral in the synagogue? How has tradition and Reform Judaism treated this subject? (Rabbi N. Hirsh, Seattle, WA)

ANSWER: Your letter has mentioned Solomon B. Freehof's responsum on the subject (*Reform Responsa for Our Time*, pp. 95 ff). This responsum favors the restriction of funerals in the main synagogue to leaders of the congregation and important communal figures, while small chapels or assembly halls usually connected with the synagogue may be utilized for other funerals. The appropriate references in post Talmudic codes and Talmudic literature are cited for this decision.

As we look at the notions behind the Talmudic restrictions, we can see that the scholars considered death as the ultimate separation from God, for the dead are unable to serve God or to carry out his *mitzvot* (Shab. 30a, 151b). For that reason, no person should discuss any Biblical verses on a cemetery or near a corpse, nor should one wear *tefilin* or carry a *Torah* in the cemetery (Sem. 13; Ber. 3b, 18a; *Midrash Genesis Rabbah* 96; *Midrash Qohelet Rabbah* 7, 2.5). The *Torah*, after all, is designated as *etz hayim*, the tree of life. The *Bible* also constantly deals with the theme of lifeless idols in contrast to the living God (Is. 42.19 - 21, 44.12-21, etc.). These thoughts have been given practical expression through the exemption of mourners before burial (*onen*) from most acts of prayer. They do not wear *tefilin*, recite the *sh'ma*, the blessing before or after meals, nor do they respond with *amen* after any benediction. The *Talmud* also exempts them from the need to execute any positive commandments (Ber. 17b; *Shulhan Arukh* Yoreh Deah 341.1).

As we proceed further, we will see that the question of ritual defilement is also involved. A human corpse represents the highest category of defilement (*tumah*) (B. K. 2b; Pes. 14b) and is the source of the ritual uncleanliness. It defiles for seven days (M. Oh. 1.14). One authority claimed that even distress upon hearing about the death of a relative without any contact with the corpse produced defilement (J. Pes. 8.7). Clearly there were strong negative feelings about death, and the dead were kept as far from anything sacred as possible. The only exception lay in the rabbinic treatment of a *met mitzvah*, a corpse without relatives. The high priest, who could not defile himself even for his own mother and father, was obligated to participate in the burial of the *met mitzvah* (*Meg.* 3b; *Yad* Hil. Ovel 3.8). A full treatment of the Biblical and rabbinic concepts of death, mourning and defilement maybe found in Emanuel Feldman's *Biblical and Post-Biblical Defilement and Mourning*.

This long standing aversion to any contact between the dead and the sacred has influenced the use of the synagogue for funerals. When this was discussed in the *Talmud* (Meg. 28b), there was a division of opinion between the Babylonian and Palestinian authorities, with the former more permissive than the latter. Later, Rashi stated that any funeral which involved the entire community, in other words communal leaders, was permitted from the synagogue. His decision was made on practical grounds as no other facility in the Jewish community could accommodate the crowd.

By the time of Maimonides (12th century), communal leaders were regularly buried from the synagogue (*Yad* Hil. Tefilah 11.7). The *Shulhan Arukh* (16th century) extended the privilege to scholars and their wives (Yoreh Deah 344.19). Sixteenth century Poland was more democratic and permitted others to be buried from the synagogue (*Ohalei Yaaqov*, p. 74). The centuries have witnessed a gradual relaxation of the ancient restrictions as the apprehension over the "separation" between God of the dead diminished. I should, however, add that some modern Orthodox authorities strongly oppose funerals for women in the synagogue (W. Leiter, *Bet David* #198; Greenwald, *Kol Bo Al Avelut* pp.96 ff; A. Yudelewitz, *Bet Av* 357.4).

The American Reform movement has gradually relaxed the restrictions on the use of the synagogue for funerals as indicated by the patterns set within your congregation. My congregation has followed the same pattern and has permitted funerals of members and their dependent children. We have not gone further as all other adults should and can join the congregation. This path is open to all as we regularly waive dues in instances of financial hardships and welcome all to affiliate.

In summary, there is no reason to restrict the use of the synagogue for funerals from the point of view of the development of Jewish tradition. A congregation may, however, limit the use of its facilities to members as in all other matters.

October 1983

90. FUNERAL WITHOUT RABBI OR CANTOR

QUESTION: Is is appropriate for a funeral service to be conducted by a family member or a friend of the family without a rabbi or cantor present? Does this diminish in any way the authentic Jewishness of the service when family members or friends conduct the service? (Rabbi D. Polish, Hollywood, CA)

ANSWER: There is absolutely nothing in traditional literature or in modern Reform decisions which demand the presence of a rabbi or cantor at a funeral, or for that matter, at any other Jewish religious occasion. State or provincial law may require an "ordained clergyman" to preside over a wedding ceremony, but Jewish law has no such stipulation. We have been, and remain, a religion without clergy, and we continue the historic role of the rabbi primarily as a teacher, judge, and religious leader rather than a functionary at specific occasions.

The evolution of the rabbinate to its present state in which the rabbi leads services and conducts weddings, funerals, etc., is part of the specialization of modern society as well as the feeling of inadequacy on the part of many Jews, Orthodox, Conservative or Reform, in conducting Jewish ceremonies. The desire to have matters go smoothly, to remove the burden of preparation and the anxiety for specific life cycle occasions has led most Jews to rely completely on the rabbi or a cantor for rites of passage and other ceremonies. This may be useful, but as a long term trend it is not healthy, for our vigor lies in the ability of the ordinary Jew to execute any Jewish rite and thereby to perpetuate Judaism wherever he may happen to be.

There is nothing in our tradition which would in any way diminish the authentic Jewishness of a funeral service conducted entirely by family and friends.

June 1986

91. OPEN CASKET

QUESTION: What is the attitude of Reform Judaism to an open casket prior to the funeral service? The casket is closed during the service. Would this attitude change if the entire funeral were held at a chapel located in the cemetery? (Rabbi R. Walter, Houston, TX)

ANSWER: We have become accustomed to closed caskets, and that has become a uniform practice throughout the country, at least after the funeral service has begun. The coffin is always closed when funeral services are held in the synagogue. In most cities, the casket also remains closed during the time before the service. Visiting before the service has been discouraged. Some modern Orthodox rabbis have objected very strongly to the open casket as an imitation of Gentile practices (J. Greenwald, *Kol Bo Al Avelut*, p. 36 and W. Leiter, *Bet David* 198b). There are also some earlier traditional objections, so the *Talmud* (M. K. 72a) stated that the faces of the poor should be covered because they would display their poverty and the surviving relatives would be put to shame, a reason also given by the *Shulhan Arukh* (Yoreh Deah 353.1). The *Talmud* (Hor. 13b) also stated that a man may forget all that he has learned if he looks upon the face of the dead. Similarly, the *Sefer Hassidim* (Margolis, ed., p. 103) prohibited kissing the dead. We must, of course, remember that most dead in ancient times were simply buried in shrouds and not in a coffin. In fact, there is a considerable discussion among the authorities whether closing a coffin is not the equivalent of burial, and therefore, may lead to the beginning of official mourning. This discussion hinges on the interpretation of a phrase *yisasem hagolel* (M. K. 27a; Shab. 152b). Rabbenu Tam insisted that this meant the grave had to be covered, while Rashi thought it referred to the closing of the coffin. Various later authorities have quoted one or the other in their opinions.

It is clearly our custom to have the coffin closed at the cemetery and generally at the funeral home in accordance with tradition. We insist on it when services are conducted in the synagogue itself and at the cemetery chapel. The coffin should be closed before and during the service.

August 1979

92. BURIAL OF A YOUNG CHILD

QUESTION: A-four-year-old-child, daughter of a Jewish father and a Gentile mother, died, and they wish her buried in the congregational cemetery, which restricts burial to Jews. The child was named in the synagogue, and it was the clear intent of the parents to raise this girl and all subsequent children as Jews. Both parents had brought the little girl to some pre-school holiday activities and to various services intended for young children. Is this child to be considered Jewish? Would a somewhat older child not enrolled in our school be considered Jewish? (D. F., Baltimore, MD)

ANSWER: We base our decision on the resolution of the Central Conference of American Rabbis, March, 1983, and on the responsum "Patrilineal and Matrilineal Descent" (November 1983). The Resolution reads:

"The Central Conference of American Rabbis declares that the child of one Jewish parent is under the presumption of Jewish descent.

This presumption of the Jewish status of the offspring of any mixed marriage is to be established through appropriate and timely public and formal acts of identification with the Jewish faith and people. The performance of these *mitzvot* serves to commit those who participate in them, both parents and child, to Jewish life.

"Depending on circumstances, *mitzvot* leading toward a positive and exclusive Jewish identity will include entry into the covenant, acquisition of a Hebrew name, *Torah* study, *Bar/Bat Mitzvah*, and *Kabbalat Torah* (Confirmation). For those beyond childhood claiming Jewish identity, other public acts or declarations may be added or substituted after consultation with their rabbi."

The Resolution indicates that acts of identification after birth are necessary to establish the Jewishness of the individual involved. In this instance, all acts of identification appropriate to the age have been observed, and the child has had no identification or affiliation with any Christian observances. We, therefore, consider this youngster as Jewish, and she is to be treated as a Jew in every way. In other words, although the cemetery has some restrictions on the burial of non-Jews, they would not apply to this youngster, who may be buried as any other Jew.

October 1983

93. BURIAL OF A DIVORCED WIFE

QUESTION: A man was married, had a child by his wife; he was then divorced. He remarried and the second marriage led to no further children. Subsequently he died after a considerable number of years of marriage to his second wife. Both the first wife and second wife are elderly women. The question of their burial sites has now arisen. The only child of the family wishes to have his mother, in other words the first wife, buried alongside his father. On the other hand, the second wife feels that it is her prerogative to be buried there. Which woman should be buried next to this man? (Rabbi R. Benjamin, Davenport, IA)

ANSWER: All formal relationships between this man and his first wife were broken by the divorce as you indicated. The two may even have been enemies for some time. The *Shulhan Arukh* states that two individuals who are enemies should not be buried alongside each

154

other (Yoreh Deah 362.6; Ezekiel Landau, *Nodah Biyehudah* II Even Haezer 79). This general statement has been applied to a husband and wife who continually quarrel with each other and never bothered to get a divorce. They, too, should not be buried next to each other (Aaron Meir Gordon, *Shaarei Daat*, p. 95, #5).

Some confusion may have arisen in the mind of the child who may remember some discussion about a similar question when dealing with a widow. In that case, in contrast to divorce, there is some discussion as to whether a second marriage completely annuls any relationship which existed previously. Moses Sofer certainly thought so (*Hatam Sofer* Yoreh Deah #355). However, there are other authorities who disagree (J. Greenwald, *Okh Letzarah*, p. 145 ff). As this question deals with divorce, it is completely different.

According to the spirit of tradition, the second wife should be buried with her husband, and the first wife should be buried somewhere else. However, there is nothing which would prevent burial in the same cemetery so that the child of these two individuals may readily visit their graves.

August 1982

94. BURIAL OF A WOMAN TWICE MARRIED

QUESTION: A woman was married to her first husband for twenty-three years, and had children by him. She subsequently became widowed, moved across the country, and now has been married to her second husband for more than twenty years. When she dies, should she be buried together with her first or her second husband? (L. B., Pittsburgh., PA)

ANSWER: There is custom (*minhag*), but no clear law on this matter. The general custom is that an individual is buried with that spouse with whom she had children, especially if that has been requested by the children (J. Greenwald, *Kol Bo Al Avelut*, p. 188 f). Some traditional authorities have felt that some special ties with that spouse continue even after her death. For example, according to them, it would be her duty to commemorate the *yahrzeit*, although in a fashion which will not sadden the second spouse (W. Leiter, *Bet David*, #134). On the other hand, the Hungarian Moses Sofer (*Hatam Sofer* Yoreh Deah #55) has stated that no further relationship exists with the first husband and there is no need to commemorate the *yahrzeit* (see also M. K. 21b and Rashi; *Shulhan Arukh* Yoreh Deah 385.2; *Menuhat Mosheh* #114).

If there are no children by either marriage, then generally burial is recommended with her first husband, as in that marriage she became "one flesh" with her husband (Lev. 21.2; Yeb. 55b; *Shulhan Arukh* Yoreh Deah 300). In most discussions of this problem, it is assumed that the graves are in the same city or at least in close proximity. Here the two burial sites are quite distant from each other. Greenwald, under those circumstances, feels that burial should take place in the city in which she died and has lived for the last years (J. Greenwald, *op. cit.*, p. 188). We would add that in our highly mobile society, it is important that burial take place close to some relatives who may be able to visit the grave (W. Jacob, *American Reform Responsa*, # 102).

Tradition, in this instance, gives preference to burial with the first husband, but it is clear that other options may be followed. This woman who would like to plan in advance should consult her children, and be buried wherever her grave can be visited by some surviving family members.

March 1984

95. BURIAL WITH FIRST OR SECOND HUSBAND

QUESTION: A Jewish woman in her seventies recently married a non-Jew. She advised me that she asked to be buried next to her first husband, a Jew, in a Jewish cemetery. The rabbi said she could not do so out of respect for her present husband. Is there any basis for this? (Rabbi H. Gelfman, Jacksonville, FL)

ANSWER: The classical discussion of whether a wife should be buried with her first or second husband is based upon the statement in the *Talmud* which understood husband and wife to "kin" even after the wife's death, (Lev. 21.2; Yeb. 55b). The general conclusion of rabbinic authorities is that the wife should be buried with her first husband unless she had children by her second husband (Wolf Leiter, *Bet David*, #134; J. Greenwald, *Kol Bo Al Avelut*, p. 188 f). However, the Hungarian authority Moses Sofer came to a completely different conclusion. He felt that the death of a woman's first husband, and her subsequent remarriage, broke those initial bonds entirely. He based his conclusion upon the a *fortiori* argument that if marriage can break the bond of brother-sister relationship (Lev. 21.3), in the case a priest who may mourn an unmarried but not a married sister, then surely remarriage would break the lesser relationships of husband and wife (*Hatam Sofer* Yoreh Deah 355).

In both of these instances, we are dealing with cases in which both husbands are deceased and the wife has survived them. In this case, the second husband is alive and she may predecease him.

A somewhat similar question was asked of Dr. Freehof some years ago. In that instance, the second wife wished to be buried alongside her deceased husband who was buried alongside his first wife. In that responsum he gave permission for such a burial provided that there was sufficient space for the interment (*Responsa for Our Time*, pp. 172 ff). This question is, of course, somewhat different, as the second husband is alive and as he is a non-Jew and may wish to be buried alongside his second wife.

If it is agreeable with the second husband that the wife be buried alongside her first husband, then there is no problem. Nor does the fact that he is a Christian present a problem if he wishes to be buried in the same cemetery as this woman as in most Reform Jewish cemeteries the burial of a Christian spouse is permitted (W. Jacob, *American Reform Responsa*, #99). If the second husband wishes to be buried in the Jewish cemetery, would we permit this woman to be buried between her two husbands? We would answer positively as such a burial reflects the reality of their lives.

We may proceed along the lines suggested above if it is agreeable with her present husband, both under the circumstances in which he may wish to be buried with his first wife (in their Christian cemetery) and if he wishes to be buried alongside his present Jewish wife in the Jewish cemetery if the cemetery permits this. Local cemetery rules, must, of course, be observed

July 1986

96. BURIAL OF A TEENAGER OF DOUBTFUL DESCENT

QUESTION: A couple has recently joined a congregation. The man is Jewish; the wife is Christian. They had two children, one sixteen and one eleven. Both have been raised in "a vaguely religious small town atmosphere" with attendance at various Protestant Sunday schools. Neither child has been baptized or formally entered into a Christian church. Now, as the parents live in a large city with a Jewish community, they wished to raise their children as Jews. Unfortunately, the older daughter was killed in an automobile accident. May she be buried in the congregation's cemetery? (D. M., Los Angeles, CA)

ANSWER: Most of our congregations have been lenient about the burial of an unconverted spouse of a Jew. They have done so by considering each individual plot in the cemetery as a separate family section, akin to the caves or small plots of land which were originally used for burial in the land of Israel (B. B. 102a). This meant that although the entire cemetery is considered as holy, sanctity actually lies with each section of graves. A non-Jewish burial in one section would, therefore, not impinge on the sanctity of any other grave. It is also clear that occasionally non-Jews have been buried in Jewish cemeteries throughout our history beginning with the Mishnaic period (M. Git. 5.8, 61a). For both of these reasons, most Reform Congregations have granted permission for the burial of a non-Jewish spouse or any other non-Jewish family member.

On these grounds alone, we may readily grant permission for burial in the sad case of this young woman. The specific rules of the local cemetery should, of course, be consulted.

March 1984

97. NON-JEWISH BURIALS

QUESTION: The Congregation owns a cemetery which is managed according to *halakhah*; no non-Jews are permitted to be buried in it. Recently the congregation had a number of mixed-married families join. One of the privileges of membership is the entitlement to two graves in the cemetery. This now leads to a problem. Is it possible to declare a segment of the cemetery "non-sectarian?" There is a section on the other side of the road which could be separated by a hedge. (Rabbi B. Lefkowitz, Taunton, MA)

ANSWER: Although there is a great amount of discussion of burial law, there is very little on the nature of the cemetery itself. It is mandated that every community should set up its own cemetery in order to honor the dead (Meg. 29a; *Shulhan Arukh* Yoreh Deah 34). If it is not possible to establish a separate cemetery, then a distinctive section is to be set aside in a general cemetery (*Dudaeh Hasadeh*, #66 and 89.) The cemetery in its entirety has always been considered as holy and deserving the respect and protection of the Jewish community. So, for example, unused sections may not be rented out for grazing (Meg. 29a; San 46a; *Shulhan Arukh* Yoreh Deah 368.1). Anyone who visits the cemetery, even the unused section, must behave in a dignified fashion (*Shulhan Arukh* Yoreh Deah 368.1). Respect given to a cemetery is akin to that extended to a synagogue (Azariah Fano, *Responsa* #56).

Once the land has been consecrated as a cemetery, it may not be sold or used for any other purpose. So, Moses Sofer asked a community to resist the government's request for a new wall around a cemetery, as the plans also called for a diminution of its grounds (*Hatam Sofer* Yoreh Deah #335). A similar opinion was provided by David Hoffman (*Melamed Lehoil* Yoreh Deah #125).

The only circumstances under which it is permissible to sell or dispose of a cemetery are: (1) if it is condemned by the government and the graves are moved; (2) if it is no longer possible to guard against vandalism. Then the dead may be disinterred and moved to another cemetery (Mosheh Feinstein, *Igrot Mosheh* Yoreh Deah 246 and 247; Moses Sofer, *Hatam Sofer*, Yoreh Deah #353). According to traditional *halakhah*, it would *not* be possible to simply set aside a portion of the existing cemetery for the burial of non-Jews.

There are two other paths which may be followed. Some adjacent land can be purchased. There would be no objection to utilizing it for Gentile burials as this ground has not been dedicated as a cemetery yet. It would also be possible to change the by-laws of the cemetery to agree with Reform practice. This would permit the burial of non-Jews in accordance with general Reform Jewish practice, as described in W. Jacob's *American Reform Responsa* (#98 ff). If the interments of Gentiles are permitted only in a separate section, then those who own plots in the old section have no reason to object.

January 1985

98. DOUBTFUL LINEAGE AND BURIAL

QUESTION: The following tragic situation presented itself to me.

A couple came to me in the midst of their sorrow. The husband had a Jewish father and a Catholic mother. He was raised as a Catholic but later in life identified more with his Jewish side, though he never converted and practiced both Jewish and Christian traditions. His spouse was Protestant. She identified herself with her Christian heritage but with the principles of Judaism. Tragically, their seven-month-old daughter has died. Is it permissible to bury this child in a Jewish cemetery with Jewish rites? (Rabbi S. Akselrad, Columbus, OH)

ANSWER: Let us approach this question both from a traditional and a Reform point of view. Tradition would consider the husband a Catholic as only his father was Jewish and so the entire family would be considered as Christian. Our Reform point of view would approach the whole matter in accordance with our resolution on patrilineal descent.

"The Central Conference of American Rabbis declares that the child of one Jewish parent is under the presumption of Jewish descent. This presumption of the Jewish status of the offspring of any mixed marriage is to be established through appropriate and timely public and formal acts of identification with the Jewish faith and people. The performance of these *mitzvot* serves to commit those who participate in them, both parents and child, to Jewish life.

"Depending on circumstances, *mitzvot* leading toward a positive and exclusive Jewish identity will include entry into the covenant, acquisition of a Hebrew name, *Torah* study, *Bar/Bat Mitzvah*, and *Kabbalat Torah* (Confirmation). For those beyond childhood claiming Jewish identity, other public acts or declarations may be added or substituted after consultation with their rabbi."

This Resolution raises the possibility of a Jewish identity irrespective of which parent was Jewish. However, this Resolution requires appropriate and timely acts of identification. In this instance, the father and mother have undertaken some rather vague steps toward Judaism. However, as they practice both Jewish and Christian tradition, these can not be considered as positive acts of identification. As neither parent is Jewish by any definition, and the child can not be considered a Jew and may *not* be buried with Jewish rites or in a Jewish cemetery.

We should do everything possible to help the family through this tragic period and comfort them in keeping with our long rabbinic tradition of aiding the comforting all those who need our help. If the parents wish to consider conversion to Judaism, they, of course, would be welcome. An act of formal conversion would be necessary before we could consider them as Jews.

January 1987

99. JEWISH FUNERAL FOR NON-JEWISH SPOUSE

QUESTION: A non-Jewish wife of a prominent member of the community has died. Although she was sporatically active in her church, she has maintained only vague ties with her Presbyterian affiliation. She will be buried in the Jewish cemetery with her Jewish husband's family. She has requested that a rabbi conduct the funeral. Can such a service be conducted for a nonJew? (D. S., Philadelphia, PA)

ANSWER: It is clear from the rabbinic sources (Gitin 61a; Yeb. 15a; *Shulhan Arukh* Yoreh Deah 367.1; S. B. Freehof, *Current Reform Responsa*, pp. 175 ff), that we bury Gentile dead *mipnei darkhei shalom*. In the Talmudic statements and in the subsequent elaboration of the medieval codes, nothing is said about any ritual which might accompany such burials. For that matter, little was stipulated about the ritual of a Jewish funeral. It has become traditional to recite a few psalms, *el male rahamim* and the *qadish*. As we may have some qualms about reciting the *el male rahamim* for a non-Jew, it may therefore be omitted. Nothing would preclude the recital of the psalms or *qadish* for non-Jewish dead. A convert has, traditionally, been specifically permitted to recite *qadish* for his deceased non-Jewish parents (E. Oshry, *Mema'amaqim*, pp. 69-72; Walkin, *Zeqan Aharon*, Yoreh Deah 877). We also often include non-Jews who have provided significant leadership in the general community on our *qadish* list and our memorial service as was done in past centuries when special services were held for deceased rulers (A. Hertzberg, *The French Enlightenment and the Jews*, pp. 203 ff).

It would, therefore, be perfectly appropriate to conduct a slightly modified Jewish service for the non-Jewish spouse of this member. This procedure should only be followed if it meets the wishes of the deceased and of her surviving husband and children, as it does in this instance.

April 1983

100. BURIAL OF AN APOSTATE

QUESTION: The following tragic situation has presented itself to me. A woman was murdered by her husband who then in turn shot himself. There is also a possibility of a suicide pact on which they had agreed. This was a second marriage; both parties were Jewish, however the wife converted to Christianity two years ago. The children by a former marriage have also converted. The husband will be buried in another city; the children (who are Christian) would like a minister to officiate at the funeral but would like the burial to take place in a Jewish cemetery with a rabbi officiating. Is this permissible? (Rabbi S. Akselrad, Columbus, OH)

ANSWER: This tragic situation raises a number of questions, however the main issue is whether we consider this woman to be Jewish or not. When an apostate has died, she has always been given the benefit of doubt as it was felt that on her deathbed she may have repented and reverted to Judaism. Although such individuals were considered sinners while alive, they nevertheless were be considered to be Jews (San. 44a). We bury sinners (Semahot II; San. 47a; *Yad* Hil. Avel 1.10; *Tur* Yoreh Deah 334; *Shulhan Arukh* Yoreh Deah 333.3 ff), but do not accord the honors of the dead to them. There has been some disagreement about the nature of such honors. We would not provide shrouds, stand in line at the cemetery to console the mourners, or have a mourning period.

In this instance as the surviving family members are Christian the ritual at the cemetery should be very simple. The woman may, however, be buried in a Jewish cemetery.

January 1987

101. RESTRICTING BURIAL IN THE CONGREGATION'S CEMETERY

QUESTION: The Congregation owns a cemetery with a limited amount of space. We would, therefore, like to restrict burial to members. Is this in keeping with Jewish tradition or should a cemetery be open to the entire community? (Rabbi R. Walters, Houston, TX)

ANSWER: Jewish burial sites can be divided into categories. The

Bible knew private burial plots, so for example, Abraham selected a grave for Sarah, the cave of Machpela, and the subsequent generations of his family were buried there as well (Gen. 23; 25.9; 49.31; 50.13). Furthermore, the Kings of Israel also seemed to have had burial sites of their own (II Kings 13.13, 15.7). Family plots also appear in the Talmudic Period (B. B. 100a, b; San. 47a; *M.* Shek. II.5; Erub. V.1). On the other hand, we should note that communal cemeteries were already in use in Biblical times (II Kings 23.6; Jer. 26.23) and of course, later on in the Talmudic period (Hag. 3b; Nid. 17a; Sem. 49b). In none of this literature or the subsequent responsa literature is there a discussion of a congregational cemetery, for virtually all cemeteries belonged to the entire community and, therefore, it was the communal responsibility to care for them and to see to it that they were maintained. Every effort was made to do so (Ezekiel Landau, *Noda Biyehudah* I Yoreh Deah #89; Isaac Spector, *Ein Yitzhoq* Yoreh Deah #34). Even when a community abandoned the city, it remained the responsibility of the neighboring communities to look after the cemeteries (Greenwald, *Kol Bo Al Avelut*, p. 164 f).

In each of the communities of previous centuries, the entire community supported the congregations and the cemetery. Such support could be forced (W. Jacob *American Reform Responsa*, # 9), therefore all of its members had the right to expect every service. The support either came through direct taxation by the secular government, as in modern central Europe, or through internal taxation, as in the earlier ghetto communities. A new resident was responsible for providing support for the poor after six months and for other charities after nine months (B. B. 8a; *Tos* Peah IV 9; *Yad* Hil. Matnat Aniyim 9.12).

The modern American congregation is different as it depends entirely on voluntary support. It, therefore, has the right to expect that such support will be forthcoming from those who wish to be served. Those who are unwilling to join in such support can expect no services. The congregation may, of course, offer its services to the general community, but it is not obligated to do so. This is in the spirit of tradition, as long as membership in the congregation is open to all irrespective of their financial condition. In other words, proper provisions must be made for the needy and indigent, so no one is excluded from congregational membership for financial reasons.

The congregation may, therefore, restrict the use of its cemetery to those who belong to the congregation.

December 1985

102. BURIAL OF ASHES IN A MAUSOLEUM

QUESTION: What does *halakhah* say about the burial of a body or ashes in a mausoleum? (Rabbi I. Neuman, Champaign, IL)

ANSWER: In this instance we are not concerned with the question of cremation but with burial of either a body or ashes in a mausoleum. Cremation itself has been discussed elsewhere (W. Jacob, *American Reform Responsa*, #100). There is good precedent for burying the dead in a mausoleum and not in direct contact with the soil, as in the cave of *Makhpelah* (Gen. 23.8), chosen by Abraham for his wife, Sarah. Subsequently, some Israelite kings were buried in cave tombs, as that traditionally associated with David. Later, in Tanaitic times, cave tombs became common and have been mentioned in the *Mishnah* (B. B. 5.8; Erub. 5.1; Shek. 2.5). Numerous such tombs have been discovered and described at great length (see particularly E. R. Goodenough, *Jewish Symbols in Greco-Roman Period*). The *Talmud* also mentioned a built up tomb (*kever binyan* - see San. 47b), which may have been a mausoleum.

In later periods, burial directly in the soil was preferred. This was influenced by the thought that the decay of the body acted as atonement for sin (*M. San 6.6, 46b; Tur; Shulhan Arukh* Yoreh Deah 362). In order to speed the decomposition, coffins were made of loose boards so that the body would be in close contact with the soil (*Shulhan Arukh* Yoreh Deah 362). If that was not possible, then some earth was deposited within the coffin. There has been considerable discussion among Orthodox authorities whether it was permissible to bury in a closed coffin altogether (J. Greenwald, *Kol Bo Al Avelut*, pp. 183 ff). Isaac Elhanan Spector of Kovno was the only authority who permitted a temporary interment in a mausoleum during a time when it was too dangerous to bury the body in the ground (*Ein Yitzhoq*, Yoreh Deah #33). Mosheh Feinstein rejected burial in a mausoleum completely as there would be no contact of the body with soil (*Igrot Mosheh* Yoreh Deah #143).

We conclude that at the present time tradition emphasizes burial in the ground. However, at an earlier time, burial in a mausoleum or cave was certainly permissible. Furthermore, traditional Judaism has changed its attitude toward the utilization of completely closed coffins and now permits them. So, direct contact with the soil seems less important. There is nothing in Reform Judaism which would preclude burial in a mausoleum.

December 1981

103. BURIAL IN THE GARDEN

QUESTION: A family who lost a child has made the request that the burial take place in their garden rather than a congregational cemetery. Is this permissible? (O. F., Atlanta, GA)

ANSWER: Communal cemeteries have been used since Mishnaic times and perhaps even earlier. It seems that our people already used them in the days of Jeremiah (Jer. 26.23; II Kings 23.6). The *Talmud*, of course, takes such community cemeteries for granted and discusses them as if they had always existed (Hag. 3b; Nid. 17a; Sem. 49b). During the Middle Ages when Jewish communities lived in restricted ghettos, the community cemeteries either were part of the ghetto or just outside the city walls. Often they were small, and so the custom arose of burying individuals in rows as they died rather than in individual family plots or even on top of each other, separated only by six hand breadths (*Shulhan Arukh* Yoreh Deah 362.4). However, special provisions were made for rabbis and communal leaders who were buried together in a separate location of the cemetery.

In our time, we have returned to family plots, and these are now used in virtually all American cemeteries. The Mishnaic and Talmudic periods also knew of interment in such family plots, crypts or mausoleums (*M. B. B. 6.8, 100a, b; San. 476; M. Erub. 6; Shek. 2.5). A number of regulations about such family plots appeared. For example, the family was obliged to care for them (B. B. 100b; Bekh. 52b), and upon the death of the individual who originally arranged for them, these lots were not divided among the heirs (*M. Sem. 14).

It is not clear whether the Talmudic family lots were part of larger burial sites or whether they simply existed on family estates. We do know from earlier Biblical times that the kings of Israel had burial sites of their own (II Kings 10.35, 13.9, 15.5) and, of course, we have the much earlier story of Abraham selecting a grave for Sarah in the cave of Makhpelah in which other members of the family were buried later (Gen. 23, 25.9, 49.31, 50.13). Therefore, it would seem appropriate for a family to establish a private gravesite on part of their own property.

If this is done, the family should, however, be aware of the fact that such a gravesite must receive permanent care; it places some perpetual restrictions upon the use of the property. That segment of the property must remain as a family possession into the future. It must also not be used for any joyful purposes. One may not eat, drink or be festive on or near it (Meg. 29a; *Shulhan Arukh* Yoreh Deah 364.1, 368). These restrictions, which are difficult in our mobile society, may make it hard to consider such an individual gravesite as practical. In addition, consideration of local and zoning laws will have to be investigated.

We should, of course, consider the psychological implications of a family living perpetually near its beloved dead. Jewish custom has tried to limit visitation to the cemetery in order to enable the family to overcome its grief. There is, for example, no visitation among us until the seventh day after the funeral, and again after thirty days (*Shulhan Arukh* Yoreh Deah 344.20), in addition to penitential days and *yahrzeit* (Yeb. 122a); among Sephardic Jews more frequent visiting is customary. It would be difficult to fulfill this period of healing under the circumstances described. So, for these reasons, and for the problems associated with perpetual care of this gravesite, such individual burial on the family property near their home should be discouraged, although it is not prohibited.

May 1977

104. BURIAL AT SEA

QUESTION: An individual has died on a cruise ship, and as he had a great love for the sea his wife has decided to bury him at sea. This avoided international complications as the ship was ten days from port. What is the attitude of Jewish tradition to burial at sea and to the subsequent mourning rites? (M. G. S., Pittsburgh, PA)

ANSWER: Jewish tradition takes the obligation of burial in the earth for granted; burial in the ground was considered part of the process of atonement. When *Gesher Hayim* discussed the question of death on the high seas, it permitted embalming to preserve the body until land had been reached. Embalming is generally prohibited by Jewish tradition (*Gesher Hayim* 1.73).

It is true that burial is usually required to take place immediately following death, i.e., on the same day or the following day (San. 46b;

Shulhan Arukh Yoreh Deah 357.11). Tradition permits the family to wait in order to do proper honor to the deceased and to permit individuals who may live at a distance to attend the funeral services (M. K. 22a; *Shulhan Arukh* Yoreh Deah 357.2). Burial in the ground, however, takes precedence over the need to bury immediately.

There have been occasions in the past when immediate burial was not possible. Rashi mentioned a siege in which bodies could not be buried; they were placed in coffins and stored (Rashi to Shab. 152a). Similar situations occurred when our forefathers were faced with various government regulations (*Shulhan Arukh* Yoreh Deah 375.5, 7), or in wartime.

In our instance, it would have been proper to hold the body until burial on land could have taken place. However, as the burial has taken place, the normal mourning rites should be carried out as with any other deceased.

Burial at sea is prohibited by Jewish tradition and is not appropriate except under emergency conditions.

November 1984

105. BURIAL IN A CHRISTIAN CEMETERY

QUESTION: A Jewish family, living in a small isolated rural community, feels a strong attachment to that community and would like to be buried there. It is likely that the children will live in that community, and so, their family will be located there in the foreseeable future. Is it permissible to Jews to be buried in a general cemetery? (Rabbi A. Task, Greensboro, NC)

ANSWER: The custom of establishing a separate Jewish cemetery has deep roots. It has always been felt as an obligation even for very small communities (*Ein Yitzhoq* Yoreh Deah 34). This practice has meant that cemeteries have often antedated congregations. That was so here in Pittsburgh where a cemetery plot was purchased in the Troy Hill section of the city more than a dozen years before the chartering of the Rodef Shalom Congregation. Your question, however, deals with a place so small that there is no congregation.

The oldest Jewish burial traditions, going back to Talmudic times in the land of Israel, simply indicated that the dead were buried in their own property - *betokh shelo* (B. B. 112a). Frequently these were family caves, some of which have been discovered by archaeologists in modern times, or small family gravesites on local farms. In more recent times, military interments have been permitted in National Cemeteries, but of course, these are not specifically Christian. There has never been any problem about the burial of Jewish dead in a general cemetery near a battlefield. Even subsequently, when the emergency was over, burial in a non-denominational cemetery has been sanctioned by the chaplaincy commission consisting of Orthodox, Conservative and Reform rabbis (Burial in National Cemeteries, *Responsa in Wartime*, 1947, p. 83).

We should also note that in places where it was impossible for the community to acquire a separate Jewish cemetery, a situation which arose frequently in Europe, a section of the general cemetery was set aside for Jewish burial. If possible, it was separated from the rest of the cemetery by a wall. In any case, a distance of four feet was left between the Jewish graves and non-Jewish graves (*Tov Taam Vadaat* III, #150; *Haderet Qodesh*, p. 34; *Ein Yitzhoq* Yoreh Deah 34).

In our instance, it would be possible to create a small separate section, even if it is only for a single family. They should purchase a lot sufficiently large to separate the graves completely from their non-Jewish neighbors. They should also clearly indicate that it is a Jewish burial site through the use of a Hebrew inscription tombstone. As this would create a small Jewish burial site in a larger general cemetery, this would be in keeping with the authorities cited above.

It would, of course, be preferable to continue the long standing custom of burial in a Jewish cemetery. If members of the immediate family have permanently settled in a large Jewish community, burial there would be preferable. In the circumstances indicated by your question, burial in a general cemetery in the way described would be in keeping with tradition, and nothing should preclude any rabbi from officiating at such a burial.

July 1985

106. BURIAL OF MISCARRIAGES, STILLBORN CHILDREN AND INFANTS

QUESTION: What is the traditional approach to burial for miscarriages, still-born children and infants who die shortly after birth?

What burial procedure and mourning customs are appropriate in the Reform Movement in this matter? (Rabbi R. J. Orkand, Westport, CT)

ANSWER: Jewish law is quite clear on the status of an infant who dies before reaching the age of thirty days. After that time, formal burial is required; before that time it is not. The child who dies before that time is considered a *nefel* and for such a child (strictly speaking considered stillborn if he does not survive thirty days), no burial and no mourning rites are required (Ket. 20b; Shab. 135b; *Evel Rabati* I; *Shulhan Arukh* Yoreh Deah 266; Ettlinger, *Binyan Zion* #133; Jacob Reischer, *Shevut Yaaqov* Vol. II, #10). A further statement by the *Shulhan Arukh* gives us some idea of the attitude to the death of children in our tradition. The question asked whether a eulogy *(hesped)* can be given for a young child, and the conclusion is for the children of the poor it may be done from age of five and onward, and for the children of the rich, six and onward (M. K. 24b; *Shulhan Arukh* 344.4). All of this indicates that relatively little was made of infant deaths or abortions. They occurred frequently and the communities would have been in a constant state of mourning if rites had been required.

A *nefel* was, therefore, treated in the same way as amputated limbs, and buried in the general section of the cemetery (Ket. 20.b). This was done to avoid ritual uncleanliness for the priests (M. Edut 6.3; *Yad* Hil. Tumat Hamet 2.3; *Pahad Yitzhaq*, Ever). Strictly speaking, it was not necessary to bury amputated limbs (Jacob Reischer, *Shevut Yaaqov* II, #10; Ezekiel Landau, *Noda Biyehudah* II, *Shulhan Arukh* Yoreh Deah #209; J. Greenwald *Kol Bo Al Avelut*, p. 184).

In our time matters have, however, changed and most families have very few children, so all the events in a child's life have become significant and magnified. That, of course, includes the tragic death of a young child, a still-birth, or miscarriage. We would, therefore, suggest that there be a simple burial of a still-born infant or a child who dies at an early age. This will provide a way for the family to overcome its grief. A miscarriage may, however, be disposed of by the hospital or clinic in accordance with its usual procedures. No burial is necessary but it is also not prohibited; we would suggest it for infants and possibly for still-births.

October 1983

107. BURIAL OF HUMAN SKIN FROM HOLOCAUST VICTIM

QUESTION: The Congregation recently acquired an antique lamp, and it turns out that the lampshade is made of human skin which has survived from the Nazi period. Should the lampshade be buried? May it be displayed in a museum? What should be done with it? (Rabbi E. Silver, Salt Lake City, UT)

ANSWER: The lampshade of which you write has survived from one of the most tragic periods of our history. It should not be displayed but treated reverently and buried.

We would urge burial of this small portion of a body as a sign of reverence and respect for the victims of the Holocaust. Tradition would suggest burial for this reason and as a precaution against ritual uncleanliness for *kohanim* (*Yad*, Tumat Met 16.8; Jacob Reisher, *Shevut Yaaqov* II, #10). We are primarily concerned with the honor of those who were murdered during the Nazi period. As this may be the only portion of that unfortunate individual's body which has survived, we should bury it with the simplest of rituals. We do not know whether this was a Jew or a non-Jew, but that would make no difference, as we have long ago been mandated to bury the dead of our neighbors (*Shulhan Arukh* Yoreh Deah 151.12). The lampshade should, therefore, be buried in the congregation's cemetery.

January 1984

108. BURIAL OF OLD BIBLES AND PRAYERBOOKS

QUESTION: If a scholar dies, is it permissible to bury a worn *Tanakh* which had been part of her library along with the body? This would be done in keeping with the custom of burying old Bibles and prayer-books (Rabbi L. Englander, Mississauga, ON).

ANSWER: The custom of "hiding" or burying a worn *Torah*, *Bible* or prayerbook is, of course, connected with the basic prohibition against misusing or erasing the name of God (Deut. 12:3, 4; *Sifre*, ed. Friedman, p. 87b; *Sefer Hahinukh* #437). A *Torah* or other sacred book which was no longer fit to use was not to be kept (Rashi to Ket. 19b). It was to be buried in an earthen jar in the grave of a scholar (*Shulhan Arukh* Orah Hayim 154.5; Rashi to Ber. 47b explained that this meant a scholar who may only have studied *Bible* and *Mishnah*, not necessarily *Gemarah*). In other words, there is a well-established custom of burying a worn *Torah* or Hebrew book in the grave of a scholar. It has been mentioned in the *Tur* and earlier. I do not know whether the custom is Ashkenazic or Sephardic in origin, but I would suspect it to be Ashkenazic.

One might ask the further question whether this custom could also be carried out for a scholarly woman. Certainly tradition would not permit it, but we as Reform Jews seek to treat men and women equally and would, of course, permit this practice for women as for men.

May 1978

109. BURIAL OF A *SEFER TORAH*

QUESTION: The congregation has a *Torah* that can no longer be repaired. Must it be buried in the congregation's cemetery, or may it be buried on the grounds of the synagogue itself? (Rabbi E. L. Sapinsley, Bluefield, WV)

ANSWER: A *Torah* is buried out of respect. Traditionally it is placed in an earthen urn and buried in the cemetery near a scholar (Meg. 26b; *Shulhan Arukh* Yoreh Deah 282.10; *Shulhan Arukh* Orah Hayim 154.5). A *Torah* could, of course, also be placed in an absolutely safe spot; that was done in the Cairo Geniza into which not only *Torah* scrolls but all kinds of documents which mention the name of God were placed in order to assure that the name of God and holy writings would not be desecrated. A *pasul Sefer Torah* in which eighty-five consecutive letters remain continues to be holy (Sab. 115b), and so must be treated in a reverent manner. According to one strand of the tradition, such a defective *Torah* could be retained in the Ark, but not used. This was generally not followed, because it was easy to forget which was the defective *Torah* and to embarrass the congregation through its use (Jacob Ettlinger, *Binyan Zion*, 1.97; *Magen Avraham* to *Shulhan Arukh* Orah Hayim 154.8; Gedaliah Felder, *Yesodeh Yeshurun*, 2.142).

Burial of a *Torah* on the grounds of a synagogue has not been discussed. It would certainly be possible, but would represent a second best choice, primarily because the ground in which the *Torah* is buried may also be put to another use later, for example, as a playground, picnic site or parking space, etc. In other words, it is easy for the next generation to forget that a *Torah* has been buried there, and so, not treat it reverently. That is unlikely to occur in a cemetery. I would, therefore, suggest that if the burial is to take place on the grounds of the synagogue, that the site be appropriately marked. Otherwise, it would be preferable to bury the *Torah* in the cemetery in keeping with tradition.

May 1985

110. DISINTERMENT FOR LEGAL EVIDENCE

QUESTION: May the body of a young person who was murdered be disinterred after a number of years have passed? New evidence has arisen, and it is the contention of the attorney representing the husband of the person who was convicted of murder that this disinterment will provide additional clues about the real killer. (H. B., MA)

ANSWER: This sad inquiry actually contains three separate questions. First, we must ask about criminal procedures, especially in cases which might lead to the death penalty. How far can we go to obtain evidence? Secondly, we must turn to the general question of disinterment, and finally, to that of autopsy.

It is clear from the *Mishnah* (Makot, Sanhedrin) that every precaution was taken in the case of capital offenses. The accused was provided with all conceivable opportunities to prove his innocence, and all possible evidence must be examined. He had to be specifically warned by two witnesses (*M.* Makot 9.6), etc. A court of twenty-three had to be used (*M.* San. 4.1) Akiba and others sought to eliminate the death sentence entirely (*M.* Makot 10.6); the Talmudic line of reasoning made it very difficult to execute anyone. The crime and sentence were publicly announced with a plea for evidence which might prove the accused's innocence. Furthermore, an elaborate communications system was arranged between the courtroom and the place of execution so that any new evidence, even at the last minute, could prevent the execution (*M.* San. 6.1 ff). As our case is a capital offense, the statements and the intent of tradition apply. These indicate that in order to save the life, or to prevent an error in judgment in a capital offense, every effort to gain evidence on behalf of the accused must be undertaken.

Now let us turn to exhumation. Disinterment is not undertaken lightly in Jewish tradition. The prohibition rests upon a Talmudic incident in which disinterment was suggested in order to establish whether the deceased was a child or an adult, and thereby settle a quarrel over property rights. In that instance, it was disallowed (B. B. 155a). Akiba felt that the dead should not be disturbed, but that was not a capital case. It has also been prohibited in almost all instances with the exception of the following:

a. in order to reinter in the land of Israel;
b. in order to reinter in a family plot, especially if the deceased died away from the city in which he normally resided;
c. in those instances in which the grave was threatened by hostile individuals or by an unforeseen natural event (*Shulhan Arukh* Yoreh Deah 363.1 ff).

Whenever burial has taken place in a coffin, rather than merely in shrouds, disinterment has been more readily acceptable as the dead are disturbed less. In our case we are not dealing with the usual cases of disinterment, but with a more serious reason. In view of the intensive search for evidence in all capital cases, disinterment should be permitted in this instance.

Each cemetery has its own regulations, and every effort should be made to abide by them. However, in this instance, as an individual's freedom is at stake, disinterment should be encouraged.

Autopsy has been thoroughly discussed by J. Z. Lauterbach (W. Jacob, *American Reform Responsa*, # 82) and S. B. Freehof (*Reform Jewish Practice* Vol. I, pp. 115 ff). As this autopsy will be of immediate benefit in a criminal case, even the more hesitant traditional authorities would permit it.

June 1982

111. DISINTERMENT AND REBURIAL

QUESTION: Is it possible to exhume and reinter a member of a family who is now buried outside of his family plot? The family would like to have all of their deceased in one location. (Rabbi I. Blum, Dayton, OH)

ANSWER: The statements which you have made based on *Shulhan Arukh* (Yoreh Deah 363) are perfectly correct. Moses Sofer (*Hatam Sofer* 6.37) also permitted such reinterment in a place where relatives, who had previously died, had already been buried (Mak. 11a). There is a good deal of discussion about this by various Orthodox authorities, but most of the instances of reinterment deal with problems of temporary burial, the need to move a body from a place which is no longer safe, or which has been condemned by the government for some public use. (See also W. Jacob, *American Reform Responsa*, # 106, 115).

The classic American legal case on this question arose in 1900 and involved the burial or reinterment of the wife who had predeceased her husband to the family plot in which her husband had been buried some two years later. The children, in accordance with the wish of the father, sought permission from Congregation Sheerit Yisrael, and the matter went to court (Howard Cohen against Congregation Sheerit Israel, Appellate Division of the Supreme Court, New York.) A large number of authorities presented their opinion on both sides. Those aligned against granting permission were Rabbi Mendes of Congregation Sheerit Yisrael, Rabbi Louis Ginsburg, Rabbi Solomon Schechter, Rabbi Benjamin Drachman, Rabbi De Sola of Montreal, Rabbi Herman Adler and Rabbi Moses Gaster of England. Those who gave testimony in favor of this disinterment and reburial consisted of both Reform and Orthodox rabbis. Among the Reform were Rabbi Kaufmann Kohler; among the Orthodox were Rabbi de Sola of St. Louis, Rabbi Rudolf Plaut, Rabbi Samuel Zeil, and Rabbi Eisenstein. The court decision favored disinterment and reburial.

June 1984

112. PRAYERS AT REINTERMENT

QUESTION: The parents of a member of our congregation are buried in a cemetery in New York City much plagued by vandalism. He would like to transfer these caskets to our cemetery. When the caskets are reinterred, need any kind of service be conducted? (Rabbi M. Silverman, Albany, NY)

ANSWER: Although Judaism generally frowns upon disinterment and reburial in a new site, it permits it for several reasons, including the one cited in this question. In fact, under some circumstances disinterment and the movement of a body to another grave is obligatory (*Shulhan Arukh* Yoreh Deah 363; Haham Z'vi Ashkenazi, *Responsa* #50).

When such reinterment occurs, no ritual of any kind is required, although some pious commentators suggest that mourning rites (*qeriah, qaddish,* etc.) be carried out for one hour (*Shulhan Arukh* Yoreh Deah 403). This might be done either at the site of the reinterment itself or just as appropriately in another setting, i.e. at home or in the synagogue. When Moses Sofer, in the last century, was faced with the government's confiscation of a large cemetery, he prohibited anyone from informing close relatives when the disinterment and reinterment would take place, so that they would feel no obligation to mourn even for one hour (*Responsa* Yoreh Deah #184).

We, of course, are concerned both with tradition and with the feelings of respect and honor of the individuals involved. Obviously, if the children wish to have the bodies of their parents transferred to a safer site, there is a strong feeling about the memory of these parents. It would be appropriate to recite a few psalms and *qaddish* at the synagogue, at home or at the cemetery. This should be done at some time on the day of the reinterment, or a few days after it has taken place. While this is not obligatory, it reflects the respect of children for their parents.

October 1985

113. RESPONSIBILITY FOR CEMETERIES

QUESTION: What responsibility does the community have towards the care of Jewish cemeteries? What is the responsibility for graves which have subsided or not been filled properly? Can soil other than that removed from the grave be used to fill a grave? (M. Witkin, Reseda, CA)

ANSWER: Traditionally one of the first acts of any Jewish community was that of setting aside land for a cemetery. This often preceded the creation of a congregation or the building of a synagogue, as for example, here in Pittsburgh, where the Troy Hill cemetery antedated the charter of the Rodef Shalom Congregation by more than a dozen years. Congregations made every effort to own their cemeteries outright (Ezekiel Landau, *Noda Biyehudah*, I, Yoreh Deah #89; Isaac Spector, *Ein Yitzhoq* Yoreh Deah #34). After purchase, the land of the cemetery was treated with great respect, both the sections which had already been used for graves and those which were still vacant (Meg.

29a; *Shulhan Arukh* Yoreh Deah 368; Moses Sofer, *Responsa* #335). Some authorities, like David Hoffmann, prohibited the sale of a segment of a cemetery if other sections had already been utilized for graves (*Melamed Lehoil* Yoreh Deah #125). Only if there was no possible future utilization of the cemetery could segments which had not yet been used for burial be sold (Abraham Gumbiner *Magen Avraham* to Orah Hayim, 153.12).

It is incumbent upon the Jewish community to look after cemeteries even if they have been abandoned by their community or those who originally founded them (Greenwald, *Kol Bo Al Avelut*, p. 164; Mosheh Feinstein, *Igrot Mosheh* Yoreh Deah #246). If all Jews have moved from a town this duty must be borne by a nearby community.

Such care refers to the cemetery generally. It means that damage caused by flooding or subsidence must be properly repaired. Furthermore, the entire cemetery must appear neat. Lawns, shrubs, trees and fences must be appropriately maintained. Any individual grave should be filled with earth taken from it, or similar soil if this is not feasible.

Most states have provided for permanent funds which must be set aside for the perpetual care of cemeteries. These endowments are designed to provide general care for the cemetery; frequently provisions for the maintenance of individual graves may also be made in perpetuity in accordance with the local cemetery's policy. Such funds placed in trust must be utilized only for the maintenance of the cemetery or individual graves.

May 1985

114. SETTING OF A TOMBSTONE

QUESTION: Is there a specific time after the funeral when the tombstone should be set? Must one wait twelve months, or may this be done sooner?

ANSWER: There is no fixed time period which must elapse before the tombstone may be set. It has become customary among some modern Orthodox Jews to wait twelve months (Akiva Eger, *Hidushei* to *Shulhan Arukh* Yoreh Deah 376.4). However, there are many opinions which state that the tombstone may be set as early as the conclusion of the *shivah* period (Tos. to Ket. 5a). In fact, a mourner may interrupt the period of mourning to concern himself with the tombstone (*Sifsei Kohen* to *Shulhan Arukh* Yoreh Deah 375, note 12). In Israel tombstones are often erected at the end of the thirty days of mourning (*sh'loshim*).

Greenwald, after citing all the customs which have been followed in both ancient and modern times, quite properly declares that the tombstone itself is erected to honor the dead. As we feel that we honor our dead more (*kibud hamet*) by waiting a year, that should be done. It would, however, be within the framework of tradition to erect a stone earlier. Both ways agree with custom and tradition (J. Greenwald, *Kol Bo Al Avelut*, p. 370). For guidance on a consecration service for the stone, see *Gates of Mitzvah* (p. 64). As waiting twelve months has become a wide-spread custom among us in America, we should generally wait until that period has elapsed.

June 1979

115. FALLEN GRAVESTONES

QUESTION: The gravemarkers in a Central European cemetery have been neglected for many years. Some have fallen over; others are broken. Can they be re-erected on the sites of the original graves, or should fallen gravemarkers simply be left as they are? (J. Spear, Pittsburgh, PA)

ANSWER: Jewish cemeteries have long been accorded a special status in Jewish life, and every effort has been made to maintain them properly. This meant that already in Talmudic times Jewish tombs were considered "more beautiful than royal palaces" (San. 96b). Every possible effort was made through the ages to protect the graves of the beloved dead, although often in the wake of persecution this failed and many medieval cemeteries were totally destroyed (Israel Abraham's *Jewish Life in the Middle Ages*, pp. 93 ff; L. Zunz *Geschichte*, pp. 396 ff). Walls were usually placed around the cemeteries to protect them, and every effort was made to maintain the cemeteries, although communities were not to tax themselves too heavily in order to protect the cemetery from rapacious government officials (S. B. Freehof, "The Vandalized Cemetery," in W. Jacob, *American Reform Responsa*, # 115).

This meant that whenever possible tombstones in vandalized cemeteries were restored or replaced by new stones. Tombstones which were replaced because of their poor condition, or because the family could now afford a better stone, could not be sold for individual profit. They may be given to the poor in order to be refashioned into a stone for someone who could normally not afford a tombstone, or they may be sold for the benefit of the cemetery and the total community (San. 47b, Asher ben Yehiel to *M. K.* 3.79; *Shulhan Arukh* Yoreh Deah 348 and commentaries; Shalom Schwadron *Responsa*, Vol. 2.122; Moses Taubesh *Hayim Shel Shalom* 2.104). When tombstones have collapsed, it is a *mitzvah* and appropriate to set them up again. If they are broken, they may be replaced.

November 1985

116. NAMES ON A TOMBSTONE

QUESTION: A woman who has been married twice recently died. Her second husband is unwilling to pay for a tombstone to be erected on her grave. Her children, born of her first husband, are willing to erect such a stone but do not want to put the second husband's name on it. Is it appropriate for them to omit any recognition of the second marriage? (Rabbi P. Knobel, Evanston, IL)

ANSWER: Let us begin by dealing with the entire matter of tombstones. From the fourteenth century on it was considered a husband's obligation to provide a tombstone for his wife (Asher ben Yehiel, *Responsa* #13, 19; Solomon ben Aderet, *Responsa* #375; *Shulhan Arukh* Even Haezer 89.1; Joel Sirkes to *Tur* Yoreh Deah 348). The *Shulhan Arukh* went even further and states that the heirs of a man are compelled to provide a tombstone (Yoreh Deah 348.2). All of this indicates that it is the absolute duty of the husband to provide such a stone.

It seems that the children do not want to pursue the matter further and force the second husband to erect such a stone. They want to erect the stone themselves. Can they now omit the name of the second husband?

The traditional literature on this subject deals primarily with the Hebrew names inscribed on the tombstone. Some inscriptions in case of both men and women simply list their names and their descent with a reference to the father only (S. E. Blogg, *Sefer Hahayim*, pp. 258 ff). They sometimes mention the name of the husband, but on other occasions, do not (Greenwald, *Kol Bo Al Avelut*, pp. 381 ff). In our communities, of course, the individual is known by her English first name and surname. If the woman who died used the last name of her second husband during her lifetime, then that name should also be mentioned on the tombstone. Tradition even goes so far as to indicate that a name be changed to "avoid the angel of death," in other words, during the last illness as was folk custom in medieval times, must be inscribed on the stone if used for more than thirty days (Greenwald, *op. cit.*, p. 382). Of course the old name was given as well. There would be nothing wrong with indicating the other family name as well or to indicate the second marriage through a hyphen or parentheses.

October 1985

117. THE *SH'MA* AS A TOMBSTONE INSCRIPTION

QUESTION: Would it be permissible to inscribe the verse *Sh'ma Yisrael* on a tombstone? (R. W., Pittsburgh, PA)

ANSWER: Inscriptions on Jewish tombstones may be found as early as Greek and Roman times. Usually they were confined to the name of the deceased and a brief description of his life. This practice was continued in subsequent centuries. Only rarely were any quotations from Biblical or later literature found on stones until modern times. There would be no problem with such inscriptions, even with those intimately connected with the synagogue service. In fact, the more familiar synagogue psalms are used most frequently for such statements. Tradition has, of course, prohibited the conducting of a formal service on a cemetery and the building of a synagogue with a *Torah* on a cemetery. The general statement made in connection with these prohibitions was that we do not mock the inability of the dead to praise God (Ber. 18a; *Shulhan Arukh* Yoreh Deah 367.2). Everything is done to help overcome sorrow and not to reemphasize it. Nothing would prohibit the use of this verse which has become so central to Judaism on a tombstone inscription.

June 1983

118. TOMBSTONE WITH CHRISTIAN MARKINGS

QUESTION: The Christian spouse has placed a tombstone with crosses upon it on the tomb of her Jewish husband, who is buried in the Jewish cemetery. Should this tombstone be permitted to stand in the Jewish cemetery? (Rabbi K. White, Lincoln, NE)

ANSWER: We should begin by looking briefly at the historical background of tombstones. Some Biblical graves were marked, so Jacob placed a pillar on the tomb of his beloved wife, Rachel, (Gen. 35.20). Similarly we find various Biblical and post-Biblical kings marking their graves (II Kings 23.17; Mac. 13.27). Tombstones were, of course, also used to warn priests (*kohen*) so that they would not become ritually unclean (*Tos.* Ohalot 17.4). Tombstones were also mentioned in the Talmudic period, but nothing indicated that their erection was a universal custom (*M.* Shek. 2.5; Hor. 13b; Er. 55b). Some of the medieval authorities considered a tombstone as customary on every grave (Solomon ben Aderet, *Responsa* #375). He also felt its erection was an obligation to be met by the family (*Responsa*, Part 7, #57). Joseph Caro followed this thought (*Shulhan Arukh* Even Haezer 89.1; Yoreh Deah 348.2) and stated that a husband is duty bound to provide a stone along with burial for his wife. The commentaries continue that emphasis. It is clear, therefore, that the grave must be marked.

We must now ask whether it is permissible to use a stone with a Christian symbol in a Jewish cemetery. There is, of course, no discussion of this in the traditional literature, for such a stone would have been unthinkable in the past and the question would not have arisen. We can, however, be guided by it in a lengthy discussion of Moses Schick of the nineteenth century (*Responsa* Yoreh Deah #171) which dealt with inscriptions of the date from the Christian calendar on the tombstone. He was outraged and felt that this violated the commandment of Deuteronomy (18.20), "The name of other Gods shall not be mentioned." Others, however, felt that this system of dating had become completely secular, and therefore, could be used on a Jewish tomb along with the Hebrew date. I cite this instance simply to indicate sensitivity on a the matter which is peripherally Christian.

The cross, however, is the central symbol of Christianity. It is sacred and universally recognized. It would, therefore, be absolutely wrong to have this or any other Christian symbol in the Jewish cemetery. In our instance it is also misleading as the individual buried there was a Jew.

When we permit a non-Jewish spouse to be buried in our cemeteries, it is a courtesy to the family. This can not be extended to non-Jewish services in our cemeteries or to Christian symbols on any grave. Anyone who is uncomfortable with these conditions should be buried in a Christian cemetery.

Many of those buried in the cemetery already, and their survivors, would feel that their religious status had been violated by such a stone.

In our instance, it seems quite likely that the widow simply ordered the stone without giving the matter any thought, and would be willing to alter it or replace it. If, for some reason, the widow is adamant and insists upon having her husband's grave marked with a cross, then her husband should be be reinterred in the general cemetery where she can mark the grave in any way that she wishes.

May 1983

119. *SHIVAH* FOR A DELAYED FUNERAL

QUESTION: Two parents have been tragically killed while on vacation in Africa. The funeral has been delayed by ten days due to various government regulations. Do the children need to sit *shivah* for the week after burial, or can their mourning period begin earlier? (R. R., Pittsburgh, PA)

ANSWER: In this instance we are concerned not only with the mourning period but also with the period before burial. Generally no one should try to console individuals during this time called *aninut* (M. K. 23b; *Shulhan Arukh* Yoreh Deah 341). Of course, these traditional regulations dealt with the usual circumstances in which burial took place the next day or shortly thereafter, not following a long interval.

Technically the mourning period begins when the body has been interred and the grave is closed. The Talmudic term for this is *golel* (Shab. 152a; M. K. 27a; *Yad* Hil. Avel 1.2; *Tur* Yoreh Deah 375; *Shulhan Arukh* Yoreh Deah 375). There was considerable discussion in the literature about the precise meaning of that term; it reflected a disagreement between Rashi and Rabenu Tam. Rabenu Tam felt that it meant that the grave needed to be covered, while Rashi felt that it indicated that a lid had been placed upon the coffin.

Normally this disagreement is of no consequence, as both acts follow each other in rapid succession. But when burial is not immediate, as for example, when a city is under siege or if weather conditions do not permit it, then traditional authorities have followed Rashi's decision and begun the mourning period when the coffin is closed (*Shulhan Arukh,* Yoreh Deah 375.4 ff). Furthermore, if burial is to take place in another locale, then whenever the mourners in the original place turn from the procession honoring the deceased, the official mourning period begins (*Yad* Hil. Avel 1.5; *Shulhan Arukh* 375.17 and Isserles).

In this tragic instance, mourning may begin as soon as the bodies have been placed in their appropriate coffins in Africa. After the funeral itself, the period of *sheloshim* will naturally continue (Deut. 34.8; Ket. 103a).

We would advise the children in these tragic circumstances to continue to receive mourners for several days after the funeral. Jewish tradition does not demand it, but it will help the young people through their difficult adjustment, and enable their friends to comfort them.

December 1984

120. NAME OF THE DECEASED ON TWO TOMBSTONES

QUESTION: A family would like the ashes of a recently deceased member interred in one family plot in our cemetery; they have also requested that her name be engraved on stones in two family plots. This represents an effort to keep peace within the family. The plots are only a few feet apart, and there is no animosity between the two families. Would this be permitted? (V. Kavaler, Pittsburgh, PA)

ANSWER: We should look briefly to the history of tombstones in Judaism, which began when Jacob set up a pillar upon the grave of his beloved wife, Rachel (Gen. 35.20). Tombs were similarly marked by the kings of Israel (II K 23.17), by some of the Maccabees (I Mac. 13.27 ff), and in the Mishnaic and Talmudic periods (San. 96b; Shek. 47a). Tombstones were generally erected, but they were not absolutely obligatory, so some graves in cemeteries remained unmarked (*Shulhan Arukh* Yoreh Deah 364). If the precise place of burial is not known, as has happened recently in the cases of cemeteries destroyed by the

Nazis during the Second World War, then one may erect a tombstone on a site which is not the actual grave (*Memaamakim* 1.28). It is permissible to memorialize the deceased on a general memorial plaque in another location, as on a monument for those who died in wartime or on a plaque in the synagogue. However, on the cemetery itself, there should be only one tombstone for a specific individual, and the name should not be inscribed on the stones of two different families.

September 1982

121. MOURNING FOR A NON-JEWISH SPOUSE

QUESTION: What traditional mourning custom should be observed for a non-Jewish partner? In this instance the couple in this mixed-marriage has spent a lifetime together. (Rabbi D. Polish, Hollywood, CA)

ANSWER: Jewish mourning customs are intended to help the living overcome their grief for the dead and are to honor the deceased. It is clear that immediately after death virtually nothing helpful can be done, and so, during the period of *aninut* the mourner is exempt from all positive religious acts such as the recital of fixed prayers, etc. (*Shulhan Arukh* Yoreh Deah 341.1; Orah Hayim 341.1). The Talmudic reasoning behind this indicated that the mourner should not be interrupted from looking after the needs of the deceased as she prepares for the funeral (Suk. 26a; Sotah 44b; *Yad* Hil. Avel 4.6). It is for the same reason that no visitation occurs during this period. Later, however, the *shiva, sheloshim*, etc., are intended to help the mourner overcome her grief.

Let us look at a number of distantly related matters which may help us. There is some discussion of this question in connection with proselytes. Maimonides ruled that a convert does not have to mourn a non-Jewish parent (*Yad* Hil. Avel 2.3) and Caro commented that this decision stemmed from the fact that a convert was considered like a "new-born child." However, Maimonides also stated that a convert is duty-bound to provide a measure of honor for his non-Jewish parents (*Yad* Hil. Mamrim 5.11). This means that some of the mourning practices would be considered obligatory upon a convert for his non-Jewish parent, while others would not. Somewhat later, Ibn Ezra stated that one should, for plain human reasons, honor one's non-Jewish parents (Commentary to Deut. 21.13 and Yeb. 47b; Kid. 21b). This consideration, and others, led Oshry (*Memaamaqim* pp. 69-72) and Aaron Walkin, (*Zeqan Aron*, Yoreh Deah #877) to decide that one could recite *qaddish* for non-Jewish parents, but should make some distinction between mourning for a Jewish parent and a non-Jewish parent.

We would, however, make no such distinction as the non-Jewish parent has presumably also influenced her child for good, and therefore, deserves to be honored through *qaddish*. Family loyalty would demand the recitation of *qaddish*.

Now, let us turn to a different situation in which there is no family relationship between the Jew and the Gentile for whom *qaddish* has been requested. This might occur when a Gentile has made a gift to the Jewish community. Gifts by non-Jews to the ancient Temple in Jerusalem were considered under certain conditions (Ar. 6a). In this century Abraham Klein was asked whether a Gentile who made a gift to the synagogue could be memorialized by the *el male rahamim* on the days of *yiskor*, and he assented (*Beerot Avraham* #11). Gifts to the synagogue which possessed a different degree of sanctity than the ancient Temple were always acceptable as long as the community could use them as needed (*Yad* Hil. Matnat Aniyim VIII, 8; *Tur* Yoreh Deah 258; Isserles to *Shulhan Arukh* Yoreh Deah 254.2; *Shulhan Arukh* Yoreh Deah 259.4). In fact, it was considered permissible to solicit such gifts from the general community and to maintain an honor role for that purpose (Abraham Cohen, *Kol Aryeh*, Orah Hayim #14; Moses Sofer, *Responsa*, Yoreh Deah #225; Joseph Messas, *Mayim Hayim* #82).

Another useful analogy can be made with the prayers recited for governmental figures. This custom, based on Jeremiah 29.7, was already mentioned by Philo (*Against Flaccus* 7). This led to special services of mourning for deceased government leaders in various periods. We have some from the eighteenth century which contain all the traditional prayers of mourning (A. Hertzberg, *The French Enlightenment and the Jews*, pp. 203 ff). It would, therefore, be appropriate to recite *qaddish* for righteous Gentiles who have aided the Jewish or general community.

Each of these matters is, of course, different from the non-Jewish spouse in a mixed-marriage, yet the same basic reasoning would apply, for it is family loyalty and a wish to honor the dead which leads us to *qaddish* as well as the other mourning customs. These customs are, of course, primarily intended to help the living through the period of grief.

Although none of the traditional mourning customs are obligatory for a non-Jewish spouse, we would, nevertheless, encourage observance which will help overcome grief, do honor to the deceased, and stress the family ties.

June 1986

122. RECITING QADDISH FOR A CONVICTED CRIMINAL

QUESTION: Is it appropriate to recite *qaddish* for a convicted criminal even if the crime was heinous? (J. Brown, Long Beach, CA)

ANSWER: The background of the *qaddish* and those for whom it is obligatory has been provided elsewhere. Although sons are generally obligated to recite *qaddish* for their parents, if we are dealing with a convicted criminal, matters may be somewhat different. Let us begin with the question of burial for convicted criminals.

It is clear from the statement in Deuteronomy (21.23) that those who are executed should be buried even though the body may have been left to lie for a few hours. In Mishnaic times, it often occurred that a special place was set aside for the temporary burial of those executed (*M.* San 4.5), but after his flesh had decayed in atonement, the bones were interred in the family cemetery (*M.* San. 4.6). Later those who had committed a crime were simply buried in a Jewish cemetery, however, at some distance from individuals who were considered righteous (San. 47a; *Shulhan Arukh* Yoreh Deah 362.52; Hatam Sofer, *Responsa,* Yoreh Deah 333). This practice was also followed for those under the ban. If they had committed a serious crime, then funeral honors were withheld, otherwise the coffin might be stoned by the *bet din,* or they placed a single stone on it. Yet, even for serious offenders, *takhrihim* were permitted (Solomon Aderet, *Responsa,* Vol. 5, #236), and his grave was placed in the cemetery in the normal fashion (Caro in *Bayit Hadash* to *Tur* Yoreh Deah 334; *Shulhan Arukh* Yoreh Deah 334.3). This pattern was followed for criminals, apostates and individuals of doubtful character. Therefore, any Jew who committed a crime, no matter how grave, must be buried in a Jewish cemetery. The normal honors like eulogy, cutting one's garment, etc. are, however, withheld.

It remains the responsibility for the son to recite *qaddish* for such an individual as for a righteous father or mother. For a division of opinion on this matter see "Incest and Parental Responsibility." This thought is reinforced by the fact that death is considered to bring atonement (San. 44a, 56a); the recital of *qaddish* is traditionally considered as a way of furthering such atonement through one's own good deeds (San 104a). *Qaddish* should, therefore, be recited for an executed or deceased criminal by those normally obligated to do so. The obligations of children do not change through any act committed by the parent.

February 1981

123. INCEST AND PARENTAL RESPONSIBILITIES

QUESTION: What is the duty of young parents toward their dying father who was guilty of incest with his granddaughter? This tragic incident occurred four years ago. Both the family and the youngster have been helped psychologically in the interval. Are the parents required to recite *qaddish* and in any other way honor him or his memory?

ANSWER: The question which you have asked is, of course, especially tragic as family ties and many early childhood memories have been permanently destroyed. The obligation of children toward an evil parent has been discussed since Talmudic times; a division of opinion is found in some discussions, which are incidental to other matters (Yeb. 22a f; B. K. 94b; San. 85a; Kid 32a). By medieval times there was a clear division of opinion between Maimonides and Alfasi on the one hand, and the exegetes of Northern France (Rashi and the Tosafists) on the other. Maimonides and Alfasi felt that the obligation of children to honor their parents was biological and had nothing to do with the moral status of the parents (*Yad* Hil. Mamrin 6.8 ff; Alfas to Yeb. 22b). Rashi and Rabenu Tam felt that honor depended on the moral status of the parent and a wicked parent need not be honored (Commentaries to Yeb. 22b; San. 85b; Mak. 12b). In each of these instances the medieval authorities dealt with parents who were considered absolutely wicked and not individuals who had sinned in a minor way (Maimonides *Sefer Hahinukh* 48; Moses of Coucey *S'mag* Lo

Taaseh 219; *Yad* Hil. Malveh Veloveh 4.4). In the medieval period, such individuals, of course, included apostates (David Hakohen *Responsa Radak* Bayit 11.1 -2).

The *Shulhan Arukh* continued this division of opinion, so Caro insisted that honor due to a parent was biological, while Isserles felt that it is dependent upon the moral status of the parents (*Shulhan Arukh* Yoreh Deah 240.18, 241.4). In the final analysis tradition would require *qaddish* even for convicted criminals (see "Reciting *Qaddish* for a Convicted Criminal") as death brought atonement and *qaddish* added to such atonement (San. 44a, 56a, 104a).

As you have asked specifically about *qaddish*, we must ask what additional purpose it serves in our age. We normally recite *qaddish* in order to overcome our sorrow and to make us feel at peace again with God and the world around us (see W. Jacob, *American Reform Responsa*, #117). In this instance, upon the father's death it will not only be necessary to make peace with religious feelings about God, but also with the feelings toward the father and the memories of the past. The recital of the *qaddish* should help in this regard. Therefore, despite all personal bitterness and the division of opinion in our tradition on this matter, the recital of the *qaddish* upon the father's death would be appropriate and should be beneficial.

July 1984

124. *QADDISH* FOR A PET

QUESTION: A pet of a family quite active in the congregation has died; the entire family has been very much attached to it for years. They would, therefore, like to recite *qaddish* for it. What does Jewish tradition say about this use of the *qaddish*? (A. S., West Virginia)

ANSWER The indulgence of pets, a recent American phenomenon, was unknown in earlier times. Animals played an important economic role in Biblical times, but there was no discussion of them beyond the need to treat them decently and kindly. For example, the commandment which deals with Sabbath rest insisted that animals rest along with man (Ex. 20.10). They are servants of man, but on a lower level. Some were not seen in a complimentary light, so dogs were mentioned disparagingly. For example, Goliath spoke of David when that lad was sent against him; "Am I a dog that you come against me with sticks?" (I Samuel 17.43). When Ecclesiastes wished to indicate the value of even a meager life, it stated, "A living dog is better than a dead lion" (9.4).

Dogs were traditionally considered unclean, mainly through their contact with corpses (Lev. 22.4). The dog was seen primarily as a scavenger, as already shown in Exodus. Cattle which had been killed by wild animals were thrown to the dogs. Elsewhere, male pagan religious prostitutes were referred to as "dogs" (Deut. 23.18). When the *Talmud* wished to be derogatory about Goliath, it provided him with a genealogy in which he is called the son of a loose woman, who had intercourse with dogs (Sotah 42b; Rashi and Commentaries).

Only in the post-Biblical book, *Tobit*, were there some favorable references to dogs (5.16, 11.4). The Mishnaic and Talmudic literature understood the danger of certain kinds of dogs being indistinguishable from wolves, especially in the evening (M. Kil 8.6, 1.6; Ber. 9b). A dog was considered among the poorest of all creatures and often had to subsist entirely on scraps and as a scavenger (Shab. 155b). Dogs used in sheep herding were viewed more favorably (M. Hul. 1.8)

On the other hand, the *Talmud* appreciated the atmosphere of safety created by dogs and suggested that one should not live in a town where the barking of dogs was not heard (Pes. 113a; Betza 15a). The potential danger of rabies was also recognized (Hul. 58b; Yoma 83b). Dogs were to be chained as they were considered dangerous (B. K. 79b; *Yad* Hil. Nizqei Mamon 5.9; *Shulhan Arukh* Hoshen Mishpat 409), and it was considered sinful to maintain a dog that was known to bite people (B. K. 15b), but one could let a dog run loose in harbor cities, presumably as an additional safeguard against lawless seamen (B. K. 83a). Enmity between human beings and dogs was mentioned in at least one passage of the *Jerusalem Talmud* (J. Ber. 8.8).

Hunting dogs were not mentioned in the *Talmud* but later by Rashi in his commentary to B. K. (80a). Dogs were sometimes kept as pets and the *Talmud* in one place mentioned that if a woman spends her time entirely with lap dogs or on games (possibly chess), this was grounds for divorce (Ket. 61b).

Although cats were certainly known to ancient Israelites, after all they were considered sacred animals in Egypt, there is no mention of the domesticated cat in the *Bible*. The single reference in the post-Biblical book of *Baruch* (6.22) may refer to a wild cat. The *Talmud* considered cats as loyal (Hor. 13a) in contrast to the dog. The principle purpose of keeping cats was to rid a building of mice (B. K. 80a) as well as other small animals (San. 105a), including snakes (Pes. 112b; Shab. 128b). They were, of course, dangerous to chickens and domesticated birds, as well young lambs and goats (Hul. 52b, 53a; Ket. 41b). Cats also endangered babies (B. K. 80b). The limited intelligence of cats was blamed on their consumption of mice, which were supposed to decrease memory (Hor. 13a). In nineteenth century Russia, a folk myth warned Yeshivah students from playing with cats because that might diminish their memory. Cats were, on the other hand, seen as a model of cleanliness and modesty (Er. 100b). Once cats established themselves in a house, they rarely left and remained very loyal (Shab. 51b). Sometimes their fur was used as it was particularly soft (B. K. 80b).

Nothing in the *halakhah* has dealt with the affection felt for animals. This feeling is understandable, but we should not confuse it with the greater love and respect for a human life. We should not use a prayer which is dear to the heart of every Jew to commemorate a dead animal. It would be absolutely wrong, and a mockery, to include the name of the pet in the weekly *qaddish* list. Mourners would be shocked and angered to see their father and mother listed alongside a dog or cat.

Whatever mourning for a pet which may occur should be conducted privately and outside of the purview of Judaism.

December 1984

125. *YAHRZEIT* FOR A BROTHER

QUESTION: An uncle has asked a young lady to recite *qaddish* upon the occasion of the *yahrzeit* of her deceased brother. The brother died before the young lady was born. Is the woman, according to tradition, required to observe this *yahrzeit*? (Rabbi H. Greenstein, Jacksonville, FL)

ANSWER: We must make a distinction here between mourning and *yahrzeit*. Mourning is obligatory for eight relatives, father, mother, sister, brother, son, daughter, husband and wife (Lev. 21.2; M. K. 20b; *Shulhan Arukh* Yoreh Deah 374.4 ff). This obligation does not, however, carry over to *yahrzeit*. *Hazkarat neshamah* originally began as a way of honoring deceased teachers and was used only to commemorate them. Eventually the memorial date was also used to recall parents

(Ned. 12a; Sheb. 14a) and this was usually connected with a fast.

Yahrzeit, as we now know it with the lighting of a candle, the recital of *qaddish* and fasting, was first mentioned by Isaac of Tyrnau in the sixteenth century (Mordechai Jaffe, *Levush Hatekhelet* #133). It has eventually become a very widespread custom (*Shulhan Arukh* Yoreh Deah 402.12). The order of precedence among mourners for the recital of the *qaddish* at services has been much discussed in Ashkenazic circles. When *yahrzeit* is included, it is always mentioned as commemorating a mother or father. The obligation of reciting *qaddish* exists for parents and not other members of the family. As with all matters connected with mourning and *yahrzeit,* there has been a slow movement to include other members of the family, especially through local customs. I am sure that the uncle in this family is thinking along those lines.

Although there is no obligation to recite *qaddish* on the *yahrzeit* date for a brother or sister whom one knew, nor for a sibling who died before one's birth, it is, however, a worthy custom. It will continue the memory of the deceased and honor that memory.

September 1985

126. TWO *YAHRZEIT* CANDLES

QUESTION: Two individuals have died in an accident. Should they be honored by two commemorative candles, which will burn for the *shivah* week and subsequently by two *yahrzeit* candles, or will a single candle suffice? What does tradition recommend? (R. R., Pittsburgh, PA)

ANSWER: It is difficult to trace the origin of both customs. Baer, in *Totzaot Hayim,* felt that the custom of lighting candles during the *shivah* was Talmudic. He recalled that Judah Hanasi wanted a light to continue to burn in his home, and everything else in his household to go on as before his death (Ket. 103a), yet that is hardly likely to be the origin of this custom. Its source must still be discovered.

As far as a *yahrzeit* candle is concerned, this old custom may have spread from the lighting of a candle in the synagogue on *Yom Kippur* (Isserles, Darkhei Mosheh to *Tur* Orah Hayim 610).

In each of these instances, the light commemorates a single individual. We should in this tragic case utilize two lights, one for each of the individuals who is mourned, both during the *shivah* period and in future years for their *yahrzeit*.

December 1985

127. LEAP YEAR *YAHRZEIT* OBSERVANCE

QUESTION: How is *yahrzeit* treated in a leap year when there is a second month of Adar? What occurs if the person commemorated died in a leap year during Adar II? What occurs if the person commemorated died during the First Adar in an ordinary year? Is the *yahrzeit* shifted as the festival of Purim? (Rabbi R. B. Davenport, IA)

ANSWER: As *yahrzeit* has traditionally been observed by fasting, visiting the grave, reciting *qaddish*, lighting a candle, studying *Torah*, giving to charity, etc., there is considerable discussion on the matter of dates, not only in connection with the Adar II, but also with a death that fell on *Rosh Hodesh* (see especially Abraham Gombiner to *Shulhan Arukh* Orah Hayim 568.7; *Sefer Hassidim* #723; *Shulhan Arukh* Yoreh Deah 220.8). One of the main problems over whether Adar I or Adar II should be used to commemorate the dead is the tradition of reciting *qaddish* for eleven months for the righteous. If it is recited for twelve months, that characterizes a person as wicked. Therefore, Adar I is certainly used for *yahrzeit* in the first year, even if that year is a leap year.

In subsequent years *yahrzeit* would, according to Sephardic and some other authorities, shift to Adar II whenever a leap year occurs (Bet Yosef to *Tur* 403; Maharil *Hilkhot Semahot;* Mahari Weil *Responsa* #68; etc.).

Caro, in the above cited section of the *Shulhan Arukh,* stated that we move the *yahrzeit* from Adar I to Adar II whenever a leap year occurs, but Isserles disagrees and leaves it in Adar I. In other words, there is a conflict of *minhag* between the Mediterranean Jewish community and that of Northern Europe. We also see that Jacob Mölln went one step further and indicates that it should be commemorated both during Adar I and Adar II, which is still done by some pious individuals.

As Reform Jews, we would follow the Northern European tradition and commemorate the *yahrzeit* in Adar I, if the death occurred in Adar

I, irrespective of whether the year was an ordinary year or leap year. If the death occurred in Adar II, we would commemorate it in Adar II during leap years and in Adar I during ordinary years.

March 1984

128. MOVING DATE OF *YAHRZEIT*

QUESTION: A family will be together approximately two weeks before the *yahrzeit* for their father. They would, therefore, like to move the *yahrzeit* and commemorate it two weeks early during this year. Is that permissible? (D. F., Pittsburgh, PA)

ANSWER: The *yahrzeit* has become an honored and established custom among Jews throughout the world. Its historic development and practices have been dealt with elsewhere (W. Jacob, *American Reform Responsa*, #127). There has been discussion about commemorating it on the day of death or burial, and tradition decided that the day of death should be used, except in the first year. If that date is not known, then a date may be arbitrarily set. However, the same date should be used in subsequent years (*Shulhan Arukh* Orah Hayim 568.8; Maharil *Responsa* #7).

A fair amount of custom and *halakhah* have developed around the commemoration of *yahrzeit*. All of it indicates that once the date has been fixed, it should not be arbitrarily moved. The family in this instance should continue to commemorate the *yahrzeit* on the appropriate date. There is, however, no reason for not doing something a few weeks earlier when the family happens to be together. In fact, we would encourage that as the mobility of the present day American Jewish community makes such family gatherings rare. The family should visit the grave of their beloved father and attend a synagogue service together, as they normally would on the *yahrzeit*; this should be done either on any day they are together or on a *shabbat* when they are in the city. In this way, they will honor the memory of their father as a family, but also not disturb the regular commemoration of *yahrzeit* from year to year.

March 1984

129. THE DIRECTION OF THE READER DURING PUBLIC SERVICES

QUESTION: Should the reader of a public service face the Ark while conducting the service, or face the congregation? What is the traditional and the Reform point of view on this matter? (Rabbi D. Prinz, Teaneck, NJ)

ANSWER: In the traditional synagogue, the reader (rabbi, cantor or layman) of the service faces the Ark both when the *bimah* is placed in the center of the synagogue or at the end of the building nearest the Ark (For a discussion of both possibilities, see W. Jacob, *American Reform Responsa*, # 18). However, even in a traditional synagogue, the leaders of the congregation are often seated facing the congregation with their backs to the Ark (*Tur* Orah Hayim 150; *Shulhan Arukh* Orah Hayim 150.4). The preacher similarly faces the congregation during his address. There are, of course, various places in the service during which these leaders would turn and face the Ark (the *amidah, Torah* service, etc.). In addition, we should note that when the priests (*kohanim*) bless the people they, too, face the congregation.

We should remember that the reader of the service only gradually achieved his dominant role in the Ashkenazic service. In the Middle Ages, he only led the service during the *amidah*, and otherwise simply indicated the conclusion of each paragraph through slightly louder recital. The service was in the hands of the congregants (I. Elbogen, *Der jüdische Gottesdienst*, p. 501). Abraham Gumbiner indicated that a reader was only necessary for the service because of the *piutim* (*Shulhan Arukh* Orah Hayim 53, #2).

The custom of the reader continually facing the congregation, with perhaps a few exceptions, represents a nineteenth century Reform innovation. As the Reform synagogues were larger and sought to increase the available seating space, they, as well as many traditional synagogues, have placed the *bimah* close to the Ark. This means that the reader of the service can be understood more readily when he faces the congregation. The innovation is probably American, but I have been unable to find a source or date for it. In most Reform, and some Conservative congregations, the rabbi and cantor face the congregation for the entire service. In other Reform and Conservative congregations, they do so for major portions of the service, except for those sections during which orientation toward the Ark is specifically indicated.

October 1985

130. PULPIT ROBES

QUESTION: Some members of the congregation feel that it would be more appropriate for the rabbi and cantor to appear on the pulpit in robes. At the present time it is the *minhag* of the congregation to have them conduct services wearing a dark suit. Is there some Jewish tradition which favors robes? (L. Brody, Pittsburgh, PA)

ANSWER: In recent centuries, Hassidic Orthodox authorities have opposed any change in the garb worn by their followers; for that reason, their members continue to wear garments commonly used in Eastern Europe during the eighteenth and nineteenth centuries (Sofer, *Mahaneh Hayim,* Vol. II, #2; Joseph Schwartz, *Vayitzbor Yosef,* 12.7, etc.). These authorities have also opposed the innovation of rabbi and cantor wearing robes, which was introduced into the liberal congregations of Hungary. They felt that this followed the customs of the Gentile community around us, and that has always been prohibited (Zeph 1.8; *Yad* Hil. Akum 11.1; *Shulhan Arukh* Yoreh Deah 178.1). This, however, was a later interpretation of these citations, for both Caro and Isserles refer to garments which were overly decorative or ostentatious (*Shulhan Arukh* Yoreh Deah 178.1).

It is, therefore, clear that although in a large number of congregations rabbis and cantors wear robes, there is nothing in tradition which would encourage it. In fact, the democratic tradition of Judaism which gives no special liturgical role to rabbi or cantor would indicate robes as inappropriate garb of distinction. The *minhag* of the congregation should, therefore, be followed.

September 1983

131. WEARING A *TALLIT* WHILE CONDUCTING THE FRIDAY EVENING SERVICE

QUESTION: May a *tallit* be worn by the individual who conducts a late Friday evening service? (Rabbi D. R. Prinz, Teaneck, NJ)

ANSWER: The Biblical injunction which deals with the *tallit* (Nu. 15.39) indicates that the fringes are to be seen as a reminder of God's commandment. This led later authorities to decide that the *tallit* should be worn during daytime only as they could then "be seen" (*Shulhan Arukh* Orah Hayim 18). Maimonides, however, indicated that a *tallit* may be worn at night if no blessing is recited (*Yad* Hil. Tzitzit 3.8). A difference of practice between Ashkenazim and Sephardim arose over the wearing of the *tallit* for the *minhah* (afternoon) service. The Sephardim have been influenced by Kabbalistic practice which places an emphasis on *tallit*. In the Mediterranean Basin and Sephardic congregations elsewhere, as in Holland, everyone wears the *tallit* during the *minhah* service. In Northern Europe only the reader and anyone called to the Torah (on *shabbat* afternoon) wears the *tallit* (*Keter Shem Tov*, Vol. I, p. 5). Even in those Ashkenazic congregations in which the *tallit* is worn during *minhah*, the authorities urge that care be taken to remove it before *maariv*.

The *tallit* has, however, been worn by Ashkenazim and Sephardim during the *Kol Nidre* service (*Shulhan Arukh* Orah Hayim 619; see Bach and Magen Avraham). Isserles suggested that the *tallit* be put on in the afternoon before the *Kol Nidrei* service so that the appropriate blessings could still be recited (Isserles to *Shulhan Arukh* Orah Hayim 18.2).

Despite this, the *minhag* of the reader wearing a *tallit* for an evening service became widespread (Epstein, *Arukh Hashulhan* Orah Hayim 18.7). Those who recited the orphans' *qaddish* also began to wear a *tallit*. Both of these practices were deemed as necessary for the "honor of the congregation" by the eighteenth century (*Shulhan Arukh* Orah Hayim 18; see *Magen Avraham*; Schneer Zalman of Ladi *Shulhan Arukh* Orah Hayim 18.4).

Although originally the *tallit* was worn only during the daylight hours, eventually through Kabbalistic and Hassidic customs it came to be worn by the reader for all public services. It is appropriate for a Reform Rabbi to wear the *tallit* at all public services.

October 1985

132. NON-JEWISH VOICES IN CONGREGATIONAL CHOIR

QUESTION: May non-Jewish voices be used in a synagogue choir? Would there be a distinction whether the choir is visible or invisible, or composed of male or female voices? (S. J. S., Akron, OH)

ANSWER: Traditionally, from Talmudic times to the late Middle Ages, solo or choral voices in the synagogue were limited to males, for it was felt that female voices might lead to sexual arousal of the male worshipper (Ber. 24a; Sotah 48a; *Shulhan Arukh* Orah Hayim 75; *Hatam Sofer* Hoshen Mishpat #190; L. Löw, *Die Lebensalter,* p. 311).

The Reform Movement has insisted in the equality of men and women since the nineteenth century (W. G. Plaut, Report to the Breslau Conference, *The Rise of Reform Judaism,* pp. 253 ff), and makes no distinction between male and female voices or the emotion which they might arouse in the opposite sex. These concerns have dealt only with Jewish singers. Non-Jewish singers have only recently been used in synagogue choirs. Despite their frequent use, we feel that every effort should be made to organize a Jewish choir. Even if the vocal quality of its voices is limited, the *kavanah* of such a choir will add beauty to the service. It should be possible to organize a Jewish choir even in small congregations. If this is not possible, then we must view the non-Jewish choir member like any other non-Jews participating in a Jewish service.

When we dealt with non-Jewish participants in a Jewish service earlier, we insisted that such participation be limited to sections which were not essential to the service (W. Jacob, *American Reform Responsa,* #6). All public services must be led by Jews, and it would be inappropriate for a non-Jew to lead a service from the pulpit.

We may, however, look at a choir in a somewhat different light. We would have no objection to a non-Jew attending a Jewish service and worshipping alongside a Jew. From the days of King Solomon onward (I K, 8.41 f), non-Jews have been welcomed at Jewish services and their sacrifices could be brought alongside those of Jews (Men. 73b).

As we consider prayer to be a substitute for a sacrifice, there is nothing wrong with a non-Jew reciting the traditional words of prayer alongside those of a Jew, especially Christians who have been considered *benei noah* since the early Middle Ages (*Yad* Hil. Melakhim 2; *Moreh Nivukhim* 1.71; Tosafot to Bekh 2b). There would be no objection to non-Jewish choir members in a choir which sings with the congregation in the general congregational worship.

Let us now look at the choir in its role of presenting solo pieces in which no congregational participation is anticipated. If those pieces are not a major part of the liturgy, and do not deal with essential matters of Jewish belief or practice, then we would permit non-Jewish choir members to sing them, just as we would permit a non-Jewish layman to recite such a prayer as part of a service. The line of division is between the essential elements of the service and other segments.

We continue to feel that every effort should be made to have Jewish choir members, even if the quality of their voices is less desirable. If no Jews are available, then it would be possible to use non-Jews, within the limitations mentioned.

January 1985

133. ABBREVIATING THE SERVICE

QUESTION: What are the minimal prayers to which *shabbat* or daily service may be abbreviated when the occasion demands a very abbreviated service? (Rabbi H. Waintrup, Abington, PA)

ANSWER: As we review the simplification of the religious services undertaken by our Reform forefathers we shall see that they were primarily interested in removing archaic *piyutim* which were no longer understood, avoiding repetition, introducing ideological changes, and substituting vernacular prayers. Sometimes this was accomplished by spreading the historic liturgy over several services as in the American *Union Prayer Book* and *Gates of Prayer*. The history of our liturgy has been beautifully discussed by Jakob Petuchowski (*Prayerbook Reform in Europe*, New York, 1968). The reformers, however, did not wish to limit the service to the absolute minimum; in fact many added prayers which they considered appropriate for their age.

Let us therefore turn to the basic structure of Jewish service for guidance; it is simple and consists of the following sections:

1. the *shema* and its benedictions (M. Tamid 5; M. Ber. 1; Ber. 1a ff);

2. the *amidah* and *tahanun*; the *amidah* has 18 or 19 benedictions on weekdays and 7 on *Shabbat* and holidays (M. Ber. 6.3; M. Taanit 2.2; Ber. 33a; R. H. 32a).

3. On *Shabbat*, holidays, Monday and Thursday, a *Torah* reading is added.

4. The concluding prayer and the *qaddish* (Pes. 50a; *Sifrei* to Deut. 306; Ber. 3a).

The practice of recital of the *qaddish* for all deceased was at first limited to great teachers, but eventually in a move toward democracy it was recited for everyone (Nachmanides *Torat Ha-adam*, p. 50; *Kol Bo* 114; *Siddur* of *Amram Gaon*).

The outline presented above is much akin to the briefer services in the *Gates of Prayer*; they would provide an adequate minimal service for the occasions you have described.

November 1986

134. VIDEO-TAPING IN THE SYNAGOGUE*

QUESTION: Is there any objection to video-taping a *Bar/Bat Mitzvah* at a service or a wedding ceremony?

ANSWER: The custom of video-taping family celebrations in the synagogue has grown during the recent years. We would generally discourage it as it is often intrusive. This does, however, provide a permanent family record of notable occasions in an individual's life. Furthermore, this often enables individuals who are too old or frail to witness the ceremony to do so at home or in the hospital.

This method is less intrusive than the earlier use of photography. We have always considered it important to maintain the decorum of the synagogue service, both public services and private occasions like weddings. Nothing may distract the worshipper from worship (Meg. 28a; *Yad*. Hil. Tefilah 6; *Shulhan Arukh* Orah Hayim 151.10; Abraham Meir Israel *Vayaan Abraham*, 7; I. Elbogen, *Der jüdische Gottesdienst*, pp. 397 ff; W. Gunther Plaut, *The Rise of Reform Judaism*, pp. 152 ff). It is essential to keep the video-taping as a recording of what has occurred and not "stage" the service for the taping. The latter is not acceptable to us. If the video-taping can be done unobtrusively and be invisible to the majority of the congregation, it is permissible.

November 1986

135. ENGLISH *TORAH* BLESSINGS

QUESTION: It has been a *minhag* in the congregation to recite the *Torah* blessing in Hebrew, although a major segment of the rest of the service is in English. Recently the *Torah* blessings were recited in English, to the dismay of a number of congregants. Should the congregation insist that they be recited in Hebrew by all who are called to the *Torah?* (I. A., Pittsburgh, PA)

ANSWER: Two separates issues are involved here. One is the use of the vernacular in prayer, and these prayers in particular, and second, what weight is to be given to congregational *minhag* (custom). Let us begin with the matter of prayers in the vernacular.

It is clear that a large proportion of our people were no longer familiar with Hebrew, even in the time of Ezra and Nehemiah (Neh. 8:8), so the Scriptural reading had to be translated for them. By the time of the *Mishnah*, the common people no longer used Hebrew, therefore, the *shema, tefilah* and the *birkhat hamazon* were permitted in the vernacular (*M.* Sotah 7.1). This, then, also was the later decision of the *Talmud* (Sotah 32b ff); it enabled individuals who recited petitions to pray sincerely and with full knowledge of what they were saying. A parallel stand was taken by later authorities, so the *Sefer Hassidim* of the eleventh century (#588 and #785) stated that those who did not understand Hebrew should pray in the vernacular. Maimonides provided a similar statement (*Yad* Hil. Ber. 1.6), while the *Tur* and *Shulhan Arukh* made a distinction between private and public prayers. Private prayers were preferably said in Hebrew, while those in the congregation might be recited in the vernacular. They expressed a preference but did not exclude the vernacular in either instance (*Tur* Orah Hayim 101; *Shulhan Arukh* Orah Hayim 101.4). Aaron Chorin, Eliezer Lieberman and others, who defended the changes made by the Reform Movement in the last century, and its use of the vernacular, however, insisted that a number of prayers should continue to be recited in Hebrew (*Qinat Ha-emet; Or Nogah,* Part I). Of course, they felt that nothing stood in the way of using the vernacular.

Although there is no discussion about the *Torah* blessing particularly, it is clear that they may be recited in any language, according to the traditional view, and certainly according to our Reform view.

Custom (*minhag*) has had an honored status in Jewish life for a very long time. Both the *Mishnah* and *Talmud* discuss the customs (*minhagim*) of the people and suggest that a variety of rites be guided by them (Ber. 45b; Pes. 66a; Sof. 14.18). Naturally, customs which were accepted had to lie within the general framework of Jewish life and be followed by respected individuals. In subsequent centuries, the *minhag* has played an ever increasing role in Jewish life, so that Isserles was able to state: "No custom should be abolished," (Isserles to *Shulhan Arukh* Orah Hayim 690.17; Yoreh Deah 376.4). Isserles, of course, listed hundreds of customs in his notes to Caro's work.

Generally the mood of modern Judaism has been very much in keeping with this tradition, and we have felt that customs are binding and should be followed whenever possible.

If it is the custom of the congregation to recite the *Torah* blessings in Hebrew, then every effort should be made to continue this practice. This should, however, not totally exclude those who can not recite the Hebrew blessings. If they are sufficiently young, they should be encouraged to study Hebrew in preparation for the next occasion when they may be asked to participate. If they are older, then perhaps an English recitation should be permitted despite the *minhag*. Another solution would be for the rabbi to recite the *berakhah* in Hebrew for individuals unable to do so, while they read the English translation.

September 1983

136. BLESSING FOR *MEGGILAH* READINGS

QUESTION: Why is no blessing recited before and after the reading of Ruth, Song of Songs, Lamentations and Ecclesiastes when they are read in the liturgical cycle? (Rabbi H. Waintrup, Abington, PA)

ANSWER: The public liturgical reading of these scrolls from the *ketuvim* was not known until the post-Talmudic period. All except Ecclesiastes were first mentioned liturgically in the Tractate *Soferim* (14.3 ff). Ecclesiastes was initially mentioned as part of the *Sukot* service by the *Mahzor Vitry* (p. 440 f). *Soferim* indicated that the Song of Solomon was read during *Pesah* (on *Shabbat* or an evening), and Ruth on *Shavuot*. The Tractate *Ta-anit* (30 a) indicated that Biblical studies may occur on *Tisha Beav*, and that Job, Lamentations or selections from Jeremiah may be read. When the Tractate *Soferim* was written, the custom of reading Lamentations on *Tisha Beav* had be-

come widespread (14.3). Some in the Middle Ages read it respon-
sively (*Mahzor Vitry,* p. 226).

These discussions demonstrate that all practices connected with
these books are late. *Soferim* suggested that a benediction be said for
Lamentations (14.3). In Sephardic communities it became the *minhag*
to adopt the benedictions normally used for Esther with the appropriate changes (*Mahzor Vitry,* pp. 304, 344). That remains the custom in
Sephardic lands, but not among the lands of the Ashkenazim of
Northern Europe (I. Elbogen, *Der jüdische Gottesdienst,* p. 185).

We have chosen to follow the general Ashkenazic European custom
of reading the scrolls without a benediction. There would be, however,
nothing wrong with following the Sephardic *minhag* if the congregation desires to do so.

November 1986

137. THE RIGHT TO CREATE A NEW CONGREGATION*

QUESTION: A young rabbi, who has settled in the community,
wishes to create a new congregation. Some individuals in the existing
congregations have questioned the need for another congregation
and want to know whether his efforts should be permitted and
supported. What rights do existing congregations possess in this
matter? (M. S. D., Pittsburgh, PA)

ANSWER: It is clear from some of the earlier sources that multiple
synagogues existed in many cities. We, of course, do not know
whether the numbers provided are accurate, but Jerusalem was supposed to have had 394 synagogues, while some sources give the
number as 466 or more at the time of the destruction of the Temple in
70 C.E. (Ket. 105a; J. Meg. 73d; J. Ket. 35c). Tiberias, in the year 300,
had thirteen synagogues (Ber. 8a), while eleven are known to us in
Rome, and a number existed in Alexandria in the first century (Philo
Leg. Ad. Ca. 20). In the Middle Ages Christian, and at times Moslem,
authorities prohibited the repair of synagogues and placed restrictions on the number of synagogues in a city; usually only one was
permitted although there were many exceptions to this rule (*Code of
Theodosius,* XVI 8.22, [450 C.E.]; *Pact of Omar* [655 C.E.]). However,
Baghdad in the thirteenth century had twenty-eight synagogues and
Shushan had fourteen according to Benjamin of Tudela (Alder, ed.,

pp. 51 ff). Benjamin reported multiple synagogues in various other communities, as do various medieval Jewish travelers.

We know from Jewish life in Eastern Europe that many communities possessed a number of synagogues, both for the convenience of the worshippers so that the place of worship was close to their residences, and in order to bring together people of similar professions or crafts (Harold Hammer-Schenk, *Synagogen in Deutschland*; Rachel Wischnitzer, *The Architecture of the European Synagogue*; Imre Heller & Zsigmond Vajda, *The Synagogues of Hungary*). For that matter, seating in the ancient great synagogue of Alexandria was by profession (Suk. 51b). Most European cities had a number of larger synagogues alongside smaller rooms for neighborhood worship (*shtibeleh*). Many of these synagogues were small, met in humble quarters which were owned or rented, and supplemented the large central communal synagogue.

In the lands of Western Europe in which congregations and their officials were supported by taxes, permission to establish a new congregation had to be obtained from the government. If no tax support was desired, they could be, and were, established without approval, as in most instances. There were, however, few specifically Jewish restrictions on establishing new congregations. The traditional sources made a distinction between those individuals who were unaffiliated and banded together to form a new congregation and those who left an existing congregation. The unaffiliated should be encouraged even if a synagogue already existed in the community, and no one should interfere with their desire to perform this *mitzvah* (J. M. K. 3.1; Isaac Bar Sheshet #253; *Shulhan Arukh* Hoshen Mispat 162.7) However, if the new members are going to separate themselves from an existing congregation, they should not be allowed to form a new congregation (*Pit-hei Teshuvah* to *Shulhan Arukh* Hoshen Mishpat 162.6; *Magen Avraham* to *Shulhan Arukh* Orah Hayim 154.23). That was modified by later authorities and permission was granted when the congregants were prone to quarrel if they remained in the same congregation. This allowed multiple congregations with their specific *minhagim* to flourish. The numerous editions of the Rödelheim prayerbooks, among others, attest to such diversity.

Interestingly enough, the traditional literature was much more extensive when it discussed the abandonment or closing of synagogues. From these discussions, it is clear that as long as one synagogue remains in a community which still has a *minyan*, it is possible under various conditions to dispose of the others. This is true in both small towns and in larger communities, although some additional restrictions are applied to the larger communities (Meg. 26a; J. Meg. 3.1; Moses Trani, *Responsa,* Vol. 3, #143; Meyer of Lubin, *Responsa* #59; *Shulhan Arukh* Orah Hayim 153.7, etc.). These discussions also indicate that there have always been quite a number of communities with multiple synagogues. There is virtually no discussion about their establishment in contrast to their dissolution. This also shows us that concern about support for the major synagogue of the city does not exclude the establishment of minor places of worship. Of course, one should not lightly separate oneself from an existing congregation in accordance with the warning by Hillel, "Do not separate yourself from the congregation" (*M.* Pirqei Avot 2:5).

In a large community such as Pittsburgh, nothing should stand in the way of attempting to establish a new congregation, if that seems desirable to some members of the Jewish community. Tradition favors the establishment of synagogues which will satisfy the needs of the worshippers.

In the establishment of a new congregation, the rules and procedures of the Union of American Hebrew Congregations and the Codes of Ethics of the Central Conference of American Rabbis should be followed; they provide guidance and will minimize friction with existing congregations.

November 1983

138. RABBI'S RESPONSIBILITY TO THE UNAFFILIATED

QUESTION: What is the rabbi's responsibility toward the unaffiliated? What is the financial responsibility of a Jew to his religious community? Does a Jew have the right to demand religious services from the community even if he refuses to pay membership fees? (Rabbi B. Cohn, New York, NY)

ANSWER: The financial responsibility of the adult Jew toward religious institutions was first mentioned in the discussion of the half *shekel* (Ex. 30:11 ff), which was demanded of every male above the age of twenty as an atonement. Rich and poor were to provide the same sum. According to some modern Biblical interpreters, this was intended less as a financial contribution and more as a way of taking census. Although the gifts, sacrifices and tithes were regularly contributed to the Temple, the sources did not indicate any mechanism for their collection. Actually, we learn far more from them about the distribution among priests, Levites and the poor.

We, of course, know that the Diaspora Jewish community continued to provide funds for the Temple until its destruction and that the Roman Emperor Vespasian, after 70 C.E., sought to devote those funds to the Temple of Jupiter Capitolina in Rome, causing considerable misery to the Diaspora. The measure, however, eventually lapsed. We do not know what regular contributions were demanded of all Jews who worshippped at the Temple in ancient times.

In the Middle Ages, it was clear that the community could compel (*kofin*) its members to contribute for the sake of charity (*Shulhan Arukh* Yoreh Deah 256.5). Even the poor were to give according to their means (Yoreh Deah 248.1). In matters of communal support and charity, therefore, the pressure of the community was exerted.

All this becomes even clearer when we look at direct support for synagogues. The *Shulhan Arukh* indicated that members of the community could force each other to contribute to the building of the synagogue, the purchase of *Torah* scrolls, etc. (Orah Hayim, 150.1 *kofin zeh et zeh*), and if this was not effective, various forms of excommunication could be, and were, used. The obligation of individuals toward the community went considerably further. For example if a community consisted of only ten adult males, and one of them wished to absent himself during the High Holidays, then the community could force him to attend their services or to obtain a substitute in order to complete the *minyan* (*Shulhan Arukh* Orah Hayim 55.20). In some places they could force each other to engage two, or even more individuals to complete a *minyan*, not only for the High Holidays, but for the regular synagogue services. Traditional sources have set ample precedent for obtaining proper support for religious institutions and using communal force when necessary.

In our age, *herem, nidui* and other lighter forms of punishment have lost their meaning; it would only be appropriate to use those means which are at our disposal, i.e., the restriction of services in life cycle events from the individuals in question. There is, of course, no doubt that those who withhold their support are still considered Jews. It is clear throughout the tradition that even apostate Jews were considered to be Jews in most ways and could be buried by rabbis in the Jewish cemetery at a distance from others (*Shulhan Arukh* Yoreh Deah

34.1, 151.12, 367.1), for even sinners were still considered Israelites (San. 44a). Those under the ban could be buried but with a stone on the coffin; furthermore, there was no *shiva* for them. Individuals who had deeply offended the community, or had been disloyal, were denied services by the *Hevra Qadisha* in eighteenth century Germany. This could extend to no visiting or care while ill, nor would their bodies be prepared for a funeral (Marcus, *Communal Sick-Care*, p. 129). Here, however, we are not dealing with the status of the Jew, rather with the survival of the Jewish religious institutions.

Perhaps most analogous is a nineteenth century Galician question brought to Joseph Saul Nathanson of Lemberg, (*Sheol Umeshiv*, Vol. 3, part A, #58). He was asked by a rabbi in a small community whether the ban on private home services, which then existed in that community, should remain in force. In the discussion Nathanson shows that the ban was originally pronounced as regular services in the synagogue were in danger of lapsing due to the home services — something which he felt was not restricted to the small community of the questioner, but also represented a danger in Lemberg. Even on the Sabbath and holidays, synagogue attendance had diminished. This, in turn, would lead to a shrinking of the income of the synagogue and its inability to support a cantor, the rabbis and teachers. He concluded that it was clearly the responsibility of the rabbinic authorities to control communal life in such a way that the synagogue would be strengthened.

Certainly, such a step to which Nathanson agreed was more stringent than the decision on our part to conduct no private services for unaffiliated individuals. After all, his decision dealt with regular daily religious services, not with a wedding, funeral or *brit*, which occur but seldom.

A similar kind of restriction was imposed on special services at home by the London Jewish community in the eighteenth century; someone who was ill was permitted to hold High Holiday services at home only if he paid the community one guinea and turned the proceeds of the sale of religious honors over to the community (*Taqonot*, London, 1791, in J. Marcus, *Communal Sick-Care*, p. 10).

It would seem clear that the tradition indicates that we can, and should, do everything possible to strengthen synagogue affiliation in our time and to assure the proper support for our religious institutions. Unaffiliated individuals have no right to demand religious services.

April 1975

139. SUPPORT FOR THE UNION OF AMERICAN HEBREW CONGREGATIONS*

QUESTION: Temple B'nai Jeshurun is a founding member of the UAHC and our Board of Trustees feel strongly that they should remain a member of the Union. Do they have an obligation to support our national organization? Who should decide what is an equitable level of support? (Rabbi S. Fink, Des Moines, IA)

ANSWER: The obligation of individuals to support the congregation is clear. Your question, however, deals with the obligation to support a national organization. There are a number of precedents for this, beginning with the duty to support the temple in Jerusalem. Certainly by the first century, and probably earlier, support went hand in hand with the obligations to maintain local synagogues in Babylonia, the Roman Empire and in the Land of Israel. The temple tax was fixed at one half *sheqel* in Exodus (30.11 ff; see also *New Testament*, Matt. 17.24 ff). The sums collected from the Diaspora were considerable and the Romans under Vespasian turned these contributions into the *fiscus judaicus* (Josephus, *Wars*, 7.218; Dio Cassius 66:7.2) which was continued in some form till Julian the Apostate (E. M. Smallwood, *The Jews under Roman Rule*, pp. 375 ff).

This Roman tax was subsequently leveled by various medieval authorities, particularly as the *Opferpfennig* of the Holy Roman Empire which began to be collected in 1342. It was also continued as a Jewish voluntary tax by the patriarchs of Palestine and called *aurim coronarium*.

For further illumination on this subject, we must turn to two directions, one to the system of community taxes which were imposed upon the government assessed or reassessed and collected by the Jewish community. In addition to that, we must look at various internal Jewish taxes levied by bodies broader than the local community.

In 1242 Henry II of England summoned a "Jewish Parliament" and through it allocated taxes on the various Jewish communities of England. This pattern was followed in other lands as well. We find it in Sicily (1489) and in the Spanish communities under James II of Aragon from 1300 onward. Somewhat later, in Poland and Lithuania the "Council of Four Lands" was organized for the purpose of assessing taxes, although it served other internal Jewish functions as well.

In modern times, the Jewish communities of several western lands, particularly Germany and Italy, were recognized as official bodies which could levy taxes locally or nationally and these were then collected by the civil tax authorities. Individuals could, of course, refuse payment but that was the equivalent of resigning from the Jewish community.

The authority for collecting taxes on behalf of the government was established early on the simple principle *dina demalkhuta dina* (B. B. 55a; B. M. 73b). This principle was less than wholly satisfactory, so in the post-Talmudic period the authority was based on *taqanot haqahal*, which were recognized as legal and binding although there was little or no Talmudic basis for them (Rebenu Nisim, *Responsa #2; Pisqei Harosh* B. B. 1.29; Rashba, *Responsa*, Vol. 5, #270; see also Hayim Palaggi *Masa Hayim* and Joshua Abraham Judah, *Avodat Masa*; Finkelstein, *Jewish Self Government in the Middle Ages*). Most of the *taqanot* then dealt with local and regional governmental units and established a strong basis for taxation as well as means of assessment. Regional ordinances are known to us from the Barcelona area (Rashba, *Responsa*, Vol. 3, #412) and of Vallidolid (Finkelstein, *op. cit.*, p. 349 ff) as well as a few other areas.

We should remember that throughout the Middle Ages each individual community also prized its independence. For example, although communities outside the jurisdiction of the of Four Lands approached it from time to time to adjudicate some conflict, it was not certain whether they would follow these decisions (Jacob Katz, "From Ghetto to Zionism" in Isadore Twersky, *Danzig between East and West: Aspects of Modern Jewish History*, pp. 42 ff).

We can see from these sources that although the taxes were often imposed by non-Jewish governmental bodies, the Jewish community organized a taxation system which administered the taxes and unified the communities. Every community had the obligation to support the system and its decisions.

For a discussion of the amount of the taxes and their apportionment we must look at the local community ordinances. There we find that most taxes were levied according to the financial means of the tax payer (Mordecai, B. B. #475; Meir of Rothenburg, *Responsa #497; Pisqei Harosh*, B. B. 1.22). In some instances this was mixed with per capita allocation (Rashba, *Responsa*, Vol. 5, #178, #220, etc.; Vol. 3, #401; *Shulhan Arukh* Orah Hayim 53.23 and commentaries). It was also stipulated frequently that taxes be paid even if the services provided were of no interest to the taxpayer, for example, providing education for all children, defense, police, etc., (Ramah, *Responsa* #241; *Shulhan Arukh* Orah Hayim 53.23 ff; Mahari Mintz, *Responsa* #7). There was always the possibility of appeal. However, payment was to be made before the appeal was heard (*Taqanot Medinat Mähren* #214; Maharik *Responsa* #1, #2, #17; Meir of Rothenburg, *Responsa*, #106, #915). There are complex rules regarding the rights of the individual versus those of the community.

The rabbis through the ages consistently spoke against tax evasion as they realized that this would place an undue burden on others in the community (B. B. 35b, 88b; *Sefer Hassidim*, #671, #1386, #1451). Various *taqanot* dealt with this matter (Finkelstein, *op. cit.*, p. 371; see also *Avodat Masa* and *Masa Hayim*).

These traditional sources enable us to establish that taxes on a broad basis, levied by national or regional bodies, were common. They had the approval of the authorities through the ages. As they were generally levied by representative bodies, those who belonged to the organizations were liable for the taxes and strictures for non-payment were always considered appropriate (Rashba, *Responsa*, Vol. 3, #408; Maharil, *Responsa* #12). Palagi even goes so far as to claim that those who do not pay the amount assessed forfeit their right to the world to come (*Masa Hayim*, Chapt. 15). On a personal note, I must add that my congregation has always paid the full amount of its UAHC dues since the beginning of the system. Some of our leaders have been shocked by the number of congregations who obviously do not contribute their fair share. Congregations which belong to the Union of American Hebrew Congregations are obligated to supported this national organization at the level set by duly elected representative delegates.

July 1986

140. SYNAGOGUE ARCHITECTURE

QUESTION: We are planning to construct a new synagogue and our architect wishes some guidance about synagogue architecture. Are there any specific suggestions of a traditional nature which should be followed? (O. M., Los Angeles, CA)

ANSWER: For guidance on synagogue architecture, we must look at the traditional literature and archaeology. The traditional literature is clear about the orientation of a synagogue which should always be toward Jerusalem. For us in the western world, this means an orientation toward the East (W. Jacob, *American Reform Responsa*, #18). Appropriate citations are presented in that responsum. The ark is to be placed in front of the people and facing toward Jerusalem (*Tos.*, Meg. 4.21).

The *Talmud* stipulated that synagogues be placed on the highest point within the city (Prov. 1.21; Ezra 9.10; *Yad* Hil. Deot 4.23; Shab. 11.1); furthermore, the synagogue should be taller than any other building in the city except perhaps the city hall (Shab. 11a and commentaries; *Tur*; *Shulhan Arukh* Orah Hayim 150.2; *Arukh Hashulhan* 150.1). Of course during the Middle Ages this was specifically prohibited by law, and churches were always placed higher than the synagogues. Under those circumstances the earlier stipulation could be ignored (*Shulhan Arukh* Orah Hayim 150.2 and Isserles, as well as commentaries). As our modern cities are filled with skyscrapers, this ancient specification is generally ignored.

Synagogues were to have an entrance in the East akin to the temple (Num. 3.38; *Tos.*, Meg. 3.1), but this became difficult when synagogues faced eastward in order to orient the worshipper toward Jerusalem. Therefore, the entrance began to be placed in the West (Rashi to M. Meg. 3.12; *Tosfot* to Ber. 6a; *Tur*; *Shulhan Arukh* Orah Hayim 150.5), although some controversy about this remains (Rashi Ber. 6b; Moses Sofer, *Responsa,* Orah Hayim #27). We possess archaeological evidence which demonstrates clearly that entrances of synagogues were shifted in the early centuries of our era when the orientation of synagogues toward the East became a general practice (Landsberger, "The Sacred Direction in Synagogue and Church," *The Synagogue*, ed., J. Gutmann, pp. 188 ff).

Aside from this, it was specified that a synagogue should have windows, as Daniel already prayed while looking out of his window toward Jerusalem (Daniel 6.11; Ber. 34b; *Yad* Hil. Tefilah 5.6; *Tur*; *Shulhan Arukh* Orah Hayim 90.4). Some of these windows should be oriented toward Jerusalem. The *Zohar* even stated that a synagogue without windows was inappropriate for prayer (*Zohar* Piqudei 251.1). There was some controversy about this (*J.* Pes. 1.1, Maimonides, *Responsa*, #21, ed., J. Freimann). Some felt that the synagogue should have a courtyard (*J.* Ber. 5.1; *Shulhan Arukh* Orah Hayim 90.)

As far as the interior is concerned, the ark was to be placed in the eastern wall and the *bimah* in the center, so that all could hear (*Yad* Hil. Tefilah 11.3; *Tur*; *Shulhan Arukh* Orah Hayim 150.5). If, however, the synagogue was sufficiently small, the *bimah* could also be placed at the end (*Kesef Mishnah* to *Yad* Hil. Hagigah 50.4 3.4). The description of the ancient great synagogue in Alexandria made it clear that even a centrally placed *bimah* could not always assure that the people would hear the service. Some authorities felt that the centrally placed *bimah* was akin to the placement of the altar in the ancient tabernacle or the temple (Moses Sofer, *Responsa*, Orah Hayim #19). In modern times, the placement of the *bimah* at the front of the hall is considered an imitation of non-Jewish practice by some and is to be avoided for that reasons (*Hanal Betzion* #8; *Imrei Esh* #7; *Sedei Hemed*, Bet Hak'neset #13). This matter remains controversial and there are Orthodox authorities who permit the building of a synagogue with a *bimah* at the front or worship in such a synagogue (Ezekiel Landau, *Noda Biyehuda*, II, Orah Hayim 18; Solomon Schick, *Responsa*, Even Haezer #118).

From the evidence of existing synagogues, we may see that a variety of different architectural styles were used. The synagogues in Worms and Prague followed the Gothic style. The synagogue of Seville was Moorish. That was true to a lesser extent of the ancient synagogue in Cairo. The seventeenth and eighteenth century synagogues of the small Italian towns like Sienna followed a renaissance pattern in their interior, while the exterior, because of strict Christian laws, appear like late renaissance houses. The wooden synagogues of Poland, which existed to the middle of this century, followed local architectural practices (M. and K. Piechotka, *Wooden Synagogues*). Even a cursory glance at books which deal with synagogues in the last century and a half demonstrates that no uniform architectural patterns were followed. During some periods every effort was made to fit into the general environment, therefore both Gothic and Greek Revival styles were frequent. At other times, an effort was made to establish a Jewish tradition which led to buildings which were vaguely reminiscent of Egyptian temples or Islamic mosques. In more recent times, modern architecture has been widely utilized for synagogues without any hesitation (R. Krautheimer, *Mittelalterliche Synagogen* 1927; J. Gutmann, ed., *The Synagogue*, 1975; A. Kampf, *Contemporary Synagogue Architecture*, 1966; Harold Hammer-Schenk, *Synagogen in Deutschland*, 1981; *Synagogen in Berlin* Zur Geschichte einer zerstörten Architektur, 1983).

Tradition does have some stipulations about orientation, place-ment of the main entrance, the ark, the windows, a courtyard and the *bimah*, but little else. Even these remain rather broad and permit an architect to build a synagogue in virtually any style.

April 1983

141. THE ROOMS BEHIND A SYNAGOGUE ARK

QUESTION: The synagogue ark is now in the eastern wall of the synagogue, as is the general custom. The synagogue needs to expand. It has been suggested that a series of offices and classrooms be built on the other side of the ark. Is this appropriate, or should the ark be on the exterior wall with nothing behind it? (Rabbi N. Hirsh, Seattle, WA)

ANSWER: There is a good deal of discussion on the location of the ark (W. Jacob, *American Reform Responsa*, #18), but virtually nothing about the space behind the wall of the ark. In much of our history, synagogues were part of rather crowded ghettos or tightly packed cities, in which the wall of one structure also formed the wall of the adjacent building, unlike the spacious setting of North America. It was, therefore, unlikely that control over the space on the other side of the wall could be effectively exercised.

A brief review of pictures and plans of more modern synagogues in my possession show that some were freestanding with nothing on the other side of the ark. On the other hand, there were also a large number of synagogues which had rooms for different purposes on the other side of the ark. Some Polish and Hungarian synagogues had schoolrooms located there. Some of the German synagogues show offices, a social hall or robing rooms for rabbi and cantor there (Randolph L. Braham and Ervin Farkas, *The Synagogues of Hungary*; Harold Hammer-Schenk, *Synagogen in Deutschland*; Maria and Kaimierz Piechotka, *Wooden Synagogues*; Rachel Wischnitzer, *The Architecture of the European Synagogue*; Avram Kampf, *Contemporary Synagogue Art*; Richard Krautheimer, *Mittelalterliche Synagogen*; David Davidowitz, *Batei Keneset Bepolin Vehurbanam*).

In American synagogues, both nineteenth and twentieth century, a similar pattern may be found. So, for example, the historic mid-nineteenth synagogue of Savanah, Georgia, has a school wing behind it. The synagogue of Rodef Shalom in Pittsburgh, Pennsylvania, (1907), had a classroom behind the ark and now has a weekday chapel behind it. Temple Shalom in Chicago, Illinois, has an entire school wing behind its ark. The traditional Poale Zedek, in Pittsburgh, Pennsylvania, has a school wing behind the ark. The same pattern may be seen among other Reform, Orthodox and Conservative synagogue buildings. There is, then, no restriction about what may be built behind the ark in a synagogue, especially if that section of the building is completely separated from the synagogue itself.

December 1984

142. A SYNAGOGUE NAMED AFTER A RABBI

QUESTION: May a synagogue be named after the rabbi of the congregation? (Rabbi S. Barack, Minneapolis, MN)

ANSWER: There has been a general reluctance among us to name the synagogue proper after an individual, although subsidiary buildings as school wings and auditoriums have been frequently named after outstanding individuals. Philo referred to Roman synagogues named for Roman Emperors, so there were synagogues of Augustus, Volumnius, Agrippa, Severus and even Herod (H. Vogelstein, *History of the Jews of Rome*, p. 27).

The *Talmud* did not report synagogues named after living individuals although it dealt with a number of instances in which synagogues were named in honor of Biblical figures (Eruv. 21a). There were three synagogues named after Moses in Syria, while others elsewhere were named for Elijah, Ezra, Daniel, etc. That custom has occasionally been followed in later periods, so congregations in the United States have used Biblical names.

In Jerusalem, there are various synagogues named after great Jewish scholars, so we have the Ramban Synagogue which seems to have been built by Nahmanides, after whom it is named, in the year 1267. Similarly, there is Johanan ben Zakai Synagogue, as well as the Judah Hasid Synagogue. More recently, we have the Porat Joseph Synagogue which seems to have been built in 1914 by a Sephardi from Calcutta. These synagogues and others in Israel, especially in Safed and Tiberias, represent both the Sephardic and the Ashkenazic tradition. There are several modern synagogues in Tel Aviv and elsewhere which have been named after significant individuals or generous donors.

In the Middle Ages, the city of Prague had a number of synagogues named after their donors, so the famous old Pinkas Synagogue was named after Rabbi Pinkas Horowitz and was subsequently refurbished by his descendants. There also is the Meisel Synagogue, the Popper Synagogue and the Salkind Zieguiner Synagogue. Prague, however, seems unique in establishing this particular custom in Europe.

In America, a number of congregations have dedicated their sanctuaries to a person without, however, naming them after that individual. So, for example, the Temple of Rodef Shalom Congregation in Pittsburgh is dedicated to the memory of Rabbi J. Leonard Levy, who died shortly after the last mortgage payment was made. He had insisted that there be no formal dedication until this had been done. If my memory serves me correctly, the new temple in Birmingham, Michigan, is named after its donor.

As we can see, synagogues through the ages have been named after individuals, so we must explain the reluctance of our western Ashkenazic tradition to do so. Perhaps it is due to the problem of maintaining a synagogue which had been named after a particular donor. It is probably difficult to attract gifts from others. That is a problem which has been encountered by many of us when refurbishing of a room or wing has had to be undertaken. The offspring of the original donors may not possess their interest or their means, and then the congregation may be helpless. However, this problem would not arise if a temple is named in honor of its rabbi or another outstanding, widely recognized leader.

There would be nothing in tradition which prohibits naming a synagogue after an outstanding rabbi. It would be a fine way of honoring such an individual and assuring a continuation of his ideals.

If your congregation should decide to name its temple for Rabbi Max Shapiro, my honored classmate, it would certainly represent a well-deserved tribute.

March 1980

143. SYNAGOGUE PLANTINGS AND CHRISTIAN LEGENDS

QUESTION: Would Jewish tradition prohibit the planting of certain trees and flowers as landscaping of a synagogue social hall? Is there any prohibition against using the dogwood tree because of Christian legend? (P. S. G., Pittsburgh, PA)

ANSWER: In order to provide a response within the proper framework, it is necessary to answer two broader questions. We must ask about the entire matter of imitating Christian customs (*huqat goyim*) and also discuss the matter of any plantings in connection with the synagogue. We should note that Jewish tradition is very specific about customs of non-Jews which are prohibited and those which are permitted. *Avodah Zarah* (11a) makes it very clear that only customs which are directly connected to idolatrous worship are prohibited (*Shulhan Arukh* Yoreh Deah 178.1). For this reason, it would not be wrong for a Jew to wear garments akin to those of non-Jews, but he should not wear garments which are specifically used in church ritual. The same would be true of the use of non-Jewish music in Jewish services. As long as it is folk music, and not specifically associated with a Christian service, it would be appropriate as shown by Joel Sirkes (*Bayit Hadash* 127).

When we turn to planting around the synagogue, we are faced with the objection of some Orthodox authorities based upon Deuteronomy 16.21, "You shall not plant thee an Asherah of any kind of tree beside the altar of the Lord thy God, which thou shalt make thee." This law has been fully developed in later Jewish tradition by Maimonides (*Yad* Hil. Akum 6.9), who stated that no shade or fruit tree could be planted in the Temple Sanctuary near the altar and also in the courtyards of the Sanctuary, although there was some debate about the latter. However, all this applied only to the Temple in Jerusalem, and later tradition did not connect this with any prohibition against plantings which decorated the exterior of a synagogue; the ancient synagogues at Arsinoe and Palermo had gardens (I. Kraus, *Synagogale Altertümer*, p. 315). In fact, we find no objection until Moses Schick who, in 1870, prohibited such plantings by reasoning that the synagogue is analogous to the Temple (*Responsa* Orah

Hayim 78, 79). Although this objection was widely discussed, it was not accepted by most authorities who cited Yomtov Lippman Heller's comment to *Mishnah* (Midot 2.6) as well as other scholars who felt that his reasoning was faulty. Nothing would have prohibited planting of trees, even in the court of Israel in the Temple of Jerusalem. Some historic *Haggadah* illustrations, which depict the temple, show it surrounded by plantings of shrubbery.

The great modern authority, Shalom Mordecai Schwadron (*Responsa,* Vol. 1, #127; Vol. VI, #17), specifically stated the objection to trees in the Temple of Jerusalem did not apply to synagogues, and only cautioned individuals who decorated their synagogues in this way to make sure that the planting would be somewhat different from that of neighboring churches. He quoted Joseph ben Moses Trani, a sixteenth century scholar (*Responsa* Yoreh Deah #4), who stated that gardens and plantings around synagogues were widespread during his lifetime.

We see that there are no specific prohibitions against planting of any kind of tree, shrub or flowers around the synagogue; only those items which are essential to Christian worship are prohibited.

Now let us turn to the specific matter of the dogwood. There are innumerable legends about a wide variety of flowers, bushes and plants which are connected in some way with Christianity. Medieval Christian art developed a highly sophisticated system of symbolism. There is hardly a common flower or tree which has not been connected with Jesus, Mary or a saint. Sometimes this symbolism has become wide-spread, while on other occasions its use was highly localized. When we turn to the dogwood and legends connected with it, we must distinguish among various species. Two types of dogwood were known in medieval Europe, the *Cornus sanguinea*, a small tree cultivated for its tiny fruit which was bitter. Oil from it was used for lamps. This tree was probably introduced from Siberia. There were references to it in Turner's *Herbal* (1551). In addition, there was the Cornelian cherry (*Cornus mas*). This was an ancient, hardy tree with an interesting bark, small flowers, tasty berries and exceptionally hard wood. It was widely planted in medieval and older times. Ancient legend claimed it provided wood for the Trojan Horse; another stated that Romulus set the borders of Rome by throwing a spear made of this tree, which later sprouted into a fine specimen. Neither one of these dogwoods is known for its blooms, nor has any medieval Christian legend been connected with them; in fact, the

Cornus mas was called "Jew Cherry" in some areas (I. Löw, *Die Flora der Juden*, I, p. 464).

One legend about the dogwood is connected with the spectacular native American variety (*Cornus florida*) with its grand bracts which protect small flowers; it was first described by Mark Catesby (*Natural History of Carolina*, 1731). These trees, as well as the *Cornus stolonifera*, the Western American *Cornus nuttalli*, the Siberian *Cornus alva* and the Japanese *Cornus kousa*, have rather spectacular petals. They bloom in the Middle Atlantic States around Easter; the West Coast *Cornus nuttalli*, with six flower petals, occasionally reaches a height of fifty feet.

Many Indian legends about the dogwood exist, as this spectacular tree seemed to appeal to the imagination. The Christian legend about the dogwood presents an interesting sidelight on the development of Christianity in the United States. In the eighteenth century, after the Shawnees had been converted to Christianity by the Jesuits, they continued to hold some beliefs in the nature deities. A Shawnee legend showed this mixture clearly; when Jesus was to be crucified, the gods told the trees not to participate, but the dogwood permitted itself to be used. It did not split or rot in protest. The deities, therefore, condemned the dogwood, which was then as tall as an oak, to become a small tree. Its floral petals would form a cross; its notches would bleed, and so it would forever bear witness to the Crucifixion. Later Shawnee warriors used the syrup of the dogwood to heal wounds. They thought it was effective because of the connection with Jesus (Vernon Quinn, *Shrubs in the Garden and Their Legends*, 1940, pp. 79 ff). Christian ministers eventually emended the legend slightly so that it no longer reflected pagan influence and added the element that Jesus blessed the dogwood to exonerate it and give it magnificent blooms which would open at Easter in his memory. This American legend remained local and is only rarely repeated nowadays. No medieval art or tales are connected with this story. We can see, therefore, that there is no firm or widespread basis connecting the dogwood with Christianity in the vast system of medieval Christian symbolism.

As such legends are not an essential part of Christianity and are not wide-spread, there would be no objection to planting a dogwood as part of landscaping a synagogue or its social hall. In fact, as so many plants have some loose ties to Christianity through artistic symbolism, we would have to say that if we object to one, we would have to object to all. That would clearly be wrong and contradicts the broad traditional interpretation of *huqat goyim*. Only those matters which are an essential part of the Christian service are objectionable for synagogue use.

October 1977

144. NAMING A BUILDING AFTER A NON-JEW

QUESTION: The non-Jewish widow of a prominent member of a community wishes to provide a new wing for the synagogue; it will contain administrative offices and a portion of the religious school. The wing is to bear her name and that of her deceased Jewish husband. Is it appropriate for a building connected with a synagogue to bear the name of a non-Jew?

ANSWER: It is clear from the Biblical sources which dealt with Solomon's Temple that non-Jews were welcome to worship in the temple (I Kings, 8.41 ff) and participated in its construction as did Hiram, King of Lebanon. Furthermore, non-Jewish sacrifices were acceptable (Meg. 73b), as were gifts by pagans unless made with idolatrous intent (Ar. 7b). Much later the famous Bevis Marks synagogue (1702) in London contained a roof beam which was the gift of Queen Anne. There is no mention of specific memorials requested with these gifts, but they were publicly acknowledged as the gift of non-Jews. So, gifts by non-Jews to the synagogue are acceptable as long as they are used in accordance with the desires of the congregation (*Yad* Hil. Matnat Aniyim 8.8; *Tur* Yoreh Deah 258; *Shulhan Arukh* Yoreh Deah 254.2 and Isserles, 259.4).

As far as the name of the wing is concerned, such buildings have in the past been named for individuals, for the district in which they were located, or the street on which they were found, and these were often not Jewish names. The fact that one donor is a Gentile would not preclude naming the building for this couple. This gift surely demonstrates that the generous widow is one of the *hasidei umot haolam*, and we should grant her appropriate honors.

April 1983

145. MEMORIAL GIFTS

QUESTION: The National Federation of Temple Brotherhoods Board would like to establish a way of honoring deceased members without seeking separate contributions on each occasion of sorrow. Does our tradition encourage equality, or should rank and past service be recognized? What precedent does Jewish tradition provide? (A. Raizman, Pittsburgh, PA)

ANSWER: We should divide this question into two segments, one dealing with honors due to the deceased, and the second with memorial gifts. Judaism has, for along time, stressed equal and simple treatment for all our dead. Rabban Gamliel (Ket. 8b; M. K. 27b), a wealthy Jewish leader of the second century, specified that he be buried in linen shrouds, and encouraged his disciples to follow that example. Such simplicity has been basic Jewish practice ever since. Many European communities carried this matter further and established strict regulations about grave markers to assure that they were equal in size, and in some communities even the inscription was scrutinized to avoid excessive elaboration (Maharam Schick, *Responsa* Yoreh Deah 170; J. Greenwald, *Kol Bo Al Avelut*, p. 380). We have continued to follow these customs with our deceased and try to maintain simple dignity at our funerals and in our cemeteries.

Gifts made in memory of those who are dead also have a long tradition behind them. The custom of reading names of the deceased began in the Rhineland during the Crusades, when lists of martyrs were recited on *Yom Kippur*, and eventually on the last day of the festivals. Later names of those deceased who left a gift to the congregation were added. Still later, this custom spread to the *shabbat* in the form of a *mi sheberakh* recited after the *Torah* reading. Similar blessings can, of course, be recited for the living as well as the dead.

Memorial gifts, therefore, became a way of helping maintain the synagogue and honoring the dead. Naturally, large gifts were encouraged, but we should note that the *mi sheberakh* remained the same whether it was accompanied by a large or a small gift, though at times the specific sums given were announced. A general mood of equality prevailed in most communities (*Or Zaruah* II, 21b; J. Zunz, *Die Ritus*, pp. 8 f; I. Elbogen, *Gottesdienst*, pp. 201 ff).

Equality in the maintenance of religious institutions was emphasized through the ancient Temple tax of one-half or one third *sheqel* per person levied upon Jews throughout the ancient world. It was based on Exodus (30.11-16) and is discussed thoroughly in the Talmudic tractate *Sheqalim*. After the destruction of the Temple, this tax was paid directly to Rome as the *fiscus Judaicus*. This became the basis for the special Jewish taxes in the Middle Ages.

We may conclude that our tradition has sought to honor our beloved dead while maintaining a sense of equality. Perhaps the Brotherhood Board might continue this by providing gifts of books to colleges through the Jewish Chautauqua Society. The number of volumes might vary according to the means available, but that information would remain confidential; everyone would simply know that an appropriate memorial gift had been made. Certainly other means of expressing this thought are possible.

January 1978

146. MEMORIALIZING A KNOWN CRIMINAL

QUESTION: A man has approached the synagogue with the wish to provide a fund. Through it he would like to remember his deceased brother, who died in prison as a convicted felon. Is it permissible to place a plaque bearing this name or to name a fund after him? (F. S., Chicago, IL)

ANSWER: The entire matter of memorial plaques has a dual history. On one hand we have wished from the Talmudic time onward to encourage gifts, yet we have tried to to discourage boasts about such donations. The medieval Spanish scholar Solomon ben Adret (*Responsa* #582) stated that it would be appropriate to list the name of the donor for two reasons and the *Shulhan Arukh* (Yoreh Deah 249.13) agreed:

a. in order to recall the specific wishes of the donor so that the funds would not be diverted to another use;

b. to encourage other donors through the good example of that individual.

The question of donations from people of doubtful reputation or those having a criminal record has also arisen a number of times. It was always felt that such gifts should be accepted, especially as it is a *mitzvah* to support a synagogue and it would be a sin to hinder its performance. There were objections to sacrifices of criminals, but these were not transferred to the synagogue (*Toldot Adam V'Havah*, Havah 23.1; *Shulhan Arukh* Orah Hayim 153.21 and commentaries). However, there was an equally strong feeling that such individuals of dubious reputation should not be honored; *marit ayin* and the honor of the synagogue are involved here.

It is, therefore, clear that although there is a strong tradition for memorializing the deceased through plaques, we should not mention a convicted felon by name. We might affix a plaque which read, "Given by in memory of his dear brother," without the specific name. We should not go further than this.

June 1983

147. MENORAH DECORATIONS FOR A SYNAGOGUE

QUESTION: May a seven-branched *menorah* be used to decorate a synagogue? (D. R., Columbus, OH)

ANSWER: Tradition has avoided the imitation of any object which was used in the ancient Temple in Jerusalem, so a seven branched *menorah* was prohibited (A. Z. 43a), although one with more or less branches was permissible. The *Shulhan Arukh* (Yoreh Deah 141.8) added that it was prohibited if made of any metal (in addition to gold which was used in the ancient Temple), but Sabbatai Cohen, in commenting on this verse, indicated that if it were made of wood, stone or clay, it could be used in the synagogue. In addition to these literary citations, we must be aware of the decorative motif of the *menorah* which was frequently used in ancient synagogues excavated in recent years (Dura Europa, Bet Alpha, Maon, Ostia, etc.). Whatever the Talmudic prohibition, the *menorah* was widely and popularly used in ancient times.

The responsa discussions of the *menorah* deal primarily with the decorations found on it; Zevi Ashkenazi, the eighteenth century authority (*Responsa* #60) stated that as long as the synagogue *menorah* differed from that used in the Temple, it was permissible. There would, therefore, be absolutely no objection to the use of a seven-branched *menorah* in any modern synagogue, certainly not in a Reform Temple.

February 1977

148. ARK AND TORAH PERMANENTLY IN A CHRISTIAN CHURCH

QUESTION: An informal congregation of senior citizens in a Florida retirement community has been meeting regularly for Sabbath and holiday worship services in the meditation chapel of a large Protestant church (United Church of Christ). The church is delighted to have the congregation meet there and has encouraged the group to install an *aron qodesh*, complete with several *Torah* scrolls, as a permanent fixture in the meditation chapel. The chapel, in addition to being part of the church complex, contains stained glass windows with modest cross designs inlaid therein. The size of the windows make it feasible for them to be covered during Jewish worship services. Under these circumstances, is it proper for the congregation to construct a permanent Ark for the *Torah* in this meditation chapel? (Rabbi R. Agler, Vero Beach, FL)

ANSWER: A number of ancillary issues must be discussed in order to put this question into the proper perspective. We must ask what is the relationship of Jews and Judaism to modern Christianity. Second, we should ask whether it is permissible for Jews to worship in a house of worship of another religion. Let us, therefore, turn to these two questions before we discuss the matter of the *Torah* and the Ark placed permanently in a church.

It is clear that non-Jews who are Christians or followers of Islam are not considered idolaters (Issac bar Sheshet *Responsa* #119, Yad Hil. Issurei Biah 14.7; Isserles to *Shulhan Arukh* Yoreh Deah 146.5), although Maimonides also expressed some hesitation on this matter (*Yad* Hil. Aqum 10.2, etc.; see also "Jewish Bridesmaid at a Christian Wedding"). All of this is based on the Talmudic statement which declared that those who had renounced idolatry and accepted the Noahide laws were to be considered *gerei toshav* and no longer as pagans (A. Z. 64b). The Christian Trinity is considered *shituf*; although it may impinge upon monotheism, Christians have, nevertheless, been considered monotheists (R. Tam, *Tosfot* to San. 63b).

Now let us turn to the question of using a church as a synagogue. This question has arisen a number of times in recent centuries and usually when it was necessary to use such a building temporarily for synagogue purposes. For example, the Russian government gave a mosque to Jewish soldiers when the Russians were fighting the Turks in the last century, and Isaac Elhanan Spector permitted such usage (*Ein Yitzhoq*, Orah Hayim #11). It had already been permitted earlier by Abraham Gumbiner (*Shulhan Arukh* Orah Hayim 154.11, note 17). These represented special emergency situations. Such services were, of course, permitted under emergency conditions (David Hoffman, *Melamed L'hoil*, Yoreh Deah #54). The question also has arisen when a church was to be permanently transformed into a synagogue; David Hoffman considered this acceptable (*Melamed Lehoil*, Orah Hayim #20), as did Joseph Saul Nathenson (*Shoel Umeshiv* I, part 3, #72.3,4) despite earlier hesitation (*Tur* Yoreh Deah 142). Some other authorities have provided similar answers (S. B. Freehof, *Contemporary Reform Responsa*, pp. 18 ff).

There is a very old discussion which goes considerably further. An ancient synagogue in Babylonia contained statues of the emperor, yet this synagogue was considered sacred and appropriate for Jewish services (A. Z. 43b). This, of course, was a synagogue and not a place of pagan worship.

Now let us turn to the specific question. We have seen that Christians are considered as monotheists by our tradition and that the temporary use of a church would be permissible. The modern close relations between Christians and Jews have led several Jewish and Christian congregations to use common facilities, as at the Greenwich Village Synagogue in New York, the Heinz Chapel of the University of Pittsburgh and most military chapels in the United States. This has continued for more than a generation in war and peace. We would permit such use especially when all Christian symbols are removable. In our instance, the permanent Christian and Jewish symbols would be covered, and that is acceptable.

Now let us turn to the *Torah* itself. The *Torah* has always been considered the most sacred object of Jewish worship, and every other item is considered auxiliary (*Shulhan Arukh* Orah Hayim 154). The Ark is sacred because of the *Torah* scrolls which it contains (154.1). As long as the *Torah* is treated with respect and proper demeanor, it may be kept in a synagogue or in a private home (Ber. 25b; *Shulhan Arukh* Yoreh Deah 282.8). Non-Jews also have a great respect for the *Bible* and for the *Torah*. The *Talmud* was aware of this feeling (Hul. 92b), which existed among all *gerei toshav*. Christians may handle a *Torah* (*Yad* Hil. Sefer Torah 9.8) and view it (Joseph Mesas, *Mayim Hayim*, Orah Hayim #13; Obadiah Joseph, *Yabiah Omer*, Vol.3, Yoreh Deah #15).

There would be no objection to installing an Ark in a church on a temporary basis in such a way that they may be removed when the Jewish services are over. We would in the late twentieth century, however, raise a serious objection to permanent placement there, not out of animosity towards Christianity, but because of the religious confusion of our age caused by various Christians conversionist groups like Jews for Jesus who have constantly utilized Jewish symbols and Jewish objects in order to entice Jews, both young and old, into Christian congregations. For these reasons, it would be wrong to place an Ark permanently in a church. Furthermore, we would encourage the congregation to establish its own house of worship as soon as possible no matter how humble that might be.

November 1982

149. AN *ALIYAH* TO THE *TORAH* AND CONGREGATIONAL DUES

QUESTION: Are members of a family, which have refused to meet its obligations of dues to the congregation, entitled to be called to the *Torah*? In this instance, the family has resigned from the congregation, but the male member continues to attend. May an *aliyah* be denied to this man as he is unwilling to support the congregation? (Rabbi B. Lefkowitz, Taunton, MA)

ANSWER: The answer to this question hinges on whether an *aliyah* is a right to which any Jew is entitled, a *mitzvah* which he must fulfill or a privilege provided by the congregation and which, therefore, may be restricted. In addition, we must balance the congregational honors with the obligation to maintain a congregation. The traditional literature is not clear on these matters. Those who claim that an *aliyah* is a right base themselves in part on the *Talmud* (Ber. 55a), which states that those who do not read the *Torah* regularly will suffer a shortened life.

Still others claim that it is a *mitzvah*, and of course, it would not be proper to deny anyone the opportunity to perform a *mitzvah*. Some argue that this is indicated by the blessing (*shepatrani*) which a father recites when his son becomes *Bar Mitzvah*; it frees him from further obligation for his son. It would not be possible to deny anyone, even the worst sinner, the opportunity to recite this blessing. However, there is some debate in the traditional literature whether this blessing is necessary and whether it may not be omitted (Isserles to *Shulhan Arukh* Orah Hayim 225.1). The entire matter has been dealt with at length in Efrayim Margolis' *Shaarei Efraim*. As women and children may be called to the *Torah* (Meg. 23a), we need not be too strict on this according to some scholars, including Jacob Emden.

The obligation to maintain the congregation is an ancient one and can be traced back to the Biblical tithe, which was used to maintain the Temple in Jerusalem. It is a *mitzvah* which makes it incumbent for all Jews to contribute to the maintenance of a synagogue as well as other communal institutions (*Shulhan Arukh* Orah Hayim 150.1). In the Middle Ages, wealthy individuals often sought to escape their communal obligations, especially when large assessments were made upon the community by Gentile oppressors. These individuals who possessed means and connections tried to use them to escape the assessments. In many instances the community placed them under the ban in order to force their cooperation (J. Wiesner, *Der Bann*). This clearly indicated that far more serious methods than simply the removal of some synagogue honors were used to elicit the cooperation of all Jews in the maintenance of the Jewish community.

In our age an *aliyah* is considered a special honor by all. This perception should lead us to be careful in selecting those thus honored. The modern scholar, Isaac Z. Sofer (*Mistar Hasofer* #5), has stated that it is quite possible to exclude those who are considered sinners as a way of building a fence and preventing sin from affecting the remainder of the community. He bases this on an earlier decision by Simon ben Zemah of Duran (*Tashbetz* II, #261).

The traditional literature has made no decision on this matter. However, it is also clear that the congregation has the obligation to assure its proper maintenance; those who do not help may be excluded from whatever is perceived to be an honor. It would be permissible to exclude this individual from the privilege of an *aliyah*.

December 1983

150. TICKETS FOR ADMISSION TO THE *YAMIM NORAIM* SERVICES

QUESTION: Is it proper to limit attendance at services for the *Yamim*

Noraim through tickets? May such tickets be sold? What is the traditional and Reform point of view on this? (Rabbi D. Prinz, Teaneck, NJ)

ANSWER: The question which you have asked really deals with the entire matter of support for the synagogue. We have used different ways of eliciting proper support from the Jewish community in various periods of history. The financial obligation of adult Israelites toward religious institutions was first mentioned in the discussion of the half *sheqel* (Ex. 30.11 ff). All men above the age of twenty were obligated for the sum, both rich and poor. Later, the Diaspora Jewish community provided for the regular maintenance of the Temple in Jerusalem; when that Temple was destroyed, the Romans sought to divert this financial resource to the royal treasury (*fiscus Judaius*), which caused considerable misery. That measure eventually lapsed. During the Middle Ages a Jewish community could force its members to help maintain the necessary religious institutions through taxation (*Shulhan Arukh*, Yoreh Deah 256.4; Orah Hayim 150.1). Actually, measures went considerably further, and a community which had only ten males could force them all to be present for the *Yamin Noraim* so that the community could conduct proper congregational services. Anyone who was absent had to obtain an appropriate substitute for the *minyan* (*Shulhan Arukh* Orah Hayim 55.20; Adret, *Responsa* V, #222, Isaac bar Sheshet, *Responsa* I, #518 and #531.) A community could also force an unwilling minority within it to contribute to a synagogue (*Yad* Hil. T'filah 11.1; *Tur,* Orah Hayim 10.50). In the Middle Ages wealthy individuals often sought to escape their communal obligations, especially when large assessments were made upon the community by Gentile oppressors. These individuals who possessed means and connections tried to use them to escape the assessments. In many instances the community placed them under the ban in order to force their cooperation (J. Wiesner, *Der Bann*). This indicated that far more serious methods than simply the removal of some synagogue honors were used to elicit the cooperation of all Jews in the maintenance of the Jewish community.

During the Middle Ages, in France and Germany, it became customary during the pilgrimage festivals to seek gifts for the poor in conjunction with the *Torah* reading. This custom was called *matnat yad* in keeping with the Scriptural injunction of Deuteronomy (16.17). In Spain, this method of raising funds was used only during *Simhat Torah*. Eventually it extended to every *shabbat*, and the sums were used either to help the poor or to maintain the synagogue (Isaac Or Zaruah II, 21b). In connection with this, a prayer for the individual who gave the donation, or his relatives, was recited. This practice was already mentioned in the *siddur* of Amram (I. Ellbogen, *Jüdischer Gottesdienst*, p. 548). Eventually in the Sephardic lands this led to a prayer for deceased relatives also. In some areas, it became customary to auction these synagogue honors. This was done on an annual, monthly, or weekly basis in Italy and at *Simhat Torah* in Germany (Maharil). In North Africa the honors were auctioned on the *Shabbat* of *Pesah* and in Italy, during the *Yamim Noraim* (Azulai).

In various other communities a whole series of prayers were available for an appropriate gift. So, for example, in the community of Fürth there were seven classes of such prayers. The entire practice was probably borrowed from Christianity as early as the ninth century (L. Zunz, *Die Ritus des Synagogalen Gottesdienstes*, pp. 8 ff).

In more recent times the Jewish communities in Western Europe have been supported by a system of government taxation as all other religious communities. Unless an individual specifically declares that he does not wish to support the synagogue, he is taxed; this has led to adequate maintenance for the synagogues of Western Europe.

In America each congregation is totally independent and must rely on the support of its members. Vigorous efforts have been made to assure a generous support. This has led to unusual questions, as "Collecting Synagogue Pledges Through the Civil Courts" (S. B. Freehof, *Recent Reform Responsa*, pp. 206 ff). Solomon Freehof indicated that such an effort is contrary to the spirit and letter of the Jewish tradition, but the fact that the question was asked demonstrates the problem which congregations face.

We, in the larger American cities, are troubled by the problem of support from those unwilling to join a synagogue and who, nevertheless, wish to avail themselves of the services of a synagogue for worship during the High Holidays, or for specific life-cycle events like *Bar/Bat Mitzvah*, funerals, weddings, etc. The synagogue must, therefore, maintain itself with such individuals in mind. Tickets of admission for services during the *Yamim Noraim* may be an appropriate way to do so as long as admission is not denied in cases of financial hardship. Every Jew, of course, has the right to worship in a synagogue, and the *mitzvah* of worship can not be denied to anyone, however, there is the equally important *mitzvah* of proper support for a synagogue. The obligation of worship need not be carried out in a specific synagogue. It is the prerogative of anyone to establish a *minyan* if they wish, and nothing else is necessary for a Jewish service. We must, of course, always also be sensitive to Jews who are poor and never exclude them from our services. Most of our synagogues make every effort to reach out to this group and make them feel at home in our synagogue and wave all obligations for dues. We must continue to do so.

In some congregations no tickets are sold, but are issued to all members. This system encourages synagogue membership. We have established this policy at Rodef Shalom in Pittsburgh so that individuals who have permanently settled in the city will join the congregation at whatever dues they can afford. This varies from nothing to large sums. This system eliminates the objection to the sale of tickets, however, in areas where such a system is not feasible, the sale of tickets is an acceptable way to raise revenue necessary for the maintenance of the synagogue.

May 1986

151. SYNAGOGUE DUES FOR A WIFE

QUESTION: A man of considerable means, who is quite generous to the local Jewish charities, has resigned his membership in the congregation as he finds "organized religion repulsive." His wife, however, wishes to remain a member. As she works at a minimum wage level, she wishes to pay dues commensurate with her income. Should this be permitted? Will it set a precedent for others? (Rabbi M. Shapiro, Minneapolis, MN)

ANSWER: Financial obligation of adult Jews toward religious institutions was first mentioned in the discussion of the half *sheqel* (Ex. 30.11 ff). All men above the age of twenty were obligated for the sum, both rich and poor. Later, the Diaspora Jewish community provided for the regular maintenance of the Temple in Jerusalem; when that Temple was destroyed, the Romans sought to divert this financial resource to the royal treasury, which caused considerable misery. That measure eventually lapsed. During the Middle Ages, a community could force its members, through taxation, to help maintain the necessary religious institutions (*Shulhan Arukh*, Yoreh Deah 256.4; Orah Hayim 150.1). Actually, measures went considerably further, and a community which had only ten males could force them all to be present for the High Holidays, so that the community could conduct proper congregational services. Anyone who was absent had to obtain an appropriate substitute for the *minyan* (*Shulhan Arukh* Orah Hayim 55.20; Adret, *Responsa* V, #222; Isaac bar Sheshet, *Responsa* I, #518 and #531.) A community could also force an unwilling minority within it to contribute to a synagogue (*Yad* Hil. Tefilah 11.1; *Tur* Orah Hayim 10.50).

In this instance, we are, of course, not only discussing the general obligations, but also the manner through which this obligation shall be determined. We must ask ourselves about the nature of the husband's obligation toward his wife. It is clear that he is responsible for her maintenance, i.e., clothing and food. There is only a quarrel in the rabbinic literature whether food, clothing and shelter are a Biblical or a rabbinic obligation (Ket. 47b ff; Git. 11b ff; *Sheeltot* 60; *Yad* Hil. Ishut 12.2; *Tur* Even Haezer 69; Ket. 89a, etc.)

Furthermore, the *Talmud* quite clearly stated, "The wife ascends with her husband, but does not descend with him." This indicated that a woman should be supported in accordance with her own standards, albeit those of her husband have diminished (Ket. 48a, 61a).

Clothing, and even perfumes, if the husband's means permit them, were considered the wife's due (Ket. 47b, 64a, 66b). In addition, a certain amount of spending money had to be allocated each week (Ket. 64b; *Yad* Hil. Ishut 12.10). All of these obligations were fixed unless a woman chose to support herself completely from her own earnings (Ket. 58b).

Medical obligations were included (*M*. Ket. 4.5, 51a). He also had to ransom her if she became a captive (*J*. Ket. 29a; *Yad* Hil. Ishut 14.18; Ket. 52a ff), an unfortunately frequent occurrence in the Middle Ages. He was obligated for her burial (Ket. 4.2, 48a, 46b).

All of these statements indicate that the husband is responsible for the complete maintenance of his wife. This surely includes synagogue membership in accordance with his means and status.

We must especially note that the husband was obligated to pay for various sacrifices which his wife owed to the temple (*J*. Yeb. 14a; Sotah 17d; Ket. 29a; *Tos*. Ket. 4.11; Sifrei [ed. Horowitz] #13; *M*. Edyot 2.3; Mjd. 35b; Nazir 24a; also *Tosfot* to Nazir 24a; B. M. 104a). These statements, which dealt with the obligations to the ancient Temple, are absolutely comparable to synagogue obligations in our age.

As the woman in question will not provide for herself solely from her own income for any of her normal needs, and will share the income of her husband, as is proper, then this should also be the basis for her synagogue dues in accordance with the mood of all statements cited.

June 1984

152. CONGREGATIONAL MEMBERSHIP AT THIRTEEN

QUESTION: A parent who is dissatisfied with his congregation wishes to drop his membership, but nevertheless, would like to have his thirteen-year-old son continue his education beyond *Bar Mitzvah*. The congregation's policy insists on parental affiliation for enrollment in the religious school. Should this policy be changed in order to permit a thirteen-year-old to affiliate in his own right? (Rabbi J. M. Brown, Long Beach, CA)

ANSWER: This question involves the obligation of a parent toward affiliation and education for her child as well as the obligation of a congregation to provide education for children. An accompanying responsum on *"Bar/Bat Mitzvah* Certificates" makes it quite clear that the education beyond the age of thirteen has always been encouraged by our tradition. Although technically thirteen is the age in which the individual can be viewed as an adult and reckoned toward a *minyan*, this is an unrealistically low level in a society in which secular education extends almost a decade further. As the general society mandates school attendance through age sixteen or beyond, the Jewish community can certainly demand no less. Our tradition often dealt with individuals in an environment in which the vast majority of people were illiterate or placed little emphasis on education. Nevertheless, we always stressed the need to educate at least to the age of thirteen. It is, therefore, clear that the father has an obligation to continue to educate his child and that the child has a continued obligation for his own education beyond the age of thirteen.

This obligation can, however, only be carried out by a synagogue if it possesses adequate financial means. In the modern American Jewish community, this is provided through synagogue membership. The financial obligation of adult Jews toward religious institutions was first mentioned in the discussion of the ancient half *sheqel* (Ex. 30.11 ff). All men above the age of twenty were obligated to give it, both rich and poor. Later the Diaspora Jewish community provided regular maintenance for the temple in Jerusalem. When the Temple was destroyed, the Romans sought to divert this financial obligation to the royal treasury, which caused considerable misery. That measure eventually lapsed. During the Middle Ages a community could force its members through taxation to help maintain the necessary religious institutions (*Shulhan Arukh* Yoreh Deah 256.5; Orah Hayim 150.1). Actually, measures went considerably further, and a community which had only ten males could force them all to be present for the High Holidays so that the community could conduct proper congregational services. Anyone unable to be present had to obtain an appropriate substitute for the *minyan* (*Shulhan Arukh* Orah Hayim 55.20; Adret, *Responsa* V, #222, Isaac bar Sheshet, *Responsa* I, #518 and #531). A community could force an unwilling minority within it to contribute to a synagogue (*Yad* Hil. Tefilah 1.1; *Tur* Orah Hayim 10.50).

The obligations of a congregation vary according to the nature of the community. In a large community, with many congregations and numerous unaffiliated individuals who do nothing to maintain the congregation, a congregation may properly exclude those who are unwilling to bear the necessary financial obligation from its services (as long as there is no financial need). Under those circumstances the community as a whole may need to provide some services, such as education for the unaffiliated. The same goal could be attained by levying a charge equal to that of membership for any specific services provided such as education, marriage, the naming of children or burial.

In a small community, the congregational obligations are somewhat different as the congregation virtually possesses the status of a community. Again various devices may be used to obtain the necessary financial support from the unaffiliated (W. Jacob, "Limitation of Congregational Membership," *American Reform Responsa*, #9).

Membership at age thirteen should not be among these methods. Tradition considered such a person as an adult, but did not expect financial independence from him. This would represent a bad precedent. If the parent does not wish to affiliate, and can not be dissuaded from that decision, then the charge for religious education should be equal to that of membership (providing there is no financial need); this is currently done by some congregations. Jewish education without any parental involvement is deficient, but it is far better than no Jewish education at all. Perhaps some individuals within the congregation leadership can take the place of the *bet din*, which traditionally looked after the education of orphaned or neglected children, and also provided some psychological support for their education.

In summary then, the obligation to provide an education continues to rest both upon the congregation and upon the family, and methods to finance it should be readily available.

May 1981

153. CANTILLATION OF THE TORAH

QUESTION: May the chanting of the *Torah* on the High Holidays be introduced to my synagogue? What is the reason for the Reform practice of not chanting the *Torah*? (Rabbi R. Lehman, New York, NY)

ANSWER: The question which you have asked really touches upon the entire matter of cantillation and its background. The origin of this custom is obscure. It is first mentioned in the *Talmud* (Meg. 32a) with the statement: "Rabbi Yohanan said, anyone who does not read *Scripture* with a pleasant voice or teach with song, to him applies the Biblical verse, "I have given you statutes and you have not done well with them" (Ez. 20:25). This statement was made in conjunction with a number of others that dealt with the reading of *Scripture*. All of them have the appearance of having dealt with widespread customs. In the Talmudic and Medieval periods the cantillation was taken for granted although the name under which it is known, "*tropp*," was borrowed from the Greek term *tropos*, meaning melody or mode. The cantillation both for special holidays and the ordinary Sabbath began to vary in different parts of the world as they were influenced by local music.

The only Medieval opponent to chanting the *Torah* was Maimonides, who was unfavorably disposed toward all music, and only grudgingly permitted it in the service of God (*Responsa* #224, ed., J. Blau). Rashi, in his comments to *Berakhot* (62a), provided some insight into the cantillation of the *Torah* and the prophetic portion in France in the tenth century, which was accompanied by appropriate hand motions (*cheironomy*).

During the Middle Ages, not only the Scriptural reading but also the *Mishnah* and the *Torah* were chanted. The oldest fragment of the

Talmud displays cantillation marks; a *Mishnah*, printed as late as 1553, also contains such marks.

In ancient and medieval times, without doubt, cantillation was used an an educational device as well as a way of rendering the service more beautiful. The cantillation marks for the *Torah* readings are, of course, of even greater importance as punctuation and accent marks. They have been closely studied in that sense. Musicological studies by Idelsohn and Werner show that the music used both for the Sabbath and the holidays follows old oriental modes.

Israel Jacobson, the founder of the Reform Movement, sought to remove the cantillation along with other forms of music which had become distasteful, as for example, the singing of the cantor accompanied by a bass and a soprano, one standing on each side and harmonizing. As the musical education of cantors in the eighteenth century seems to have been poor in many places synagogue music needed reform, and there was movement in this direction in Cassel, Seesen and Berlin. However, the synagogues in Seesen and Berlin soon had cantors again and presumably began the cantillation of the *Torah* once more.

In the American Reform congregations, the cantillation lapsed principally due to the fact that most congregations did not employ a cantor and relied on the rabbi or laymen to read the entire service. In those congregations which have had a cantorical tradition Biblical selections have often continued to be chanted, and there is a growing interest in returning to the cantillation in our time. We should also note a Talmudic discussion which treated both the role and the payment of a cantor. In the *Talmud* (Ned. 37a) there is a discussion about the permissibility of paying a Hebrew teacher since the teaching of the *Torah* is a mandate incumbent upon him and all of us. The *Talmud* comments (God speaking to Moses): "Just as I have a taught you without pay, so you teach without pay." In that case how can a *melamed* accept payment? Two answers are given by the *Talmud*. One stipulates that he receive pay for guarding the children. The other explanation states that he is not paid for the actual teaching of the *Torah* but for teaching the punctuation and the cantillation (*pisuk hata'amim*). Clearly this placed cantillation into a secondary rank considerably less important than the *Torah* itself. One could dispense with it.

There would, therefore, be nothing in the Reform tradition to prevent the use of cantillation for the *Torah* reading. If it is done on the holidays it should also be done on *shabbat*. There should be some consistency in the pattern which is developed by the congregation.

January 1975

154. USE OF THE *TORAH* FOR FUNDRAISING

QUESTION: A number of congregations have engaged in a "*Torah* writing project." Each letter of the *Torah* is paid for through a donation of one dollar toward the congregation. This is a fund-raising project utilizing the *Torah*. The *Torah* itself will be written by a scribe in the traditional manner. Is this method of using the *Torah* for fund-raising appropriate?

ANSWER: We should remember that the *Torah* gains a special status when transferred to a synagogue, then the officers of the community possess jurisdiction over it (Joseph Colon, *Mahariq*, Vol. 2, p. 173). This has become the classic view toward a *Torah*, unless an individual formally (before two witnesses) states that his presentation of a *Torah* is only a loan and not a gift, it remains the property of the synagogue and may not be removed, transferred or sold by any individual (Bet Yoseph, *Tur*, Yoreh Deah 259; *Shulhan Arukh* Yoreh Deah 259). This, then, makes it clear that a *Torah* once acquired is completely the possession of the synagogue, and the officers have great discretion in what is done with it.

The same section of the *Shulhan Arukh* discusses what may be done with items given to the synagogue. The degrees of sanctity attached to objects is described, and there is general agreement that a *Torah* may be sold to provide for the poor and to support the study of the *Torah*. This includes the education of adults as well as children. The *Shulhan Arukh*, of course, discusses a *Torah* which has already been completed. The discussion does indicate that fund-raising through the project described may be in keeping with tradition.

We should also remember that there is considerable tradition for making a gift when called to the *Torah* (*nedavah*), and in many Orthodox congregations the sum pledged is publicly stated, alongside with a blessing recited for the individual's family or anyone else whom he may propose. Fund-raising for the general support of the congregation has thereby been undertaken in this most sacred segment of the service. We have eliminated this practice as objectionable and an unnecessary intrusion to the spirit of the service, yet this indicates that the reading of the *Torah*, at least, may be used for fund-raising.

During the period when the *Torah* is written, the scribe must perform the task with special dedication, so he is instructed to concentrate on the sacredness of his task (Meg. 18b). When writing the name of God, he must be pure and show proper devotion (*Yad* Hil. Tif. Mez. 1-10; *Shulhan Arukh* Yoreh Deah 270 ff). Thus, a certain degree of sanctity is attached to the process of writing, yet the separate sections of the *Torah* are not given any special status until they are combined into a scroll. This is true of sections which have been completed and are free of error and those which contain errors. The latter are buried as any other book which contains the name of God.

The manner used for raising funds to obtain a *Torah* has not been discussed in detail. An individual may pay for a *Torah* and could "finish the writing of a *Torah*" by assisting in completing the last letters and, thereby, fulfill the *mitzvah* of writing it. A number of individuals may participate in that process and share the cost. There would, therefore, be nothing in our tradition which would prevent using this method of fund-raising as long as it is done in the proper spirit, especially if emphasis is given to the educational value of the project, as well as its financial assistance to the congregation.

November 1980

155. THE FORTUNE TELLER

QUESTION: The congregation is going to have a "Hungarian Night Dinner Dance," and some people have asked whether it would be permitted to have a fortune teller work there as an authentic Magyar touch. Is there anything in our tradition which would oppose this? (Rabbi L. Winograd, McKeesport, PA)

ANSWER: There are strong traditional negative statements about sorcery, witchcraft and fortune telling. They are based upon verses in Leviticus and Deuteronomy (Lev. 19.26; 31; Deut. 18.10, 11; as well as Ex. 22.17). The prohibition includes soothsayers and fortune tellers of all kinds. There are numerous discussions in the *Talmud* (Hul. 7b; 95b; Ber. 33b; Shab. 75a, 152a; San. 65a ff; Pes. 113b; Ned. 32a, etc.). The matter is also treated in the various books of *mitzvot*, for example, *Sefer Hamitzvot* (*lo ta-aseh* 8, 9, 31, 38), as well as by Maimonides' Code (*Yad* Hil. Akum V'huqotehem 11.14 ff) and the *Shulhan Arukh* (Yoreh Deah 179). There are some modern discussions which are equally negative (*Responsa Da-at Kohen* 69). It has sometimes proven difficult to remain distant from superstitious practices of our non-Jewish neighbors, but the effort was always made. The medieval discussions are summarized by Berliner (*Aus dem Leben der deutschen Juden im Mittelalter*, pp. 84-104).

It is quite clear that tradition has strongly opposed using or consulting fortune tellers, witches, sorcerers, necromancers or anyone else who utilizes magic in order to deal with the future. It would be well, therefore, to avoid the inclusion of a fortune teller in the planned synagogue party. This might make the affair less authentic Hungarian, but more authentically Jewish.

February 1984

156. SUNDAY MORNING BAR/BAT MITZVAHS*

QUESTION: It is no longer possible for the congregation to schedule the large number of *Bar/Bat Mitzvahs* which recent growth has imposed on *shabbat* morning, Friday evening or even *shabbat* afternoon, without making this a meaningless ceremony. Would it be possible, therefore, to schedule Bar/Bat Mitzvah on Sunday morning and have the *Torah* read as part of the regular week-day morning service? (Rabbi M. Winer, Commack, NY)

ANSWER: It is, of course, the desire of the *Bar/Bat Mitzvah* to proclaim publicly that the youngster can now be part of the *minyan* (Meg. 23a). Participation in a service has been used for this purpose for several millennia. For us, *Bar/Bat Mitzvah* also recognizes the youngsters' achievements in Hebrew and religious studies, encourages some knowledge of the liturgy, and tries to establish the habit of regular worship attendance for both parents and children. This means that the public service at which the festivities take place seeks to strengthen the religious life of the individual as well as the congregation. *Bar/Bat Mitzvah* should, therefore, be part of regularly scheduled public service.

Traditionally such public services at which the *Torah* was read were held on *shabbat* morning and afternoon, as well as Monday and Thursday morning. In addition, of course, the *Torah* was read on *Rosh Hodesh* and the various festivals, which are also suitable for *Bar/Bat Mitzvah*. In many Reform congregations the *Torah* is regularly read on Friday evening, an American innovation instituted in this century, which has become part of our established congregational practice.

Each of these occasions represents a normal time of regular public worship. We are interested in strengthening all public services, especially those on a *shabbat* morning so that this day will be a day of rest, worship and celebration for us and our congregants. Permission for *Bar/Bat Mitzvahs* on Sunday morning would move us away from this emphasis.

We would, therefore, urge that all *Bar/Bat Mitzvahs* be scheduled on *shabbat*, even if it means that a number of children will share this occasion.

November 1985

157. *BAR/BAT MITZVAH* CERTIFICATES

QUESTION: It is Temple policy to grant *Bar/Bat Mitzvah* certificates at the beginning of the confirmation year approximately two and a half years after the *Bar/Bat Mitzvah* and not at the ceremony itself. This represents a congregational effort to assure the continuing education of the members' children. Some children and some parents have objected and consider this as inappropriate coercion. How far should a congregation go to assure the education of its children? (Rabbi J. Brown, Long Beach, CA)

ANSWER: It is, of course, clear that the ceremony of *Bar/Bat Mitzvah* stands on its own merit and has no relationship to any certificate which may or not be issued. Certificates represent a recent innovation. On the other hand, as these parents and children are anxious about the certificates, they seem to be meaningful, and so represent an appropriate tool to encourage Jewish education. We must, therefore, ask what standards of education were set by our tradition. Is there any age when the obligation ceases for the parents or for the children?

Our tradition has encouraged education in all periods of our history. The parental duty was already presented in the well-known verse, "And you shall teach them diligently to your children" (Deut. 6.7). In

Maimonides' *Sefer Mitzvot*, this commandment stood as number seven among the positive commandments. The *Talmud* made education the father's duty (Yoma 82a; Suk. 2b; Nazir 29a, etc.). There was some controversy in Talmudic and later times about the extent of obligation for women's education (Nazir 28b, 29a; Yoma 82a; *Or Zarua* II, 48; *Yad* Hil. Talmud Torah, etc.). Generally women received little formal education until modern times. There was also controversy over a mother's responsibility for the education of her sons if her husband failed or could not provide an education (Er. 81a; *Mahatzit Hasheqel* 343; Meir b. Baruch *Responsa*, Vol. 4, #20; Hatam Sofer, *Responsa* #24, etc.). Although the mother may have limited direct responsibility, anything that she accomplished was considered praiseworthy. If the mother failed, then the *bet din* could assume the responsibility (*Terumat Hadeshen* 94; *Yad* Hil. Shevuot 12.8; *Magen Avraham* 640.3). Of course, when a boy reached thirteen and his father recited the blessing which freed him from further obligation for his child (*shepatrani*), then educational obligations also ceased (Isserles to *Shulhan Arukh* Orah Hayim 225.2). A Talmudic authority indicated that a man should struggle with the education of his son until the age of twelve (Ket. 50a), yet various medieval sources indicated that education was generally pursued to the age of sixteen (*Huqei Torah* I, 3; II, 5; III).

The eleventh century *Huqei Torah* provided extensive rules and curricula for every facet of education for children and adults. Similar rules are also found scattered through the responsa literature and the books of *minhagim* from Gaonic times onward (M. Güdemann, *Geschichte des Erziehungswesens*, Vols. I, II, III).

The innumerable injunctions on the part of the *Mishnah* and *Talmud* to continue studying make it absolutely clear that adult education is obligatory for every Jewish male with statements like, "The study of *Torah* outweighs all other commandments" (Peah 1.1); "The world rests upon three things, upon *Torah*, worship and acts of kindness" (Pirkei Avot 1.2); "He who does not increase knowledge decreases it" (Ibid. 1.13). Furthermore, a *Bet Hamidrash* always accompanies the synagogue (*Tos.* Ber. 11b, 37b; *Or Zarua* II, 3; Adret, *Responsa* I, #210; III, #318; IV, #311, #417; Simon b. Zemah, *Responsa* II, #185, #217, etc.). Those who study are honored by being called to the *Torah* or are given other communal and synagogal recognition.

Widespread communal pressure insisted on universal education for men, and it remained effective even in difficult times. Titles were used as another form of recognition for advanced study, so *rebbe, gaon* and *haver* have been used in various periods to encourage further education.

We must note that all of these statements which are largely, but not entirely, limited to boys would also apply to girls for us as Reform Jews. Equality of the sexes has been a hallmark of our movement since its beginning.

One of the concerns expressed within the Reform movement when *Bar/Bat Mitzvahs* were re-emphasized or re-introduced was the danger of stopping education at thirteen. Every discussion of *Bar/Bat Mitzvah* has stressed the need for continued education at least through Confirmation, if not through high school and beyond. The latest responsum written by this committee on *Bar/Bat Mitzvah* does so as well. Various congregations have used different methods to attain this goal. Certainly the method utilized in Long Beach effectively exerts communal pressure toward continued education. Such pressure is in keeping with our tradition and should be maintained.

May 1981

158. *BAR MITZVAH* OF A CONVERT

QUESTION: A lad, born to a Jewish father and a non-Jewish mother who has received a Jewish education through the years, has begun his preparation for *Bar Mitzvah*. May he become *Bar Mitzvah* without formal ritual conversion in our congregation, which does not accept patrilineal descent? (G. Sucov, Pittsburgh, PA)

ANSWER: According to tradition the children of such a mixed marriage follow the status of the mother (*M.* Kid. 312; Maimonides, *Yad* Hil. Issurei Biah 15, 3 and 4). Thus, this child would at birth be considered a Gentile. According to tradition, he could at that time be converted to Judaism. The process is described by Maimonides (*Yad* Hil. Issurei Biah 14) and *Shulhan Arukh* (Yoreh Deah 268, especially 268.7, 8). The necessary elements are circumcision, a ritual bath, (in the days when the temple existed, a sacrifice), and of course, the willingness to observe all the commandments. All this is based on a Talmudic discussion (Yeb. 46). Such a conversion takes place before a *bet din* consisting of three members (Yeb. 46b, 47a).

These traditional sources are explicit on the requirements, but considerable discussion about them exists in the *Talmud*. For example,

R. Eliezer stated that if a prospective male convert was circumcised *or* took a ritual bath, he was considered a proselyte. R. Joshua insisted on both, and his point of view was adopted (Yeb. 46b), but we might well agree with R. Eliezer. Furthermore, there was also an earlier controversy between Hillel and Shammai who disagreed about a prospective male convert who was already circumcised. Bet Shammai insisted that blood must be drawn from him, while Bet Hillel stated that one may simply accept his earlier circumcision without drawing blood (Shab. 135a). The rabbinic authorities decided in favor of Bet Shammai (*Shulhan Arukh* Yoreh Deah 268.1; *Yad* Hil. Issurei Biah 14.5). All sources agree that a child converted in this way may renounce that conversion upon growing up and not be considered an apostate but simply as a Gentile (*Shulhan Arukh* Yoreh Deah 278.7). Clearly, there were differences of opinion about steps necessary for the ritual of conversion in ancient times. The *Talmud* also contains a variety of opinions about the desirability of accepting converts. These reflect historic competition with Christianity, persecution, etc. in the early centuries of our era.

The ritual elements emphasized by modern Orthodoxy have been given a secondary role by the Reform movement. Emphasis instead has been placed upon a thorough study of Judaism, the acceptance of Jewish ideas and the Jewish way of life. For this reason, the Central Conference of American Rabbis, in 1892, decided that any Reform rabbi, together with two other witnesses, could accept converts without the traditional initiatory rites. A child (if a boy, presumably circumcised) would be accepted through declaration of the parents that they intend to raise their child as a Jew, the process of Jewish education, *Bar/Bat Mitzvah* and Confirmation ("Report on Mixed Marriage and Intermarriage," *C.C.A.R. Yearbook*, 1947). This has continued to be the pattern for many Reform conversions of children.

We can see from the traditional sources that there is ample ground for lenience in ritual matters, especially when a couple has made every effort to educate their child as a Jew and intend him to live a Jewish life. Our attitude might well be reflected by the Midrashic statement, "Whenever a convert comes to us we welcome him with an open hand and seek to bring him under the wings of the *shekhinaah*" (*Lev. Rabbah* 2.9). Therefore, we should welcome this lad and accept his *Bar Mitzvah* as a further step to becoming an adult Jew. That occasion should be treated like any other *Bar/Bat Mitzvah*.

October 1977

159. *BAR MITZVAH* DURING THE MOURNING PERIOD

QUESTION: A young man's mother has died and has been buried three weeks prior to the scheduled *Bar Mitzvah*. May the *Bar Mitzvah* be held, or should it be postponed? (Rabbi F. Pomerantz, Closter, NJ)

ANSWER: The traditional literature says virtually nothing about the ceremony of *Bar/Bat Mitzvah*. When signs of puberty are observed in a young male, he is considered to be an adult, and his father may recite the blessing which frees him of responsibility for his son (*Genesis Rabbah* 63.10). Eventually the age of thirteen became fixed as the age of adult religious responsibility (*M.* Pirqei Avot 5.25), although this was sometimes debated (Luria, *Yam Shel Shelomoh* to B. K. 7.37). When a young man has reached the proper age, he is permitted to put on *tefilin* and has the right to be called to the *Torah* (Meg. 23a; *Or Zarua* 2.20 #43; *Tur* Orah Hayim 37, etc.). The discussions of these matters say nothing about a special ceremony or festivals. The ceremony of *Bar Mitzvah* seems to have its origin in the Middle Ages and probably did not become wide-spread until the fourteenth century (L. Löw, *Die Lebensalter in der jüdischen Literatur*, pp. 210 ff). For this reason, there is nothing in the traditional literature which deals directly with the question which you have asked.

We must, therefore, turn to analogies in the law regarding marriage and the mourning period. It is a general rule that marriages should not take place during the period of *sheloshim*, i.e., the first thirty days of mourning (M. K. 23a) unless everything has already been prepared for the marriage. Then it may take place with subdued festivities. After thirty days, the marriage may take place with the usual festivities (*Shulhan Arukh* Yoreh Deah 392.1). In each of these cases, we are dealing with a marriage and a family in which a father or mother has died. The *Talmud* also discusses the example of a death which occurred just prior to a marriage. In that instance, as everything is ready, the marriage takes place and is followed by the funeral. Seven days of subdued marriage festivities are held and are followed by seven days of mourning (Ket. 3b, 4a). If, however, the burial has taken place prior to the marriage, then the wedding would be celebrated and be followed by the seven days of mourning and then the seven days of wedding festivities. I should add that these procedures are followed only if it is impossible to postpone the wedding. If it can be postponed, then it should be held after the *shiva* has ended (*Shulhan*

Arukh Yoreh Deah 342). All of these decisions are based on the fact that the commandment, "Be fruitful and multiply" (*peruh urvuh*), is of primary importance and takes precedence.

In the case of a *Bar/Bat Mitzvah*, there is no conflict of commandments. Therefore, there would no reason to postpone the *Bar/Bat Mitzvah*, as it simply consists of the act of being called to the *Torah*. There should, of course, be no *Bar/Bat Mitzvah* in the period between death and the funeral. This is the period of *aninut* when one does not attend the synagogue nor recite *shema* or the *tefilah* (M. K. 23b; *Shulhan Arukh* Yoreh Deah 341). In the next period, however, one may leave home to worship at the synagogue. Therefore, it would be appropriate to have a *Bar/Bat Mitzvah* during the *shiva* (*Shulhan Arukh* Yoreh Deah 393.2).

A *Bar/Bat Mitzvah* held under these circumstances should be accompanied by subdued festivities. The religious ceremony itself may be conducted as planned.

March 1984

160. NON-JEWISH PARTICIPATION IN *BAR/BAT MITZVAH* SERVICE*

QUESTION: A child of a mixed marriage is about to be *Bar Mitzvah*. It is customary for the parents to participate in the service. Would it be possible for the non-Jewish parent to also participate? In this instance, the father is Christian and the mother is Jewish. Are there any limits on participation? (Rabbi L. Mahrer, Topeka, KS)

ANSWER: The general question has been answered in a responsum entitled, "Participation of Non-Jews in a Jewish Public Service" (W. Jacob, *American Reform Responsa*, #6). We must now turn to specific participation in the *Bar/Bat Mitzvah* service. In this instance, the non-Jewish spouse has been very much involved in raising the child and may or may not have been somewhat active in Jewish life. It is clear that we want to include the non-Jewish spouse in order to make him continue to feel at home in the synagogue and to emphasize the *Bar/Bat Mitzvah* as a family occasion. There are, however, limits in which our Reform tradition and good judgment would indicate. We would recommend the following procedure:

1. It would be inappropriate for the non-Jewish spouse to lead the major segments of our service, to proclaim the traditional *berakhot*, or

phrases like, "Who has commanded us" or "Who has chosen us." Such statements which express specific Jewish sentiments and ideas should only be recited by Jews.

A minority of the Responsa Committee felt that a non-Jewish spouse should not participate in any portion of the formal service, but that such participation should be restricted to a personal prayer or statement directly connected with the *Bar/Bat Mitzvah*. In that way family feelings and the bond between parents and children could be stressed while remaining completely honest about the nature of this service which is specifically Jewish.

Some members of the committee felt that participation in the earlier part of the service is appropriate if restricted to:

a. some specific psalms or responsive readings;

b. to the preliminary portions of the service before the formal service begins, i.e., before the *barkhu;*

c. special prayers which are normally not found in the liturgy.

One member of the committee felt that it would be better to involve the non-Jew in all aspects of the service in which a Jewish family member is normally involved and simply change the blessing or prayers to conform with his status as a non-Jew through some neutral wording.

2. The non-Jewish partner should not be involved in the removal of the *Torah* from the Ark and handing it to the *Bar/Bat Mitzvah*. It would be inappropriate to involve the non-Jewish parent in this ritual as it is frequently accompanied by a statement indicating the transmission of the Jewish tradition from one generation to another. Even if nothing is said, the act itself indicates that transmission which can, of course, not occur from a non-Jew to a Jew. Therefore, the Jewish spouse should be involved in this ritual or it should be omitted. One member of the Committee felt that such participation by a non-Jew was appropriate.

3. Some private words or prayers at an appropriate point during the *Torah* service should be permitted to the non-Jewish parent.

In summary, we therefore recommend that participation of non-Jews in a *Bar/Bat Mitzvah* service be sharply restricted with one member of the committee feeling that segments of the service normally recited by a parent be modified to suit his non-Jewish status.

July 1983

161. GENTILES IN A JEWISH CONGREGATION

QUESTION: Can a Gentile who has lived a basically Jewish life, and is married to a Jewess, join a congregation in his own right? (Rabbi J. Edelstein, Monroeville, PA)

ANSWER: This Gentile would be considered a *ger toshav*, or a follower of the Noahide laws, but of course, we could not consider him to be a *ger tzedek*, or a convert to Judaism. Christians and Muslims, as monotheists, have been classified as *gerei toshav* since the Middle Ages (Meir of Rothenburg *Responsa* #386; *Yad* Hil. M'lakhim 8.11, *Shulhan Arukh* Yoreh Deah 148.2, etc.) rather than idolaters. The status of a *ger toshav* is rather clear. A *ger toshav* is considered equal to a Jew in all legal matters, but he has no status in connection with ritual obligations, for they are not incumbent upon him. He would, therefore, not be considered part of the quota for a *minyan* or for *m'zuman*, nor could he lead a worship service, etc. (*Shulhan Arukh* Orah Hayim 199.4).

We can *not* include such an individual in our synagogue membership. This would, after all, entail their participation in every aspect of synagogue life, the right to lead services, the right to help determine policy or synagogue members. It would be inappropriate to have unconverted Gentiles participate in these aspects of congregational life. If this individual feels close to the congregation and wishes to help it, then he should feel free to contribute to it, attend its services and functions; perhaps later that individual will convert and join the congregation.

July 1977

162. CONGREGATIONAL MEMBERSHIP FOR A
NON-JEWISH SPOUSE*

QUESTION: Should we reinstitute the ancient category of semi-proselyte known in the Talmudic literature as *yirei adonai, ger toshav* and *ger shaar*? Would this be a way of solving the problem of non-Jewish spouse whose Jewish husband or wife belong to our congregations while they, as non-Jews with a considerable interest in Judaism, have either no status or a status which has not been properly and clearly defined? Would this ancient Talmudic category help us with our modern problems? What kind of status should be granted to such an individual? (Rabbi G. Raiskin, Burlingame, CA)

ANSWER: The problem of the non-Jewish spouse is a serious one in many congregations. Every effort toward a solution deserves our attention and consideration. We should begin by looking at the Talmudic categories, *yirei adonai, gerei toshav* and *gerei shaar,* and try to understand their precise meaning. What rights, if any, did individuals in each category possess? How were they treated in the Temple, in the synagogue, by Jewish courts, etc.?

The general question of conversion to Judaism has been well treated by a number of our colleagues (J. Rosenbloom, *Conversion to Judaism,* Cincinnati, 1978; H. Eichorn, *Conversion to Judaism,* New York, 1965; B. Bamberger, *Proselytism in the Talmudic Period,* New York, 1939; W. Braude, *Jewish Proselyting in the First Five Centuries of the Common Era,* Providence, 1940). These volumes indicate that conversion to Judaism has continued through the centuries. They discuss what was expected of the convert, motives which led to conversion, and the way in which converts have fit into the general community. Relatively little space in these volumes is given to our categories, which existed for only a few centuries. These categories play no role in rabbinic literature after the *Talmud,* and when these terms are used they are synonymous with *benei noah,* in other words, a Gentile who had accepted basic human morality and was no longer a pagan. The terms also designate individuals who had adopted certain Jewish thoughts in the post Talmudic period. No special status has been accorded to them (S. Zeitlin, "Proselyte and Proselytism," *Harry Wolfson Jubilee Volumes,* Vol. 2, pp. 587 ff; see also A. Bertholet, *Die Stellung der Israeliten und der Juden zu den Fremden,* Leipzig, 1896). If we follow the generally accepted view, individuals characterized by these designations seem to have fallen into four categories during the Mishnaic and early Talmudic period:

1. A theoretical designation which indicated how the rabbis would have liked to treat resident aliens (*gerei toshav*) in Israel (*M.* Gerim 3.1; A. Z. 64b; San 56a ff; Arak. 29a).

2. Individuals who were on their way to becoming full proselytes but had not yet fulfilled all the conditions. In other words, they may have undergone immersion or circumcision, but not yet brought the mandatory sacrifice in Jerusalem before the destruction of the temple (Moore, *Judaism in the First Centuries of the Christian Era,* Vol. I, pp. 330

ff; *Mishnat R. Eliezer,* p. 374; Juvenal, *Satire,* XIV, 96 ff).

3. Individuals who were married to Jews, accepted basic Jewish morality and religious thought, but for a variety of reasons were unwilling to undergo complete conversion. Usually this category seemed to consist of husbands of women who had become Jewish and were unwilling to follow as this entailed the difficult operation of circumcision. Other reasons may also have been operative.

4. Individuals who had accepted some of the ethics and morality of Judaism and left their ancient pagan beliefs, in other words, a synonym for *benei noah* (A. Z. 64a; Pes. 21a; Ker. 8b; Hul. 5a; Meg. 13a; Philo, *Contra Apion;* Josephus, *Antiq.* 20.8.7; *Wars* 2.18.2, 7.3.3).

One scholar, Solomon Zeitlin, felt that these categories did not exist at all. The terms merely designated Gentiles who were no longer idolaters but in no way semi-proselytes (Zeitlin, *op. cit.*).

For the purposes of our discussion, we can forget the first two categories. As we turn to the remaining category, we must first ask about the status of these individuals within the Jewish community. It is clear from a wide variety of statements that they were considered on a level above pagans, but did not posses the status of full converts or Jews; they had no official status in either the synagogue or a Jewish court and were considered non-Jews in virtually all legal matters (Gerei Toshav, *Encyclopedia Talmudit,* Vol. 6, pp. 290 ff). They could bring sacrifices at the Temple, but so could any pagan who wished to do so (Schürer, *A History of the Jewish People in the Age of Jesus Christ,* revised by Vermez, Millar and Black, Vol. 2, pp. 309 ff). The fact that they had taken this step was recognized and praised; there was the hope that they might go further, but until this occurred, no real change of status was conferred.

These designations ceased to exist with the end of the pagan period. After the majority of the neighboring people had become Christians, or later, followers of Islam, most individuals known to Jews were *benei noah* and could be designated by the synonyms, *yirei adonai, ger toshav,* and *ger shaar.* The special categories, therefore, became meaningless.

If we nowadays accorded these designations to our Christian friends, they would provide no special status in the synagogue but simply recognize the ethical and moral teachings of their religion as akin to our own which we have done anyhow.

A revival, therefore, of the Talmudic categories of *yirei adonai, ger toshav,* and *ger shaar* would not achieve the goal desired or solve the problem of the non-Jewish spouse. It is not likely that a revival of a special designation which carries no appropriate historical overtones would help us. It would probably only confuse matters and place the non-Jewish partner in a doubtful position. We, therefore, recommend that the membership section of the constitution and the constitutions of the auxiliary bodies, such as Brotherhood and Sisterhood, read as follows:

Membership in our congregation is limited to Jews and Jewish families. A non-Jewish partner is welcome to the fellowship of the congregation and is encouraged to participate in all of its activities; however, the non-Jewish spouse may not serve on on the Board, hold office, become chairman of any committee or have the privilege of voting at congregational or committee meetings.

October 1983

163. GENTILE CHAIRMAN OF CONFIRMATION GROUP

QUESTION: The parents of each year's Confirmation Class and of *Bar/Bat Mitzvah* groups form a club which sponsors special activities for these young people; it also provides some educational programs for the parents. This year a mother who is not Jewish has been selected as chairman of the Confirmation Club. This was done inadvertently as the woman in question has identified herself closely with the Jewish community and has been very active in communal work and the Jewish Federation. She attends synagogue services regularly. Although the rabbi knew that she was not Jewish, members of the group were unaware of that fact. How should we deal with this situation? (D. L., Los Angeles, CA)

ANSWER: This Committee has decided on a number of other occasions that it is inappropriate for a non-Jew to serve in leadership positions within a congregation (see "Congregational Membership for A Non-Jewish Partner"). There is, of course, nothing which would prohibit such individuals from being active in the congregation and the Jewish community. In fact, we should encourage such activities even if full conversion to Judaism is not possible. Such efforts will eventually bring these fine individuals closer to Judaism and may lead to eventual conversion.

In the case of this individual, it would be appropriate to suggest that this might be a good time to accept Judaism formally. Her activities have taken place entirely within the orbit of Judaism; her youngest child is now to be confirmed. Her own commitment and her efforts through the years would more than suffice to qualify her for conversion without any further instruction. It has been my experience that individuals in this position are very open to such a suggestion and will often formally join the community. That would, of course, remove the problem.

April 1983

164. GENTILE MEMBERS ON CONGREGATIONAL COMMITTEES

QUESTION: My congregation contains a number of couples in which one spouse is Christian and the other is Jewish. Several of these non-Jews have indicated interest in working on the committees of the congregation. What limits to participation, if any, should be set? (K. S. Cleveland, OH)

ANSWER: We Jews have considered Christians as *benei noah* since the early Middle Ages, so all the statements made during previous periods which deal with idolatry do not apply to Christians or Moslems. Christians are monotheists who have added elements (*shituf*) to One God. We should note that even in the Talmudic period, there was considerable doubt about classifying pagans in the same category as the idolators of previous periods for it was clear to many of the Talmudic authorities that the old idolatrous religions had lost their hold on the people (Hul. 13b; *Yad* Hil. Melakhim 11; Maimonides, *Moreh Nivukhim* I.71; Responsa II, #448, ed. Blau).

This age old change in our attitude and the new mood brought by the French Revolution have led to a completely different approach to the non-Jewish world. This began with the Paris Sanhedrin of 1807, which dealt with numerous questions concerning the relationship between Jews and non-Jews (Tama, *Transaction of the Parisian Sanhedrin*, tr. F. Kirwan; W. G. Plaut, *The Rise of Reform Judaism*).

The Responsa Committee, in recent years, has addressed the question of non-Jewish participation in congregational life a number of times. We have discussed their participation in religious services and life cycle events as well as burial in our cemeteries (W. Jacob, *American*

Reform Responsa, #6, #10, #98, etc.). The Committee has stated that non-Jews should not become formal members of a congregation in a responsum (see "Non-Jews as Congregational Members"). Our congregations are established to continue and further the traditions and goals of Judaism; they are not general charities or social clubs open to everyone. In this way they differ from Hadassah, ORT, Brandeis and other groups whose constituency may be largely Jewish but has always included non-Jewish members. Many other examples could be given.

When a mixed couple joins a congregation, the membership and the voting rights should be limited to the Jewish spouse. That, of course, does not exclude the non-Jew from participation at services, educational or social functions, but means that due to the nature of the synagogue, such individuals can have no voice in its governance. This would also apply to congregational committees. Those committees which deal with matters which specifically involve Jewish knowledge or feelings must, by their nature, exclude non-Jewish participation. We must also exclude non-Jews from committees which are viewed as stepping-stones to congregational leadership.

It would, however, be perfectly possible to include non-Jews in committees of a more general nature (without a vote) which deal with community projects. For example, committees on scholarship, social action, community service, the handicapped, etc., could draw their membership from Jewish congregants as well as non-Jewish spouses. We should be careful, however, not to have non-Jews as chairpeople of these committees or as representatives of such committees to the general community.

In other words, non-Jews who wish to be active in some aspect of synagogue life should be encouraged in that direction both through membership on committees with a broad communal purpose as well as attendance at synagogue functions with the hope that they will eventually join us as fully committed Jews.

April 1983

165. MAY A NON-JEW LIGHT THE SHABBAT EVE CANDLES?

QUESTION: May a non-Jew married to a Jew light the *shabbat* eve candles? The question has arisen at the time when a son of such a couple is about to be *Bar Mitzvah*. Normally the mother of the *Bar/Bat*

Mitzvah participates in the *shabbat* eve ceremony by lighting the candles. May she do so under the circumstances? (Rabbi E. Palnick, Little Rock, AR)

ANSWER: Tradition has little to say on this specifically as the custom of lighting the candles in the synagogue is an innovation of the Reform movement. It may have been intended as a revival of an ancient custom of lighting the *shabbat* candles following the afternoon service in the synagogue (*Sidur Rav Amram*, ed., Jerusalem, 1979, p. 61, also Isaac Lamperonti, *Pahad Yitzhaq*, Hadlakhah). It came as a recent addition to the late Friday evening service created by Isaac Mayer Wise. His first congregation was not enthusiastic but did permit him to establish such a service in 1869 (W. G. Plaut, "The Sabbath in the Reform Movement," *C.C.A.R. Yearbook*, Vol. 75, p. 177). This service did not contain the ritual of lighting the candles in the synagogue, nor did the early editions of the *Union Prayerbook*. It was introduced in the newly revised edition of 1940 and has become an accepted part of our liturgy.

The lighting of *shabbat* candles at the *erev shabbat* service represents a synagogue version of the *mitzvah* of lighting *shabbat* candles at home (*M.* Shab II, 6). This was one of the three *mitzvot* specifically commanded to women (*Shulhan Arukh* Orah Hayim 263.3), although both men and women may light the candles.

The non-Jewish spouse's participation in the Friday evening ritual at home has evolved naturally. Frequently she does light the *shabbat* candles and through this indicates a wish to establish some ties with Judaism at home. Technically, of course, it is inappropriate for a Christian to recite the traditional benediction as it contains the words *asher qidshanu* - "who sanctified us with His commandments," which indicates an obligation imposed on Jews. We have, however, taken this act as a positive indication that the home is to be Jewish.

We can not apply the same reasoning to the non-Jewish mother's participation in the Friday evening service by reciting the traditional words on the occasion of her child's *Bar/Bat Mitzvah*. This is a public service and non-Jews may not lead in essential segments of the synagogue service or sections which utilize such phrases as "who has sanctified us" ("Participation of Non-Jews in a Jewish Public Service," W. Jacob, *American Reform Responsa*, #6). The non-Jewish mother may light the candles and recite a modified prayer while someone else, perhaps another family member, should recite the traditional *b'rakhah*.

January 1984

166. CHURCH WINDOW HONORING A JEW

QUESTION: A church in the community wishes to honor a Jew who has made significant contributions to the community through his efforts to help others. This is not recognition for a financial gift to the institution. Is it appropriate to have a window dedicated to this individual? Might it appear wrong or be misleading from a Jewish point of view? (Rabbi S. Rubin, Savannah, GA)

ANSWER: In the Biblical and Talmudic periods, concern about relations with idolaters was constantly voiced. The entire Tractate *Avodah Zarah* deals with every conceivable association with pagans, including worship and business matters, as well as social contacts. Although these laws continue to appear in the later codes, they are hardly applicable to anyone by the Middle Ages, as both Christians and Muslims were considered as monotheists and in the category of *gerei toshav* (Menahem Meiri, *Bet Habehira* to Avodah Zarah 20a; Meir of Rothenburg, *Responsa* #386; Isaac of Dampierre, *Tosfot* to San. 63b; Bekh. 2b; Maimonides, *Yad* Hil. Melakhim 8.11; Hil. Edut. 11.10, etc.; *Tur* Yoreh Deah 148; *Shulhan Arukh* Yoreh Deah 148.12). Orthodox authorities, as Emden, Bacharach, and Ashkenazi, at the beginning of the modern era, also stressed a positive outlook toward non-Jews (A. Shohet, "The German Jew: His Integration Within the Non-Jewish Environment in the First Half of the Eighteenth Century," *Zion*, Vol. 21, 1956, pp. 229 ff). The Reform Movement has continued this trend, and the responsa of our movement make this clear, as do numerous resolutions of the Central Conference of American Rabbis (Solomon B. Freehof, *Reform Responsa* and succeeding volumes; W. Jacob, *American Reform Responsa*).

This century has seen further development in the friendly relationship between Christians and Jews; there have been many common efforts, especially in the area of social problems. Jews and non-Jews have worked side by side in America for more than a century, and numerous examples can be named in virtually every larger American community. This has led us to honor co-workers without regard to religious background. Rabbinic seminaries have granted honorary degrees to Christians in recognition of outstanding scholarly or communal achievement. At the same time, outstanding Jews have been recognized by prominent Christian institutions. Such recognition has increased the feelings of cooperation and brotherhood. They carry out the Biblical commandment of Leviticus, "love your neighbor as yourself," and many Talmudic injunctions, like *mipnei darkhei shalom* - actions done for the sake of peace and brotherhood.

All of this has occurred without the surrender of religious identity on either side or effort at proselytization. In other words, brotherhood and friendship have been genuine.

As such a cooperative spirit continues to reign, and as we seek to strengthen common efforts in social causes, it would be fitting for a Jew, among others, to be honored through a window in a Christian house of worship. This would be appropriate in a church. We welcome such recognition as a permanent reminder of good Jewish-Christian relationships. In times of tension when other acts may be forgotten, the window will remain a visible bond between the two communities. It would be appropriate to word the statement so that it indicates honor to a Jew.

March 1985

167. A RABBI AT CHRISTIAN ORDINATION SERVICE

QUESTION: Should a rabbi participate in the service of ordination of a student as a Christian minister? Would it be possible for him to participate in one of the three following ways - attending the ordination; reading a Biblical selection; invoking the priestly blessing on the candidate? (Rabbi J. Stein, Indianapolis, IN)

ANSWER: This question involves the Jewish attitude towards Christians and Christianity. Since Medieval times Christianity and Islam were viewed as monotheistic religions. Therefore, none of the strictures which the *Bible* and *Talmud* place upon idolatry are relevant for Christianity.

The *Talmud* began to consider pagans of its day differently from the ancient heathen; it treated Christians similarly. The precise attitude toward Gentiles during the five centuries of Talmudic times depended upon specific circumstances. Thus, Simeon ben Yohai could be uncomfortably negative (J. Kid. 66c, with full reading in *Tosfot* to A. Z. 26b; Soferim 15.10). On the other hand, it was possible for Meir and Judah Hanasi to have warm friendly relationships with Gentiles (B. K. 38a). We comfort their dead, visit their sick, help their poor, etc. (Git. 29b; *Tur* Hoshen Mishpat 266). R. Hiya bar Abba said in the name of R. Johanan that Gentiles outside the land of Israel were not idolaters. They merely continued to follow the customs of their fathers (Hul. 13b).

By the Middle Ages, Christians were generally no longer classified as idolaters (Meir of Rothenburg, *Responsa* #386). Rabbi Isaac of Dampierre placed Christians in the category of Noachides and not of pagans (*Tosfot* to San. 73b and Bek. 2b). Menachem Meiri (1249-1306) went further by stating that Christians and Moslems who live by the discipline of their religion should be regarded as Jews in social and economic relationships (*Bet Habehirah* to A. Z. 20a). Maimonides stated that Christians or Muslims should be considered as *gerei toshav*. They would assist in the preparation for the Messianic era (*Yad* Melakhim 8.11 and Teshuvah 3.5; Edut. 11.10, etc.). At other times he considered Christianity as a form of idol worship (*Yad* Hil. Avodat Kokhavim 9.4; Hil. Akum 10.2; Hil. Maakhalot Asurot), although he, too, had some positive thoughts about Christianity (*Yad* Hil. Melakhim 11.4). Of course Maimonides dealt with Christianity in the abstract in contrast to the other authorities who lived in a Christian world. A French Tosafist of the same period expressed positive views akin to Meiri, and so we see that they were not restricted to Sephardic Jewry (Bekh. 2b). This point of view became normative, and Christians as well as Muslims were considered in the same category as the *gerei toshav*. This point of view was accepted by Caro in the *Shulhan Arukh* (Yoreh Deah 148.12; also *Tur* Yoreh Deah 148) and most forcefully by Mosheh Rifkes, author of the *Beer Hagolah* to the *Shulhan Arukh* (Hoshen Mishpat, 425 at the end). The statement is remarkable because the author himself had fled Vilna to Amsterdam from anti-Jewish riots. He stated: "The sages made reference only to the idolaters of their day who did not believe in the creation of the world, the Exodus, God's marvelous deeds, or the divinely given law. But these people, among whom we are scattered, believe in all these essentials of religion. So, it is our duty to pray for their welfare, and that of their kingdom, etc." The status of the Gentile in the general application of Jewish law had, therefore, changed and this positive opinion of Gentiles was reemphasized at the beginning of the modern era by Emden, Bacharach, Askenazi and other Orthodox authorities (See A. Shohet, "The German Jew, His Integration Within Their Non-Jewish Environment in the First Half of the Eighteenth Century," *Zion*, Vol. 21, 1956, pp. 229 ff) as well as Mendlelssohn ("Schreiben an Lavater," *Schriften*, 1843, Vol. 3, pp. 39 ff).

The classification of Christians as *gerei toshav* had theological implications and important economic consequences. For example, wine made by a Gentile was permitted to be handled by Ashkenazic Jews. Although it could not be consumed by Jews, they could trade in it (*Tosfot* to San. 63b; Isserles to *Shulhan Arukh* Yoreh Deah 123.1). Sephardic Jews did not follow this practice and had no pressing need to do so, as they were not involved in extensive wine growing and lived among Moslems, whose consumption of wine was limited (Maimonides, *Responsa* II, #448; *Tur* Yoreh Deah 124).

Despite these friendly views, all of the traditional authorities made it quite clear that major distinctions continue to exist between Judaism and Christianity. Maimonides felt that we should restrict our relationships with Christians (*Yad* Hil. Akum 10.2) and also prohibited Jews from dealing in Christian wine (*Yad* Maakhalot Asurot 17). He and all the other medieval authorities thought that both Christianity and Islam had strange concepts (*shituf*) which impinged on the absolute unity of God (Isserles to *Shulhan Arukh* Orah Hayim 156; Maimonides, *Peer Hador* 50, etc.). In secular relationships Christians could *be treated* as *b'nei noah*, but in religious matters, distinctions were to remain.

The factors outlined above have provided a Jewish basis for good Jewish-Christian relationships in the last centuries. They have enabled us to participate in many joint social and charitable programs. Reform Jewish thought goes one step further and permits participation in interfaith services which remain neutral and are non-Christological. They would also permit us to participate in a strictly Christian service when it is clear that our participation is limited to matters which are not offensive to us. This means that it would be possible to read a Biblical portion at an ordinary service or a service of installation for a minister in a new congregation, or at any other service as a gesture of friendship. This emphasizes our common bonds.

Additional participation at a service of ordination would be inappropriate, as such a service is by its very nature very specifically Christian. Such services usually emphasize creed and the loyalty of the minister to that creed. This emphasis on *shituf* would be inappropriate for us. In our age of extensive friendship, it is important that ties be continued and fostered, yet distinctions should not be blurred.

December 1980

168. JEWISH BRIDESMAID AT A CHRISTIAN WEDDING

QUESTION: May a Jewish girl be a bridesmaid in a Christian wedding ceremony which will be held in a Christian church? (Rabbi L. Winograd, McKeesport, PA)

ANSWER: This question involves our relationship with Christians and the nature of the bridesmaids' involvement in the wedding ceremony. Let us look at each of these matters separately.

In the Biblical and Talmudic periods, concern about relations with idolaters was constantly voiced. The entire tractate *Avodah Zarah* deals with every conceivable association with pagans, including worship and business matters, as well as social contacts. Although these laws continue to appear in the later codes, they were hardly applicable to anyone by the Middle Ages, as both Christians and Muslims were considered as monotheists and in the category of *gerei toshav* (Menahem Meiri, *Bet Habehira* to Avodah Zarah 20a; Meir of Rothenburg, *Responsa* #386; Isaac of Dampierre, *Tosfot* to San. 63b; Bekh. 2b; *Tur* Yoreh Deah 148; *Shulhan Arukh* Yoreh Deah 148.12). Orthodox authorities as Emden, Bacharach and Ashkenazi, at the beginning of the modern era, also stressed a positive outlook toward non-Jews (A. Shohet, "The German Jew: His Integration Within the Non-Jewish Environment in the First Half of the Eighteenth Century," *Zion*, Vol. 21, 1956, pp. 229 ff). The Reform Movement has continued this trend, and the responsa of our movement make this clear, as do numerous resolutions of the Central Conference of American Rabbis (Solomon B. Freehof, *Reform Responsa* and succeeding volumes; W. Jacob, *American Reform Responsa*).

This positive outlook toward Christianity has not been shared by some scholars living in the Muslim world, so for example, Maimonides sometimes considered Christianity as a form of idol worship (*Yad* Hil. Avodat Kokhavim 9.4; Hil. Maakhalot Asurot), although he, too, had some positive thoughts about Christianity (*Yad* Hil. Melakhim 11.4). Of course Maimonides dealt with Christianity in the abstract in contrast to the other authorities who lived in a Christian world. On other occasions he felt that Christians or Muslims should be considered as *gerei toshav*. They would assist in the preparation for the Messianic era (*Yad* Hil. Melahim 8.11 and Hil. Teshuvah 3.5; Edut. 11.10; see also "A Rabbi at a Christian Ordination Service" for additional references).

In more recent times, some authorities have again viewed the trinitarian element of Christianity as *shituf* in an effort to create a firmer distinction between Judaism and Christianity (David Hoffmann, *Melamed Lehoil* Yoreh Deah 2.148). Others have not felt threatened, so David Hoffmann's Berlin colleague, Marcus Horovitz, who was equally Orthodox, did not follow this line of reasoning and considered Christianity as monotheistic (David Ellenson, Jewish Covenant and Christian Trinitarianism," R. A. Brauner, *Jewish Civilization: Essays and Studies*, Volume III, pp. 86 ff).

Our general mood is to consider Christianity as monotheistic. Although assimilation represents a danger for us, conversion to Christianity is extremely rare and presents no threat. We may, therefore, associate with Christians freely.

Let us turn to the second matter at issue. Is a bridesmaid in any way an active participant in the worship element of a Christian service? Public participation in contrast to attendance in a specifically Christian service is prohibited. Acts like kneeling, bowing, etc. would be prohibited for Jews. Generally a bridesmaid simply stands in attendance and is, therefore, only in attendance but not a participant. She is singled out for this honor as a token of friendship. As long as she does not participate in any act of worship, her participation is permissible.

We can see, therefore, that as we consider Christianity as a monotheistic religion, we can be present at a Christian service, although we may not participate in the acts of worship themselves. The young lady may attend as a bridesmaid but she may not kneel or do anything which may be considered as participation in a Christian worship service.

July 1986

169. MEDITATION GROUPS AND JUDAISM

QUESTION: Several meditation groups have been formed in the community. Those who have participated say that this is not a religion but simply a way of relaxing tensions and learning to cope with personal problems. Is there a conflict between the meditation groups and Judaism?

ANSWER: There is a wide variety of such groups currently in existence in the United States. Some of them adhere to beliefs and practices which are not compatible with Judaism. This would be true of Hare Krishna, Scientology and groups which have become cults around a specific leader who has frequently been elevated above the status of a normal human being. We would consider such groups as close to idolatry and dangerous to Judaism.

A group which, however, meets solely for the purpose of meditation and solving of personal problems would not be very different from group psychology which often resorts to this method in order to resolve certain kinds of problems. We would, of course, be concerned that there is absolutely no theological activity which might be in conflict with Judaism. There would be nothing wrong with participating in such a group as long as the individuals attending are aware that sometimes matters begin in this fashion and then lead down the path of cults.

September 1983

170. FIGHTING DISCRIMINATION

QUESTION: I was recently dismissed from gainful employment with a Gentile company and have proof that this act was both anti-Semitic and retaliatory in nature. How far can I go in fighting for my rights? Does my Jewish tradition mandate that I stay within certain limits in taking legal action? (E. J. K., Washington, DC).

ANSWER: Our struggle against discrimination began in the Hellenistic period. We fought physically, not only at the time of the Maccabean revolt which dealt with outright religious oppression, but also in Alexandria and elsewhere against hatred and discrimination (Josephus, *The Jewish Wars; Against Apion; Maccabees* I, II, III, IV). We also struggled against ancient anti-Semitism as it manifested itself in statements and diatribes against Jews and Judaism in the Hellenistic and Roman literature (see M. Stern, *Greeks and Latin Authors on Jews and Judaism*, 3 vols.). These statements were answered in part by polemics recorded in the *Apocrypha* and the *Pseudepigrapha*, as well as the writings of Philo and Josephus.

With this period we began the long struggle against hatred and discrimination through whatever methods were available to us which were often dictated by our opponents. In the Middle Ages, scholars

256

and leaders were occasionally forced into public polemics against their will, for they realized that if they lost to the Christian opponents, the community would fare badly. On the other hand, if they won over their opponents, hatred would hardly diminish (*Dialogue with Tryphon; Chronicle of Ahimaaz;* J. D. Eisenstadt, *Otzar Vikukhim*). When it was not possible to conduct a struggle in this fashion, then it was carried on through philosophical polemics (Daniel J. Lasker, *Jewish Philosophical Polemics Against Christianity in the Middle Ages,* 1977). More recently, beginning with some Russian pogroms at the end of the last century, Jews again defended themselves with weapons. Clearly we have used the methods appropriate for the society in which we lived to defend ourselves (L. Poliakov, *The History of Anti-Semitism,* Vols. 1-4). As the American society provides legal redress in cases of discrimination, those should be used fully and without hesitation. If there are specific local concerns, it would be appropriate to check with the American Jewish Committee or Anti-Defamation League. Tradition places no limits on our methods of self-defense.

December 1985

171. THE LORD'S PRAYER

QUESTION: A rabbi who has joined Alcoholics Anonymous discovered that the meetings concluded with the recitation of the "Lord's Prayer." He personally does not feel uncomfortable with that prayer, but wonders whether it is appropriate for him as a rabbi to participate in the recital of that prayer.

ANSWER: As you have indicated in your letter, it is clear that the "Lord's Prayer" is Jewish in spirit and parallels a number of ancient Jewish prayers. This has been discussed at some length by a wide variety of Jewish scholars from Kaufmann Kohler to Jakob Petuchowski (Kaufmann Kohler, "The Lord's Prayer," *Jewish Encyclopedia,* Vol. VIII, pp. 183 f; C. G. Montefiore, *Rabbinic Literature and Gospel Teachings;* Jakob Petuchowski and Michael Brocke, *The Lord's Prayer and Jewish Liturgy*).

The problem does not lie with the origin of the prayer, or its Talmudic parallels (Ber. 16b f, 29b; *Tosefta* Ber. 3.7), but with the fact that Jesus taught it to his disciples (Matt. 6.9 ff; Luke 11.1 ff). Furthermore, it has become the central prayer of Christianity, and, in fact, is one of the strongest bonds between the Catholic and Protestant forms of Christianity. Although its content is neutral and it does not contain any direct reference to Christianity, its origin with Jesus and its strong Christian overtones makes its use unacceptable to Jews. It would, therefore, be better if Jews refrained from its recital even in a non-religious setting like Alcoholics Anonymous. As it is recited at the conclusion of the meeting, there is really no reason to participate. One can stand in silence, and I am sure that this would be respected and understood. An alternative would be the recital of Psalm 23 which has been used by a number of chapters at the conclusion of their meetings.

July 1985

172. HOLIDAY GREETINGS

QUESTION: The author of a monthly house organ is Jewish and wishes to know how to treat the holiday season in his magazine. What kind of religious message and what kind of religious symbols would be appropriate for use by a Jewish author in what essentially is a limited circulation magazine whose readership is largely non-Jewish? (Dr. S. Millman, Arnold, MD)

ANSWER: Jews and Christians have for many centuries worked together in business enterprises. Although the *Talmud* (Bek. 2b) prohibited business relationships between Jews and pagans, as soon as Christianity was recognized as a monotheistic religion, this prohibition was no longer in effect. The medieval Rabenu Tam (*Tosfot.* to Bek. 2b) stated that it was perfectly permissible to enter into a business partnership or other close business relationship with a Christian. There are many records of such partnerships with Christians and Muslims (I. A. Agus, *The Heroic Age of Franco-German Jewry,* pp. 130 ff; S. D. Goitein, *A Mediterranean Society,* Vol. 1, pp. 169 ff; Müller, *Mafteah,* pp. 153, 219; Israel Isserlein, *Terumat Hadeshen,* 152). Jews and Christians worked closely together and wished each other well on holidays through appropriate greetings as well as gifts (Güdemann, *Geschichte des Erziehungswesens,* pp. 144 ff; *Shulhan Arukh* Orah Hayim, 224, and *Magen Avraham*). Jews exchanged gifts with Christians and vice versa (Solomon ben Adret, *Responsa* #175; Berliner, *Aus dem inneren Leben,* pp. 18 ff; Güdemann, *op. cit.,* Vol. 3, pp. 89 ff; Isserlein

Terumat Hadeshen #195). This was part of the general social life which Jews and Christians shared.

In keeping with this spirit there would be nothing that would prevent a Jewish editor of a non-Jewish magazine from expressing either specifically Christmas or general holiday greetings. If for other reasons it seems appropriate to keep the holiday greetings neutral and not specifically religious, that may be preferable.

March 1982

173. CHRISTMAS LIGHTS CELEBRATIONS

QUESTION: A community in a Maryland county has begun a program of "Christmas" or "Holiday Luminaries." On one night during the holiday season, all the streets in the community are lit by candles. The original meaning was interpreted as "lighting the way for the return of Christ." Later it was broadened to demonstrate the "universal message of brotherhood to all men" provided by the holiday season, which includes Christmas and Hannukah. Should Jews participate in this practice? (Dr. S. Millman, Arnold, MD)

ANSWER: In order to answer this question properly we should briefly review the relationship of Judaism and Christianity, and then look at the conditions and problems of our own times.

The *Talmud* began to consider pagans of its day differently from the ancient heathen; it treated Christians similarly. The precise attitude toward Gentiles during the five centuries of Talmudic times depended upon specific circumstances. Thus, Simeon ben Yohai could be uncomfortably negative (*J*. Kid. 66c, with full reading in *Tosefot* to A. Z. 26b; Soferim 15.10). On the other hand, it was possible for Meir and Judah Hanasi to have warm friendly relationships with Gentiles (B. K. 38a). We comfort their dead, visit their sick, help their poor, etc. (Git. 29b; *Tur* Hoshen Mishpat 266). R. Hiya bar Abba said in the name of R. Johanan that Gentiles outside the land of Israel were not idolaters. They merely continued to follow the customs of their fathers (Hul. 13b).

By the Middle Ages, Christians were generally no longer classified as idolaters (Meir of Rothenburg, *Responsa* #386). Rabbi Isaac of Dampierre placed Christians in the category of Noachides and not of pagans (Tosfot to San. 73b and Bek. 2b). Menachem Meiri (1249-1306) went further by stating that Christians and Moslems who live by the discipline of their religion should be regarded as Jews in social and economic relationships (*Bet Habehirah* to A. Z. 20a). Maimonides stated that Christians or Muslims should be considered as *gerei toshav.* They would assist in the preparation for the Messianic era (*Yad* Melahim 8.11 and Teshuvah 3.5; Edut. 11.10, etc.). He expressed harsher views at other times and considered Christianity idolatrous (*Yad.* Hil. Avodat Kokhavim 9.4, etc.) A French Tosafist of the same period expressed similar views, and so we see that they were not restricted to Sephardic Jewry (Bekh. 2b). This point of view became normative, and Christians as well as Muslims were considered in the same category as the *gerei toshav.* This was the point of view accepted by Caro in the *Shulhan Arukh* (Yoreh Deah 148.12; also *Tur* Yoreh Deah 148) and most forcefully by Mosheh Rifkes, author of the *Beer Hagolah* to the *Shulhan Arukh* (Hoshen Mishpat, 425 at the end). The statement is remarkable because the author himself had fled Vilna to Amsterdam from anti-Jewish riots. He stated: "The sages made reference only to the idolaters of their day who did not believe in the the creation of the world, the Exodus, God's marvelous deeds, or the divinely given law. But these people, among whom we are scattered, believe in all these essentials of religion. So, it is our duty to pray for their welfare, and that of their kingdom, etc." The status of the Gentile in the general application of Jewish law had, therefore, changed and this positive opinion of Gentiles was reemphasized at the beginning of the modern era by Emden, Bacharach, Askenazi and other Orthodox authorities (See A. Shohet, "The German Jew, His Integration Within Their Non-Jewish Environment in the First Half of the Eighteenth Century," *Zion*, Vol. 21, 1956, pp. 229 ff) as well as Mendelssohn ("Schreiben an Lavater," *Schriften*, 1843, Vol. 3, pp. 39 ff).

We have gone considerably further in recent times as expressed by Franz Rosenzweig's philosophy which provided equal religious status to Christianity (*Star of Redemption*). He was the first Jewish philosopher to express this thought in clear terms (W. Jacob, *Christianity Through Jewish Eyes*, pp. 122 ff). The Jewish community in America has given practical expression to this thought through "non-denominational" religious services which have involved Christian clergy alongside rabbis. These services have been carefully constructed and generally celebrate public holidays like Thanksgiving.

Joint celebrations of events connected with Christmas and Hannukah can not properly fall into this neutral territory for the following reasons:

1. Christmas and Hannukah are too distinctive in emphasis and significance. Christmas is one of the two main holidays of the Christian calendar. It celebrates the birth of Jesus, considered by them as the redeemer of mankind. The messianic hope and religious rebirth stressed by this holiday is felt by every Christian. Christmas and Easter are *the* two significant holidays of Christianity universally celebrated. On the other hand, Hannukah is a minor Jewish holiday of secondary importance. Its significance has risen in modern times as Jewish families have used it to protect their children from the "Christmas spirit" and its gift-giving atmosphere. In addition, it has gained significance through Israel's struggle which parallels that of the ancient Maccabees. A joint celebration of these days is, therefore incongruous.

2. The spirit of the holidays is precisely opposite. Christmas is the season of rebirth, good will and redemption. Hannukah, on the other hand, rejects the influence of outside religions and cultures. We emphasize the Maccabean resistance against the Seleucid's Hellenistic civilization. The first martyrs for monotheism are celebrated on it. This spirit would not permit us to join in the celebration of another religion's festivities.

3. Jewish adults and children have been under considerable pressure recently through new conversionist movements. Some seek to convert us by occupying a position on the border between Judaism and Christianity, like "Jews for Jesus" and "Fulfilled Jews." These groups have used symbols of Jewish holidays and reinterpreted them along Christian lines. Jewish college students have been invited to what appeared to be a Jewish service, only to find themselves in a Christian setting. For these reasons, we should be especially careful to avoid anything which might lead to religious syncretism.

Although we wish our Christian neighbors well on their holiday and have a high regard for their religion, we can not participate in their religious ceremonies. We should especially refrain from doing so publicly. Programs like the "Holiday Luminaries" should exclude us so that religious distinctions remain clear to ourselves and our children. It would, on the other hand, be appropriate for Jews to light *menorahs* outside or in windows on Hannukah, as this is in keeping with the tradition which demands that the miracle be proclaimed publicly (Shab. 21b; *Shulhan Arukh* Orah Hayim 681.5). When Christmas and Hannukah coincide, the "Holiday Luminaries" and our *menorahs* would appropriately demonstrate our religious differences.

March 1982

174. CHRISTIAN DECORATIONS IN A BUSINESS OFFICE

QUESTION: A Jewish employee of an insurance firm has protested against the planned Christmas decorations. He is one of eight employees in his office. Most of the offices in that business building are decorated for the holiday of Christmas. Is there anything in the *halakhah* which might encourage him to object? What should our attitude be toward Christmas decorations in non-public places? (Rabbi J. Brown, Long Beach, CA)

ANSWER: This question, first of all, involves the Jewish attitude towards Christians and Christianity. Ever since Talmudic times, Christianity as well as Islam have been viewed as monotheistic religions. Therefore, none of the strictures which the *Bible* and the *Talmud* place upon idolatry are relevant for Christianity.

The *Talmud* began to consider pagans of its day differently from the ancient heathen; it treated Christians similarly. The precise attitude toward Gentiles during the five centuries of Talmudic times depended upon specific circumstances. Thus, Simeon ben Yohai could be uncomfortably negative (*J*. Kid. 66c, with full reading in Tosfot to A. Z. 26b; Soferim 15.10). On the other hand, it was possible for Meir and Judah Hanasi to have warm friendly relationships with Gentiles (B. K. 38a). We comfort their dead, visit their sick, help their poor, etc. (Git. 29b; *Tur* Hoshen Mishpat 266). R. Hiya bar Abba said in the name of R. Johanan that Gentiles outside the land of Israel were not idolaters. They merely continued to follow the customs of their fathers (Hul. 13b).

By the Middle Ages, Christians were generally no longer classified as idolaters (Meir of Rothenburg, *Responsa* #386). Rabbi Isaac of Dampierre placed Christians in the category of Noachides and not of pagans (*Tosfot* to San. 73b and Bek. 2b). Menachem Meiri (1249-1306) went further by stating that Christians and Moslems who live by the discipline of their religion should be regarded as Jews in social and economic relationships (*Bet Habehirah* to A. Z. 20a). Maimonides stated that Christians or Muslims should be considered as *gerei toshav*.

They would assist in the preparation for the Messianic era (*Yad* Melahim 8.11 and Teshuvah 3.5; Edut. 11.10, etc.). He expressed harsher views at other times and considered Christianity idolatrous (*Yad*. Hil. Avodat Kokhavim 9.4, etc.). A French Tosafist of the same period expressed similar views, and so we see that they were not restricted to Sephardic Jewry (Bekh. 2b). Maimonides dealt with Christianity in the abstract in contrast to the authorities who lived in a Christian world. A French Tosafist of the same period expressed positive views akin to Meiri, and so we see that this point of view was not restricted to Sephardic Jewry (Bekh. 2b). This point of view became normative, and Christians as well as Moslems were considered in the same category as *gerei toshav*. This view was accepted by Caro in the *Shulhan Arukh* (Yoreh Deah 148.12; also *Tur* Yoreh Deah 148) and most forcefully by Mosheh Rifkes, author of the *Beer Hagolah* to the *Shulhan Arukh* (Hoshen Mihpat, 425 at the end). The statement is remarkable because the author himself had fled Vilna to Amsterdam from anti-Jewish riots. He stated: "The sages made reference only to the idolaters of their day who did not believe in the creation of the world, the Exodus, God's marvelous deeds, or the divinely given law. But these people, among whom we are scattered, believe in all these essentials of religion. So, it is our duty to pray for their welfare, and that of their kingdom, etc." The status of the Gentile in the general application of Jewish law had, therefore, changed and this positive opinion of Gentiles was reemphasized at the beginning of the modern era by Emden, Bacharach, Askenazi and other Orthodox authorities (See A. Shohet, "The German Jew, His Integration Within Their Non-Jewish Environment in the First Half of the Eighteenth Century," *Zion*, Vol. 21, 1956, pp. 229 ff) as well as Mendelssohn ("Schreiben an Lavater," *Schriften*, 1843, Vol. 3, pp. 39 ff).

As we turn to the specific question of decorations, we must note that it would obviously be wrong for a Jew to worship symbols which are sacred to Christians, especially as we do not agree with their trinitarian concept of God (*Tosfot* to San. 63b; *Shulhan Arukh* Orah Hayim 156 and note of Isserles). In our instance, the decorations used are a general reminder of the holiday season, but they are rarely specifically religious. Christmas trees, wreaths, poinsettas, Santa Claus, etc. are not objects of worship. In fact, many devout Christians reject them as they have detracted from true religious devotion, as well as the importance of Christmas. We can, therefore, find little objectionable to such decorations in an adult business setting. Our feelings, of course, would be different if we were dealing with a public institution, or especially a public school. That represents an infringement of religious liberty and the separation of church and state in our land. It would also be an effort to influence children toward the majority religion, and we would object to that.

We might also look upon this entire matter by investigating the rights of a minority versus the majority. That has nothing to do specifically with the relationship of Jews and Christians. Let us briefly look at a Jewish view of minority rights within a totally Jewish setting. If an injustice has been done and not been rectified, then an individual may interrupt synagogue services and demand that attention be given to his case. This right, probably of Palestinian origin, was reaffirmed by a *taqanah* of R. Gershom (Finkelstein, *Jewish Self-Government*, p. 119) and was also reported in Medieval Spain (Adret, *Responsa* IV, #56). Its abuse led to some objections and the curtailment of this right (*Sefer Hassidim*, ed. Margolis, #107 f; Solomon Luria *Responsa* #20). Under other circumstances, however, the minority is required to adjust itself to the majority. For example, if an individual comes to a community and finds that their customs of reciting prayers or celebrating a holiday differ from his, he must abide by the customs of that community and can not make a nuisance of himself (*J. Pes.* 30d; *Yad Hil.* Yom Tov 8:20; *Shulhan Arukh* Orah Hayim 468; 498 also *Peri Hadash*). Actually, the question of minority rights was only urgent in those medieval lands which restricted the Jewish community to one synagogue and that threat may bring redress of complaints. A threat of defection by a large segment of the community often guaranteed a fair hearing. In our case, which of course is not a Jewish setting, the individual may seek some adjustment in the decorations, but there would be no basis for absolute objection.

In summary, the decorations involved in this business office are not religious and are not used for worship, and so the Jewish employee has little grounds for objection. He may protest and thus assure sensitivity to a minority point of view.

December 1979

175. LIGHTING THE CANDLES AND THE *QIDDUSH* — MAN'S OR WOMAN'S PREROGATIVE

QUESTION: It has thus far been customary for a woman to light the candles at the Friday evening service and for a man to recite the *qiddush*. Does the woman have a primary responsibility for lighting candles, or is this only a matter of custom? Is there value in the current synagogue practice which encourages a woman to light candles and a man to lead the *qiddush*, or is there a middle ground which would permit a man on rare occasion to light the candles and the woman to lead the *qiddush*? (N. Hirsh, Seattle, WA)

ANSWER: It is certainly clear to all that both these segments of the service have been moved from the home to the synagogue. Orthodox Judaism moved the *qiddush*, and Reform Judaism moved the lighting of the *shabbat* candles. The Orthodox rational was clearly stated by Joseph Caro, who specified that the *qiddush* should be recited wherever a meal was eaten. It was moved to a synagogue for the sake of strangers who ate in the synagogue (Pes. 10a; *Shulhan Arukh* Orah Hayim 269). He felt that the practice should have been halted in his day, as meals were no longer taken in the synagogue. However, Isserles added that it was Ashkenazic custom to continue the recital of the *qiddush* in the synagogue. This followed Natronai Gaon (*Siddur Rav Amram*, ed., Jerusalem, p. 65). As no woman participated in any public portion of the Orthodox service, the question of a woman reciting *qiddush* was never raised.

The Reform innovation of lighting the candles in the synagogue may have been intended as a revival of an ancient custom of lighting *shabbat* candles following the afternoon service in the synagogue (*Siddur Rav Amram*, ed. Jerusalem, 1971, p. 61). It came as an addition to the late Friday evening service, which had its origin with Isaac Mayer Wise. His first congregation was not enthusiastic about such a service, but permitted him to establish it in 1869 (G. Plaut, "The Sabbath in the Reform Movement," *C.C.A.R. Yearbook*, Vol. 75, p. 177). This service did not contain the ritual lighting of candles in the synagogue, nor did the early editions of the *Union Prayer Book*. It was introduced in the newly revised edition of 1940, and has become an accepted part of liturgy.

Lighting the *shabbat* candles at home is a *mitzvah* which was primarily assigned to women, but not exclusively (*M.* Shab. 2.6). It is one of the three *mitzvot* specifically commanded to women as also stressed by the *Shulhan Arukh* (Orah Hayim 263.3), yet the duty of executing this commandment rests upon both men and women. If a male is traveling alone, he is responsible for lighting the *shabbat* candles

(*Shulhan Arukh* Orah Hayim 263.2, 6).

It is not clear why this commandment, which must be carried out before a specified time on Friday evening, was recommended to women, as women are free from all positive *mitzvot* which were dependent upon time. Some authorities felt that the execution of such commandments might interfere with family responsibilities (Simon Duran, *Magen Avot* 2.6). This explanation did not deal with women without family responsibility. The commandments from which they are exempt may, of course, be performed by women, although these are not incumbent upon them. As they are not obligated to execute these *mitzvot*, they can not discharge the obligation for others (*Shulhan Arukh* Orah Hayim 106.1). This would preclude their recital of the *qiddush*. Naturally, this conclusion has been rejected by Reform Judaism in keeping with its emphasis on the equality of men and women. Either *mitzvah*, lighting the candles or *qiddush*, may be performed by women both at home and at a public service.

Although it has become customary for women to light the candles and for men to recite the *qiddush*, there is absolutely nothing within Reform tradition which would preclude a reversal of these roles. This would be appropriate both at home and in the synagogue. In keeping with the current emphasis on equality, it would be good to vary the practice in the synagogue.

December 1981

176. POVERTY PROJECT AND *SHABBAT*

QUESTION: Members of the congregation are involved in a social action program which seeks to rebuild homes in various deprived areas of the city. Plans are made for this throughout the year; the building material is gathered; hundreds of volunteers both in the Christian and Jewish community are involved in the process. The actual rebuilding takes place twice a year each time on a *shabbat*. Should members of the Jewish community be involved in this activity which violates the spirit of *shabbat*, but on the other hand helps the poor? (Rabbi J. Zabarenko, Houston, TX)

ANSWER: The commitment of Judaism to help those who are poor has been very clear from Biblical times onward. The legislation of the

Torah, and the constant exortation of the prophets, have moved us in this direction. The statements about charity by the legal literature from the *Mishnah* onward have been very specific, and makes this one of the highest priorities of Judaism. *Tzedakah* in all forms has always been important to us. Maimonides' eight steps of charity have systematized our efforts. The last of his steps is akin to the project undertaken by your community, as it enables the poor to provide for themselves with dignity, and in this case, proper homes in which their families can live.

Reform Jews have placed special emphasis on social action programs, and the eighth point of the Pittsburgh Platform of 1885 stressed this:

"In full accordance with the spirit of Mosaic legislation which strives to regulate the relation between rich and poor, we deem it our duty to participate in the great task of modern times, to solve on the basis of justice and righteousness the problem presented by the contrasts and evils of the present organization of society" (*The Changing World of Reform Judaism: The Pittsburgh Platform in Retrospect*, W. Jacob, ed. p. 109).

The efforts of the Reform Movement in this regard are clear. The resolutions of the Union of American Hebrew Congregations and the Central Conference of American Rabbis, as well as the action of hundreds of congregations, have led us in this direction for more than a century. The Social Action Center, which was established in Washington, DC, some two decades ago, has provided additional national leadership.

We must, however, ask how we can balance this goal of Reform Judaism with the equally significant tasks of honoring the *shabbat* and observing the spirit of this day of rest.

The Reform Movement has considered the *shabbat* very important and has tried to strengthen it. When the immigrant generation found it difficult to attend *shabbat* morning services, Isaac M. Wise created the late Friday evening service. The effort by some early Reform leaders to emphasize a Sunday weekday service over the *shabbat* service was vigorously rejected as an infringement on the sanctity of the *shabbat* (W. Jacob, *Pittsburgh Platform in Retrospect*; pp. 115 ff). During last decades we have placed greater emphasis on *shabbat* observance. The C.C.A.R. has done so through resolutions and publications (W. Gunther Plaut, *Shabbat Manual*; Peter Knobel, *Gates of the Seasons*). Reform Judaism has emphasized rest, worship, study and family activity rather than the details of the thirty-nine major categories of prohibited work (*M.* Shab. 7.2; *Mishnah Torah; Shulhan Arukh*).

Although rebuilding a home for the poor is a religious activity, we can not consider it restful. Furthermore, we are not dealing with an emergency situation, but with a well planned activity for which preparations have been made over a long period of time. Some Reform Jews may not live up to the ideals of *shabbat* observance, but we must, nevertheless, encourage them and discourage activities which clearly lead in other directions.

We would, therefore, encourage the Jewish community to participate in other aspects of this charitable venture. They may plan, collect the necessary materials as well as fund the project, but they should not participate on *shabbat* itself.

As the project is carried out twice during the year, one of those occasions can be a day other than *shabbat*. If Sunday seems inappropriate, then one of the national holidays can be selected.

We should participate in the project but not on *shabbat*.

March 1986

177. A HOLIDAY GIFT WRAPPING PROJECT AND *SHABBAT*

QUESTION: For six years Congregation Beth El, in Traverse City, has cooperated in a fund-raising effort by operating a Christmas gift wrap service at the local shopping mall. This activity has provided funds both for the congregation and the local United Way campaign. Is it appropriate for the congregation to sponsor such an activity during *shabbat?* (C. Carnick, Traverse City, MI)

ANSWER: Reform Judaism has continually emphasized the general mood of *shabbat*. It is a day of rest, worship, study and family activity (S. Maslin, *Gates of the Season*, pp. 18 ff). In the matter of specific prohibitions, traditional Judaism has been guided by the thirty-nine major categories of work listed in the *Mishnah* (Shab. 7.2; 49b) and their later development in the Codes (*Yad, Tur, Shulhan Arukh,* etc.) We, too, have emphasized the need to refrain from the normal routine of work.

It is clear from both the Biblical commandments and the subsequent development of Judaism that all kinds of business activities are prohibited, and it is the task of the congregation to encourage its members to live in the spirit of *shabbat* without involvement in any business activity. The fact that the activity helps to provide funds for the congregation and the United Way Campaign would make no difference. The holiday gift wrapping activity is carried out in a business setting with all the bustle and activity of the normal working week. It necessitates the involvement of individuals in a working routine, and so, in every way is a business activity. It should not be conducted by Jews, either on Friday night or on *shabbat*. After *shabbat* is over on Saturday night, there would be no objection to Jewish involvement.

October 1985

178. *ERUV*

QUESTION: What is the origin for the *eruv*? What should our Reform Jewish attitude be? (Rabbi A. Wohl, New Rochelle, NY)

ANSWER: As you know, the *eruv* has been developed by Orthodoxy as a legal way around the Sabbath restrictions which prohibited the carrying of any item beyond one's private domain. Although there are several categories of domain, the ones which concern us are *r'shut harabim* and *reshut hayahid*. The personal and private domain could be enlarged through individuals living around a courtyard or any similar enclosure, agreeing to do so, and placing items necessary for the meal in one place (Er. 17b, 61a, 82a; *Tur* and *Shulhan Arukh* Orah Hayim 336-395.)

It became the practice in the Middle Ages to consider the entire ghetto community as a private domain through the creation of an *eruv*, and of course, the area was walled in and had gates which were closed on *shabbat*. So, the necessary preconditions of an enclosure were assured. Later on, when the Jewish community spread further or no longer lived in a walled ghetto, a symbolic enclosure was created by connecting rope, wire or poles atop a post at least ten handbreadth (about 4 feet) in height (Er. 11a ff; *Tur Shulhan Arukh* Orah Hayim 362).

Although it was rather easily possible to construct such an artificial symbolic device in the towns of Poland, which were predominantly Jewish, it became much more difficult to do so in western cities, where Jews were in minority and frequently lived scattered throughout the city. In many places, therefore, no attempt was made to construct an *eruv*, and nothing was carried outside of the private domain by strictly Orthodox Jews. An attempt was made to create an *eruv* in Manhattan in the nineteen twenties. In this case, the island, of course, is entirely surrounded by water, except at the upper end and there a segment of the elevated railroad was to be used as a symbolic wall (*eruv*). This was recognized by some, but not by others. Recently, as the mood of Orthodoxy has been that of greater and greater strictness, efforts have been made to create an *eruv* in other cities as well. This can generally be accomplished without any governmental interference and done either through the use of telephone wires or cable television wire, with proper connections placed for the sake of the *eruv*.

It will be difficult to argue with the current Orthodox mood, which is one of further separation and strict adherence to the letter of the law. Certainly we, as Reform Jews, who are interested in the spirit of the law, would reject this kind of legal fiction for the observance of the *shabbat*, and we should discuss the matter in that spirit with our Orthodox colleagues.

July 1983

179. DIETS AND *PESAH*

QUESTION: Nowadays many congregants are utilizing weight-loss programs such as "The Cambridge Diet." An individual is required only to drink a nutritional liquid a number of times each day as well as a supplement with vitamins. Under what obligation is this individual in connection with the Passover *seder*? (Rabbi M. Feinstein, San Antonio, TX)

ANSWER: The diet in question has been assumed voluntarily by the individual. It has not been dictated by a health emergency or danger to life, nor has it been prescribed by a physician.

As no medical emergency is involved, such an individual should participate in the *seder* in the normal fashion; this will not violate his diet in any major manner. In other words, that person should sip from four cups of wine, consume a small portion of each symbolic food of the *seder*, and eat *matzah*. As you know, it is only commanded to eat the *matzah shemurah* at the *seder* (Pes. 38b, 120a; *Shulhan Arukh*

Orah Hayim 482 ff). Subsequently, no further *matzah* need be eaten and tradition demands only that we abstain from anything which is leavened (*hametz*).

January 1984

180. MEMORIAL LIGHTS/TABLETS ON *YOM KIPPUR*

QUESTION: Should the memorial lights and the memorial tablets be lit throughout the *Yom Kippur* service or only for the memorial service in the late afternoon? (Rabbi S. Pinskey, Tenafly, NJ)

ANSWER: The memorial light on *Yom Kippur* seems to go back to another custom which is quite old. The *Talmud* states in several places that we add honor to the Day of Atonement by using fine garments (Shab. 119a), while Asher ben Yehiel in his commentary to Yoma (the last chapter) added that aside from festive garments, we also have the custom of increasing the number of candles lit in the synagogue. This commentary sought to base itself on Isaiah 24.15, "Therefore, glorify the Lord in the region of light." Targum Jonathan translates "light" here as "candles." Later the *Kol Bo* (68) gave a much simpler reason. As people were in the synagogue all day and all night, they needed as many lights as possible. *Kol Bo* continued by stating that every individual brought a light to study *Torah* as *Yom Kippur* marked the anniversary of Moses' appearance with the second tablets. Such study was considered helpful in the redemption of the soul of each individual. This factor of "redemption" was then extended to deceased parents based on, "Atone for thy people Israel thou *hast* redeem" (Deut. 21.8). These individuals who were already dead would be provided with further atonement. The *Sifra* already found this meaning in the verse of Deuteronomy, and *Kol Bo* added it as a reason for lighting memorial candles. This custom is mentioned in the *Shulhan Arukh* (Orah Hayim 610.4), with comments by Isserles. The custom is more important to Ashkenazim than Sephardim.

It would, therefore, be appropriate to light memorial candles or memorial lights on a memorial plaque through the entire *Yom Kippur* service beginning with the *Kol Nidre*. This would be in keeping with an honored tradition.

August 1979

181. *SUKKAH* AS A *HUPPAH*

QUESTION: May a *sukkah* be used as a *huppah*? Is it possible to use a *sukkah* in this fashion in the courtyard of a synagogue? May it be used in the case of a symbolic *sukkah* on the *bimah* of a synagogue? (L. P., Pittsburgh, PA)

ANSWER: Traditionally a wedding is not conducted, except under emergency conditions, during *hol hamoed sukkot* (*Shulhan Arukh* Even Haezer 64.5; Orah Hayim 524.1). Yet, if we intend to do so, and are not constrained by the earlier prohibition, we should then inquire about the nature of the *huppah* in general. Although the term *huppah* has been used in the *Talmud*, its meaning there was quite different from the meaning which we have given it. In the *Talmud* it referred to the marriage chamber, often beautifully and generously decorated by the groom's father (San. 108a). Subsequently, there was considerable difference of opinion as to what *huppah* actually meant as indicated in the comments by Joe Sirkes (*Tur* Even Haezer 61). *Huppah* may have meant the isolation of the groom with the bride, or the mere fact that she entered his house (even in the company of others according to Rabbanu Nissim), or that some cloth, possibly a portion of the groom's coat, was placed over the girl's head during the blessings, or that the father gave the girl to the husband. These and others are all possible definitions of the *huppah*. None of them have anything to do with the small canopy which we now erect for a wedding ceremony. The canopy was probably first mentioned by Moses Halevi Mintz in the fifteenth century (*Maharam Minz* #109). There it stated that the community provided a *kipah*, or canopy, for the couple in which they were seated outside the synagogue before the ceremony. This, of course, had nothing to do with the ceremony itself. Moses Isserles first mentioned the *huppah* as used by us (*Shulhan Arukh* to Even Haezer 55.1), and it is clear that this was a novelty, symbolic of the room in which the bride and groom were later alone together. Solomon B. Freehof has concluded ("Huppah," *In the Time of Harvest*, pp. 192 ff) that this symbolic home was arranged during the period of poverty in Poland and Russia in which one could hardly expect a young student to be able to provide a home or even a room for the bride. Instead, they often resided in the home of the girl's parents. The *huppah* served to meet the ancient requirements, and the community arranged for this symbolic room on neutral ground, i.e., the courtyard of the synagogue. As the *huppah* stood for the sexual union of the bride and groom, it was considered inappropriate to bring the *huppah* into the synagogue. For that reason, the ceremony previously held within the synagogue was moved to the exterior into the courtyard.

Any kind of symbolic hut may be used, and there would be no reason for excluding a *sukkah*. The construction of the *sukkah* would not interfere with such a use. All the regulations which deal with the construction of a *sukkah* are quite specific. They treat its dimensions, the nature of its sides and the roof. The main concern, however, is the visibility of the sky through the roofing material, which may not be solid. For that reason, a *sukkah* may not be placed under a tree, does not become a permanent part of a home, etc. (*Shulhan Arukh* Orah Hayim 426 ff). The *sukkah* is to be used as much as possible during the week of the festival. The family should live in it and minimally take one meal in it (*Shulhan Arukh* Orah Hayim 439). All of this makes it clear that the *sukkah* is the equivalent of a home for that week. The symbolism of the *huppah* would fit to a *sukkah* if (a) the *sukkah* belongs to the groom, and therefore, demonstrated his intention of providing a home for his newly established family; (b) the *sukkah* belongs to the synagogue, and therefore, to the entire community. It would provide the same symbolism as the communal synagogue *huppah*.

For these reasons, it would be perfectly possible to use an outdoor *sukkah* as a *huppah* if a wedding is permitted at this time. For that matter, it would be equally appropriate to use the interior *huppah* placed on the *bimah* of many synagogues. As the *huppah* is symbolic, we may use it in this manner.

February 1979

182. DECORATION OF SUKKAH WITH FRUIT & VEGETABLES

QUESTION: Are there any specific requirements about decorating a *sukkah*? Need it be decorated with fresh and perishable fruits and vegetables? It seems that this is an inappropriate waste in a period when many individuals go hungry, and the food should be given to poor people. Would it be equally appropriate to celebrate the festival by insisting the fruit and vegetables, normally used in this fashion, simply be donated to the poor? (Rabbi M. Soifer, New Orleans, LA)

ANSWER: The decoration of *sukkot* with fruit and vegetables goes back to Talmudic discussions. There is, for example, a statement whether "branches of fig trees on which there are figs, vines with grapes, palm branches with dates, and wheat with ears on it, may be used for a *sukkah* covering." Though there is some discussion, they are considered valid (Suk. 13b). More directly, it is simply stated that a wide variety of fruit and vegetables were used to decorate the *sukkah*. This included nuts, almonds, peaches, pomegranates, grapes and ears of corn along with phials of wine, oil, fine flax and embroidered work (Suk. 10a, also 31b). In another place in the same tractate, there is a discussion of using other decorations (Suk. 28b). Some later authorities mention nuts used for beautification. It is clear, therefore, that there is some warrant for decorating the *sukkah* in this fashion, using fruit and vegetables as well as nuts, from Talmudic times onward. We find this mentioned, incidentally, in prescriptions for the *sukkah* given by Maimonides, Caro and other codifiers, as well as an occasional reference in the responsa. There is, however, no requirement that the *sukkah* be decorated in this fashion. For that matter, any type of decoration seems to have been acceptable. Some *sukkot* of wealthy European families in the last century contained painted walls. Few of those survived and one is exhibited in the Israel Museum in Jerusalem. Others were decorated with pictures made by various younger members of the family. There are no stipulations about this in the legal *halakhic* literature and we are dealing with *minhag* in this matter.

As there are no stipulations for the decoration of the *sukkah*, it would be a *mitzvah* in time of need to use the funds normally expended upon such items of food for the direct alleviation of poverty. In place of the fruit and vegetables usually hung, inedible items could be hung as decoration, such as gourds, acorns, chestnuts, etc., along with pictures made by children in the religious schools.

October 1983

183. THE NATURE OF THE *ETROG*

QUESTION: The modern nature of the *lulav* and *etrog* are quite clear, but the original text in Leviticus 23.40 is not so specific. How do we know that these items now used are those originally intended? (D. F. A., St. Louis, MO)

ANSWER: There are many uncertainties in the verse cited, "and you shall take on the first day the fruit of goodly trees, branches of palm trees, and boughs of thick trees, and willows of the brook. You shall rejoice before the Lord your God seven days" (*Holy Scriptures*, Jewish Publication Society, 1917). The uncertainty is conveyed by the more recent translation of the *Torah*, "On the first day you shall take the product of *hadar* trees, branches of palm trees, boughs of leafy trees, and willows of the brook, and you shall rejoice before the Lord your God seven days," (*The Torah*, Jewish Publication Society, 1967). The footnote for *hadar*, "leafy," states that the meaning is uncertain. It has been set for us by tradition. We must now try to establish the age of this tradition.

Let us begin with the phrase *peri etz hadar*, commonly interpreted as *etrog*. The *Targum Onkelos* translated this as *perei ilan m'shubah*. The Septuagint provided a similar translation, while the later Jewish commentaries like Rashi took it for granted that this was the *etrog*, and so followed the interpretation of the *Mishnah*. Ramban suggested that *etrog* was simply the Aramaic for the Hebrew word *hadar*. Ibn Ezra similarly relied on the earlier tradition and stated that there was no fruit as beautiful, and for that reason it was called *hadar*. It was, of course, clear from other uses of the words that it meant glorious, beautiful or grandly decorated. The modern Biblical critic, Bruno Baentsch (*Handkommentar zum Alten Testament* - Exodus, Levitikus, Numeri - 1903), suggested that it either refers to the fruit of paradise or to the citron for which the word *etrog* was used later. He also speculated that the fruit might originally have been connected with a fruit offering as mentioned in some Carthaginian rites (p. 418). We find the term *etrog* used in the Mishnaic description of the ritual connected with *Sukkot* (Suk. III.4). This would make it clear that by the second century at the very latest, the citron had been thoroughly established. Naturally, this tradition may go back to a period earlier than the written version of the *Mishnah*. We must, therefore, ask when the citron first appeared in the Near East, as it was not native to that area.

It seems that the citron was already reported by Greek authors; it reached the Mediterranean in the third century before our era (Harrison, Masefield and Michael, *Oxford Book of Food Plants*, 1969, p. 88). Immanuel Löw, the great Jewish authority on plants, arrived at his conclusions through eliminating other possible fruits, for example, the pomegranate. Although it is beautiful, the tree is not leafy. Another contender was the karob. That tree is grand, but the fruit is not. That left only the *etrog* by elimination - *rutaceae, citrus* (I. Löw, *Die Flora der Juden* III, p. 53, III, pp. 103 ff). Later Löw stated that the fruit originally was the *citrus medica* which was introduced to the Mediterranean by the administrators of Alexander the Great.

In the time of Alexander, the tree was first described by the ancient authority Theophrastus. Its use was also reported by Josephus (*Antiquities* xiii, 13, 5). He called the *etrog* a Persian apple, which would be a citron.

Probably the earliest evidence that this is a citron comes from the time of Alexander Jannaeus (104 - 78 B.C.E.), when the people pelted the high priest during *Sukkot* with their *etrogim*. The rabbinic literature made the *etrog* a tradition from the days of Sinai (*halakhah misinai*). Löw felt that the tradition went back as far as 430 B.C.E. (Löw, *op. cit.*, III, p. 289).

The fruit had first been cultivated by the Chinese who found it in the warmer regions of the Himalayas. Subsequently, the fruit was introduced to Europe through the Crusaders. It may have been introduced to Roman Italy by Jews who used it on *Sukkot* by the second century. Citrons were used in villas and gardens for decorative purposes. The fruit was definitely not known in ancient Egypt (Löw, *op. cit.*, III, pp. 278 ff). We know from the report of Jacques De Vitry, who visited Israel around 1225, that the citron had not yet been introduced into Northern Europe.

The numerous Mishnaic and Talmudic references to *etrog* do not tell us the precise nature of this citron, so it is impossible to proceed further into the species of citron available.

Many commentators have found it strange that the fruit was not given a precise name, but simply described as "the fruit of the glorious tree." The word *etrog* came from the Persian *torong* and originally from the Sanskrit *suranga*, its term for orange. Löw also noted that the German Jews frequently used *citrus limon scabiosa*, which they received from the southern lands of Europe. Currently *citrus medica* is generally used (Löw, *op. cit*, III, p. 285). Naturally greater efforts to explain the fruit were made after the appearance of the Karaites with their questioning attitude, but to no avail.

Maimonides, in the twelfth century, also sought a rational reason for the use of this particular fruit; he felt it was chosen because it remained fresh through the entire festival (*Moreh Nibukhim* 3.43; *Yad Hil. Lulav* 7.2). Both in medieval and modern times, various efforts to equate *hadar* and *etrog* have been made, but without success.

The efforts of Biblical commentators during the last centuries to find a solution can be divided into three efforts: 1. Both tree and fruit must be grand; 2. The tree possess the same taste as the fruit; 3. The fruit remain on the tree throughout the year, as is true of citrus fruit trees which bloom throughout the year, and whose leaves do not fall (Löw, *op. cit*, III, p. 288).

In conclusion, we can state that the tradition of the *etrog* is more than 2,000 years old, but its origin remains obscure.

November 1984

184. TORAH READING FOR SECOND DAY OF SHAVUOT

QUESTION: This year the second day of *Shavuot* will be celebrated on *shabbat* by Orthodox and some Conservative Jews. This means that the cycle of *Torah* readings may for the subsequent weeks be different for those Reform and Conservative Jews who celebrate only one day of *Shavuot*. What should the *Torah* reading be for us? How should we handle this situation so as to bring a minimum confusion to the Jewish community? (Rabbi S. Karff, Houston, TX)

ANSWER: Initially the answer to this question seems simple. After all, the Israeli Jewish community, both liberal and traditional, observes only one day of the holiday and so continues reading the *Torah* one portion out of step with the Diaspora community until the next double portion is reached, in this case (*huqat-balaq*). That is a possibility for us in the case of *Shavuot* or when the eighth day of *Pesah* falls on a *shabbat*.

This solution is desirable for those congregations which read the entire *Torah* portion. It is, however, not necessary for those congregations which read the *Torah* on a tri-annual cycle with only a portion of the *sidrah* read during each *shabbat*. Then it would be equally possible to read a segment of the following Scriptural portion, in this case *nasa*, and another segment on the next *shabbat*.

This solution has the advantage of not separating us from the remainder of the Diaspora Jewish community. The Israeli solution is fine, but there the entire community, Orthodox and Liberal, follows the same pattern. We would recommend a division of the *Torah* portion for most congregations, and therefore, maintain the same cycle as the rest of the Diaspora community. For congregations which read the entire portion, the other solution is equally appropriate.

August 1986

185. *HANNUKAH* AND A COMBUSTIBLE *MENORAH*

QUESTION: May a *Hannukah menorah* be constructed totally of combustible material which will be destroyed during the course of the festival? In other words, an artist intends to fabricate eight different *menorahs*, one for each night of *Hannukah*; they will be made of wax. They are intended to be lit on the eight nights and to burn until nothing remains. (M. G., Washington, DC)

ANSWER: The *Hannukah menorah* represents one of the few ritual objects of which we have a large representation from the past. We possess examples dating back to the first century, while more recent times are represented by hundreds of variations (M. Narkiss, *The Hannukah Lamp*; R. Elis, *Hannukah Lamps of the Judah L. Magnus Museum*). *Menorahs* have been made of many kinds of metal as well as stone, and occasionally wood or porcelain. There is virtually no discussion about the material of the *menorah*; its purpose is to "publicize the miracle." This can be done in a humble or grand manner according to the means of the household involved. My synagogue museum contains a small traveling *menorah* no larger than a matchbox, as well as an eighteenth century *menorah* six feet in height. Tradition has been indifferent to the material used. There is some discussion about the manner in which the lights should be displayed, although that is also minimal (S. B. Freehof, "A Non-Linear Menorah," *Modern Reform Responsa*, pp. 86 ff).

Considerable attention is given to the material used as fuel for the light. Theoretically, virtually any fuel which clearly proclaims the miracle is allowed; this excludes a wood burning fire, whose appearance does not indicate the observance of the holiday (Sab. 21b). There are Orthodox objections to gas and electric *menorahs* (S. Z. Auerbach, *Meorei Esh*, Chap. 3; Frank, *Har Zevi*, Orah Hayim #143; Eliezer Waldenberg, *Tzitz Eliezer* I, #20, Chapt. 12). Those objections rest on very doubtful bases, i.e., that the appropriate amount of fuel is not immediately available, that throwing a light switch is not akin to kindling a flame, or that a wick is necessary for the *menorah*.

The real objection to the use of gas or electricity is aesthetic and our love of tradition. We wish to celebrate *Hannukah* through lighting candles or oil as did our forefathers. If oil is used then olive oil is preferred; among candles, wax candles are suggested (*Shulhan Arukh* Orah Hayim 673.1). The sources, however, indicate that any fuel may be used. Tradition is primarily concerned with publicizing the miracle in an appealing manner.

It would, therefore, be appropriate to utilize the eight separate *menorahs*, one for each night, under conditions in which each will be completely consumed.

October 1984

186. SEQUENCE OF LIGHTING *HANNUKAH* CANDLES

QUESTION: Is there a sequence for lighting the *Hannukah* candles? Should it be done from right to left, or from left to right? (M. C., Pittsburgh, PA)

ANSWER: There are a number of ways of lighting the *Hannukah menorah* and each is appropriate. Israel Isserlein indicated that the Rhineland tradition began at the left of the *menorah* and continued in sequence day by day. On the other hand, he also stated that in Vienna, precisely the opposite sequence was used, and one moved from right to left, in other words, in the fashion of the Hebrew writing (*Terumat Hadeshen* #105). To the best of my knowledge, there is no earlier discussion of this matter and there is no Talmudic or Mishnaic basis for any decision. The *Shulhan Arukh* decided that the candles should be inserted from the right, with one added each night, but lit from the left, with the newest lit first, a kind of compromise (*Shulhan Arukh* Orah Hayim 676.5).

The *Talmud* (Sab. 21b) is concerned with another problem, i.e., should one add a light each night or diminish the number each night? The School of Shammai began with eight candles and diminished the number until on the last night only a single candle was lit. On the other hand, the School of Hillel began with one candle and built to a climax of eight candles. Tradition has chosen to follow the School of Hillel, and we continue in this pattern.

Clearly then, family tradition in this matter may be followed, though the path of the *Shulhan Arukh* has become a general custom, and we should follow this pattern along with the majority of the Jewish community.

October 1984

187. VIRGINITY AND THE *KETUBAH*

QUESTION: The traditional *ketubah* classifies a bride as a virgin or places her in a number of other categories. Nowadays, many couples have lived together before marriage. Should this fact be taken into account in writing the *ketubah*? Should an inquiry be made by the officiating rabbi? What would the consequences be if the bride is called a "virgin" and this is not so? (Rabbi R. Marcovitz, Pittsburgh, PA)

ANSWER: Chastity before marriage has been urged by both the *Bible* and the *Talmud* (Proverbs; Lev. 19.29, 20.10; *Tos.* Kid. 1.4, etc.). These and other sources, of course, apply to both men and women. However, virginity has only been mentioned in the marriage document in the case of women. Virginity determines the *mohar,* in other words, the amount of the legal purchase agreement, which has been an age old portion of the marriage document. A difference in the sum to be provided exists between virgins and those who are not virgins. In the *Bible* the price seems to have been fifty *sheqel* for virgins (Ex. 22.15; Deut. 22.29; Ket. 10, 29b, 30b). In the later rabbinic periods, the *mohar* for a virgin was two hundred *zuzim,* which seems to have been the equivalent of fifty *sheqel* (Ket. 10a, 110b), while a non-virgin had a *mohar* of one hundred *zuzim* (B. K. 36b; Ket. 10a, b; *Tos.* to Ket. 10a - 11a ff; *Yad* Hil. Ishut 11.3). The priestly aristocracy established a *mohar* of double this amount (L. M. Epstein, *The Jewish Marriage Contract,* pp. 73 ff). In more recent times, the ring symbolizes the former cash *mohar* without the prejorative overtones of a purchase agreement. We have interpreted the ring as a symbol of mutual love.

The status of the bride is not only reflected in the *mohar* but also through the descriptive term used with her name in the *ketubah*. We must now ask whether the *ketubot* of the past made an effort to accurately reflect the status of each bride. They were, of course, to contain no false material (Git. 10b, 87b; *Yad* Hil. Ishut 3.8). No problem ever existed for women who were widowed or divorced; they were so designated in the *ketubah*. Their status was public knowledge and there was no reason to hide it or to be ashamed of it. If a woman was no longer a virgin, due to accident or intercourse, this should have been so designated. Yet we find that in ancient Judea, where premarital intercourse seems to have been frequent, the Judeans did not permit such a reflection to be cast on their women and insisted on a *mohar* of two hundred *zuzim* for everyone including the widowed and divorced. In other words, all women were automatically classified as virgins. It seems that at this time it was not customary to mention the status of the bride when her name appeared in the *ketubah* (Ket. 10b, 12a; *Tos.* Ket. 1.4; J. Ket. 25c). There were a number of other periods in Jewish history when loose standards of conduct were widespread. However, this does not seem to have affected the wording of the *ketubot* (Isaac b. Sheshet quoting Nahmanides #6, 395, 398, 425; L. Epstein, *Sex Laws and Customs in Judaism*, p. 128). There is some likelihood that the joining together of *erusin* and *nisuin*, which occurred in the Middle Ages, was due to illicit intercourse which took place during the longer interval between the two ceremonies, which were often separated by as much as a year (Z. W. Falk, *Jewish Matrimonial Law in the Middle Ages*, pp. 43 ff; A. Freiman, *Seder Qidushin Venisuin*).

Let us now look at the document itself and the various categories of non-virgins, such as widows and divorcees. In the case of a divorcee, this designation is placed in the *ketubah* in order to indicate that she is prohibited from marrying a priest. In the case of someone who has been raped or seduced, this lack of virginity may be omitted in the *ketubah* in order to refrain from shaming her through this memory; some scholars insisted that it be mentioned and made public knowledge (*Nahalat Shivah* 12.15). However, we should also note that no authorities demand an inquiry to see whether the individual involved is in fact a virgin. B. Schereschewsky states that if the bride is neither widowed nor divorced, the *ketubah* should indicate "virgin" (*Dinei Mishpahah*, p. 99).

We should also note that the traditional *ketubah* makes no demands of virginity upon the groom. There is no statement about his virginity or lack of it, nor was this reflected in the economic segment of the *ketubah*.

Now let us go one step further and see what is the consequence of writing "virgin" in a *ketubah* when this is not so. It is clear from the Biblical text (Deut. 22.14) that an accusation of non-virginity could be brought by the groom after the wedding night. The parents would then proceed with the defense of their daughter. If indeed she was not a virgin, the death penalty was involved (Deut. 22.20, 21). If she had been accused erroneously, then her husband was fined a hundred pieces of silver and forfeited the opportunity of ever divorcing her (Deut. 22.13 - 19). All of this has been discussed further by the *Talmud* and later literature (Ket. 10a, 46a; etc.) One authority, however, indicated that if such an accusation was brought before him, the young man was to be whipped, as the accusation indicated that he himself had engaged in illicit intercourse earlier. Another limited such a challenge to a man previously married since he possessed legitimate experience (Ket. 10a). Furthermore, after a girl is more than twelve years and six months old (*bogeret*), the hymen may disappear naturally and no sign of virginity remains (Ket. 36a). Should she have lost her virginity by accident, then the only change would be a reduction in her *ketubah* by 100 *zuzim*; no such reduction is made if she claims rape after bethrothal (*Yad* Hil. Ishut 11.10 ff). It was generally made almost impossible for a groom to file a complaint of non-virginity (Ket. 10a b; *Yad*; *Shulhan Arukh*).

We should also note that if there was any kind of misrepresentation of a physical defect on the part of the wife, without the knowledge of the husband, then this is grounds for divorce or for the annulment of the marriage (*Tos.* Ket. 7.8 - 9; Ket. 72b ff). This is also true if the groom found that his wife was not a virgin. In order to accuse her, he had to show that he had never been together with her without a chaperon. The laws concerning chaperonage are extremely strict (Ned. 20a; *J.* Kid. 66b; Git. 81a; Ket. 27b ff; *Yad* Hil. Is. Biah 21.27; *Arukh Hashulkhan* Even Haezer 119.25 - 28).

The husband has to bring his complaint to a court immediately (Ket. 3b, 11b, 12a; Yeb. 111b). Such an accusation does not necessarily reflect illicit intercourse. The woman could claim that she lost her virginity due to an accident, without intercourse (Ket. 13a). Her only penalty then is a reduction in the *mohar*.

Before we leave the subject we should note that the Gaonim composed a special *berakhah* to be recited by the groom on his wedding night if his wife was a virgin (B. Lewis, *Otzar Hagaonim*, Vol. 8, Ket. pp. 14-15; Lawrence A. Hoffman, *The Canonization of the Synagogue Service*, p. 136). The recital of such a blessing if the wife was not a virgin would be *levatalah*. The ritual was, however, not continued and no post-Gaonic discussions exist.

From this we can see that with our modern system of dating it would be absolutely impossible for any man to bring a successful accusation of non-virginity against his wife. Therefore, there are no legal consequences which can be drawn from a statement of virginity made in the *ketubah* or represented by the *mohar* when, in fact, the bride is not a virgin.

In summary, we realize that there were periods in our history when female virginity was very important. However, we can also see that during other times looser moral standards prevailed, and the *ketubot* written during them were not changed.

We must also express our modern concern for equal rights for men and women. If we expressly name the status of the female, we should also do so for the male.

We might also view the entire matter differently and see the marriage as already taken place, through the intercourse of the couple who lived together. This form of marriage is legal, *bediavad*, although frowned upon since the Talmudic period (Kid 9b; *Shulkhan Arukh* Even Haezer 33.1, 42.1). The marriage subsequently conducted in the synagogue, and the resultant *ketubah*, would confirm an already existing status. The bride may very well have entered into the original relationship as a virgin.

On all these grounds, it would be wise either to refrain from any kind of designation of status for the woman in the *ketubah* (for which there is ample precedent), or simply to use the designation "virgin" as part of a standard formula. We may standardize it in exactly the same spirit as some of the economic elements of the *ketubah* which no longer possess significance for us.

March 1984

188. BRIDE AND GROOM ON THEIR WEDDING DAY

QUESTION: May a bride and groom see each other on their wedding day? (L. F. and W. R., Pittsburgh, PA)

ANSWER: Let us begin with a discussion of the relationship between bride and groom during their engagement. There was a strong feeling that the couple should not be permitted to be alone subsequent to their formal engagement. This was the Galilean custom which became normative for Jewish life (*M. Ket.* 1.5, 12a); the Judean knew no such prohibition (*M*. Kallah 1.1; Ket. 7b). In the Talmudic and Gaonic period, an engaged man and woman could not be together alone (Yeb. 69b; Kid. 75a, *Otzar Hagaonim*, Ket. 18 ff; Yeb. 166). This became the law and was reflected in the later Codes (*Yad* Hil. Ishut 101, *Shulhan Arukh* Even Haezer 55.1). There are discussions of violations in the responsa literature, and they were treated with greater or lesser severity depending upon the period and the general environment.

Nowhere does this literature restrict the groom and bride from seeing each other on the wedding day, or prior to it, as long as they are chaperoned. In fact, the groom and bride see each other immediately before the wedding. If they fasted, and the wedding was late in the day, then they are permitted to break their fast together before the ceremony, as long as they are chaperoned and do not partake of any intoxicating liquor (*Hokhmat Adam* 129.2). More important is the custom of covering the face of the bride by the groom before the wedding, usually in the presence of both sets of parents (*M*. Ket. 2.1; *Shulhan Arukh* Even Haezer 31.2).

The current prohibition is, therefore, a recent American *minhag*, probably from non-Jewish sources. There is no reason for the couple not to see each other, or to participate in such honors as being called to the *Torah* upon the *shabbat* before their wedding, when the wedding is to be held on *motzei shabbat*.

December 1981

189. A MINYAN AT A WEDDING CEREMONY

QUESTION: Is a *minyan* required to be present at a wedding ceremony? (P. L., Pittsburgh, PA)

ANSWER: The traditional requirement for a *minyan* is based upon the Talmudic interpretation (Ket. 7b) of Ruth (4.2), "He took ten men of the elders of the city." The *Talmud* felt that they were taken to act as witnesses. Eight of these may be relatives, and two must be unrelated so that they can attest to the value of the ring and the propriety of the *ketubah*. Jacob Moelln (*Hilkhot Nisuin*) required two additional witnesses for the *ketubah*. The assembled witnesses and relatives could later be called as witnesses in case the legality of the wedding was questioned.

Two witnesses are used for our *ketubah* in keeping with the tradition.

A *minyan* provides a more formal and public setting for the wedding (A. Freimann, *Seder Qidushin Venisuin*, p. 16; P. Dykan, *Dinei Nisuin Vegerushin*, p. 29). Medieval authorities repeatedly felt the need for a *minyan* in order to prevent misrepresentation and deception (Adret and others; see Freimann, *op. cit.*, pp. 50 f, 102 ff, 160 f). Although every effort to have a *minyan* should be made, it is not essential that a *minyan* be present in keeping with the old tradition that a service can also be conducted with a lesser number, and it is certainly valid *b'diavad* (Sof. 10.8; *Shulhan Arukh* Even Haezer 34.4). If a *minyan* is constituted, men and women would count equally in keeping with our Reform traditions.

February 1977

190. DUAL WEDDING CEREMONIES

QUESTION: A couple in which one party is Jewish and the other is non-Jewish wish to be married. They would like to have two separate ceremonies, a Christian ceremony and a Jewish ceremony. What is our attitude toward this kind of a situation? (Rabbi H. Sherer, Mission Viejo, CA)

ANSWER: The position of the Central Conference on mixed marriage is very clear, and the Conference has been strongly opposed to such marriages as stated through resolutions passed in 1909 and 1973 (*C.C.A.R. Yearbook*, 1909, Vol. 19, pp. 170; 1973, Vol. 57, p. 161). I have written detailed responsa on mixed marriages for the Conference (*C.C.A.R. Yearbook*, 1980, Vol. 90, pp. 86 ff; 1982, Vol. 92; W. Jacob, *American Reform Responsa*, pp. 445 ff). For the reasons cited in these responsa, both traditional Judaism and Reform Judaism have been, and continue to be, opposed to mixed marriage. This means that no Jewish ceremony could be conducted under the circumstances described in the question.

The Central Conference has stated its utter opposition to rabbis co-officiating with Christian clergy at mixed marriages in a special resolution passed in 1982. This would certainly apply to two separate ceremonies, one Christian and one Jewish. We vigorously reject this attempt at religious syncretism suggested by the question and can in no way condone Jewish participation in such dual ceremonies in which one party is Jewish and the other Christian.

January 1982

191. PERMANENT *HUPPAH*

QUESTION: A sculptor has created a permanent *hupah* with a brass top simulating leaves and vines. May this stand as a synagogue ornament, or must it be disassembled between weddings? (Rabbi J. Glaser, New York, NY)

ANSWER: Let us begin by looking at the origin of the *hupah* and its placement. The *hupah* is referred to the room to which the bride and groom retired after the marriage ceremony in order to consummate the marriage (Psalms 19.7; Sotah 49b; Gen. Rabbah 114; *Yad* Hil. Ishut 10.10; *Tosfot* to Sukah 25b and Yoma 13b, etc.) Usually this was in the house of the groom. Therefore, the act of bringing the bride to the *huppah* indicated the transfer of the bride into the groom's household. This is the generally accepted meaning; some consider the ceremony of veiling the bride as *huppah*, for it established a new relationship between bride and groom (Isserles to *Shulhan Arukh* Even Haezer 55.1; Ezekiel Landau to *Shulhan Arukh* Yoreh Deah 342.1; see Taz to Yoreh Deah 342 for a contrary opinion). In any case, it is clear that the older usage of the *huppah* does not refer to the simple canopy now used during wedding ceremonies. This was introduced in the late medieval period, possibly just before the time of Moses Isserles, as he refers to it as something used "nowadays" (*Shulhan Arukh* Even Haezer 55.1). The custom itself may have come from the earlier medieval *minhag* of spreading a *talit* over the bride and groom during the wedding ceremony, or of the groom simply spreading his *talit* over the bride during the ceremony (*Hamanhig* 91b ff). The placement of a *huppah* within the synagogue has not been accepted by all authorities. Moses Sofer objected to it as a Gentile custom (*Hatam Sofer* Even Haezer #65). Isserles knew its use in the synagogue courtyard (Isserles to *Shulhan Arukh* Even Haezer 61.1). We see, therefore that this new symbolic use of the *huppah* during the wedding ceremony is relatively recent. Nowadays, a *huppah* may be beautifully embroidered. There would be nothing wrong with having a permanent sculptured floral *huppah*.

There is nothing in literature which deals with the storage of the *huppah* or its placement when not in use. As it mostly consists of a cloth placed on four staves held by four friends, the question does not arise. Even when placed on poles, there still is no reason to display it after the wedding.

Such work of art may be displayed permanently. It would be a beautiful addition to the ritual items of a synagogue. Many synagogues have had a permanent chair for Elijah for use during a *berit*, so they may now have a permanent *huppah*. It would form an appropriate reminder of the *mitzvah* of marriage.

April 1982

192. ADULTERY AND MARRIAGE

QUESTION: One of the partners in a marriage has engaged in an adulterous relationship, and the marriage has terminated in acrimonious divorce. Subsequently, the adulterous party has asked the rabbi to officiate at the marriage to "the other person." Should the rabbi comply with the request?

ANSWER: The sources are clear in their prohibition of adultery (Ex. 20.13) and of marriage between the adulterous party and her lover (Sot. 27b; *Shulhan Arukh* Even Haezer 11.1, 178.17). The traditional statements, of course, deal primarily with the adulterous woman and her lover. They are very strict in this regard and even prohibit remarriage to her former husband, though she may not have been married to anyone else subsequent to the divorce (*Shulhan Arukh* Even Haezer 11.1). The prohibition against marrying her lover holds true not only after divorce but even after the death of her former husband (Yev. 24b; *Shulhan Arukh* Even Haezer 11.1).

Despite these strictures the reality of the situation, which usually led the adulterous parties to live together and possibly to marry, brought rabbinic recognition of this status. Tradition gives its grudging consent by stating that if, nevertheless, the adulterous parties marry, they are not compelled to divorce (*Shulhan Arukh* Even Haezer 11.2 ff and commentaries, 159.3; *Otzar Haposqim* Even Haezer 11.1, 44).

A rabbi may, in this instance, find herself in a difficult position as she is dutybound to strengthen family life and defend the sanctity of marriage. If she, however, refuses to marry this couple, they may simply opt to live together, as is frequent in our time; that will not help their situation or the general attitude towards family life. Therefore, the rabbi should officiate at such a marriage, while at the same time discussing her own hesitation in keeping the tradition. She may insist on some special counseling before the ceremony. She should insist that it be a simple ceremony and one which places special emphasis on the seriousness and sanctity of marriage.

March 1986

193. SOME QUESTIONS ON WEDDING PROCEDURES

QUESTION: Must the *ketubah* be signed prior to the ceremony? May the bride and groom see each other prior to the wedding in order to perform the ceremony of *bedecken*? Is there any objection to guests rising as the bride enters in the processional? Is this a Jewish custom? (Rabbi B. Lefkowitz, Taunton, MA)

ANSWER: The *ketubah* must be written before the wedding ceremony (Ket. 82b; *Shulhan Arukh* Even Haezer 61.1; P. Dykan, *Dinei Nisuin V'gerushin,* pp. 134 ff). It must be signed by two witnesses who will be present for the ceremony. Normally the witnesses also sign it immediately prior to the ceremony. But as far as I know, there would be no objection to their signing it following the ceremony, after they have actually witnessed it. As the *ketubah* deals with the obligations which the groom and bride assume upon marriage, they must sign it beforehand, but need not see each other at that time.

Now let us deal with the custom of *bedecken*. This *minhag* was already mentioned in the *Mishnah* (Ket. 2.1) and also found in later books of *minhagim* (*Liqutei Mahari* 3.130; *Minhagei Yisrael*, p. 360; *Shulhan Arukh* Even Haezer 31.2; Isserles, etc.) This custom is optional and need not be undertaken even in an Orthodox ceremony. If done, it would take place just before proceeding to the *huppah*. As that time the groom places a veil over the bride's face. This is usually done in the families' presence. As this act forms an immediate prelude to the ceremony under the *huppah*, it could be designated as the beginning of the ceremony. The bride and groom would see each other at that moment and then proceed to the *huppah*. It should be noted that there is nothing in Jewish custom or law which prohibits the bride from seeing the groom on the wedding day as long as they are chaperoned.

As far as the assembled individuals rising when the bride enters, I have not heard of this custom, nor is it mentioned in any books of *minhagim* available to me. There is no harm in doing it, but why bother?

April 1982

194. JEWISH WEDDING IN A NON-JEWISH HOME

QUESTION: A young couple wishes to be married in the home of her parents. The young man is Jewish by birth and the young woman is Jewish by conversion. The parents are Catholic and the wedding is to be performed in their home which contains Christian symbols in virtually every room, including a beautiful Andrea della Robbia *terra cota* depicting the Virgin and Jesus over the mantelpiece of the living room where the wedding will occur. Is it appropriate to hold a wedding in such a setting? (L. R., New Jersey)

ANSWER: We should begin by recognizing the obvious willingness of the parents to accept the conversion and the fact that they are agreeable to have a Jewish wedding in their Catholic home. The fact that the wedding will be held in the home suggests strong family ties and, of course, everything should be done to encourage a good relationship between the young couple and both sets of parents. As you suggested in your conversation, if the weather permits, the wedding will be held outside. Although there is considerable specifically Catholic statuary in the garden, it would be quite possible to locate the wedding site in such a way that the statuary would only be incidental to the ceremony and attention would not be focused upon it.

The situation would be more difficult in the living room where this beautiful work of art is the central point of the entire room. As it is not possible to remove it, perhaps one should begin by seeking to cover it as much as possible through a *huppah* and floral decorations. Certainly if a floral *huppah* of considerable size is placed into the living room, this would largely remove the problem.

Similar problems have arisen in the past. Many a Jewish traveller in former days found himself lodged at night in an inn with Christian images on its walls. When he wished to pray, he faced another direction away from them, and turned his heart to Jerusalem (Abraham Danzig, *Hayei Adam* 23.5). Occasionally a group of Jews needed a temporary site for services. A non-Jewish house of worship could be used if nothing else is available (Abraham Gumbiner, *Orah Hayim* 154.11, note 17; Joseph Teomim, *Peri Megadim* to the above reference). Many of our modern American Jewish congregations have begun their existence in church buildings temporarily borrowed and it was not always possible to remove every Christian symbol and decoration.

If no floral screen can be put up, and the wedding must be held there, then the wedding should simply proceed, and we should take the plaque on the wall as a piece of art. After all, it decorates a home and not a church which is a place of normal public worship. We should remember as well that the wedding service is a private ritual generally conducted before a *minyan* for the sake of public knowledge and witnesses. It does not, however, possess the character of a formal Jewish service. It would, therefore, be possible to conduct the wedding in this setting, preferably under a *huppah* which would hide the plaque.

June 1983

195. CHRISTIAN MUSIC AT JEWISH WEDDING

QUESTION: A couple, in which one member is a Jew by birth and the other by conversion, is going to be married in the synagogue. They have made several musical requests, classical in nature. Some of the pieces are specifically written for church service. Should this music be permitted at the wedding? (G. M., Boston, MA)

ANSWER: We should begin by looking at the nature of synagogue music for weddings. Tradition has virtually nothing to say about wedding music. There are reports of musicians from Talmudic times onward (*Gen. Rab.* 23, 50) playing at weddings, but it is presumed that this occurred principally at the subsequent celebration. In Prague, organ or other music was provided in the synagogue prior to the wedding ceremony. This may also have been true in some of the renaissance synagogues of Italy and early authorities, like Mordecai, permit non-Jews to play music at weddings (Mordecai, Betzah 5;

Shulhan Arukh Orah Hayim 338.1 ff; Roth *History of the Jews in Venice*, pp. 200 ff). Efforts were made to prohibit music at weddings in Palestine although the people liked it. Radbaz fought against the custom (*Responsa #6*, 132). However, no specific pieces of music are mentioned in the literature.

We should also recognize that throughout our history we have frequently borrowed from the musical tradition of our neighbors. In this way, some Christian pieces entered the Jewish repetoire. In the sixteenth century, Joel Sirkes felt that only music which was a fundamental part of the Christian liturgy was prohibited to us (*Responsa #127*). Such borrowing also occurred during the last century when many who sought to create a Jewish hymnal included pieces by Christian composers. Even when we have not taken music from the Christian liturgical tradition, we have borrowed heavily from the popular and secular tradition throughout the ages. In our century when much fine Jewish music has been composed, we should be particularly careful and use it whenever possible.

In this instance, we should exercise special care as one member of this couple has converted to Judaism. Everything connected with the wedding should, therefore, reflect this religious choice. If the couple wishes to introduce the wedding through some classical music, it should not be too difficult to find appropriate pieces which will properly reflect the mood of the day as well as the taste of the young couple.

June 1983

196. TWENTY-FIFTH ANNIVERSARY OF A MIXED MARRIAGE*

QUESTION: A couple, in which the husband is Jewish and wife is Christian, has been happily married for twenty-five years. Their children have been raised as Jews and the oldest among them is now a member of the congregation. The family has participated in the life of the congregation in every way, including a term of service by the husband on the Board of the Congregation. The rabbi is a friend of the couple. The couple was originally married by a judge. Now they have asked the rabbi to participate in the anniversary celebration by performing a service of rededication, before a party at home, after twenty-five years. Should the rabbi participate or should he decline on the grounds that he does not officiate at mixed marriages? (J. F., Miami, FL)

ANSWER: There is, of course, nothing in the traditional literature which deals with this subject. For a full discussion of mixed marriage and the *halakhic* basis for not officiating, let me refer you to the resolutions of the C.C.A.R. and W. Jacob, *American Reform Responsa* (#148 ff). There is also no discussion in any literature about a ceremony of rededication. Nothing akin to it seems to have been used in the past. As the couple has participated actively in the congregation throughout their married life, this might be an appropriate time to suggest the conversion of the non-Jewish spouse, especially as her entire family is Jewish. Under these circumstances, no formal period of study would be necessary; conversion would indicate official acceptance into the Jewish community. Following that, a marriage ceremony, with appropriate modifications, could take place.

If the non-Jewish spouse does not wish to convert, a simple prayer of rededication, rather than a service, would be appropriate; the rabbi may participate in the private setting. We make this decision on the principle that *lehat-hilah*, we can not officiate in a mixed marriage, but *bediavad*, we will accept the couple, work with them and help them lead a Jewish life. The occasion should have no overtones of a marriage ceremony and should stress the couple's participation in Jewish life and in the congregation. Everything should be done in a way which would stress that there has been no change in the rabbi's policy on mixed marriage, nor should it have the appearance of representing any change.

October 1984

197. CHILD BORN THROUGH ARTIFICIAL INSEMINATION

QUESTION: Should a parent whose child has been born through artificial insemination tell the child that the child has been conceived in this fashion? If the semen used in the process of artificial insemination is a mixture of that of the father and of a volunteer, is the husband to be considered the actual father of the child? Is it permissible to use a donor in the case of artificial insemination? (Rabbi S. Ezring, Elkins Park, PA)

ANSWER: Let me begin with your second question which deals with the status of the father. In many instances artificial insemination merely uses the semen of the husband. Then there is absolutely no question. If, as you indicated, a mixture has been used, there would also be no question about the father. In accordance with Jewish law, the husband is presumed to be the father unless there is proof that this is not so (Hul. 11b; Sotah 27a; *Shulhan Arukh* Even Haezer 4.13 ff and commentaries). The husband would be presumed to be the father even if there was some suspicion that the woman had intercourse with someone else, or that the child was the result of rape. In this case, as there was no other intercourse, and a mixture of semen was used, the husband is definitely considered as the father.

The only reason for not using a Jewish donor for artificial insemination lies in the possibility that the child may marry incestuously without realizing it (C. F. Epstein, *Teshuvah Shelemah*, Even Haezer #4). In our very large, widely dispersed American Jewish community, this likelihood is minimal and for that reason both Jewish and non-Jewish donors may be used.

There is no reason to tell the child that he is the result of artificial insemination. After all, such a child is in every way part of the family from gestation and is genetically part of the family. Such knowledge can not benefit the child or its relationship with the parents. Such a discussion would be as absurd as telling a child conceived naturally that he may have been the result of intercourse in anger, or under other unusual circumstances. Conception is a private matter between the parents and the child has no right to that information. The child, therefore, should not be told about his conception through artificial insemination.

March 1986

198. VASECTOMY

QUESTION: A young couple, with three children and a fourth on the way, has asked about the Jewish view on vasectomy as a means of contraception. They have been married for five years, have tried all other methods, and rejected them either as painful, dangerous or inconvenient. Does Reform Judaism agree with the *halakhic* restrictions on sterilization? (Rabbi B. Lefkowitz, Taunton, MA)

ANSWER: As you have stated, the *halakhah* prohibits sterilization based upon the verse in Leviticus (22.24), which was subsequently discussed in the *Talmud* (San. 70a; Kid. 25b; Hag. 14b, 13; Shab. 110b ff); these sources prohibit the castration of male human beings as well as animals. Vasectomy is somewhat different, but the intent of removing the reproductive capacity permanently is the same. Rabbinic discussions on this matter continue and explicitly prohibit all forms of male sterilization (*Yad* Hil. Issurei Biah 16; *Shulhan Arukh* Even Haezer 5). The more recent commentaries and responsa agree (*Hatam Sofer*, Even Haezer #20; *Noam*, Vol. 1, pp. 257 ff; *Otzar Haposqim* Even Haezer, Vol. 1, #68 ff).

While we disagree with tradition on matters of temporary birth control and are more permissive than many of the traditional authorities, we would agree with tradition on this prohibition against permanent sterilization. This is an irreversible act, and should not be undertaken. There are other methods of birth control which are safe and which are sanctioned by us and also by the more liberal Orthodox authorities.

February 1984

199. MARRIAGE OF TRANSEXUALS*

QUESTION: May a rabbi officiate at a marriage of two Jews, one of whom has undergone a surgical operation which has changed his/her sex? (Rabbi D. Gluckman, Family Life Committee)

ANSWER: Our responsum will deal with an individual who has undergone an operation for sexual change for physical or psychological reasons. We will presume (a) that this has been done for valid, serious reasons and not frivolously; (b) that the best available medical tests (chromosome analysis, etc.) have been utilized as aids; (c) that this in no way constitutes a homosexual marriage.

There is some discussion in traditional literature about the propriety of this kind of operation. In addition, we must recall that tradition sought to avoid any operation which would seriously endanger life (*Shulhan Arukh* Yoreh Deah 116; Hul. 10a). The *Mishnah* has dealt with the problem of individuals whose sex was undetermined. It divides them into two separate categories, *tumtum* and *androginos*. A *tumtum* is a person whose genitals are hidden or undeveloped and whose sex, therefore, is unknown. R. Ammi recorded an operation on one such individual who was found to be male and who then fathered seven children (Yeb. 83b). S. B. Freehof has discussed such operations most recently; he *permits* such an operation for a *tumtum, but not* for an *androginos* (*Modern Reform Responsa*, pp. 128 ff). The *androginos* is a hermaphrodite and clearly carries characteristics of both sexes (M. Bik., IV, 5). The former is a condition which can be corrected, and the latter, as far as the ancients were concerned, could not. So, the *Mishnah* and later tradition treats the *androginos* sometimes like a male, sometimes like a female, and occasionally as a separate category. However, with regard to marriage, the *Mishnah* (Bik 4.2) states unequivocally, "he can take a wife, but not be taken as a wife." If married, they are free from the obligation of bearing children (*Yad* Hil. Yibum Vehalitzah 6.2), but some doubted the validity of their marriages (Yeb. 81a; *Yad* Hil. Ishut 4.11; *Shulhan Arukh* Even Haezer 44.6). The *Talmud* has also dealt with *ailoni,* a masculine woman who is barren (Nid. 47b; Yeb. 80b; *Yad* Hil. Ishut 2.4). If she marries and her husband was aware of her condition, then this is a valid marriage (*Yad* Hil. Ishut 4.11), although the ancient authorities felt that such a marriage would only be permitted if the prospective husband had children by a previous marriage, otherwise he may divorce her in order to have children (*M.* Yeb. 24.1; Yeb. 61a). Later authorities would simply permit such a marriage to stand.

We, however, are dealing with a situation in which either the lack of sexual development has been corrected and the individual has been provided with a sexual identity, or the psychological makeup of the individual clashes with the physical characteristics, and this has been corrected through surgery. In other words, our question deals with an individual who now possesses definite physical characteristics of a man or a woman, but has obtained them through surgical procedure and whose status is recognized by the civil government. The problem before us is that such an individual is sterile, and the question is whether under such circumstances he or she may be married. Our question, therefore, must deal with the nature of marriage for such individuals. Can a Jewish marriage be conducted under these circumstances?

There is no doubt that both procreation and sexual satisfaction are basic elements of marriage as seen by Jewish tradition. Procreation is considered essential as already stated in the *Mishnah*: "A man may not desist from the duty of procreation unless he already has children." The *Gemarah* to this concludes that he may marry a barren woman if he has fulfilled this *mitzvah*; in any case, he should not remain unmarried (Yeb. 61b). There was a difference between the schools of Hillel and Shammai about what is required to fulfill the *mitzvah* of procreation; tradition followed Hillel who minimally required a son and a daughter, yet the Codes all emphasize the need to produce children beyond that number (*M.* Yeb. 6.6; Ket. 8a; Yeb. 61b; *Tos.* Yeb. 8; Yeb. 8; *Yad* Hil. Ishut 15.16, etc.) The sources also indicate that this *mitzvah* is only incumbent upon the male (*Tos.* Yeb. 8), although some later authorities would include women in the obligation, perhaps in a secondary sense (*Arukh Hashulhan*, Even Haezer 1.4; Hatam Sofer, *Responsa*, Even Haezer #20). Abraham Hirsh (*Noam*, Vol. 16, 152 ff) has recently discussed the matter of granting a divorce when one party of a married couple has had a transexual operation. Aside from opposing the operation generally, he also stated that no essential biological changes had taken place and that the operation, therefore, was akin to sterilization (which is prohibited) or cosmetic surgery.

Hirsh also mentioned a case related to our situation; a male in the time of R. Hananel added an orifice to his body, and R. Hananel decided that a male having intercourse with this individual had committed a homosexual act. This statement was quoted by Ibn Ezra in his commentary on Lev. 18.22. We, however, are not dealing with this kind of situation, but with a complete sexual change operation.

Despite the strong emphasis on procreation, companionship and joy play a major role in the Jewish concept of marriage. Thus, the seven marriage blessings deal with joy, companionship, the unity of family, restoration of Zion, etc., as well as with children (Ket. 8a). These same blessings are to be recited for those beyond the child-bearing age or those who are sterile (Abudraham, *Birkhot Erusin*, 98a).

Most traditional authorities who discuss childless marriages were considering a marriage already in existence (*bediavad*), and not the entrance into such a union. Under such circumstances, the marriage would be considered valid and need not result in divorce for the sake of procreation, although that possibility existed (*Shulhan Arukh* Even Haezer 23, see Isserles' note to 154.10). This was the only alternative solution since bigamy was no longer even theoretically possible after the decree of Rabbenu Gershom in the eleventh century in those countries where this decree was accepted; we should remember that Oriental Jews did not accept the *herem* of Rabbenu Gershom. Maimonides considered such a marriage valid under any circumstances (*Yad* Hil. Ishut 4.10) whether this individual was born sterile or was sterilized later. The commentator Abraham di Boton emphasized the validity of such a marriage if sterility has been caused by an accident or surgery (*Lehem Mishneh* to *Yad* Hil. Ishut 4.10). Yair Hayim Bacharach stated that as long as the prospective wife realized that her prospective husband was infertile though sexually potent, and had agreed to the marriage, it was valid and acceptable (*Havat Yair* #221). Traditional *halakhah* which makes a distinction between the obligations of men and women (a distinction not accepted by Reform Judaism) would allow a woman to marry a sterile male since the obligation of procreation do not affect her (as mentioned earlier).

There was some difference of opinion when a change of status in the male member of a wedded couple had taken place. R. Asher discussed this, but came to no conclusion, though he felt that a male whose sexual organs had been removed could not contract a valid marriage (*Besamim Rosh* #340 - attributed to R. Asher). The contemporary Orthodox authority, E. Waldenberg, assumed that a sexual change has occurred and terminated the marriage without divorce (*Tzitz Eliezer*, X, #25). Joseph Pellagi came to a similar conclusion earlier (*Yosef et Ahab* 3:5).

Perhaps the clearest statement about entering into such a marriage was made by Isaac bar Sheshet who felt that a couple is permitted to marry and then should be left alone, although they entered the marriage with full awareness of the situation (*Ribash* #15; *Shulhan Arukh* Even Haezer 1.3; see Isserles' note). Similarly, traditional authorities who usually oppose contraception permit it to a couple if one partner is in ill health; the permission is granted so that the couple may remain happily married, a solution favored over abstinence (Mosheh Feinstein, *Igrot Mosheh*, Even Haezer #63 and #67; he permits marriage under these circumstances).

Our discussion indicates that individuals whose sex has been changed by a surgical procedure, and who are now sterile, may be married according to Jewish tradition. We agree with this conclusion. Both partners should be aware of each other's condition. The ceremony need not be changed in any way for the sake of these individuals.

September 1977

200. LESBIANS AND THEIR CHILDREN

QUESTION: Two women who are in a lesbian relationship have raised a child who has been adopted by one of them. The child has been formally converted to Judaism with *berit milah* and *miqveh*. This was done like any other conversion and posed no problems. Now, however, the child is about to be *Bar Mitzvah* and the two women want to participate in the service as any parents. Should they be permitted to do so? (Rabbi M. Staitman, Pittsburgh, PA)

ANSWER: Although Jewish tradition from the Bible onwards strongly condemns homosexuality, it has rather little to say about lesbianism. Some of the sources indicate that it may have been treated as a temporary phenomenon, rather than as a permanent condition among women. So, the *Talmud* (Shab. 65a; Yeb. 76a) and the *Sifrei* (9.8) prohibit sexual intercourse between women, but do not specify any punishment. They state that such a woman was permitted to marry even into the priesthood. As lesbianism was considered obscene, later sources demanded punishment (*makot mardut*) for those involved (*Yad* Hil. Issurei Biah 21.8; *Shulhan Arukh* Even Haezer 20.2). As, however, there was no Biblical basis for such punishment, there was also little further discussion in responsa literature.

We should be guided by these feelings and by our tradition's strong support of normative family life. Everything which we do should strengthen the family. We should, therefore, ignore the lesbian relationship and feel no need to deal with it unless the individuals involved are flagrant about their relationship and make an issue of it. If they do not, then their lesbian relationship is irrelevant; it should not be recognized. They should be permitted, along with other individuals both male and female, to participate in the *Torah* readings as well as other portions of the Friday-*shabbat* service. This will indicate to both the congregation and this household that we recognize the love and care given to the child and do not focus on or recognize the lesbian relationship.

March 1986

201. HOMOSEXUAL MARRIAGE*

QUESTION: May a rabbi officiate at the "marriage" of two homosexuals? (Rabbi L. Poller, Larchmont, NY)

ANSWER: The attitude of our tradition and of Reform Judaism toward homosexuals is clear. For a full discussion, see the responsa by S. B. Freehof and W. Jacob (*American Reform Responsa*, # 13, 14). The resolution of the Central Conference of American Rabbis on homosexuality deals exclusively with the civil rights and civil liberties of homosexuals and seeks to protect them from discrimination. It does not, however, understand it to be an alternative lifestyle which is religiously condoned.

Judaism places great emphasis on family, children and the future, which is assured by a family. However we may understand homosexuality, whether as an illness, as a genetically based dysfunction or as a sexual preference and lifestyle -we cannot accommodate the relationship of two homosexuals as a "marriage" within the context of Judaism, for none of the elements of *qiddushin* (sanctification) normally associated with marriage can be invoked for this relationship.

A rabbi can not, therefore, participate in the "marriage" of two homosexuals.

October 1985

202. PARENTAL OBLIGATION TO A SEVERELY RETARDED CHILD

QUESTION: A couple with two healthy, normal children has a third child who is severely malformed and retarded. The child is not aware of people around him, and his intelligence is limited to a few reflexes. His face will occasionally form what appears to be a smile, and if food is placed in his mouth he will swallow by reflex. There is no hope for a future beyond this, however. The child has, for several years, simply lain in a fetal position in a crib in a nursing home. Do the parents have a continued obligation to visit this child or is it sufficient that they see to it that he is cared for in the institution where he now resides? Does the tradition provide some guidelines for determining the degree of medical care to be given to this child in a crisis? Physicians are generally surprised that the child has lived this long. If the reflex by which the child eats stops functioning, how far should the medical staff intervene to preserve life? Is there the obligation to feed him through a stomach tube, for example? (Rabbi M. Remson, Naperville, IL)

ANSWER: Let us begin by dealing individually with each question which you have asked. Traditional Judaism places an obligation for the maintenance of children upon the father; it is his duty to provide for all of his children's needs in accordance with his ability (*Yad* Ishut 13.6; *Shulhan Arukh* Even Haezer 73.6 ff). This includes formal education, learning a trade or anything else which will enable a child to take her place in the adult world (Kid. 29a ff; *Shulhan Arukh* Yoreh Deah 245.1, 4). There is some discussion about the number of years for which this obligation exists. Originally tradition limited it to six years (Ket. 49b, 65b; *Shulhan Arukh* Even Haezer 71.1) and indicated that after that time, the father was duty-bound to maintain the child as an act of *tzedaqah* (*Yad* Hil. Ishut 12.14, 15, 21.17; *Shulhan Arukh* Yoreh Deah 251.4). However, the demands of *tzedaqah* were to be enforced rigidly according to the actual needs of the child (*Yad* Hil. Ishut 13.6; *Shulhan Arukh* Even Haezer 73.6). This obligation then continues until age thirteen or in modern times until the child reaches an independent adult status.

Little has been said in our legal tradition about the emotional needs of the child, but such thoughts have been conveyed through the *aggadic* literature.

Nothing in the traditional literature limits such care to normal children. In other words, the obligation is universal and applies to every child regardless of her mental or physical abilities.

Tradition, therefore, indicates that this child, despite its very limited abilities, deserves both the maintenance and affection which the parents can provide. As I view this problem through my personal experience with a severely handicapped daughter and that of others who have dealt with parents of handicapped children, it is clear that unless ongoing relationships of some kind are established with such a handicapped child, the parents and other children will always feel guilty. Obviously this child can not be made part of the normal family life, but ongoing visits and continued concern with his welfare rests as any obligation upon all the members of the family. Practically speaking, such visits also assure a higher standard of care for such an individual, as those institutionalized children who receive no visits are frequently neglected.

Now, let me turn to the second portion of your question which asks about medical procedures in case this child's normal reflexes stop. We should follow the advice of the *Mishnah*, which states that no positive action which will hasten death may be instituted (*M*. Shab 23.5, 151b; *Shulhan Arukh* Yoreh Deah 339). On the other hand, the same sources indicate that we need not impede the individual's death when no recovery is possible. This matter has been discussed at some length by Solomon B. Freehof (W. Jacob, *American Reform Responsa*, # 77). Nothing unusual needs be done by the attending physician; there would be no obligation to feed this individual through a stomach tube, etc. We followed the decision with our own child.

In summary, as long as this handicapped child remains alive, he should be given all care and affection possible. If his reflexes stop and no recovery is possible, he should be permitted to die peacefully.

February 1984

INDEX

This is an index to the volumes *American Reform Responsa* (I) and *Contemporary American Reform Responsa* (II). The index indicates the volume and number, not the page of the responsum.